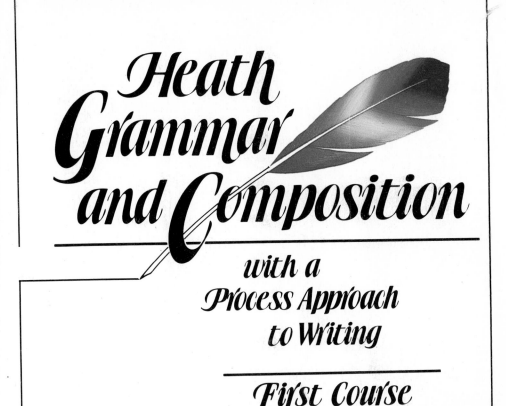

# Heath Grammar and Composition

## with a Process Approach to Writing

## First Course

*Authors*
Carol Ann Bergman
J. A. Senn

*Contributing Author*
Margaret M. Withey

D.C. Heath and Company
Lexington, Massachusetts / Toronto, Ontario

**Series Titles**

Heath Grammar and Composition: Introductory Course
Heath Grammar and Composition: First Course
Heath Grammar and Composition: Second Course
Heath Grammar and Composition: Third Course
Heath Grammar and Composition: Fourth Course
Heath Grammar and Composition: Fifth Course
Heath Grammar and Composition: Complete Course

**Supplementary Materials (for each course)**

Annotated Teacher's Edition
Teacher's Resource Binder
Writing Transparencies
Workbook
Tests

**Contributing Writer**

Florence Harris

*Editorial* Sue Martin (Managing Editor), Barbara Brien (Project Editor), Carol Clay, Lynn Duffy, Kathleen Kennedy, Peg McNary, Mary Ellen Walters; *Freelance Assistance:* Karen Gabler, Anne Jones, Dale Lyle, Linda Nowicki, William Ray, Ellen Whalen
*Editorial Services* Marianna Frew Palmer (Manager), K. Kirschbaum Harvie
*Design by* Dawn Ostrer Emerson
*Production* Maureen LaRiccia

Acknowledgments: page 588



Printed in the United States of America
Published simultaneously in Canada

International Standard Book Number: 0-669-15965-4

4 5 6 7 8 9 0

First Course

# Heath Grammar and Composition

with a Process Approach to Writing

## Series Consultant

Henry I. Christ
Former Chairman of the English Department
Andrew Jackson High School
St. Albans, New York

## Reviewers

**Arkansas**

Joy Leatherwood
Lake Hamilton Junior High School
Pearcy, Arkansas

Elizabeth A. McDuff
Cloverdale Junior High School
Little Rock, Arkansas

**California**

Joan B. Greenberger
Jean Strauber
Suzanne M. Woods
Portola Junior High School
Tarzana, California

Linda Kaye
Gompers Middle School
Los Angeles, California

**Florida**

Faithia T. Clayton
Sixteenth Street Middle School
St. Petersburg, Florida

Patricia A. Davey
Osceola Middle School
Seminole, Florida

Rebecca Hight Miller
Westridge Junior High School
Orlando, Florida

**Illinois**

Helen Glass Fulce
Haven Middle School
Evanston, Illinois

**Iowa**

Nathan James Weate
Lamoni Community School
Lamoni, Iowa

**Louisiana**

Diane Marusak
Campti Junior High School
Campti, Louisiana

**New Jersey**

Kathleen Kayser
Pequannock Valley School
Pompton Plains, New Jersey

Michael Napurano
Terrill Middle School
Scotch Plains, New Jersey

Jennifer Pasculli
Readington School
Readington, New Jersey

**New York**

Geraldine C. Charney
Center School
New York, New York

Carol S. Lotz
Booker T. Washington Junior High School
New York, New York

**North Carolina**

Ruth L. Hudson
Ligon Gifted and Talented Middle School
Raleigh, North Carolina

Wilma M. Roseboro
Kingswood Sixth Grade Center
Cary, North Carolina

**Oregon**

Vicki Jefferson
Briggs Middle School
Eugene, Oregon

**Pennsylvania**

Bonnie Burns Guarini
Saint Paul School
Norristown, Pennsylvania

**Tennessee**

Shelia A. Duncan
Margaret A. Moore
Central Middle School
Murfreesboro, Tennessee

Rebecca Harrelson
Brainerd Junior High School
Chattanooga, Tennessee

**Washington**

Steven Berry
Carmichael Junior High School
Richland, Washington

Evelyn Blatt
Islander Middle School
Mercer Island, Washington

# Contents

## UNIT 1 *Grammar*

## Chapter 3 Verbs 38



## Chapter 4 Adjectives and Adverbs 50



## Chapter 5 Other Parts of Speech 66

# UNIT 2 Usage

## Chapter 10 Using Verbs 134



## Chapter 11 Using Pronouns 150



## Chapter 12 Subject and Verb Agreement 168

## UNIT 3 Mechanics

## Chapter 15 End Marks and Commas 222



## Chapter 16 Underlining and Quotation Marks 238



## Chapter 17 Other Punctuation 250

# UNIT 4 Composition
## Part One

## UNIT 5 Composition Part Two

## UNIT 6 Composition Part Three

### Chapter 26 Essays 410



### Chapter 27 Reports 430

## Chapter 28 Letters 460



# UNIT 7 Related Language Skills

## Chapter 29 Speaking and Listening 484

# To the Student

This book is about communication—the act of expressing yourself. Think of how much of your day is spent speaking with your family, friends, and many others in your school and community. Speaking, however, is only one means of communication. Writing is another. Writing clearly is an important skill. In today's world more and more businesses are using computers to communicate information. The written word—whether displayed on a screen or printed on paper—is the backbone of communication.

The different units in this book have one main goal. That goal is to help you speak and write clearly. The first unit, on grammar, shows the structure of English and gives you choices for your speaking and writing. The next unit, on usage, explains ways to speak and write clearly. The third unit, on mechanics, shows the importance of punctuation and capitalization in writing. The fourth, fifth, and sixth units show how to find, organize, and communicate your ideas in writing. The seventh unit gives important study tips and other language skills that you will need in school.

The composition units in this book are unique. The chapters include all the help you need to understand and write different kinds of compositions—from single paragraphs through reports. Within chapters you are taken step by step through the four stages of the writing process. In the *prewriting* stage, you choose and limit a subject and organize your ideas. In the *writing* stage, you learn how to write a draft based on your prewriting notes that includes a topic sentence and a concluding sentence. In the *revising* stage, you learn how to improve your work and to look at it from a reader's point of view. Finally, in the *editing* stage, you learn how to polish your work by applying what you have learned in the first three units.

Going through these writing stages is like having someone steady you as you learn how to ride a bike. If you are unsure of yourself, there are many helps, including practice exercises, models, and checklists. These will show you exactly what to do, how to do it, and when to do it. Following these stages in the writing process will help you write well on your own.

As you go through each unit in this book, remember its goal: to help you speak and write clearly. Each chapter has been written with this goal in mind. The skills you build today will help you in tomorrow's world.

## Special Helps

Your teacher will probably go through some of the chapters in this book with you. All of the chapters, however, have been written and organized so that you can refer to them and use them on your own throughout the year. You may find some of the following features of the book particularly helpful.

***Keyed Rules*** All the rules are clearly marked with keyed blue arrows. An index at the back of the book tells you where to find each rule.

***Tinted Boxes*** Throughout the text, important lists, summaries, and writing steps are highlighted in tinted boxes for easy reference.

***Application to Writing*** These sections in the first three units of the book clearly show you how you can use the various grammatical concepts you have learned to improve your writing.

***Diagnostic and Mastery Tests*** You can use the diagnostic and mastery tests to measure your progress. The diagnostic test at the beginning of a chapter will show you what you need to learn; the mastery test at the end of a chapter will show you how well you learned it.

***High-Interest Exercises*** Many of the exercises throughout the book are based on interesting topics. You will not only practice learning a particular skill, but you will also find the material in these exercises informative and interesting.

***Composition Models*** Clearly marked models in the composition chapters provide interesting examples by professional writers.

***Spotlight on Writing*** Fun activities at the end of each composition chapter give you many writing projects. Some ask you to write about a picture. Some give you information to work with. All of them give you more practice in growing as a writer.

***Composition Checklists*** Almost all the composition chapters end with a checklist that you can follow—step by step—when you are writing a paragraph, an essay, or a report.

***Standardized Tests*** Standardized tests, which follow all seven units, give you practice and build your confidence in taking tests.

***Study Skills*** You will find information on note-taking, using the library, taking tests, and other topics that will help you succeed in school. A special chapter on speaking and listening will sharpen your oral skills.

# UNIT 1

# Grammar

1. The Sentence
2. Nouns and Pronouns
3. Verbs
4. Adjectives and Adverbs
5. Other Parts of Speech
6. Parts of Speech Review
7. Complements
8. Simple and Compound Sentences
9. Sound Sentences

1

# The Sentence

## Diagnostic Test

Number your paper 1 to 10. Make two columns on your paper. Label the first column *subjects* and the second column *verbs*. Then under the proper heading, write each subject and each verb. (Some subjects and verbs are compound.)

EXAMPLE Sarah and Paul are studying in the library.

ANSWER

| subjects | verbs |
|---|---|
| Sarah, Paul | are studying |

1. Most people have 12 pairs of ribs.
2. The library will close on Mondays this winter.
3. Dust and gas from meteoroids add a few tons a day to the weight of the earth.
4. Tony fished all day and caught only two bass.
5. To the top of the barn soared the crow.
6. The Hoover Dam controls floods along the Colorado River.
7. Did Rosa and her family find a new apartment?
8. Andrea has always walked to school.
9. At times snow falls in the Sahara Desert.
10. From behind the curtain, Julie couldn't see the audience.

# Kinds of Sentences

A sentence has one of four purposes. A sentence can make a statement, ask a question, give a command, or express strong feeling. The purpose of a particular sentence determines what end mark will go at the end of that sentence.

1a A **declarative sentence** makes a statement or expresses an opinion and ends with a period.

The Miami Dolphins played in the Super Bowl on Sunday**.** [statement]
Football is a very exciting game**.** [opinion]

1b An **interrogative sentence** asks a question and ends with a question mark.

Do you like football**?**
How many first downs did the team make in last Saturday's play-off game**?**

1c An **imperative sentence** makes a request or gives a command and ends with either a period or an exclamation point.

Follow me along Route 6 to the football stadium**.** [This imperative sentence ends with a period because it is a mild request.]
Catch that pass**!** [This imperative sentence ends with an exclamation point because it is a strong command.]

1d An **exclamatory sentence** expresses strong feeling and ends with an exclamation point.

That's the best play I have ever seen**!**
What a thrilling football game that was**!**

## EXERCISE 1 Classifying Sentences

Number your paper 1 to 10. Write each sentence, using the correct end mark. Then label each sentence *declarative, interrogative, imperative,* or *exclamatory.*

EXAMPLE Gold is a precious metal
ANSWER Gold is a precious metal. declarative

Gold

1. What an amazing place gold has had in legend and history
2. It was partly responsible for the rapid settlement of the West
3. Do you know when the Gold Rush started
4. Is gold still mined in the United States
5. Gold is a metal that never rusts or tarnishes
6. Read the story about Croesus
7. Wasn't he a wealthy ruler in ancient times
8. Yes, gold filled every room in his house
9. How proud he was of his golden throne
10. At the library look for pictures of the throne

## EXERCISE 2 Classifying Sentences

Number your paper 1 to 10. Write each sentence, using the correct end mark. Then label each sentence *declarative, interrogative, imperative,* or *exclamatory.*

1. Did you sign up for the whale watch
2. The year of the first 500-mile race at the Indianapolis Motor Speedway was 1911
3. How well that quarterback played
4. Have you finished your science report
5. Fraternal twins are more common than identical twins
6. When will the assembly start
7. Elephants reach old age at about 65
8. What an amazing feat that was
9. The driver tossed the newspapers from the truck onto the stoop in front of the store
10. Dallas, Texas, was incorporated as a city in 1871

# Subjects and Predicates

Learning to recognize sentences is one of the most important keys to good speaking and writing.

1e A **sentence** is a group of words that expresses a complete thought.

In order to express a complete thought, a sentence must have two parts. The first part, the *subject,* names the person, place, thing, or idea the sentence is about. The second part, the *predicate,* tells what the subject is or does.

| **SUBJECT** *(names whom or what the sentence is about)* | **PREDICATE** *(tells what the subject is or does)* |
|---|---|
| My brother's friend | works at a garage. |
| The chicken for dinner | smells delicious. |

### EXERCISE 3 Combining Subjects and Predicates

Number your paper 1 to 10. Match a subject in column A with a predicate in column B. Then combine them to form a sentence that makes sense. Begin each sentence with a capital letter and end each one with a period.

| A | B |
|---|---|
| 1. orange juice | slid across the grass |
| 2. the rocket | belongs to Kent |
| 3. a snake | paints with oils |
| 4. a baby leopard | has many potholes |
| 5. the road to our house | protects trees |
| 6. the book on the table | roared into the sky |
| 7. that famous artist | rarely curls its tail |
| 8. bark | has noisy fans |
| 9. a sick pig | tumbles like a kitten |
| 10. hockey | contains vitamin C |

## Complete Subjects

Some of the subjects in the previous exercise—such as *the road to our house*—have more than one word. They have more than one word because they are *complete subjects.*

1f A **complete subject** includes all the words used to identify the person, place, thing, or idea that the sentence is about.

To find a complete subject, ask yourself, *Who or what is doing something?* or *About whom or what is some statement being made?*

complete subject
**The boy in the last row** answered the question correctly. [Who or what answered the question? *The boy in the last row* is the complete subject.]

complete subject
**The peanut butter in that jar** is homemade. [What is homemade? *The peanut butter in that jar* is the complete subject.]

### EXERCISE 4 Finding Complete Subjects

Number your paper 1 to 10. Then write each complete subject.

Water Creatures

1. Schools of fish stay together for protection.
2. An average goldfish lives for four years.
3. The horseshoe crab existed 500 million years ago.
4. A small trout swims faster than a person.
5. The upside-down catfish floats on its back.
6. The huge whale shark eats only small plants and small water animals, not people.
7. The world's smallest frog fits inside a thimble.
8. The common sponge is a sea animal with a soft skeleton.
9. The basket starfish has more than 80,000 arms.
10. Scientists around the world have identified about 21,000 different kinds of fish.

## Simple Subjects

As you have seen, a complete subject often includes several words. Within each complete subject, however, there is one main word. This one main word is called the *simple subject*. It most clearly answers the question *Who or what is doing something?* or *About whom or what is some statement being made?*

1g A **simple subject** is the main word in the complete subject.

complete subject: That big black **dog** with the bushy tail

That big black **dog** with the bushy tail followed me home. [What is the main word in the complete subject? Who or what is doing something in this sentence? The simple subject is *dog*.]

Sometimes the simple subject can have more than one word. Usually these subjects are the names of persons or places.

complete subject: **Sports Plus** in the mall

**Sports Plus** in the mall has a sale on baseball bats.

Sometimes a complete subject and a simple subject are the same.

**Marianna** scored the final points.

NOTE: Throughout the rest of this book, the simple subject will be called the *subject*.

### EXERCISE 5 Finding Complete and Simple Subjects

Number your paper 1 to 10. Write each complete subject. Then underline each simple subject.

EXAMPLE The coat on the chair needs a button.
ANSWER The coat on the chair

1. A heavy shower ended a month-long drought.
2. The apples from our tree make wonderful applesauce.
3. China is the third largest country in the world.

4. The winner of the race accepted the trophy with a howl of glee and a huge grin.
5. *Viking 1* took pictures of the surface of Mars.
6. A person can take 12 to 18 breaths per minute.
7. My younger brother cautiously entered the attic.
8. Hair on your head daily grows about 1/100 of an inch.
9. The large trees next door survived the storm.
10. Robert Fulton built the first successful steamboat.

### EXERCISE 6 Finding Complete and Simple Subjects

Number your paper 1 to 10. Write each complete subject. Then underline each simple subject.

1. A movie about dinosaurs is playing at the Plaza.
2. The red sweater with blue stripes is mine.
3. The Statue of Liberty is almost 152 feet in height.
4. Chinese inventors of the twelfth century created the compass.
5. The tall, handsome man over there is my father.
6. The first transatlantic journey in a balloon was in 1978.
7. The huge building on Boylston Street is the Prudential.
8. Today's portable computers are battery-powered.
9. The big white house with black shutters belongs to Mario.
10. William Armstrong wrote the book *Sounder*.

## Complete Predicates

In addition to a subject, every sentence must have a *predicate*.

1h A **complete predicate** includes all the words that tell what the subject is doing, or that tell something about the subject.

To find a complete predicate, first find the subject. Then ask yourself, *What is the subject doing?* or *What is being said about the subject?*

complete predicate

The clock **ticked loudly in the quiet room.** [The subject is *clock.* What did the clock do? *Ticked loudly in the quiet room* is the complete predicate.]

complete predicate

Our kitchen **has a fresh coat of paint.** [The subject is *kitchen.* What is being said about the kitchen? *Has a fresh coat of paint* is the complete predicate.]

### EXERCISE 7 Finding Complete Predicates

Number your paper 1 to 10. Then write each complete predicate.

Crazy Critters

1. That zany zebra plays the zither.
2. A big bear with a balloon bolted through the barn.
3. Furry foxes with four feet fought fiercely until five.
4. The giant giraffes greeted me graciously.
5. Lazy llamas from Liberia licked the lemons.
6. Chilly chipmunks chattered cheerfully.
7. The brown baboons banged on the bongo drums.
8. The round raccoons raced the reindeer.
9. The timid tiger tripped on a torn tuxedo.
10. Pudgy pandas played the piano with precision.

## Simple Predicates, or Verbs

Each complete predicate has one main word or phrase that tells what the subject is doing, or that tells something about the subject. This main word or phrase is called a *simple predicate,* or *verb.*

1i A **simple predicate,** or **verb,** is the main word or phrase in the complete predicate.

Some verbs tell what the subject is doing. These are action verbs. Some action verbs—such as *run, talk,* and *drive*—show physical action. Other action verbs—such as *dream, think,* and *worry*—show mental action.

complete predicate
My father **cooked** Italian food last night. [What is the main word in the complete predicate? What did the subject do? The verb is *cooked.*]

complete predicate
Jody **wants** a kite for her birthday.

Sometimes verbs do not show action. These verbs tell something about a subject. Following is a list of some common verb forms that are used to make a statement about a subject.

**Verbs That Make Statements**

am is are was were

complete predicate
My umbrella **is** in the trunk of your car.

complete predicate
The math test **was** unusually long yesterday.

NOTE: A complete predicate and a simple predicate can be the same.

The happy child **giggled.**

### EXERCISE 8 *Finding Complete Predicates and Verbs*

Number your paper 1 to 10. Write each complete predicate. Then underline each verb.

EXAMPLE The windbreakers are in Cheryl's backpack.
ANSWER are in Cheryl's backpack

1. All ants live in colonies.
2. I thought about your suggestion for a new character in my short story.
3. The largest state in the United States is Alaska.
4. Lafayette sailed from the country of France to America on March 26, 1777.

5. The infielder caught the ball for an out.
6. Some violins contain about 70 pieces of wood.
7. Dad was a member of the school board last year.
8. Paper is a Chinese invention.
9. I am always hungry before lunch.
10. White tigers are extremely rare.

### EXERCISE 9 Finding Complete Predicates and Verbs

Number your paper 1 to 10. Write each complete predicate. Then underline each verb.

1. The officer quickly followed the suspect down the street.
2. The Alaskan pipeline transports crude oil over land.
3. The Underground is the name of London's subway system.
4. Levi Strauss originally designed his jeans for miners.
5. The United States bought Alaska from Russia in 1867.
6. Their brothers are the referees for tonight's game.
7. The Pyrenees Mountains separate France from Spain.
8. Paul worried about his driver's test.
9. Edgar Allan Poe wrote the first detective story.
10. The Black Sea is along the northern coast of Turkey.

**Verb Phrases.** The verb of a sentence sometimes needs help to make a statement or to tell what action is taking place. Words that help a verb are called *helping verbs,* or auxiliary verbs. The main verb and any helping verbs make up a *verb phrase.* Following is a list of common helping verbs.

**Common Helping Verbs**

| | |
|---|---|
| ***be*** | am, is, are, was, were, be, being, been |
| ***have*** | has, have, had |
| ***do*** | do, does, did |
| **other verbs** | may, might, must, can, could, shall, should, will, would |

The helping verbs in the following examples are in heavy type.

verb phrase

The team **is** practicing hard for next week's game.

verb phrase

The Baldwins **must have** taken the wrong exit.

Sometimes one or more words may separate the parts of a verb phrase. In the following examples, the verb phrases are in heavy type.

A calculator **can** easily **multiply** large numbers.
I **have** never **given** a public speech before.

*Not* and its contraction *n't* are never part of a verb phrase.

Pearl **is** not **going** with us.
Paulo **did**n't **hear** the weather report.

In some questions the subject comes in the middle of a verb phrase. To find the verb phrase in a question like this, turn the question around to make a statement.

**Does** Terry **know** the date of his birthday? [Terry *does know* the date of his birthday.]

NOTE: Throughout the rest of this book, a verb phrase will be called a verb.

## EXERCISE 10 Finding Verb Phrases

Number your paper 1 to 10. Then write each verb phrase.

EXAMPLE My cousin will graduate from college in May.
ANSWER will graduate

1. Drew might audition for a part in the school play.
2. By the end of Saturday's football game, our quarterback had completed six touchdown passes.
3. The Kansas City Royals did win the 1985 World Series.
4. My brother has forgotten his locker key again this week.
5. My family has invited John to a party in June.
6. Sarah may be running in the relay race tomorrow.

7. Many sea otters do live off the coast of California.
8. Karen can memorize almost anything.
9. Next month I will volunteer at Children's Hospital.
10. The swim team does practice an hour every morning.

### EXERCISE 11 Finding Verb Phrases

Number your paper 1 to 10. Then write each verb phrase.

EXAMPLE My family has never camped beside this lake.
ANSWER has camped

1. An ostrich can cover 25 feet in one stride.
2. We couldn't find his football helmet.
3. No life would exist on Earth without the sun.
4. Will your mother drive us to the concert?
5. A porcupine does not throw its quills.
6. The weather forecaster should have warned us.
7. Coastlines can affect the level of tides.
8. Does practice begin at three o'clock?
9. A bloodhound can easily follow a day-old trail.
10. Starfish will often eat baby oysters.

### EXERCISE 12 Writing Sentences

Number your paper 1 to 5. Write a sentence for each of the following verbs. Include the helping verb *has* or *have* in at least two of your sentences. Then underline each subject once and each verb twice.

1. paddled 2. tumbled 3. raced 4. waded 5. sank

## Position of Subjects

When the subject comes before the verb, a sentence is in natural order. In the following examples, each subject is underlined once, and each verb is underlined twice.

The captain navigated the ship to safety.

In summer the Tanners visit Cape Cod.

When the verb comes before the subject, the sentence is in inverted order. To find the subject, turn the sentence around to its natural order.

INVERTED ORDER Near the fire slept the dachshund.
NATURAL ORDER The dachshund slept near the fire.

In some questions part of the verb phrase comes before the subject. To find the subject, turn the question into a statement.

QUESTION Has Roberta operated this computer before?
STATEMENT Roberta has operated this computer before.

When a sentence begins with the word *here* or *there,* it is in inverted order. To find the subject in such a sentence, turn the sentence around to its natural order.

INVERTED ORDER Here is the chalk.
NATURAL ORDER The chalk is here.

INVERTED ORDER There are some mittens in the chest.
NATURAL ORDER Some mittens are in the chest. [Sometimes *there* must be dropped for the sentence to make sense.]

In a command or a request, the subject *you* is not stated. *You* is called an *understood subject.*

COMMAND (you) Wait for me!
OR (you) Smile for the camera.
REQUEST (you) Have a nice day.

### EXERCISE 13 Finding Subjects and Predicates

Number your paper 1 to 10. Then write the subject and the verb in each sentence.

1. Over the beam vaulted the gymnast.
2. There are three pizzas for you at Tom's Pizza Shop on Elm Street.
3. Did Allison finish her homework?

4. Down the hill swooped the skier.
5. With a timid grin, the new student approached the group in the cafeteria.
6. From the auditorium came a boisterous cheer in response to the candidate's speech.
7. Is the faculty rehearsing the skits with the seventh graders for the comedy hour tonight?
8. There are not many tickets available for the rock concert on Saturday night at the college arena.
9. Do you agree with the student council's decision for a longer lunch period?
10. Beyond the rim of the canyon, the brilliant orange sun was slowly sinking.

### EXERCISE 14 *Finding Subjects and Verbs*

Number your paper 1 to 10. Then write the subject and the verb in each sentence. If the subject is an understood *you*, write *you* in parentheses.

1. At the age of three, Mozart was playing the harpsichord with quite a bit of skill.
2. Did Nathan see a snowflake under his microscope during lab period today?
3. Along the river's edge by several small docks were dozens of sailboats.
4. Every day at the corner of the street, Sandy met the mail carrier.
5. Can Gloria mail this package for me after her conference with her guidance counselor?
6. Read to the class your poem about your trip to the mountains.
7. During a roundup each cowboy uses three or four horses.
8. Is Dennis buying season tickets to the hockey games again this year?
9. Write an entry in your journal every day this week about your reactions to nature.
10. Does an octopus have eight arms?

## TIME-OUT FOR REVIEW • • • • •

Number your paper 1 to 20. Then write the subject and the verb in each sentence. If the subject is an understood *you,* write *you* in parentheses.

How Football Began

1. Have you ever heard the name *William Webb Ellis?*
2. Without this man people might not be enjoying football today.
3. This little-known athlete of long ago scored football's first touchdown.
4. Listen to this interesting story.
5. In 1823, Ellis was eagerly playing a game of soccer at the Rugby School in England.
6. Soccer players could use only their feet and heads.
7. Team members couldn't touch the ball with their hands in that rugged game.
8. All of a sudden, Ellis grabbed the ball.
9. Toward the goal line at the opposite end of the field ran the young man.
10. Many spectators criticized him.
11. Some people, however, liked the idea.
12. Didn't the strange, new play make the game even more exciting?
13. A new game had just begun.
14. The members of Ellis's school called the game rugby after their school.
15. American football was on its way.
16. Several teams organized the first American professional team in 1895.
17. In the early days of football, players didn't wear any equipment, not even helmets.
18. In the last 75 years, many changes have occurred in football, however.
19. For example, college coaches developed the forward pass in 1906.
20. Now football captures the attention of millions of spectators.

## Compound Subjects

Some sentences have two or more subjects joined by the conjunction *and* or *or.* These subjects together are called a *compound subject.*

1j A **compound subject** is two or more subjects in one sentence that have the same verb and are joined by a conjunction.

Notice that each subject in the following examples shares the same verb—*attended.*

| | |
|---|---|
| ONE SUBJECT | The principal attended the meeting. |
| COMPOUND SUBJECT | The principal and the teachers attended the meeting. |
| COMPOUND SUBJECT | The principal, the teachers, and many parents attended the meeting. |

### EXERCISE 15 *Finding Compound Subjects*

Number your paper 1 to 10. Then write each compound subject.

EXAMPLE Heavy rain and harsh winds ruined our hike.
ANSWER rain, winds

1. At the Music Hall, songs and speeches will be featured.
2. Rattlesnakes and copperheads do not often appear in our woods.
3. Jupiter and Saturn were photographed during the *Voyager* missions.
4. Bananas or grapes would taste good in that salad.
5. Did Ann, Ruth, Gary, and Fred enter the track meet?
6. Only female wasps and female mosquitoes can sting.
7. A trapeze performance and a clown act are scheduled.
8. A magazine and a newspaper have arrived.
9. A jacket or a light coat will be warm enough.
10. In my garden are tomatoes, peas, and squash.

## Compound Verbs

Some sentences have two or more verbs joined by the conjunction *and, or,* or *but.* These verbs together are called a *compound verb.*

1k A **compound verb** is two or more verbs that have the same subject and are joined by a conjunction.

Notice that each verb in the following examples shares the same subject—*Patty.*

ONE VERB Patty is reading that book.

COMPOUND VERB Patty is reading that book and will write a book report afterward.

A sentence can include both a compound subject and a compound verb.

The parents and their children talked with the teachers and toured the school.

### EXERCISE 16 *Finding Compound Subjects and Verbs*

Number your paper 1 to 10. Make two columns on your paper. Label the first column *subjects* and the second column *verbs.* Then under the proper heading, write each subject and each verb.

1. Kate takes pictures for the school newspaper and also develops them.
2. The pitcher stopped the grounder and threw the ball to first base.
3. Mark will take the tire to the repair shop or will fix the leak himself.
4. The coaches and several teachers planned the field day and judged the different events.
5. Janet and Carlotta have packed a lunch and will spend the day at the beach.
6. Jean has run the mile and will try the 100-yard dash.

7. A few people lose their second set of teeth and grow a third set.
8. The umpire took a whisk broom from his pocket and swept home plate.
9. The beaver leveled a tree, chopped it into logs, and dragged it to the water's edge.
10. Babe Ruth and Lou Gehrig played for the New York Yankees and broke many baseball records.

### EXERCISE 17 *Writing Sentences*

Write five sentences that describe a school hallway just before the class bell. At least one sentence should have a compound subject, and at least one sentence should have a compound verb. Then underline each subject once and each verb twice.

## TIME-OUT FOR REVIEW • • • • •

Number your paper 1 to 10. Then write the subject and the verb in each sentence.

Two Instead of One

1. In 1951, a powerful hurricane was heading for Bermuda.
2. Weather forecasters and the people of the island were waiting for the hurricane with fear.
3. By noon the storm had almost reached the coast.
4. Trees and poles were swaying in the fierce wind.
5. Then a weather forecaster noticed something very strange.
6. A second hurricane was also traveling toward the island.
7. Eventually the second storm reached the first storm and smashed into it.
8. The collision weakened both hurricanes and threw them off course.
9. The storms changed course and headed toward the ocean.
10. The buildings and the people of the island survived both hurricanes.

# Diagraming Subjects and Verbs

A diagram to a buried treasure would show you where the roads and landmarks that lead to the treasure are. A *sentence diagram* is very similar. It uses lines and words to help you find and identify all the parts of a sentence.

***Subjects and Verbs.*** All sentence diagrams begin with a baseline. A straight, vertical line then separates the subject (or subjects) on the left from the verb (or verbs) on the right. Capital letters are included in a diagram, but punctuation is not. In the second example that follows, notice that the whole verb phrase is written on the baseline.

Flies buzzed.

Flies | buzzed

John had been winning.

John | had been winning

***Questions.*** A question is diagramed as if it were a statement.

Was Donna listening? (Donna was listening.)

Donna | Was listening

***Understood Subjects.*** When the subject of a sentence is an understood *you,* as in a command or a request, place *you* in parentheses in the subject position.

Listen.

(you) | Listen

***Compound Subjects and Verbs.*** Place the parts of a compound subject or a compound verb on parallel horizontal lines. Then put the conjunction connecting each part on a broken line between them.

Canoes and kayaks were drifting.

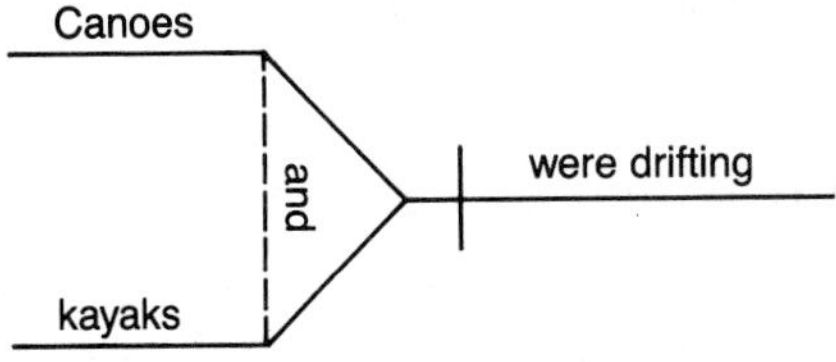


Lee hums or whistles.

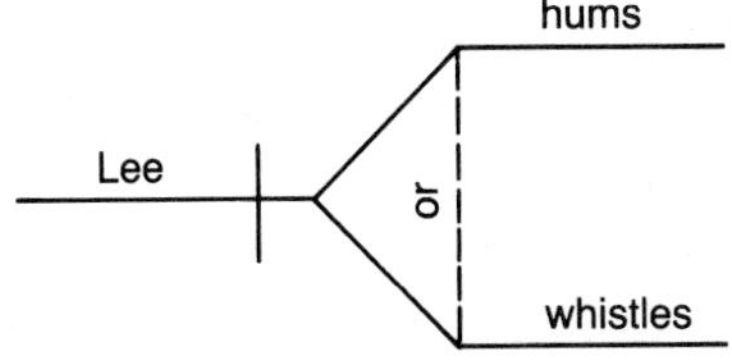


Maria and Rita studied and read.

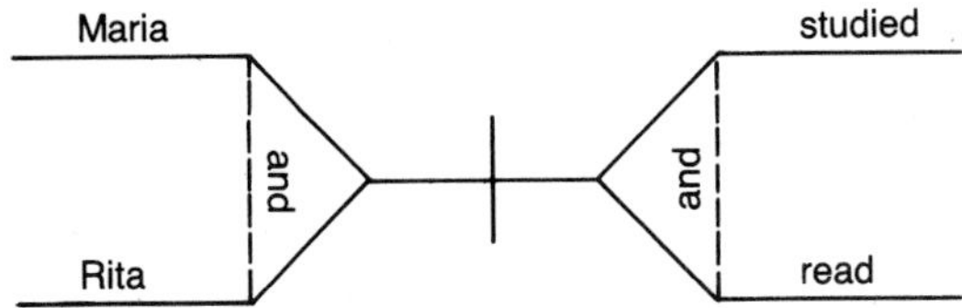


## EXERCISE 18 *Diagraming Subjects and Verbs*

Diagram the following sentences or copy them. If your teacher tells you to copy them, draw one line under each subject and two lines under each verb. If the subject is an understood *you,* write *you* in parentheses.

1. Weeds grew.
2. Babies are crying.
3. Were people laughing?
4. Jump!
5. Rachel has remembered.
6. Mother and Father are working.
7. Jake tripped or stumbled.
8. Is José pitching?
9. Children and dogs were wading.
10. Windows and doors creaked and rattled.

## Application to Writing

In a well-written paragraph, the sentences flow in a natural rhythm. One way to make your writing flow is to combine short sentences into longer ones. If two sentences have the same verb but different subjects, you can combine them by using a compound subject.

| | |
|---|---|
| TWO SENTENCES | Those pencils belong to me. Those books belong to me. |
| COMBINED SENTENCES | Those pencils and books belong to me. [combined with a compound subject] |
| TWO SENTENCES | Ancient pyramids in Mexico attract many tourists. Ancient temples in Mexico attract many tourists. |
| COMBINED SENTENCES | Ancient pyramids and temples in Mexico attract many tourists. [combined with a compound subject] |

NOTE: Some repeated words can be dropped when sentences are combined.

You can also combine two short sentences that have the same subject but different verbs by using a compound verb.

| | |
|---|---|
| TWO SENTENCES | Jeff auditioned for the school play. Jeff won the leading role. |
| COMBINED SENTENCES | Jeff auditioned for the school play and won the leading role. [combined with a compound verb] |
| TWO SENTENCES | Lori finished her science project. Lori left it at home. |
| COMBINED SENTENCES | Lori finished her science project but left it at home. [combined with a compound verb] |

### *EXERCISE 19 Combining Sentences*

Number your paper 1 to 10. Then combine each pair of sentences into one sentence with a compound subject or a compound verb. Use the word in brackets to join the compound subject or compound verb.

EXAMPLE Cora walked through the woods. Cora sketched some of the wild flowers. [and]

ANSWER Cora walked through the woods and sketched some of the wild flowers.

1. Hawks kill many rodents. Owls kill many rodents. [and]
2. Some fish leave the water. These fish climb up the roots of trees with their fins. [and]
3. Captain Robert Scott competed in the race to the South Pole. Roald Amundsen competed in the race to the South Pole. [and]
4. Tim missed the first pass. Tim later ran 60 yards for a touchdown. [but]
5. Two mother ducks were swimming in Huntington Pond. Their 12 ducklings were swimming in Huntington Pond. [and]
6. Buds are formed on trees in the fall. Buds remain on the branches throughout the winter. [and]
7. A hockey game will be on television at noon today. A basketball game will be on television at noon today. [and]
8. The woodpecker does not kill trees. The woodpecker simply destroys the harmful insects inside the tree. [but]
9. During halftime the cheerleaders performed. The band also performed. [and]
10. The horses hobbled across the stony riverbed. The horses then broke into a trot across the field on the other side. [and]

# Chapter Review

**A** **Finding Subjects and Verbs.** Number your paper 1 to 10. Then write the subject and the verb in each sentence.

1. A housefly will live for only about 15 days.
2. The umpire threw a new ball to the pitcher.
3. Directly over our house flew the WCRN helicopter.
4. Is Sandy singing in the variety show?
5. The cowboy swung into the saddle and headed for the range.
6. That movie has been playing at Cinema 1 for weeks.
7. Has Jamie or Franklin ever read *Treasure Island*?
8. From the basement came a loud noise.
9. An average hen will lay about 200 eggs a year.
10. Nancy raced to the telephone and called the fire department.

**B** **Finding Subjects and Verbs.** Number your paper 1 to 10. Then write the subject and the verb in each sentence. If the subject is an understood *you,* write *you* in parentheses.

1. Didn't camels live in North America at one time?
2. Tennis and soccer are very popular sports in many countries.
3. The mail and the newspaper have always arrived on time.
4. Pour some more water onto the fire.
5. Hadn't Andy ever tasted eggplant before?
6. Both parrots and mynas can whistle and can imitate speech.
7. Is Albany the capital of New York?
8. In the clear stream swam some fish.
9. Look at those beautiful pink clouds.
10. Right in the center of the distant target quivered the arrow.

**C** **Finding Subjects and Verbs.** Number your paper 1 to 10. Then write the subject and the verb in each sentence.

1. Have you ever heard this true story?
2. For weeks a young boy had begged his father for a dog.
3. During this time the terrier down the block had puppies.
4. Shortly afterward the boy's father came home with one of the puppies.
5. The father and the mother put the little dog in the basement for the first two nights.
6. Throughout both nights the puppy howled and howled.
7. The neighbors could also hear its sad cries.
8. Next morning the mother heard a noise and opened the front door.
9. There stood the pup's mother.
10. The dog walked in, grabbed her pup by the scruff of the neck, and returned home with it.

## Mastery Test

Number your paper 1 to 10. Make two columns on your paper. Label the first column *subjects* and the second column *verbs*. Then under the proper heading, write each subject and each verb. (Some subjects and verbs are compound.)

1. The Vikings founded the city of Dublin, Ireland.
2. The Dutch have played ice hockey since 1670.
3. The baby raccoon and its mother carefully washed their food in the clear stream.
4. In front of the curtain, the actors took their bow.
5. The musicians will perform in the Fourth of July concert.
6. The hikers followed the trail and came to a hut.
7. Charles couldn't have known about the award.
8. Did Pam bring her lunch to school today?
9. On the top of the mountain above us stood one tree.
10. Uranus and Neptune probably have rocky cores.

2

# Nouns and Pronouns

## Diagnostic Test

Number your paper 1 to 10. Write each underlined word. Then label each one *noun* or *pronoun*.

EXAMPLE My teacher gave me extra help after school.
ANSWER teacher—noun, me—pronoun

1. Will you drive us to the game?
2. Those are my baby pictures.
3. Mount Rushmore is a spectacular monument.
4. Who is substituting for Mr. Mason?
5. I lived in New Jersey for three years.
6. Does John think this is a good price for a camera?
7. On their next hike, the Andersons are taking a compass.
8. Everyone in my class is going on the field trip.
9. Excitement filled the stadium as our team appeared.
10. She didn't say anything but the truth.

# Nouns

The thousands of words in the English language can be divided into eight groups called the *parts of speech*. Each part of speech does a different job in a sentence.

**The Eight Parts of Speech**

| | |
|---|---|
| **noun** [names] | **preposition** [relates] |
| **pronoun** [replaces] | **conjunction** [connects] |
| **verb** [states action or being] | **interjection** [expresses strong feeling] |
| **adjective** [describes, limits] | |
| **adverb** [describes, limits] | |

The most common part of speech is the *noun*. Nouns are sometimes called naming words, because they name people, places, things, and ideas.

2a A **noun** is a word that names a person, a place, a thing, or an idea.

| | |
|---|---|
| PEOPLE | boy, pilot, teachers, Mr. Jenkins, Pamela |
| PLACES | classrooms, park, theater, Arizona, lake |
| THINGS | bells, water, Mars, oxygen, memory, science |
| IDEAS AND QUALITIES | honesty, kindness, peace, truth, wisdom, hope, independence, freedom, loyalty |

### EXERCISE 1 *Finding Nouns*

Number your paper 1 to 10. Then write each noun. There are 33 nouns.

Dinosaurs

1. At one time dinosaurs were rulers of the earth.
2. Some of these creatures were as big as houses.
3. Other dinosaurs were as small as turkeys.
4. Many of these animals walked on two legs and used their hands to hold things.

5. Their brains were tiny—no bigger than a walnut.
6. We know about these reptiles from footprints and from fossils such as eggs, bones, and teeth.
7. Some bones have been formed into whole skeletons.
8. By studying fossils, experts can tell if dinosaurs ate plants or meat.
9. Many questions, however, still have no answers.
10. One such mystery is that we have no knowledge of what color these ancient creatures were.

## Common and Proper Nouns

Nouns can be divided into two groups: common nouns and proper nouns. A *common noun* names any person, place, or thing. A *proper noun* names a particular person, place, or thing. All proper nouns begin with a capital letter.

| | |
|---|---|
| COMMON NOUNS | teacher, lake, language, relative |
| PROPER NOUNS | Mrs. Gray, Lake Erie, French, Aunt Kay |

NOTE: Although a proper noun sometimes includes more than one word, it is considered *one* noun.

### EXERCISE 2 Finding Common and Proper Nouns

Number your paper 1 to 10. Make two columns on your paper. Then write the common nouns in one column and the proper nouns in the other. There are 33 nouns.

*The Call of the Wild*

1. Buck did not read the newspapers, or he would have known what was going on in California.
2. When gold was found, prospectors eagerly rushed to the area.
3. They needed dogs with strong muscles and warm coats.
4. Buck was the son of a huge Saint Bernard.
5. He lived in a house owned by Judge Miller.
6 On the night that Buck was kidnapped, the judge was at a meeting of the Raisin Growers' Association.

7. The stolen dog would never return to his warm home in the Santa Clara Valley.
8. He was taken for a long ride on a train and sold to several different people.
9. Once he even pulled a sled that delivered mail between the towns of Dawson and Skagway.
10. After his last master died, he joined several wolves and roamed freely throughout the wilderness.

### EXERCISE 3 Writing Sentences

Write five sentences that describe what a deep-sea diver might find in the hull of a sunken ship. Then underline each noun.

### TIME-OUT FOR REVIEW • • • • •

Number your paper 1 to 10. Then write each noun. (A date is a noun.) There are 33 nouns.

Circus Greats

1. In 1785, Thomas Pool presented the first circus in the United States.
2. It is not the popcorn or elephants that have made circuses last all these years.
3. The excitement has come from original acts and amazing performers.
4. Five brothers once gathered together some entertainers and traveled by wagons to various cities.
5. Their name was Ringling.
6. Later P. T. Barnum offered three shows at the same time in different rings.
7. Americans always loved Emmett Kelly, a clown with a sad face.
8. Miguel Vazquez first performed four somersaults through the air to a catcher.
9. Tom Thumb was less than a yard tall.
10. President Lincoln once invited him to the White House.

## Application to Writing

When you are writing, always choose specific nouns. They will make your writing more interesting to read.

GENERAL NOUN I want a **pet.**
SPECIFIC NOUNS **puppy, kitten, parakeet, hamster**

### EXERCISE 4 Listing Specific Nouns

Number your paper 1 to 10. Then write at least two specific nouns for each general noun.

EXAMPLE flower
POSSIBLE ANSWERS rose, aster, daisy, lily

1. machine
2. teacher
3. street
4. insect
5. store
6. sport
7. bird
8. gift
9. tool
10. tree

### EXERCISE 5 Using Specific Nouns

Number your paper 1 to 10. Then substitute a specific noun for each underlined word or group of words.

EXAMPLE I would like to live in a big city.
POSSIBLE ANSWER Chicago

1. Would you like some dessert after dinner?
2. We went to the animal shelter to look for a dog.
3. Someday I would like to meet a famous person.
4. Stacy and Mark climbed a mountain last summer.
5. A foreign country would be an exciting place to visit.
6. Does your sister go to that college?
7. The item of clothing has shrunk in the dryer.
8. We invited my relatives for dinner on a holiday.
9. The school is being renovated.
10. Having a job as a type of worker would be interesting.

### EXERCISE 6 Writing Sentences

Write five sentences that describe your school cafeteria at lunchtime. Use specific nouns whenever possible.

# Pronouns

Notice the differences between these sentences.

Rafael asked Jill if Jill would help Rafael with Rafael's math homework.

Rafael asked Jill if she would help him with his math homework.

The second sentence is shorter and clearer because pronouns have been substituted for nouns.

2b A **pronoun** is a word that takes the place of one or more nouns.

## Personal Pronouns

There are several different kinds of pronouns. *Personal pronouns* are the kind used most often.

**Personal Pronouns**

| | Singular | Plural |
|---|---|---|
| FIRST PERSON (speaker) | I, me<br>my, mine | we, us<br>our, ours |
| SECOND PERSON (person spoken to) | you<br>your, yours | you<br>your, yours |
| THIRD PERSON (person or thing spoken about) | he, him, his<br>she, her, hers<br>it, its | they, them<br>their, theirs |

| | |
|---|---|
| FIRST PERSON PRONOUNS | **I** have **my** luggage with **me**.<br>**We** left **ours** at the cottage. |
| SECOND PERSON PRONOUNS | Did **you** take **your** library books back?<br>The papers must be **yours**. |
| THIRD PERSON PRONOUNS | **She** played all **her** albums.<br>**They** like **their** eggs soft-boiled. |

## EXERCISE 7 Finding Personal Pronouns

Number your paper 1 to 10. Then write each personal pronoun. There are 20 pronouns.

1. Our tickets are for the second balcony.
2. I am scheduled to speak before she arrives.
3. Did he bring the paper in and put it on the counter?
4. We wanted her to be the umpire.
5. The blue car is ours, not theirs.
6. Give me the note, and I will take it to him.
7. Yours is on the shelf beside my trophy.
8. The small notebook is mine.
9. She and they will meet us at the library.
10. The red jacket is his.

***Antecedents.*** The word that a pronoun refers to is called an *antecedent*. An antecedent usually comes before the pronoun. The antecedent may be in the same sentence or in another sentence.

Rosalie watered the plant and hung **it** outside.

Tim has a nice smile. **He** once wore braces.

Sometimes a pronoun will have more than one antecedent.

Mary and Dan sang **their** duet perfectly.

## EXERCISE 8 Finding Antecedents

Number your paper 1 to 10. Then write each personal pronoun and its antecedent.

EXAMPLE Anna saw Fred and gave him the book.
ANSWER him—Fred

1. The dog broke its leash last night.
2. Aaron asked Sue if she would like to go skating.
3. Nina lost a contact lens. Fortunately, she also has a pair of glasses.
4. When the lights came on, their glare hurt Ed's eyes.

5. Rob displayed three of his favorite paintings.
6. The book fell on the plate and broke it.
7. Frank and Robert work in their father's restaurant.
8. Would Marilyn and her friends like to go for a swim?
9. Jason watched the balloons before they floated away.
10. On a fishing trip, don't overlook the bass. They often hide among the weeds.

## Other Kinds of Pronouns

In addition to personal pronouns, there are also indefinite pronouns, demonstrative pronouns, and interrogative pronouns.

*Indefinite pronouns* refer to unnamed persons or things. Indefinite pronouns do not usually have definite antecedents as personal pronouns do.

INDEFINITE PRONOUNS **No one** was late for the meeting.
I've told you **everything** I remember.

**Common Indefinite Pronouns**

| | | | |
|---|---|---|---|
| all | both | few | nothing |
| another | each | many | one |
| any | either | most | several |
| anybody | everybody | neither | some |
| anyone | everyone | none | someone |
| anything | everything | no one | something |

*Demonstrative pronouns* point out persons and things.

DEMONSTRATIVE PRONOUNS **This** is my best score so far.
I want to buy **these** for my father.

**Demonstrative Pronouns**

| | | | |
|---|---|---|---|
| this | that | these | those |

*Interrogative pronouns* are used to ask questions.

| | |
|---|---|
| INTERROGATIVE PRONOUNS | **What** did you do then? |
| | **Who** was invited to the party? |

**Interrogative Pronouns**

what which who whom whose

## EXERCISE 9 Finding Indefinite Pronouns

Number your paper 1 to 10. Then write each indefinite pronoun.

EXAMPLE Each of the students taking part in the playoffs was presented a trophy.

ANSWER Each

1. Someone left the living room lights on after the party.
2. All of the plans of the decorating committee will be announced at the class meeting.
3. Most of the audience cheered at the end of the film.
4. Some of the meatloaf should be saved for Greg.
5. Midge spoke to another of her brothers about her parents' anniversary.
6. Neither of the drivers knows the way.
7. The sea divers were disappointed to find nothing in the sunken ship.
8. Everyone in the club wants to attend the picnic next weekend.
9. Stephen listened to a few of the new records.
10. No one in the group knew the time of the game.

## EXERCISE 10 Finding Other Kinds of Pronouns

Number your paper 1 to 10. Then write each pronoun.

1. All of the pencils have sharp points.
2. Which is the bus schedule for North Station?
3. A dash of this will add spice to the sauce.

4. Either of the candidates would make a good class president.
5. Rebecca has said nothing about moving.
6. Three of these were made in Japan.
7. Who is knocking at the back door?
8. Not many of the students finished the test.
9. What did Gregory do last weekend?
10. David saw something strange streak across the sky.

## TIME-OUT FOR REVIEW • • • • •

Number your paper 1 to 20. Then write each pronoun.

1. No "moon germs" were found on *Apollo II* or its astronauts.
2. The judges spoke with each of the contestants.
3. This is the poster Tara wants.
4. The ancient Egyptians curled their hair with heated irons.
5. Which is the best buy?
6. Craig invited Tamara to the volleyball game. She has an excellent serve.
7. Who just called for Paulo?
8. The Great Wall of China is one of the greatest human achievements in the world.
9. That is Brian's poster.
10. Both of the twins want a large birthday party.
11. These just arrived in the mail.
12. A few of the reasons for heart attacks include bad diet, smoking, and high blood pressure.
13. Richard could not think of anything to say.
14. What is the correct time?
15. Tansy found everybody at the mall.
16. Lulu mailed a letter to her pen pal in Taiwan.
17. Douglas collects baseball cards as well as those.
18. The students ate nothing for dessert.
19. Whom will the cheerleaders choose?
20. Seals swim mainly with their hind legs.

# Chapter Review

**A** **Finding Nouns.** Number your paper 1 to 10. Then write each noun. There are 33 nouns.

1. King Louis XIX ruled France for only 15 minutes.
2. The scouts camped near a lake in the White Mountains.
3. The dentist told Matthew that he must wear braces on his teeth for three years.
4. Pure gold is rarely used in jewelry.
5. My sister plays in the band at Warren High School.
6. Timothy admires her humor and confidence.
7. Vitamins, film, and batteries will keep longer if stored in the refrigerator.
8. Have you ever seen Venus through a telescope?
9. Pat will cook pancakes or waffles for breakfast.
10. The pool in Elizabeth Park will be closed on Friday for repairs.

**B** **Finding Pronouns and Antecedents.** Number your paper 1 to 10. Write each personal pronoun. Then beside each one, write its antecedent.

1. Are Andrew and Emily visiting their cousin?
2. Emma's parents can't see the play, for they will be out of town.
3. No United States coin shows its denomination in numbers.
4. Are Cora and Lily still good friends? Lately they don't spend much time together.
5. Tonight Jim is eating dinner with the Wilsons. His parents are working late.
6. Jonathan said that he won't be taking the bus tomorrow.
7. Fleas don't have wings; they have powerful legs.
8. On Saturday Tara will fly her kite in the park.
9. Joshua and Kevin have expanded their paper routes.
10. Dawn waited until she heard the school bell.

**C** **Finding Other Pronouns.** Number your paper 1 to 10. Then write each pronoun. There are 15 pronouns.

1. In science we learned about hurricanes.
2. Frogs must close their eyes when they swallow.
3. Has everybody eaten breakfast?
4. That is a very funny story.
5. Who sent Melissa the flowers?
6. She carried the groceries into the house and placed them on the table.
7. Someone saw her ten minutes ago.
8. He doesn't like anything to disturb him during a mystery on television.
9. Most of the people enjoyed the play.
10. These are the decorations for the school party.

# Mastery Test

Number your paper 1 to 10. Write each underlined word. Then label each one *noun* or *pronoun*.

1. Mother called a plumber to fix the broken pipe.
2. Meryl and she will go with them to the ballet.
3. The happy winners threw their hats into the air.
4. The puppy licked its paw.
5. Patriotism was felt by all when the national anthem of the United States was played before the game.
6. What is the best remedy for a bad cold?
7. The coach spoke with each of us.
8. When the rain started, no one left the stadium.
9. Is this the magazine you wanted?
10. He reads everything about the stars.

# 3

# Verbs

## Diagnostic Test

Number your paper 1 to 10. Write each verb or verb phrase. Then label each one *action* or *linking*.

EXAMPLE The evenings have been quite cool lately.
ANSWER have been—linking

1. The teacher has chosen six ushers for the play.
2. Fresh corn tastes best in the summer.
3. An ant can crawl at the rate of 12 feet a minute.
4. Our history book this year is very large.
5. Did you smell this perfume?
6. Today Ronnie tasted clams for the first time.
7. Laura has been a baton twirler for many years.
8. Eric and Rosa are members of the soccer team.
9. In 1923, you could buy a Model T Ford for $295.
10. The first capital of the United States was New York.

# Action Verbs

Without a *verb* a group of words cannot be a sentence. One kind of verb is called an *action verb.* Action verbs are easy to recognize. They often show some kind of action.

3a An **action verb** tells what action a subject is performing.

To find an action verb, first find the subject of the sentence. Then ask yourself, *What is the subject doing?*

Carl **pitched** the first game. [The subject is *Carl.* What did Carl do? *Pitched* is the action verb.]

Some action verbs show physical action. Others show mental action.

PHYSICAL ACTION Sandy **put** a dime in the meter.
The large vase **tipped** over.

MENTAL ACTION Belinda always **thinks** positively.
We **believed** her story.

Other action verbs, such as *have* and *own,* show ownership or possession.

OWNERSHIP Lilly **has** two tickets.
The Russos **own** a canoe.

### EXERCISE 1 *Finding Action Verbs*

Number your paper 1 to 10. Then write each action verb.

EXAMPLE Phil dodged the tackle.
ANSWER dodged

1. With a wide grin, Dad placed the huge fish on the table.
2. A comet's tail always points away from the sun.
3. The swimmer dived from the dock at the end of the lawn into the clear lake.

4. Most spiders have eight eyes.
5. Everyone hoped for a sunny day.
6. Last summer I visited my grandparents in Idaho for three weeks.
7. The telephone rang all morning.
8. The sailboat skimmed across the bay.
9. Five minutes later Paul remembered the answer.
10. Thomas Edison invented wax paper.

### EXERCISE 2 *Finding Action Verbs*

Number your paper 1 to 10. Then write each action verb.

A Chilly Race

1. Every year dogsled drivers race across the frozen landscape of Alaska.
2. The course stretches more than a thousand miles from Anchorage to Nome.
3. Weather conditions often create hazards for the racers.
4. Snow and storms sometimes hide the trails.
5. Each driver carries snowshoes, a sleeping bag, and food for the dogs.
6. Drivers even take boots for the dogs' feet.
7. Veterinarians examine the dogs at checkpoints along the route.
8. Host families welcome the racers into their homes.
9. They feed the drivers and dogs at resting points.
10. Most competitors complete the race within 12 or 13 days.

### EXERCISE 3 *Writing Sentences*

Number your paper 1 to 20. Then write a sentence for each of the following action verbs.

1. wrote
2. spilled
3. studied
4. caught
5. glided
6. carved
7. thought
8. carried
9. roared
10. had
11. hiked
12. rode
13. step
14. knew
15. swam
16. pushed
17. jumped
18. ran
19. dived
20. skied

# Linking Verbs

Some verbs show being instead of action.

Therese **was** at the library.

Some being verbs, called *linking verbs,* link the subject with another word in the sentence.

3b A **linking verb** links the subject with another word that renames or describes the subject.

Joan **was** captain of the softball team. [*Was* links *captain* with *Joan. Captain* renames the subject.]

The rain **will be** heavy tomorrow. [*Will be* links *heavy* with *rain. Heavy* describes the rain.]

**Common Forms of *Be* Used as Linking Verbs**

| | | | |
|---|---|---|---|
| be | was | could be | have been |
| is | were | should be | has been |
| am | shall be | may be | could have been |
| are | will be | might be | must have been |

### EXERCISE 4 *Finding Linking Verbs*

Number your paper 1 to 10. Write each linking verb. Then write the two words that the verb links.

EXAMPLE They are the winners of the race.
ANSWER are—they, winners

1. A snake's skin is quite dry.
2. You might be right.
3. They are the officers of the Honor Society.
4. Frank has been ill all week.
5. A glider is an airplane without any engines.

6. That story could be true.
7. That rope must have been old.
8. They were the winners of the art contest.
9. Should the lights on the stage be brighter?
10. The largest bone in the body is the thighbone.

### EXERCISE 5 Finding Linking Verbs

Number your paper 1 to 10. Write each linking verb. Then write the two words that the verb links.

1. Will you be warm in that jacket?
2. Carrie should be the editor of the newspaper.
3. Earth's first space traveler was a dog.
4. We may be late.
5. Most people are healthiest from age 5 to 15.
6. The Taylors have been our neighbors for six years.
7. I am nervous about the interview.
8. Marlene must have been happy.
9. The giraffe is the world's tallest animal.
10. In some parts of the world, cattle are still wild.

## Additional Linking Verbs

Forms of the verb *be* are not the only linking verbs. The following words can also be used as linking verbs.

**Additional Linking Verbs**

| | | | | | |
|---|---|---|---|---|---|
| appear | feel | look | seem | sound | taste |
| become | grow | remain | smell | stay | turn |

Lucy **became** the new treasurer. [*Became* links *treasurer* and *Lucy*. *Treasurer* renames the subject.]

The chili **tasted** very spicy. [*Tasted* links *spicy* and *chili*. *Spicy* describes the subject.]

### EXERCISE 6 Finding Linking Verbs

Number your paper 1 to 10. Write each linking verb. Then write the two words that the verb links.

1. The strange object appeared solid from the outside.
2. Your muscles grow firm with exercise.
3. This tuna casserole tastes wonderful.
4. Mrs. Jones became president of the local bank.
5. That cold watermelon looks delicious.
6. Those books smell musty.
7. Last week the nights turned colder.
8. Randy seemed cheerful to me.
9. The down comforter feels light.
10. They remained friends for many years.

## Linking Verb or Action Verb?

Some of the linking verbs listed on page 42 can also be action verbs. If the verb links two words, it is a linking verb. If the verb shows action, it is an action verb.

LINKING VERB His shoes **looked** new. [*Looked* links *new* and *shoes. New* describes the shoes.]

ACTION VERB Angie **looked** into the closet. [*Looked* shows action. It tells what Angie did.]

### EXERCISE 7 Distinguishing between Linking Verbs and Action Verbs

Number your paper 1 to 10. Write each verb. Then label each one *action* or *linking*.

EXAMPLE She grew fond of our family.
ANSWER grew—linking

1. That siren sounds extremely loud.
2. The lost child remained silent.
3. Did you feel the rabbit's soft fur?

4. All of us smelled the roses.
5. Your car looks so shiny.
6. The people remained in their seats.
7. I feel absolutely great today.
8. The bugle sounded the beginning of the race.
9. The roses smelled delightful.
10. We looked under the bed.

### EXERCISE 8 Writing Sentences

Write two sentences for each of the following verbs. First use the verb as a linking verb. Then use it as an action verb. Label each one *linking* or *action*.

1. look 2. feel 3. taste 4. smell 5. sound

## TIME-OUT FOR REVIEW • • • • •

Number your paper 1 to 10. Write each verb. Then label each one *action* or *linking*.

EXAMPLE The blue whale is the world's largest animal.
ANSWER is—linking

The Blue Whale

1. The biggest dinosaur was smaller than a blue whale.
2. Blue whales are toothless.
3. They eat mainly tiny creatures of the sea.
4. These huge animals stay underwater for periods as long as 20 minutes.
5. During the summer blue whales approach Arctic and Antarctic icebergs.
6. During the winter, however, they migrate to subtropical waters.
7. On rare occasions blue whales have twins.
8. Blue whales are very intelligent.
9. Unfortunately, blue whales became an endangered species some time ago.
10. Many people hope for a change in this situation.

# Helping Verbs

*Helping verbs,* or auxiliary verbs, are used with a main verb to form a *verb phrase.*

3c A **verb phrase** is a main verb plus one or more helping verbs.

Following is a list of common helping verbs.

| Common Helping Verbs | |
|---|---|
| ***be*** | am, is, are, was, were, be, being, been |
| ***have*** | has, have, had |
| ***do*** | do, does, did |
| **others** | may, might, must, can, could, shall, should, will, would |

A verb phrase may have one or more helping verbs.

Critics **have nominated** that movie for an Oscar.
The homeroom lists **will be hanging** outside the office.

Like action verbs linking verbs may have helping verbs.

By tomorrow the weather **will turn** cold.

Sometimes a verb phrase is interrupted by other words.

Carol **has** always **seemed** calm before swim meets.
Julio **must** not **be coming** to the meeting.
I **have**n't **heard** his latest record yet.

To find the verb phrase in a question, turn the question around to make a statement.

QUESTION Have they joined the camera club?
STATEMENT They **have joined** the camera club.

NOTE: Remember that a verb phrase is called a verb.

## EXERCISE 9 Finding Verbs

Number your paper 1 to 10. Then write each verb.

1. As long ago as Colonial times, American children were playing hopscotch and leapfrog.
2. Newspapers will turn yellow in the sunlight.
3. Dan has never been on a houseboat.
4. My grandparents should be visiting us soon.
5. Have you met my brother?
6. Rachel is painting her bedroom.
7. I haven't seen Yvonne all day.
8. Our class has recently been reading that wonderful novel *The Red Pony*.
9. Will Kara be happy with this sweater?
10. The weather has not turned cooler today.

## TIME-OUT FOR REVIEW • • • • •

Number your paper 1 to 15. Write each verb. Then label each one *action* or *linking*.

Disney's Dream on Day One

1. In 1955, Disneyland became the first theme park.
2. Disney built the fantastic park in Anaheim, California.
3. Nearly 30,000 people attended the grand opening.
4. The first day could have been the end for Disneyland.
5. Fantasyland temporarily closed because of a gas leak.
6. Refreshment stands didn't have enough food.
7. Some of the buildings were still wet with fresh paint.
8. The asphalt on Main Street was soft from the hot sun.
9. Shoes stuck in the asphalt.
10. Millions saw these problems on news shows.
11. Newspapers gave Disneyland very bad reviews.
12. "Walt's Dream Is a Nightmare."
13. Disneyland's future would soon look brighter.
14. After only seven weeks of operation, Disneyland welcomed its one-millionth guest.
15. At the close of its first year, 3.8 million people had gone through the gates of Disneyland.

## Application to Writing

Many verbs have *synonyms,* words that mean nearly the same thing. Some of these synonyms are colorful, action-packed verbs. When you write, use the dictionary or a thesaurus to find substitutes for dull, overused verbs.

### EXERCISE 10 Substituting Colorful Verbs

Number your paper 1 to 10. Then for each blank, write a different substitute for the verb *walk.* Use the following words in your answers.

| hiked | glided | marched | plodded | strolled |
|---|---|---|---|---|
| paced | limped | paraded | trudged | strutted |

1. Last week we ______ to the top of Mount Clinton.
2. With plenty of time to spare, the young couple ______ along the busy street.
3. The man ______ back and forth in the waiting room.
4. The ballerinas ______ across the stage.
5. The band members ______ proudly in the parade.
6. The injured player ______ off the field.
7. The weary hikers ______ into camp.
8. The models ______ down the ramp.
9. Having missed the bus, Jerry ______ the two miles to school.
10. In his new suit, Gregory ______ past his friends.

### EXERCISE 11 Listing Colorful Verbs

Number your paper 1 to 5. Then write two colorful synonyms for each overused verb.

1. sit 2. say 3. go 4. watch 5. run

### EXERCISE 12 Writing Sentences

Write five sentences that describe an airplane taking off. Use colorful verbs.

# Chapter Review

**A** **Finding Action and Linking Verbs.** Number your paper 1 to 10. Write each verb. Then label each one *action* or *linking.*

1. Magellan began his trip around the world in 1519.
2. For short distances lizards are very fast.
3. Does anyone smell smoke?
4. The gymnasts appeared nervous before the match.
5. Tony gently felt the pony's side.
6. Benjamin Franklin founded the world's first take-out library.
7. The first female driver in the Indianapolis 500 was Janet Guthrie.
8. From end to end, the Great Wall of China stretches about 1,500 miles.
9. Canada is the second largest country in the world.
10. A dog's weakest sense is its eyesight.

**B** **Finding Verb Phrases.** Number your paper 1 to 10. Write each verb. Remember that words may interrupt a verb phrase.

1. My brother will be home by noon.
2. Because of the storm we might not go to the concert.
3. During your lifetime your brain may store up to 100 million bits of information.
4. Front-wheel-drive cars are becoming very popular in the United States.
5. At sunset the fire was still burning out of control.
6. The first public railroad was not built until 1825.
7. Robins have been appearing early this spring.
8. Haven't they become friends quickly?
9. Don't those lilies smell wonderful?
10. People have been wearing glasses for over 700 years.

**C** **Finding the Verb.** Number your paper 1 to 10. Write each verb. Then label each one *action* or *linking*.

A Huge Dinosaur

1. For millions of years, dinosaurs ruled the land.
2. The brontosaurus was a huge animal.
3. This dinosaur reached a weight of 30 or 40 tons!
4. Because of its weight, it became a water animal.
5. Water took the pressure of its weight off its feet.
6. In fairly deep water, a brontosaurus could even float.
7. The water was also protection from its enemies.
8. The brontosaurus looked fierce and mean.
9. Actually, it was never a threat to other dinosaurs.
10. This huge animal ate only vegetation.

## Mastery Test

Number your paper 1 to 10. Write each verb or verb phrase. Then label each one *action* or *linking*.

1. Sally looked very happy at her birthday party.
2. The turkey in the oven smells delicious.
3. Will Sherry be attending the meeting today?
4. That could have been George in the car.
5. Their dog plays gently with the little kitten.
6. Squirrels come down trees headfirst.
7. Missy looked everywhere for her watch.
8. The diameter of the sun is 864,000 miles.
9. Everyone could smell the carnations in her corsage.
10. An owl's eyes do not move in their sockets.

4

# Adjectives and Adverbs

## Diagnostic Test

Number your paper 1 to 10. Write each underlined word. Then label each one *adjective* or *adverb*.

EXAMPLE The three cheerleaders yelled loudly.
ANSWER three—adjective, loudly—adverb

1. The happy cat purred softly.
2. The British ship sailed past.
3. The bright sun was quite hot.
4. A cheetah can run very swiftly.
5. Kerry finally bought two tickets.
6. The tree, tall and straight, reached above the house.
7. Unexpectedly the baseball team won.
8. Those young children are not playing noisily.
9. That old clock works quietly and accurately.
10. Which red flower is a zinnia?

# Adjectives

Two of the eight parts of speech are called modifiers. A *modifier* makes the meaning of another word more precise. Modifiers are very important because they add color and exactness to writing and speaking. One kind of modifier is an adjective.

**4a** An **adjective** is a word that modifies a noun or a pronoun.

An adjective answers the question *What kind? Which one? How many?* or *How much?* about nouns and some pronouns. The adjectives in the following examples are in heavy type. An arrow points to the noun or the pronoun each adjective modifies.

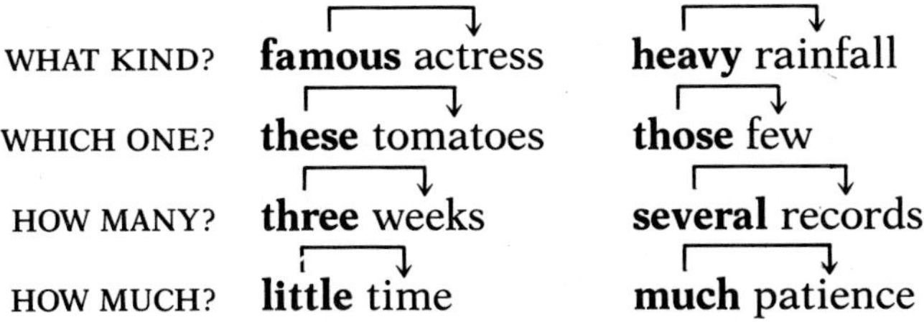

| | | |
|---|---|---|
| WHAT KIND? | **famous** actress | **heavy** rainfall |
| WHICH ONE? | **these** tomatoes | **those** few |
| HOW MANY? | **three** weeks | **several** records |
| HOW MUCH? | **little** time | **much** patience |

An adjective usually comes right in front of the word it modifies. Occasionally, however, an adjective will follow the word it modifies. An adjective can also follow a linking verb. *(See pages 41 and 42 for lists of common linking verbs.)*

| | |
|---|---|
| BEFORE A NOUN | A **huge, ugly** monster was the star of the movie. |
| AFTER A NOUN | A monster, **huge** and **ugly,** was the star of the movie. |
| AFTER A LINKING VERB | The monster was **huge** and **ugly** in the movie. |

Notice that more than one adjective can modify the same noun or pronoun.

The words *a, an,* and *the* form a special group of adjectives called *articles.* These words are the adjectives that you use most often.

ARTICLES Did you eat **an** omelet at **the** brunch?

### EXERCISE 1 *Finding Adjectives*

Number your paper 1 to 10. Write each adjective. Then beside each one, write the word it modifies. There are 20 adjectives. (Do not list *a, an,* and *the.*)

EXAMPLE Dangerous hurricanes can cause much trouble.

ANSWER dangerous—hurricanes, much—trouble

Big Winds

1. A fierce hurricane begins over the ocean in the hot parts of the world.
2. Strong winds come from opposite directions and smash together.
3. Then the wild winds move in a circular pattern.
4. The center of the hurricane, called the eye, is calm and quiet.
5. The eye is an area of light breezes and puffy clouds.
6. If the mighty winds of a hurricane hit land, they can cause severe damage.
7. Tall, sturdy buildings have collapsed because of the huge waves or terrible winds of a hurricane.
8. With a hurricane comes heavy rain that often causes additional damage to property.
9. The rains often cause many rivers to overflow.
10. After a hurricane hits land, the powerful storm begins to weaken.

### EXERCISE 2 *Writing Sentences*

Write five sentences that describe a character in a story, TV show, or movie. Describe the person's appearance and personality. Then underline each adjective.

## Proper Adjectives

A proper noun is the name of a particular person, place, or thing. A *proper adjective* is formed from a proper noun. A proper adjective always begins with a capital letter.

| PROPER NOUNS | PROPER ADJECTIVES |
|---|---|
| China | **Chinese** history |
| Europe | **European** countries |
| Democrat | **Democratic** candidate |

### EXERCISE 3 Finding Proper Adjectives

Number your paper 1 to 10. Write each proper adjective. Then beside each one, write the word it modifies.

1. Mr. Taylor speaks with an English accent.
2. The Chinese embroidery was very delicate.
3. A Congressional committee was formed to study the issue.
4. José bought a souvenir at the Italian festival.
5. We could see the Mexican coast from the boat.
6. Can you name the Canadian provinces?
7. My neighbor was a delegate to the last Republican convention.
8. Nancy Coleman owns a German clock.
9. We ate Greek food at the fair.
10. They just won a Hawaiian vacation.

## Adjective or Noun?

A word's part of speech depends on how it is used in a sentence. That is why one word can be a noun in one sentence and an adjective in another sentence.

NOUN Let's go to the **beach** today.

ADJECTIVE Did you lose your **beach** towel?

NOUN The baby caught my **cold.**

ADJECTIVE I like **cold** weather.

### EXERCISE 4 Distinguishing between Adjectives and Nouns

Number your paper 1 to 10. Then label each underlined word *adjective* or *noun*.

1. How many gallons of paint did you buy?
2. I will need a new winter coat this year.
3. The baseball soared into the bleachers.
4. Will you travel by train or by car?
5. Finding time to study is a major problem for me.
6. Can the paint stains be removed from the rug?
7. The train station was crowded at six o'clock.
8. Last winter we had 20 inches of snow.
9. Chet's father is a major in the army.
10. Did you join the baseball team this year?

### EXERCISE 5 Writing Sentences

Write two sentences for each of the following words. The first sentence should use the word as an adjective. The second sentence should use the word as a noun. Then label the use of each one.

1. radio 2. art 3. silver 4. city 5. apple

## Adjective or Pronoun?

Some words can be used as pronouns or adjectives. A word such as *these* is a pronoun if it stands alone and takes the place of a noun. The same word can be an adjective if it modifies a noun or a pronoun.

ADJECTIVE **That** dog belongs to me. [*That* modifies *dog*.]

PRONOUN **That** belongs to me. [*That* takes the place of the noun *dog*.]

ADJECTIVE **Which** pen do you want?
PRONOUN **Which** do you want?

ADJECTIVE **Many** fans left the game early.
PRONOUN **Many** left the game early.

All of the following words can be used as pronouns or adjectives.

**Words Used as Pronouns or Adjectives**

| Demonstrative | Interrogative | Indefinite | |
|---|---|---|---|
| that | what | all | many |
| these | which | another | more |
| this | whose | any | most |
| those | | both | neither |
| | | each | other |
| | | either | several |
| | | few | some |

## EXERCISE 6 Distinguishing between Adjectives and Pronouns

Number your paper 1 to 10. Then label each underlined word *adjective* or *pronoun.*

1. That is Morgan's stamp collection.
2. Ken has seen the movie several times.
3. I'll take three of those cucumbers.
4. I saw a few things in the museum shop that I liked very much.
5. Those should be stored in the cabinet in the corner of the basement.
6. At what time should we meet?
7. That bicycle is on sale.
8. We need several for the salad.
9. What did he say to you?
10. By the end of class, few had finished the test.

## EXERCISE 7 Writing Sentences

Write two sentences for each of the following words. The first sentence should use the word as an adjective. The second sentence should use the word as a pronoun. Then label the use of each one.

1. some 2. this 3. which 4. these 5. all

## TIME-OUT FOR REVIEW • • • • •

Number your paper 1 to 15. Write each adjective. Then beside each one, write the word it modifies. There are 33 adjectives. (Do not list *a, an,* and *the.*)

EXAMPLE Many movies have pictured gorillas as ferocious animals.

ANSWERS many—movies, ferocious—animals

Gorillas

1. Gorillas, shy and gentle, are peaceful animals.
2. A gorilla may reach a height of six feet.
3. The arms, long and powerful, almost touch the ground.
4. Gorillas live in small family groups.
5. They roam many miles each day in search of food.
6. They eat fruits and green leafy plants.
7. Toward evening they construct several platforms.
8. The male leader sleeps on the bottom platform.
9. The leader is the strongest and protects the other members.
10. The females and the young gorillas sleep on the top platforms on high branches.
11. Every day gorillas build new shelters.
12. Gorillas with short hair live in the hot, damp areas of the Congo River valley.
13. The faces of these gorillas are hairless and shiny.
14. Gorillas with coarse hair live in the cool air of the African mountains.
15. Most gorillas live in and around the Albert National Park in Africa.

## Application to Writing

When you write, choosing the right adjective can make a difference. Use a dictionary or thesaurus to select adjectives that create a clear picture for your readers.

UNCLEAR The car sped past.
CLEAR The **sleek black** car sped past.
The **red compact** car sped past.
The **noisy old** car sped past.

### EXERCISE 8 *Finding Specific Adjectives*

Number your paper 1 to 5. Find at least three specific adjectives that would describe each noun. Create a clear picture with each adjective.

EXAMPLE street
POSSIBLE ANSWERS shady, wide, noisy, slippery

1. friend 2. dancer 3. bridge 4. bear 5. tree

### EXERCISE 9 *Expanding Sentences*

Expand each sentence by adding two specific adjectives.

EXAMPLE The boys opened the door.
POSSIBLE ANSWER The curious boys opened the squeaky door.

1. A light shone through the window.
2. The wind damaged the barn.
3. The boat sailed across the ocean.
4. Skaters gathered around the bonfire.
5. The class decorated the room with streamers.

### EXERCISE 10 *Writing Sentences*

Write five sentences that describe what a creature from outer space might look like in a science-fiction movie. Use fresh, specific adjectives.

# Adverbs

Another kind of modifier is an adverb. Adverbs make your writing more precise. Notice in the following examples how the second sentence gives more information just by adding two adverbs.

Jonathan is writing his report.
Jonathan is **carefully** writing his report **now.**

4b An **adverb** is a word that modifies a verb, an adjective, or another adverb.

Many adverbs are easy to recognize because they end in *-ly*.

Write **neatly** and answer the questions **carefully.**
Did Ruth **finally** complete her swimming test **successfully?**

The following chart shows, however, that some common adverbs do not end in *-ly*.

**Common Adverbs**

| | | | |
|---|---|---|---|
| again | ever | outside | somewhere |
| almost | here | quite | soon |
| already | just | rather | still |
| also | never | seldom | then |
| always | not | so | there |
| away | now | sometimes | too |
| down | often | somewhat | very |

NOTE: *Not* and its contraction *n't* are always adverbs.

The washing machine is **not** working.
I have**n't** eaten lunch.

## Adverbs That Modify Verbs

Most adverbs modify verbs. To find these adverbs, first find each verb. Then ask yourself, *Where? When? How?* or *To what extent?* about each one. The answers to these questions will be adverbs. Notice that an adverb can appear anywhere in the sentence.

WHERE? The old fence fell **down.**

WHEN? **Then** the phone rang.

HOW? The council meeting ended **abruptly.**

TO WHAT EXTENT? Stacy **almost** won the race.

If the verb contains helping verbs, the adverb modifies the entire verb phrase.

He has packed the dishes **carefully.**

**Soon** the heavy rains will begin **again.**

Uncle Ray has **not** met my soccer coach.

Does the river **often** overflow its banks?

Notice in the previous examples that an adverb can interrupt a verb phrase.

### EXERCISE 11 *Finding Adverbs*

Number your paper 1 to 10. Then write each adverb and the word or words it modifies.

EXAMPLE I have seldom seen a raccoon.
ANSWER seldom—have seen

1. Female birds rarely sing.
2. The huge crowd rushed forward.
3. Lately I have been watching the evening news.
4. Danny was quickly eating his dinner.
5. Did you really forget her birthday?

6. Finally the cold weather has ended.
7. The track team is practicing again.
8. We have looked everywhere for her contact lens.
9. A hard-boiled egg will spin easily.
10. A raw egg will not spin.

## EXERCISE 12 Finding Adverbs

Number your paper 1 to 10. Write the two adverbs in each sentence. Then beside each one, write the word or words it modifies.

EXAMPLE Kate swims quickly but gracefully.
ANSWER quickly—swims, gracefully—swims

1. Ellis will never go there.
2. The panther stalked its prey quietly and cautiously.
3. Don't look down!
4. You should always write neatly.
5. Sometimes I also sing a solo.
6. We often eat here.
7. Nancy always sings superbly.
8. Franklin hasn't arrived yet.
9. I have already read the assignment thoroughly.
10. We can collect our paycheck weekly or monthly.

## EXERCISE 13 Writing Sentences

Number your paper 1 to 5. Using an adverb, write a sentence that follows each direction. Underline each adverb.

EXAMPLE Describe how a bird flies.
POSSIBLE ANSWER A bird flies <u>gracefully</u>.

1. Describe how a friend talks.
2. Describe how a detective enters a dark, scary house.
3. Describe how a toddler walks.
4. Describe how you do your homework.
5. Describe how you eat spaghetti.

## Adverbs That Modify Adjectives and Other Adverbs

An adverb can modify an adjective or another adverb. When it does, it usually comes before the word it modifies.

MODIFYING AN ADJECTIVE Barry's compliments were **truly** sincere. [*Sincere* is an adjective. *Truly* tells how sincere Barry's compliments were.]

MODIFYING AN ADVERB Ada finished her homework **very** quickly. [*Quickly* is an adverb. *Very* tells how quickly Ada finished.]

### EXERCISE 14 Finding Adverbs

Number your paper 1 to 15. Write each underlined adverb. Then beside each one, write the word it modifies.

EXAMPLE Ken rode very fast around the bicycle track.
ANSWER fast—rode, very—fast

1. The actors were extremely nervous.
2. You should drive very carefully.
3. It rains quite often during the month of April.
4. Your turkey dinner tasted truly delicious.
5. Rita arrived too early.
6. Snow fell quite heavily for an hour.
7. Lenny has an unusually powerful pitch.
8. The truck was moving rather slowly.
9. The music was exceptionally loud.
10. The assembly seemed somewhat long.
11. The audience is usually enthusiastic.
12. Joyce is often absent from practice.
13. The toddler grew curiously silent during dinner.
14. This orange tastes strangely bitter.
15. Despite the parade the horses appeared totally calm.

## TIME-OUT FOR REVIEW • • • • •

Number your paper 1 to 10. Write each adverb. Then beside each one, write the word or words it modifies. There are 15 adverbs.

The Giraffe

1. Giraffes glide gracefully and noiselessly across the plains of Kenya in Africa.
2. There they search eagerly for the acacia tree.
3. A family of giraffes often feeds from the same tree.
4. Drinking water is the most difficult job.
5. This unusually tall animal drinks slowly and awkwardly.
6. The giraffe's very long neck contains the same number of bones as the neck of a guinea pig.
7. These neck bones are much longer in the giraffe.
8. The giraffe seldom uses its quite unusual voice.
9. A giraffe will not attack other creatures.
10. Other animals rarely threaten its survival.

## Application to Writing

When you write, begin some of your sentences with an adverb for variety.

| | |
|---|---|
| REGULAR ORDER | The pilot changed direction **suddenly.** |
| VARIETY | **Suddenly** the pilot changed direction. |

### EXERCISE 15 *Creating Sentence Variety*

Number your paper 1 to 10. Use each word as an adverb in a sentence. Then change five of the sentences around so that they begin with the adverb.

1. calmly
2. soon
3. finally
4. quickly
5. never
6. later
7. proudly
8. carefully
9. often
10. mysteriously

# Diagraming Adjectives and Adverbs

In a sentence diagram, adjectives and adverbs are both diagramed on a slanted line below the words they modify.

The tall tree leaned over.

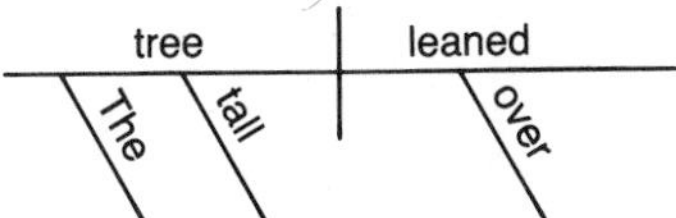


***An Adverb That Modifies an Adjective or Another Adverb.*** This adverb is also connected to the word it modifies. It is written on a line parallel to the word it modifies.

The unusually bright stars glittered quite intensely.

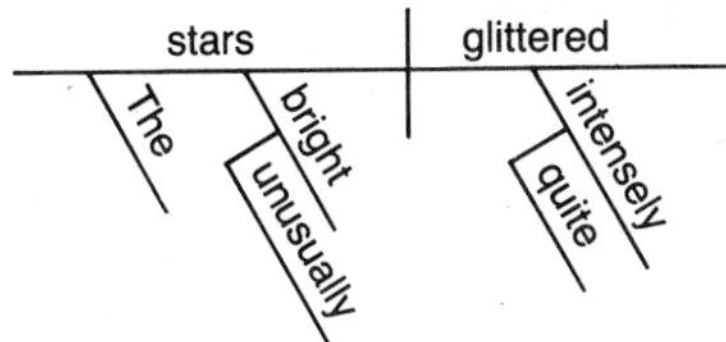


### EXERCISE 16 Diagraming Adjectives and Adverbs

Diagram the following sentences or copy them. If your teacher tells you to copy them, draw one line under each subject and two lines under each verb. Then label each modifier *adjective* or *adverb*.

1. Three chickens have escaped.
2. Julia worked steadily.
3. Suddenly the brilliant sun disappeared.
4. Fierce winds blew daily.
5. An elephant can move noiselessly.
6. The strong batter grinned confidently.
7. The rather large ball bounced high.
8. She writes quite often.
9. Have the three workers finished so soon?
10. Very young kittens run quite awkwardly.

# Chapter Review

**A** **Identifying Adjectives and Adverbs.** Number your paper 1 to 10. Make two columns on your paper. Label the first column *adjectives* and the second column *adverbs.* Then under the proper heading, write each adjective and each adverb. (Do not list *a, an,* and *the.*)

EXAMPLE A bright light suddenly flashed.
ANSWER *adjectives* *adverbs*
bright suddenly

1. Finally we finished the new doghouse for Tex.
2. The Irish soccer team has often won.
3. Lee spoke slowly and calmly.
4. A car skidded dangerously on the icy road.
5. The French diplomats were formally introduced.
6. The ride was too scary for me.
7. Did you bring that warm jacket?
8. They left the dance unusually early.
9. You should not drive the car through the deep water.
10. The English nurse is extremely thoughtful.

**B** **Identifying Adjectives and Adverbs.** Number your paper 1 to 10. Write each adjective and each adverb. Then write the word or words each one modifies.

1. Jody answered the first question correctly.
2. The spring concert will begin soon.
3. Slowly Jeff opened the old window.
4. Karen has never tasted a green apple.
5. Occasionally Mom does research for large companies.
6. I haven't seen that movie.
7. Muffy often eats small grasshoppers.
8. Now we should listen to the latest news.
9. Everyone has worked eagerly on the magazine drive.
10. There is the first star of the night.

**C** **Noun, Pronoun, or Adjective?** Number your paper 1 to 10. Write each underlined word. Then label each one *noun, pronoun,* or *adjective.*

1. The words of that song are funny.
2. Use these to wash the car windows.
3. I always enjoy watching the news on television.
4. Which is the best buy for each of us?
5. Several of the musicians knew the song title.
6. We will need a bicycle rack for the car.
7. These news bulletins just arrived for the President.
8. Which television station do you watch?
9. That is the bicycle for me.
10. Each runner ate several bananas.

## Mastery Test

Number your paper 1 to 10. Write each underlined word. Then label each one *adjective* or *adverb.*

1. Four satellites of Jupiter can be easily seen with a good pair of binoculars.
2. The skaters performed most gracefully.
3. Does that coat come in a small size?
4. The Mexican chili was hot!
5. He drove slowly and cautiously through the parking lot.
6. What class do you have now?
7. They arrived very late.
8. Those chairs look extremely comfortable.
9. The small plane flew dangerously close to the church steeple.
10. The music, loud and shrill, gave Marty a headache.

5

# Other Parts of Speech

## Diagnostic Test

Number your paper 1 to 10. Then label each underlined word *preposition, conjunction,* or *interjection.*

EXAMPLE Wow! Look at that painting.
ANSWER Wow—interjection, at—preposition

1. Penguins have wings like flippers.
2. I listened to the records, yet I still can't speak French.
3. A cow has a special stomach with four parts.
4. Patsy's dog is large and friendly.
5. Hey! Don't leave without me.
6. The time had come, but no one was there.
7. On Tuesday morning Jorge will leave for Nevada.
8. Take a sweater or your jacket.
9. During the concert will you sit beside me?
10. Oops! Kim just dropped the sandwiches in the river.

# Prepositions

*Prepositions* can change the entire meaning of a sentence.

Please hand me the book { **on** / **near** / **under** } the table.

**5a** A **preposition** is a word that shows the relationship between a noun or a pronoun and another word in the sentence.

Following is a list of the most common prepositions.

**Common Prepositions**

| | | | | |
|---|---|---|---|---|
| about | before | during | of | toward |
| above | behind | except | off | under |
| across | below | for | on | underneath |
| after | beneath | from | over | until |
| against | beside | in | past | up |
| along | between | inside | since | upon |
| among | beyond | into | through | with |
| around | by | like | throughout | within |
| at | down | near | to | without |

## EXERCISE 1 *Supplying Prepositions*

Number your paper 1 to 10. Then write two prepositions that could fill each blank in the following sentences.

EXAMPLE The cat was sleeping ______ the couch.

POSSIBLE ANSWERS on, behind

1. The narrow road ran ______ the cliffs.
2. A huge boulder was lying ______ the path.
3. The scouts camped ______ the lake.
4. I found my watch ______ the stream.

5. Kathleen found the missing fork ______ the kitchen table.
6. The dog looked for its bone ______ the bushes.
7. The huge jet flew ______ the clouds.
8. The stunt man dived ______ the high rocks.
9. That quilt was made ______ Kathy.
10. This trail leads ______ the river.

## Prepositional Phrases

A preposition is always the first word of a group of words called a *prepositional phrase*.

5b A **prepositional phrase** is a group of words made up of a preposition, its object, and any words that modify the object.

PREPOSITIONAL PHRASES **In July** the creek is often dry. [*July* is the object of the preposition *in*.]

Lee came **with us.** [The pronoun *us* is the object of the preposition *with*.]

Put the tractor **inside the small barn.** [*Barn* is the object of the preposition *inside*. *The* and *small* modify *barn*.]

Sometimes a preposition has more than one object. Then the prepositional phrase has a *compound object of the preposition.*

COMPOUND OBJECT OF A PREPOSITION All players **except Kevin and Brian** have arrived.

Some sentences may include more than one prepositional phrase.

The tulips **in our garden** usually bloom **around May.**
**After dinner** we went **to the library.**

## *EXERCISE 2 Finding Prepositional Phrases*

Number your paper 1 to 10. Write each prepositional phrase. Then underline the preposition and circle its object. There are 15 phrases.

EXAMPLE The roads in our town were covered with ice.
ANSWER in our (town) with (ice)

1. The East Indian water lizard can run across water.
2. The Smithsonian Institution contains items of historical interest.
3. You can find toadstools beneath trees and bushes.
4. Your science book is underneath the newspaper.
5. During the last period, I wrote my report about George Washington.
6. Hakan built a tree house for his younger brother and sister.
7. Before her performance, Cindy waited nervously behind the curtain.
8. At the theater Benita can sit between you and me.
9. Can the players on the other team bring extra hockey sticks with them?
10. From the shore we watched the sun sink below the horizon.

## *EXERCISE 3 Finding Prepositional Phrases*

Number your paper 1 to 10. Write each prepositional phrase. Then underline the preposition and circle its object. There are 15 phrases.

Elephants

1. The trunk of an elephant is like a hose.
2. Elephants inhale water through their trunks.
3. Then they curl their trunks inward and shoot the water into their mouths.
4. Elephants eat food in a similar way.
5. With their trunks elephants also spray water on their backs.
6. They like water and can swim for six hours.

7. During the hottest hours, elephants often huddle under trees.
8. Elephants also throw mud over their bodies.
9. With their trunks elephants can break large branches from trees.
10. In a wildlife park, an elephant can live for 65 years.

## Preposition or Adverb?

Certain words, such as *inside,* can be a preposition in one sentence and an adverb in another. Such a word is a preposition when it is part of a prepositional phrase. It is an adverb when it stands alone.

| | |
|---|---|
| PREPOSITION | We all went ***inside*** *the house. [Inside the house* is a prepositional phrase.] |
| ADVERB | We all went **inside.** [*Inside* is an adverb that tells where we went. It is not part of a prepositional phrase, and it has no object.] |
| PREPOSITION | Climb ***up*** *the ladder.* |
| ADVERB | Climb **up.** |
| PREPOSITION | His quarter rolled ***down*** *the aisle.* |
| ADVERB | She wound the window **down.** |

### Exercise 4 Distinguishing between Prepositions and Adverbs

Number your paper 1 to 10. Then label each underlined word *preposition* or *adverb.*

1. We drove through Chicago in less than an hour.
2. The mountains stood a long way off.
3. We ate our lunch near the falls.
4. Every morning Scott and Betsy jog around the football field.
5. Can you crawl through?
6. Lisa left the tickets behind.

7. The melon rolled off the table.
8. Don't come so near!
9. Did you look around?
10. The dog's ball may have rolled behind the couch in the family room.

## Exercise 5 *Writing Sentences*

Write two sentences for each of the following words. The first sentence should use the word as a preposition. The second sentence should use the word as an adverb. Then label the use of each one.

1. in  2. up  3. across  4. along  5. below

## Time-Out for Review • • • • •

Number your paper 1 to 15. Then write the prepositional phrases in the following paragraphs.

The Loch Ness Monster

Does a monster really hide under Loch Ness? For many centuries people have reportedly seen this strange creature. The Loch Ness monster first had its picture taken in 1934. Dr. R. K. Wilson was driving along the shore. Suddenly he saw movement in the water and grabbed his camera. The result is a very famous, very blurry photograph of a mysterious object. The fuzzy picture just *might* show a strange animal with an extremely long neck. Some people, however, are not convinced by this photograph.

With special underwater cameras, scientists have searched more recently for the Loch Ness monster. Unfortunately, the new pictures also show little except fuzzy shapes. Most scientists do not believe in the monster. Possible explanations for the monster reports include a large fish, an unusual wave, and a giant seal. Believers, though, think that a dinosaur may have survived from prehistoric times. Without better evidence the Loch Ness mystery will remain unsolved.

## Adjective Phrases

Like an adjective, a prepositional phrase can modify a noun or a pronoun. This kind of phrase is called an *adjective phrase.* Adjective phrases answer the questions *Which one?* and *What kind?*

ADJECTIVE A **prickly** hedge lined the walk.

ADJECTIVE PHRASE A hedge **with sharp thorns** lined the front sidewalk.

An adjective phrase usually comes directly after the word it modifies.

5c An **adjective phrase** is a prepositional phrase that modifies a noun or a pronoun.

A sentence can have one or more adjective phrases.

ADJECTIVE PHRASES The lamp **on the desk** never works.
James liked the story **about wild horses.**
One **of my friends** wrote an essay **on energy.**

### EXERCISE 6 Finding Adjective Phrases

Number your paper 1 to 10. Write each adjective phrase. Then beside each one, write the word it modifies.

EXAMPLE The package by the door is a gift for you.
ANSWER by the door—package, for you—gift

1. The most dangerous animal in the Far North is the polar bear.
2. The first batter on the home team hit a home run.
3. The McFarlins own the apartment below us.
4. The brontosaurus was a tremendous dinosaur with a long tail and a small head.
5. The valley beyond those hills is excellent farmland.

6. The space creature with beady red eyes approached the astronaut.
7. The small box inside the larger box contained an antique ring.
8. Paloma's essay about Indian pottery explains some methods of decoration.
9. A mechanic at the gas station is buying the car with faulty brakes.
10. One of my friends owns a collection of model trains.

### EXERCISE 7 Finding Adjective Phrases

Number your paper 1 to 10. Write each adjective phrase. Then beside each one, write the word it modifies.

1. The cottage across the lake is vacant.
2. I would like a notebook like that blue one.
3. The 1980 eruption of Mount St. Helens destroyed huge areas of forest.
4. The path through the pine woods was narrow.
5. Six students on the committee organized the pancake breakfast.
6. The sailboat with the torn sail left the race.
7. The day after tomorrow should be a good time for us.
8. The windows in our school have double panes of glass.
9. The three tiny bones in your ear are the smallest bones in your whole body.
10. Together the three bones are approximately the size of your thumbnail.

### EXERCISE 8 Writing Sentences

Number your paper 1 to 5. Write a sentence that uses each of the following prepositional phrases as an adjective phrase. Remember to place each phrase directly after the noun or the pronoun it modifies.

1. of students
2. with the green stripes
3. near the ocean
4. on the table
5. from my aunt

## Adverb Phrases

Like an adverb, a prepositional phrase can modify a verb. This kind of phrase is called an *adverb phrase.* An adverb phrase answers the questions *Where? When?* or *How?*

| | |
|---|---|
| ADVERB | Everyone went **there.** |
| ADVERB PHRASE | Everyone went **to the game.** |
| ADVERB | My sister left **early.** |
| ADVERB PHRASE | **Before intermission** my sister left. |
| ADVERB | Maria responded **pleasantly.** |
| ADVERB PHRASE | Maria responded **with a smile.** |

5d An **adverb phrase** is a prepositional phrase that is used mainly to modify a verb.

The same adverb phrase may be located in different places in a sentence.

ADVERB PHRASES We had an assembly **during the afternoon.**

**During the afternoon** we had an assembly.

If the verb has a helping verb, the adverb phrase modifies the entire verb.

**In art class** I must finish a picture.

Tomorrow the game will be played **in the evening.**

Two adverb phrases can modify the same verb.

**On several occasions** I have gone **to the city library.**

I have gone ***to*** **the city library *on* several occasions.**

## EXERCISE 9 *Finding Adverb Phrases*

Number your paper 1 to 10. Write each adverb phrase. Then beside each one, write the word or words it modifies.

EXAMPLE He had already put his bicycle in the garage.
ANSWER in the garage—had put

1. The baseball whizzed by the pitcher.
2. The parade marched down Main Street.
3. Within an hour we will know the winners.
4. A narrow road wound around the steep cliff.
5. I must finish my report before Friday.
6. Toward morning the rain finally stopped.
7. Dark clouds have appeared in the western sky.
8. Nai worked without a break.
9. After the game we will have a light dinner and watch the movie.
10. You can store it in the cellar or the attic.

## EXERCISE 10 *Finding Adverb Phrases*

Number your paper 1 to 10. Write each adverb phrase. Then beside each one, write the word or words it modifies.

EXAMPLE At noon a fire engine raced by our house.
ANSWER at noon—raced, by our house—raced

1. The weary Mountain Club hikers scrambled down the steep trail.
2. That piano will not fit through the door.
3. Christopher hurried down the stairs.
4. A cat was sleeping in the store window.
5. Have you ever gone to a rodeo?
6. On Washington Boulevard you will find the Primitive Art Museum.
7. Jack brushed the lint off his coat.
8. Until last week I had never ridden on a plane.
9. In the valley snow fell on the fields and farmhouses.
10. My sister Pauline dived from the high board without any fear.

## EXERCISE 11 Finding Adverb Phrases

Number your paper 1 to 10. Write each adverb phrase. Then beside each one, write the word or words it modifies. There are 15 adverb phrases.

EXAMPLE Snails live on land and in water.
ANSWER on land—live, in water—live

Snails

1. A snail lives inside a tough spiral shell.
2. On its slow travels, a snail drags its shell on its back.
3. A snail creeps on a large footlike structure.
4. Many snails have a slimy fluid under this foot.
5. With this fluid snails can crawl up vertical surfaces.
6. A snail can climb safely over a razor blade.
7. In a dangerous situation, a snail pulls its head inside its shell.
8. Within the shell it hides from most enemies.
9. Land snails usually live in shady, damp places.
10. With a long, toothed "tongue," a snail scrapes its food off surfaces.

### Punctuation with Adverb Phrases

If a short adverb phrase comes at the beginning of a sentence, usually no comma is needed. However, a comma should be placed after an introductory adverb phrase of four or more words.

NO COMMA **From the deck** you can see the lake.
COMMA **From the front deck,** you can see the lake.

## EXERCISE 12 Writing Sentences

Number your paper 1 to 5. Write a sentence using each phrase as an adverb phrase. Begin three of the sentences with an adverb phrase. Use commas where needed.

1. during intermission
2. from the big picture window
3. around the track
4. within a few weeks
5. in the old trunk

## *TIME-OUT FOR REVIEW* • • • • •

Number your paper 1 to 20. Write each prepositional phrase. Then label each one *adjective* or *adverb*.

EXAMPLE Basketball was invented in 1891.
ANSWER in 1891—adverb

Birth of a Sport

1. At that time no major sport was played during the winter months.
2. A man at a Massachusetts YMCA school had a wonderful idea.
3. This person was James A. Naismith, the father of basketball.
4. Basketball provided a sport between the football season and the baseball season.
5. The origin of its name is an interesting story.
6. Naismith had no money for fancy equipment.
7. In a large hall, he nailed peach baskets on opposite walls.
8. The game's name came from the peach baskets.
9. Another necessary piece of equipment for the new game was a tall ladder.
10. The bottoms of the peach baskets were not taken out.
11. At the start everyone used an old soccer ball.
12. The players were divided into two teams.
13. Each of the teams defended a basket.
14. For a score a player would throw the ball into the opposite basket.
15. Sometimes each side had 50 players on a team.
16. With that many players, there wasn't much space for team play or skill.
17. Eventually the number on a basketball team decreased to five.
18. Basketball soon spread to other countries throughout the world.
19. Twenty nations played basketball in the 1936 Olympics.
20. Today basketball hoops are commonly found in schools and parks.

# Diagraming Prepositional Phrases

An **adjective phrase** is connected to the noun or the pronoun it modifies. An **adverb phrase** is connected to the verb it modifies.

The boy on the red bike waved.

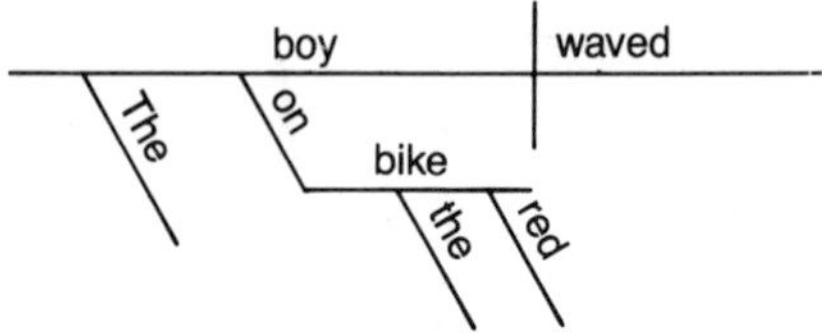


For an hour the wind blew steadily.

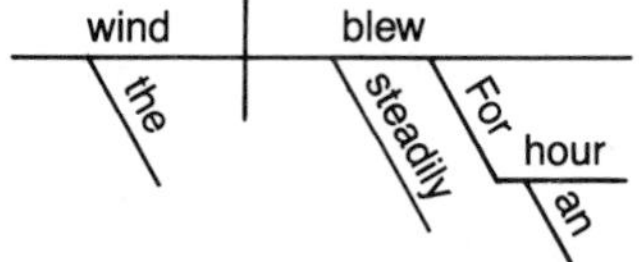


### EXERCISE 13 Diagraming Prepositional Phrases

Diagram the following sentences or copy them. If your teacher tells you to copy them, draw one line under each subject and two lines under each verb. Then underline each prepositional phrase and label it *adjective* or *adverb.*

1. The ducks flew toward the lake.
2. The band on his new watch has already broken.
3. Some guests at the birthday party stayed late.
4. The plane from Chicago will soon arrive.
5. Five students volunteered for the speech contest.
6. Mack slowly walked into the room.
7. During the play the telephone on the desk must ring.
8. Patches of tulips are blooming in our backyard.
9. The baseball players sat gloomily in the dugout.
10. The light from the hall shines under my door.

## Application to Writing

Varying the length of your sentences adds sparkle and interest to your writing. You can create variety by using prepositional phrases to combine short, choppy sentences.

| | |
|---|---|
| TWO SENTENCES | A car stalled. The car was nearby. |
| ONE SENTENCE | A car **near ours** stalled. [adjective phrase] |
| TWO SENTENCES | Karen went home. She rode her bicycle. |
| ONE SENTENCE | Karen went home on her bicycle. [adverb phrase] |

### *EXERCISE 14 Combining Sentences*

Number your paper 1 to 10. Then combine each pair of sentences into one sentence. Put the information in one sentence into a prepositional phrase.

1. Each morning several of my friends jog. They jog around the track.
2. We watched the TV special about Halley's Comet. It was on Channel 6.
3. The quarterback hesitated and then threw the ball. He threw it to the right end.
4. Two dogs barked all night. They live in the next apartment.
5. We should meet at the gym. We should be there at six o'clock.
6. My mother works at the Millard Building. It is on Temple Avenue.
7. That painting is very old. It pictures a mysterious castle.
8. Last Friday I gave my report. It was about nature photography.
9. I just bought this sweatshirt. I bought it at the discount store.
10. The old shack collapsed last night. It had a leaky roof.

# Conjunctions and Interjections

You have learned that prepositions show relationships between words. Conjunctions connect words. Interjections show strong feeling.

5e A **conjunction** connects words or groups of words.

Following is a list of some coordinating conjunctions. These conjunctions connect single words and groups of words.

| Coordinating Conjunctions | | | |
|---|---|---|---|
| and | but | or | yet |

WORDS
I have *paper* **and** *pens.* [connects nouns]
*He* **or** *I* will meet Tim. [connects pronouns]
The telephone *rang* **and** *rang.* [connects verbs]
Get *blue* **or** *green* paint. [connects adjectives]
He spoke *firmly* **yet** *kindly.* [connects adverbs]

GROUPS OF WORDS
Tad looked *in the house* **and** *outside the house.* [connects prepositional phrases]
*Everyone was here early,* **but** *the honored guest was late.* [connects sentences]

5f An **interjection** is a word that expresses strong feeling.

An interjection at the beginning of a sentence is followed by an exclamation point or a comma.

**Wow!** That was the best pass of the game.
**Oh,** I forgot my homework!
**Great!** We can leave now.

NOTE: Do not use too many interjections, or they will lose their force.

## EXERCISE 15 *Finding Conjunctions*

Number your paper 1 to 10. Then write each conjunction.

1. Gladys or Brenda will give the next report.
2. A rainbow can be seen only in the morning, during the late afternoon, or in the early evening.
3. The actress wore an old but beautiful dress.
4. Nani will bake or broil the freshly caught fish.
5. Tyler answered the question quickly and correctly.
6. A male walrus may weigh 3,000 pounds, but a female rarely exceeds 2,000 pounds.
7. You and I are responsible for the party decorations.
8. The miners blasted a large pit but found little coal.
9. You taste with your tongue, your nose, and your brain.
10. The storm was severe, yet no one was injured.

## EXERCISE 16 *Writing Sentences*

Number your paper 1 to 10. Then write ten sentences that follow the directions below.

1. Use *and* to connect two subjects.
2. Use *or* to connect two verbs.
3. Use *but* to connect two sentences. (Place a comma before *but.*)
4. Use *and* to connect two prepositional phrases.
5. Use *and* to connect two adverbs.
6. Use *but* to connect two adjectives.
7. Use *and* to connect two nouns.
8. Use *yet* to connect two sentences. (Place a comma before *yet.*)
9. Use *or* to connect a noun and a pronoun.
10. Use *and* to connect two adjectives.

## EXERCISE 17 *Writing Sentences*

Number your paper 1 to 5. Then write a sentence for each of the following interjections.

1. Aha! 2. Surprise! 3. Ugh! 4. Oops! 5. Wow!

# Chapter Review

**A** **Finding Prepositions, Conjunctions, and Interjections.** Number your paper 1 to 10. Make three columns. Label the first column *prepositions,* the second column *conjunctions,* and the third column *interjections.* Then under the proper heading, write these parts of speech.

1. Pineapple and watermelon were served after dinner.
2. Underneath our car a small kitten was sleeping.
3. Congratulations! You won first prize for your sculpture.
4. Roberto will sing or dance at the variety show.
5. All members were present, yet no vote was taken.
6. Ouch! A hornet just bit me on the arm.
7. On a long journey, wild geese often fly in a V-shaped formation.
8. Those strawberries were big but tasteless.
9. Within five minutes the fire fighters had the fire under control.
10. Some bananas are picked green and fried in batter.

**B** **Finding Prepositional Phrases.** Number your paper 1 to 10. Then write each prepositional phrase.

1. New York was named after an English royal family.
2. Goliath beetles in Africa can reach a length of over four inches.
3. The horse went to the creek and took a drink.
4. Jamie owns a cat without a tail.
5. The fruit with the highest number of calories is the avocado.
6. Little League Baseball began in 1939.
7. A grove of cherry trees grew along the riverbank.
8. The bark of the white birch was often used for Indian canoes.
9. The big oak door near us slowly swung open.
10. Comets travel around the sun in egg-shaped paths.

**C Finding Adjective and Adverb Phrases.** Number your paper 1 to 10. Write each prepositional phrase. Then next to each one, write the word or words it modifies.

1. The symbol of peace is the dove.
2. Buddy has run the race in one hour.
3. Alfonzo opened the door to the hall.
4. Since breakfast Lisa has been painting the porch.
5. Tim limped into the nurse's office.
6. On the blackboard the teacher wrote several questions about the 13 colonies.
7. Indians make adobe bricks from clay and straw.
8. Through the telescope we could see the rings around Saturn.
9. Most of the people sat beneath the trees.
10. During English class we saw a film about famous poets.

## Mastery Test

Number your paper 1 to 10. Then label each underlined word *preposition, conjunction,* or *interjection.*

1. Golf balls were once stuffed with feathers.
2. No! Don't lean against the wet paint.
3. We will get a ride or take the bus.
4. Within ten minutes I will be ready.
5. That box is large but light.
6. Hurray! We won the championship for the second year.
7. Pepper, nutmeg, and mustard are all made from seeds.
8. That wonderful story was written by Raymond.
9. Well, I didn't expect you until this afternoon.
10. An anteater is nearly six feet long, yet its mouth has a width of only an inch.

6

# Parts of Speech Review

## Diagnostic Test

Number your paper 1 to 10. Write each underlined word. Then beside each one, write its part of speech: *noun, pronoun, verb, adjective, adverb, preposition, conjunction,* or *interjection.*

EXAMPLE Where did you put the hammer?
ANSWER you—pronoun hammer—noun

1. Three large boulders stood at the edge of the cliff.
2. Everyone will meet us at the basketball court.
3. That tall but young tree was planted by my father.
4. That was an unusually heavy downpour for this time of year.
5. Which answer is correct?
6. Ann clipped the picture of her dog from the newspaper.
7. A quarterback must think and move quickly.
8. The melon is still too hard.
9. A friend from Georgia sent me a pound of pecans.
10. Right! We should take some action immediately.

# Parts of Speech Review

Along with the definitions of words, the dictionary includes abbreviations like *n.*, *adj.*, and *v.* The word *work*, for example, would first be labeled *n.* for *noun*. This label, however, does not mean that *work* is always a noun. It means that *work* may be used as a noun. A word does not become a part of speech until it is used in a sentence. *Work*, as a matter of fact, can be used as three different parts of speech.

NOUN Our success will depend on hard **work.**
VERB I **work** best in the morning.
ADJECTIVE Have you seen the **work** schedule?

To find a word's part of speech, ask yourself, *What is the word doing in this sentence?*

NOUN Is the word naming a person, a place, a thing, or an idea?

The **boy** with the red **bicycle** lives on this **street.**

**Freedom** is important to all **Americans.**

PRONOUN Is the word taking the place of a noun?

**That** is the best color for **me.**

VERB Is the word showing action? Does it link the subject with another word in the sentence?

Everyone **signed** the card.

The weather today **was** very muggy.

ADJECTIVE Is the word modifying a noun or pronoun? Does it answer the question *What kind? Which one? How many?* or *How much?*

The **new** gym will be **larger.**

**That** one has **two** stripes.

ADVERB Is the word modifying a verb, an adjective, or another adverb? Does it answer the question *How? When? Where?* or *To what extent?*

**Unusually** long hair tangles **quite easily.**

PREPOSITION Is the word showing a relationship between a noun or pronoun and another word in the sentence? Is it part of a phrase?

***During** the afternoon,* we watched a film ***about** South America.*

CONJUNCTION Is the word connecting words or groups of words?

Find the yardstick **and** some string.
I left early in the morning, **but** I was still late.

INTERJECTION Is the word expressing strong feeling?

**Wow!** I received the nomination.
**Whew!** I just ran five miles.

## EXERCISE 1 *Identifying Parts of Speech*

Number your paper 1 to 10. Write each underlined word. Then beside each one, write its part of speech: *noun, pronoun, verb, adjective, adverb, preposition, conjunction,* or *interjection.*

EXAMPLE Laurie saw the spout of a whale.
ANSWER saw—verb, of—preposition

1. The only animal with a straight backbone is the camel.
2. Everything is tasty but cold.
3. An earthworm in Australia sometimes grows to 12 feet.
4. Amazing! Inside the green glass bottle was a tiny clipper ship.

5. We must take the injured cat to the animal hospital immediately.
6. Great! Vacation begins next week.
7. The old football sailed through the air and landed out-of-bounds.
8. Have you purchased the blue sweater yet?
9. My cousin will visit me during the summer.
10. Popular sports in China are baseball, basketball, soccer, and volleyball.

### EXERCISE 2 *Identifying Parts of Speech*

Number your paper 1 to 33. Write each underlined word. Then beside each one, write its part of speech: *noun, pronoun, verb, adjective, adverb, preposition,* or *conjunction.*

What's in a Name?

The study of the names of people (1) is (2) fun. (3) During the Middle Ages, for example, (4) most people (5) had only a first name. (6) That was (7) fine as long as (8) everyone stayed in (9) his or her own village. Cities were (10) finally formed, however, (11) and people moved (12) from place to place. Five Henrys or (13) five Marys in the same place (14) became confusing. The solution (15) was easy. Most people added more information to their names. (16) They used one of four methods.

First, a (17) son might take the (18) name of his father. As a result, *Henry* would become *Henry, son of John.* (19) Through time, this became *Henry Johnson.*

Second, (20) people were named (21) for some of their features. A strong person could be named Henry Strong or Henry Hardy. A person with (22) red hair might take the last name of Reed or Reid. The family names of Wise, Grim, Moody, and Sharp resulted (23) for the same reason.

Third, people became identified with the place (24) of their birth. The Woods (25) or the Atwoods, for example, (26) lived near a forest. The Fairbanks family would have come from the edge of a (27) lovely river or stream.

Fourth, people were named for their (28) occupations. In fact, all the major occupations of (29) Europe in the twelfth century are presented in names today. A town's (30) blacksmith might be called Henry the Smith. (31) Later this would be changed to *Henry Smith.* The roofmaker would be called Henry Thatcher, (32) but the village grain (33) merchant would be called Henry Miller.

### EXERCISE 3 Determining Parts of Speech

Number your paper 1 to 10. Write each underlined word. Then beside each one, write its part of speech: *noun, pronoun, verb, adjective, adverb, preposition, conjunction,* or *interjection.*

1. That plant needs some water.
2. Well! That certainly was a surprise.
3. What time do you have?
4. Please don't leave your records around.
5. Did you plant any flowers?
6. What is for dinner?
7. Where should we dig the well?
8. Did you buy any plant food?
9. Each day I jog around the track.
10. They work well together.

### EXERCISE 4 Determining Parts of Speech

Number your paper 1 to 10. Write each underlined word. Then beside each one, write its part of speech: *noun, pronoun, verb, adjective, adverb, preposition,* or *conjunction.*

1. During the storm all of the commuters went inside the bus station.
2. Our class toured the state capitol.
3. That car has a nice look to it.
4. This would be a good spot for a picnic.

5. Which of these belongs to you?
6. Look out the car window.
7. Are these the class pictures?
8. Which state lies north of Colorado?
9. Did you look inside?
10. This pitcher has already struck out three batters in one inning.

## EXERCISE 5 Labeling Parts of Speech

Number your paper 1 to 5. Copy the following sentences, skipping a line after each one. Then above each word, label its part of speech, using the following abbreviations. Remember that the articles *a, an,* and *the* are adjectives.

| | | |
|---|---|---|
| noun = *n.* | adjective = *adj.* | conjunction = *conj.* |
| pronoun = *pron.* | adverb = *adv.* | interjection = *interj.* |
| verb = *v.* | preposition = *prep.* | |

EXAMPLE You should buy the blue shirt and sweater.

pron. v. v. adj. adj. n. conj. n.

ANSWER You should buy the blue shirt and sweater.

1. Rico walked slowly toward the empty bleachers.
2. The moss below the waterfall covered the rocks.
3. Quick! The game will begin in five minutes.
4. I will draw that barn and horse.
5. Rembrandt was a Dutch painter.

## EXERCISE 6 Writing Sentences

Number your paper 1 to 5, skipping a line after each number. Then write sentences that follow the directions below.

1. Use *baseball* as a noun and an adjective.
2. Use *this* as a pronoun and an adjective.
3. Use *one* as a pronoun and an adjective.
4. Use *outside* as a preposition and an adverb.
5. Use *watch* as a noun and a verb.

# Chapter Review

## A

**Identifying Parts of Speech.** Number your paper 1 to 10. Write each underlined word. Then beside each one, write its part of speech: *noun, pronoun, verb, adjective, adverb, preposition,* or *conjunction.*

The Young King

1. Louis, a young boy of five, became the king of France in 1643.
2. He was the king, but he didn't rule.
3. His mother and other adults made the decisions.
4. During much of his childhood, his life was in danger.
5. A group of people wanted a change in the government.
6. Once the royal family was trapped in the palace.
7. Outside, people yelled and threatened the young king and his family.
8. At 16 Louis finally became king.
9. He was called the Sun King, and his court was very fancy.
10. During his reign he acquired much land for France.

## B

**Identifying Parts of Speech.** Number your paper 1 to 10. Write each underlined word. Then beside each one, write its part of speech: *noun, pronoun, verb, adjective, adverb, preposition, conjunction,* or *interjection.*

1. Which picture should we hang above the fireplace?
2. My family members have a special whistle for our dog.
3. All of us have taken a few.
4. Excellent! The profits from the fair were great.
5. Is your family going away all summer?
6. What's that noise above?
7. The food at the banquet was fair.
8. Can you whistle a few bars of that song?
9. Which is better, this or that?
10. That food store has excellent buys.

**C** **Identifying Parts of Speech.** Number your paper 1 to 10. Write each underlined word. Then beside each one, write its part of speech: *noun, pronoun, verb, adjective, adverb, preposition, conjunction,* or *interjection.*

1. The western sky was purple after sunset.
2. Frequently hikers camp by the brook.
3. Wow! Glass was made in prehistoric times.
4. They rang the bell, but no one was at home.
5. Haiku is an ancient form of Japanese poetry.
6. Mozart wrote the music to "Twinkle, Twinkle, Little Star" at the age of five.
7. Do you read the cartoons in the local newspaper?
8. I enjoy juice or half a grapefruit with my breakfast.
9. Hey! Let's put a scarecrow in the garden.
10. Anna sailed the boat safely through the choppy bay.

## Mastery Test

Number your paper 1 to 10. Write the underlined words. Then beside each one, write its part of speech: *noun, pronoun, verb, adjective, adverb, preposition, conjunction,* or *interjection.*

1. An ostrich may weigh as much as 300 pounds.
2. Long-distance runners do not tire quickly.
3. Daniel remembered his books but forgot his notebook.
4. An actor's life is not for me.
5. Steve or I will introduce the speaker at the assembly.
6. An African eagle often hunts over a territory of 250 square miles a day.
7. Fantastic! Everyone is coming to my party.
8. Our neighbors in Tulsa were very friendly.
9. School pennants and bumper stickers are on sale in the office.
10. The base of the Great Pyramid in Egypt would cover ten football fields.

7

# Complements

## Diagnostic Test

Number your paper 1 to 10. Then label each underlined complement *direct object, indirect object, predicate nominative,* or *predicate adjective.*

EXAMPLE For breakfast I had cereal.
ANSWER direct object

1. Everyone enjoyed the clowns at the circus.
2. The appetite of a young bird is enormous.
3. Jerry made us cheese sandwiches.
4. Mom planted a birch tree in our front yard.
5. One of the largest animals of all time is the whale.
6. Did Mr. Rodale give you any homework?
7. The downpour was quite heavy.
8. During the weekend Eric seemed unusually energetic.
9. Have you ever owned any goldfish?
10. Last year Mr. Gleason was my English teacher.

# Kinds of Complements

A sentence must have a subject and a verb. Some sentences, however, need another word to complete the meaning of the sentence. By themselves, the following subjects and verbs are not complete statements.

Paul built. Barney seems.

A *complement,* or completer, is necessary to complete the meaning of these statements.

Paul built **models.** Barney seems **healthy.**

There are four common kinds of complements. *Direct objects* and *indirect objects* follow action verbs. *Predicate nominatives* and *predicate adjectives,* called *subject complements,* follow linking verbs.

## Direct Objects

All direct objects are usually nouns or pronouns.

7a A **direct object** is a noun or pronoun that answers the question *What?* or *Whom?* after an action verb.

To find a direct object, first find the subject and the action verb in a sentence. Then ask yourself *What?* or *Whom?* after the verb. The answer to either question will be a direct object. In the following sentences, subjects are underlined once, and verbs are underlined twice. Notice in the following examples that the direct object comes after the verb.

DIRECT OBJECTS

d.o.
I have a math **test** tomorrow. [I have what? *Test* is the direct object.]

d.o.
My brother knows **them** very well. [My brother knows whom? *Them* is the direct object.]

To find the direct object in a question, change the question into a statement.

QUESTION Did you make dinner?

STATEMENT You did make **dinner.** (d.o.)

Two or more direct objects together are called a *compound direct object.*

COMPOUND DIRECT OBJECT Adam bought a **hammer** (d.o.) and **nails.** (d.o.) [Adam bought what? The compound direct object is *hammer* and *nails*.]

## EXERCISE 1 Finding Direct Objects

Number your paper 1 to 10. Then write each direct object.

EXAMPLE Tony scraped his knee in soccer.
ANSWER knee

1. Ducks will lay eggs only in the morning.
2. Has Mom found them yet?
3. You can make 11½ omelets with an ostrich egg.
4. Will you sell your bicycle?
5. A robin has almost 3,000 feathers.
6. Egyptians used bricks 7,000 years ago.
7. The river overflowed its banks during the storm.
8. Have you seen my scarf anywhere?
9. I invited everyone in the class.
10. Did Mrs. Lewis sell any tickets?

## EXERCISE 2 Finding Direct Objects

Number your paper 1 to 10. Then write each direct object. (Some sentences have a compound object.)

1. Some earthworms have ten hearts.
2. The hungry hikers ate pancakes and oranges.
3. You'll need some paper and a pencil for this quiz.
4. Lemon sharks grow new teeth every two weeks.

5. You can telephone your mom and dad from here.
6. The modern piano contains nearly 12,000 parts.
7. We saw the Braves and the Astros yesterday at the new stadium.
8. One type of spider can spin a web in 20 minutes.
9. Ann uses mostly oils and acrylics in her art.
10. The committee hung posters and lists in the stores.

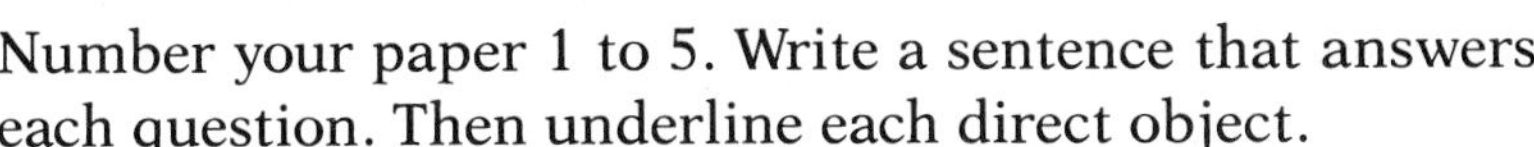

### EXERCISE 3 Writing Sentences

Number your paper 1 to 5. Write a sentence that answers each question. Then underline each direct object.

1. What do you see directly in front of you?
2. Whom did you visit recently?
3. What did you eat for dinner last night?
4. How many pencils and pens do you have with you?
5. What kind of books do you like best?

## Indirect Objects

If a sentence has a direct object, it can also have an *indirect object.* An indirect object is a noun or a pronoun.

**7b** An **indirect object** is a noun or pronoun that answers the question *To* or *for whom?* or *To* or *for what?* after an action verb.

To find an indirect object, first find the direct object. Then ask yourself, *To whom? For whom? To what?* or *For what?* about the direct object. The answer to any of these questions will be an indirect object. Remember that in order to have an indirect object, a sentence must have a direct object.

INDIRECT OBJECT — Ken bought **Nathan** (i.o.) three tickets (d.o.). [*Tickets* is the direct object. Ken bought the tickets for whom? *Nathan* is the indirect object.]

INDIRECT OBJECT — The yellow paint gave the i.o. **room** a bright d.o. appearance. [*Appearance* is the direct object. The paint gave a bright appearance to what? *Room* is the indirect object.]

NOTE: Notice that an indirect object always comes before a direct object in a sentence.

To find the indirect object in a question, change the question into a statement.

QUESTION — Will you show everyone that trick?

STATEMENT — You will show i.o. **everyone** that d.o. trick.

Two or more indirect objects together are called a *compound indirect object.*

COMPOUND INDIRECT OBJECT — Dad gave i.o. **Gene** and i.o. **Lani** his old d.o. coins. [Dad gave the coins to whom? The compound indirect object is *Gene* and *Lani*.]

## EXERCISE 4 *Finding Indirect Objects*

Number your paper 1 to 10. Then write each indirect object.

1. Ella built the birds a large feeder.
2. Dad cooked us hamburgers on the grill.
3. Our teacher read the class several chapters from *The Red Pony.*
4. Will you pass me that dictionary?
5. The guide found everyone on the walking tour a shady spot for lunch.
6. Did Steve build Mary that desk?
7. You must show him your class picture.
8. Have you given the computer an answer?
9. Please send your sister this letter.
10. That latest plan for a new library will save the city a million dollars.

## EXERCISE 5 Finding Indirect Objects

Number your paper 1 to 10. Then write each indirect object. (Some sentences have a compound indirect object.)

1. Mr. Gómez read the committee his report.
2. The coach taught the players a new play.
3. David cooked his mother and father a Chinese dinner for their anniversary.
4. Did you give Alex your new address?
5. The judges awarded Chet first prize.
6. This summer Juan will teach Harry and me Spanish.
7. Rona saved me a seat at the concert.
8. Read your little sister and brother a story.
9. We bought Flora this present.
10. I brought Willa and Betsy their books.

## TIME-OUT FOR REVIEW • • • • •

Number your paper 1 to 10. Write each complement. Then label each one *direct object* or *indirect object*.

EXAMPLE Chester sent me a beautiful bouquet.
ANSWER bouquet—direct object
me—indirect object

1. Eagles keep the same nest throughout their lives.
2. I saw Jeannie and him before homeroom.
3. Antón played everyone a Mexican song.
4. Grandmother knitted Martina and me matching sweaters.
5. For privacy people often put fences around their homes.
6. Please pass us the sandwiches and fruit from the picnic basket.
7. Did you show him the new band uniforms?
8. Two young rabbits were nibbling dandelions and clover in our yard.
9. Anna showed Peter and Maria her woodworking project.
10. Have you ever eaten an artichoke or an avocado?

## Predicate Nominatives

Direct objects and indirect objects follow action verbs. Two other kinds of complements follow linking verbs. They are called *subject complements* because they identify, rename, or describe the subject. One kind of subject complement is called a *predicate nominative.*

7c A **predicate nominative** is a noun or a pronoun that follows a linking verb and identifies, renames, or explains the subject.

In order to find subject complements, you must be able to recognize linking verbs. *(See page 41 for a more complete list of linking verbs.)*

**Common Linking Verbs**

| | |
|---|---|
| *BE* VERBS | is, are, am, was, were, be, being, been, shall be, will be, can be, should be, would be, may be, might be, has been, etc. |
| OTHERS | appear, become, feel, grow, look, remain, seem, smell, sound, stay, taste, turn |

To find a predicate nominative, first find the subject and the verb. Check to see if the verb is a linking verb. Then find the noun or the pronoun that identifies, renames, or explains the subject. This word will always be a predicate nominative. In the following examples, the arrows point to the subjects and the predicate nominatives.

PREDICATE NOMINATIVES

That horse is a **palomino.** (p.n.) [*Palomino* renames the subject *horse.*]

Kate has become a strong **swimmer.** (p.n.) [*Swimmer* renames the subject *Kate.*]

Two or more predicate nominatives together are called a *compound predicate nominative.*

COMPOUND PREDICATE NOMINATIVE The stars of the play were **Eliza** and **you.** [Both predicate nominatives rename the subject *stars. Eliza* and *you* = *stars.*]

NOTE: A predicate nominative can never be part of a prepositional phrase.

Elroy was **one** of the winners. [*One* identifies the subject *Elroy. Winners* is not the predicate nominative because it is part of the prepositional phrase *of the winners.*]

## EXERCISE 6 *Finding Predicate Nominatives*

Number your paper 1 to 10. Then write each predicate nominative. (Some sentences have a compound predicate nominative.)

EXAMPLE Sarah is a good student and a fine writer.
ANSWER student, writer

1. Diamonds are extremely hard stones.
2. The prairie sunsets were spectacular sights.
3. Those trees are oaks and maples.
4. The exchange student may be a speaker at the assembly program.
5. The main resources of South Asia are soil, water, and climate.
6. Jean remained the top runner during her three years in junior high school.
7. The longest rivers in the world are the Amazon and the Nile.
8. Nina has become one of the candidates for treasurer of the 4-H Club.
9. Mercury is the smallest planet.
10. My favorite subjects are English and science.

### EXERCISE 7 Supplying Predicate Nominatives

Number your paper 1 to 10. Then write a predicate nominative that completes each sentence. (If you use a pronoun as a predicate nominative, use only *I, you, he, she, it, we,* or *they.*)

1. My favorite holiday is ______.
2. Two of my best friends are ______ and ______.
3. My brother Roy will become a (an) ______.
4. The items on sale are ______ and ______.
5. Their car is a (an) ______.
6. Eric will remain ______ of our class.
7. Mrs. Davis is my ______.
8. The soloist in Sunday's concert will be ______.
9. My favorite beverage is ______.
10. The drummers in the band are ______ and ______.

## Predicate Adjectives

The second kind of subject complement is the *predicate adjective.*

**7d** A **predicate adjective** is an adjective that follows a linking verb and modifies the subject.

To find a predicate adjective, first find the subject and the verb. Check to see if the verb is a linking verb. Then find an adjective that follows the verb and describes the subject. This word will be a predicate adjective.

PREDICATE ADJECTIVES

p.a.
The baby's skin was very **smooth.** [The predicate adjective *smooth* describes the subject *skin. (smooth skin)*]

p.a.
Recently the weather has become **warmer.** [The predicate adjective *warmer* describes the subject *weather. (warmer weather)*]

Two or more predicate adjectives together are called a *compound predicate adjective.*

| | |
|---|---|
| COMPOUND PREDICATE ADJECTIVES | These shoes are **sturdy** and **comfortable.** [Both *sturdy* and *comfortable* describe the subject *shoes.*] |

(p.a. marks *sturdy* and *comfortable*.)

### EXERCISE 8 Finding Predicate Adjectives

Number your paper 1 to 10. Then write each predicate adjective. (Some sentences may have a compound predicate adjective.)

EXAMPLE The guides were pleasant and helpful.
ANSWER pleasant, helpful

1. Mom was right again.
2. The tail of the opossum is long and scaly.
3. This radiator feels cold.
4. The stage lights were bright and warm.
5. Our basement smelled musty after the storm.
6. In the winter the fur of the ermine turns white.
7. Amon appeared calm during his speech.
8. The tiny shrew is fearless.
9. Your fruit salad tastes fresh and sweet.
10. The top of the table was smooth and shiny.

### EXERCISE 9 Supplying Predicate Adjectives

Number your paper 1 to 10. Then write a predicate adjective that completes each sentence. Avoid overused adjectives like *good, nice,* or *wonderful.*

1. All of Terry's poems are ______.
2. The mayor looked ______ and ______ during the news conference.
3. The wooden box is ______.
4. After waiting 30 minutes for the concert to start, the audience became ______.

5. After finishing swimming laps, Natalie always seems so ______.
6. Alana appeared ______ after the race even though she placed third.
7. That new hit record sounds ______.
8. The volume on the television is too ______.
9. Ray and Alice were ______ during the assembly.
10. The vegetables from Fraser's market taste ______ and ______.

### EXERCISE 10 Writing Sentences

Write four sentences. Two sentences should include a predicate nominative. Two sentences should include a predicate adjective. Label each complement *p.n.* or *p.a.*

## TIME-OUT FOR REVIEW • • • • •

Number your paper 1 to 10. Write each complement. Then label each one *predicate nominative* or *predicate adjective.*

The Fifties

1. Television became very popular in the 1950s.
2. *Howdy Doody* was a favorite program of the time.
3. The characters Howdy Doody and Clarabelle the Clown were comical.
4. For over 20 million teenagers, the most popular show was *American Bandstand.*
5. Davy Crockett was one of the most admired TV characters of the 1950s.
6. Davy Crockett was a frontiersman.
7. Popular clothes for boys during those years were chino pants and motorcycle jackets.
8. Pedal pushers, bobby socks, and short skirts were fashionable for girls.
9. Hula-Hoops, large colorful plastic circles, became a fad in 1958.
10. TV dinners in little aluminum-foil dishes first grew popular in 1954.

# Diagraming Complements

A subject, a verb, and sometimes a complement make up the *sentence base.* Complements are diagramed on the baseline or are attached to it.

***Direct Objects.*** A direct object is placed on the baseline after the verb. The direct object and the verb are separated by a short vertical line. Notice in the second example that the parts of a compound direct object are placed on parallel horizontal lines. The conjunction is placed on a broken line.

That camera takes clear pictures.

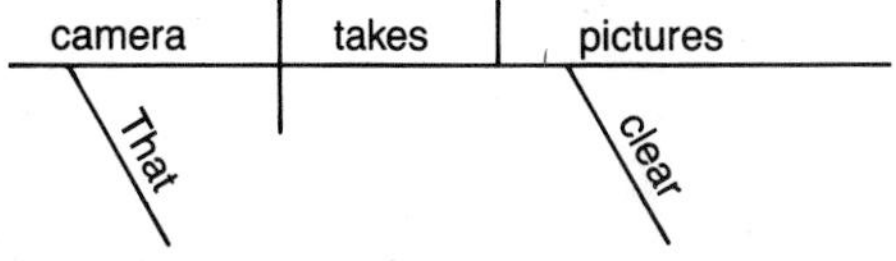


The team manager thoroughly cleaned the uniforms and the equipment.

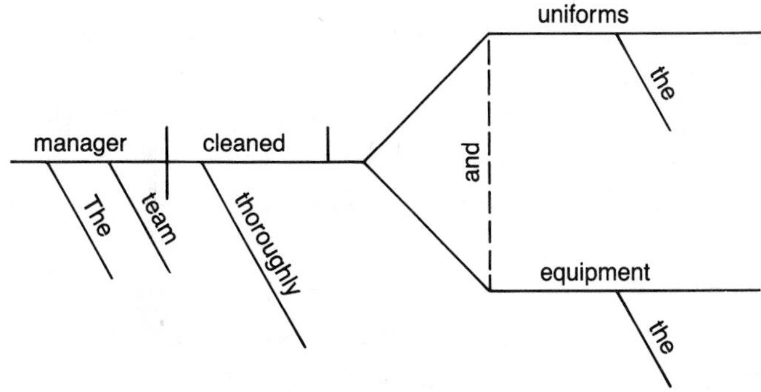


***Indirect Objects.*** An indirect object is diagramed on a horizontal line that is connected to the verb by a slanted line. Notice in the second example that the parts of a compound indirect object are diagramed on parallel horizontal lines. The conjunction is placed on a broken line.

The school counselor gave Beth some good advice.

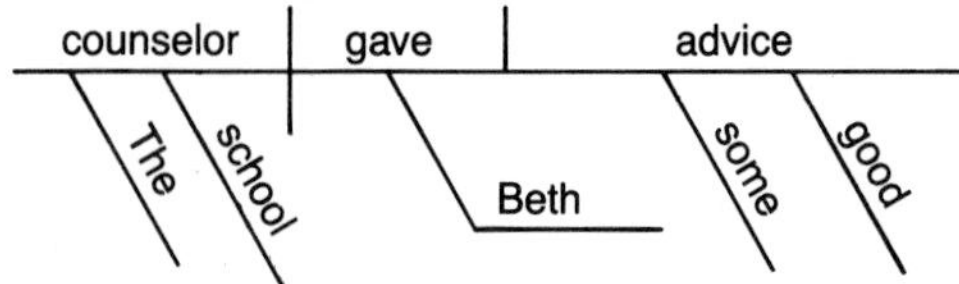


Give Carla and Rick our concert tickets.

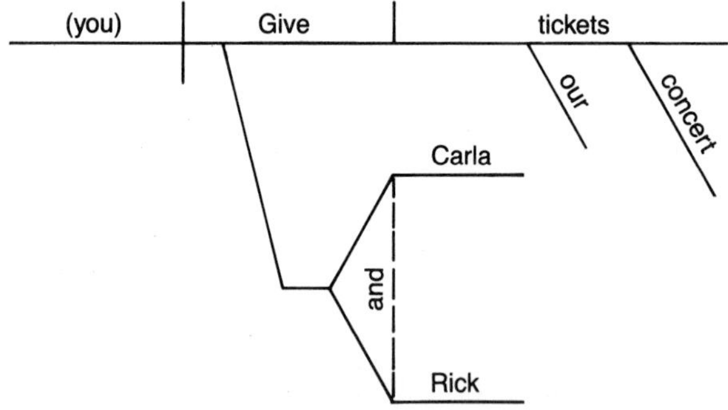


***Subject Complements.*** The predicate nominative and the predicate adjective are diagramed alike. They are placed on the baseline after the verb. These subject complements are separated from the verb by a slanted line that points back toward the subject.

Notice in the second example on page 105 that the parts of a compound subject complement are placed on parallel lines. The conjunction is placed on a broken line.

The trophies were small bronze statues.

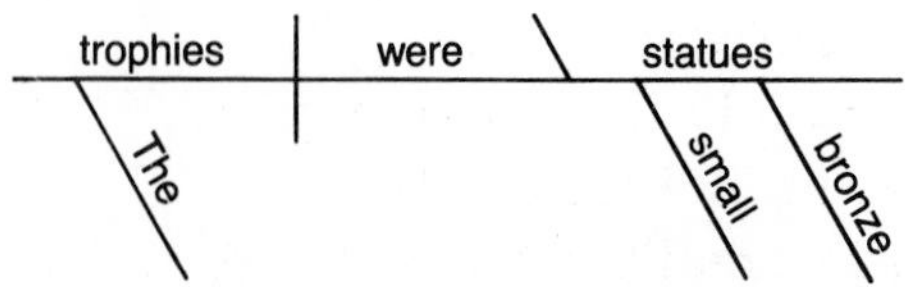

Our house is very old.

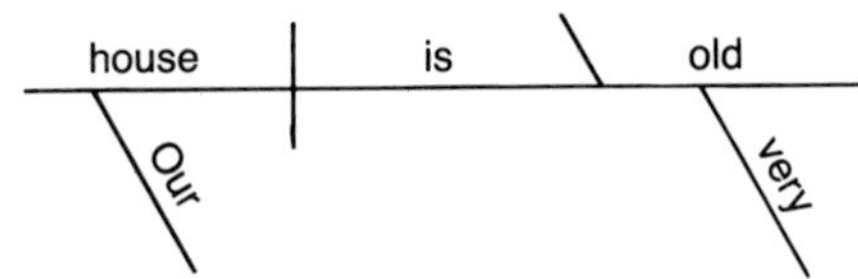


The leather belt feels soft and smooth.

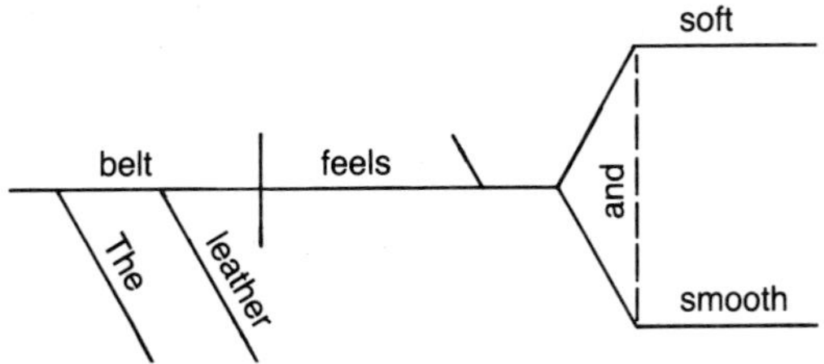


## EXERCISE 11 Diagraming Complements

Diagram the following sentences or copy them. If your teacher tells you to copy them, draw one line under each subject and two lines under each verb. Then label each complement, using the following abbreviations.

direct object = *d.o.* predicate nominative = *p.n.*
indirect object = *i.o.* predicate adjective = *p.a.*

1. The jackrabbit is a hare.
2. The sunrise was quite hazy.
3. Liang gave an excellent report.
4. Patsy sang us a song.
5. Did you bring your watch?
6. Send me a free sample.
7. Last night was clear and crisp.
8. Recently I sold my bicycle and my skates.
9. Bella promised Delores and me a ride.
10. My favorite courses are math and science.

## Application to Writing

Nearly every sentence you write follows one of five different patterns. Each pattern may be expanded by adding modifiers and prepositional phrases.

**PATTERN 1:** S-V (subject–verb)

Clocks (S) chime (V).

Certain clocks (S) in the store chime (V) on the hour.

**PATTERN 2:** S-V-O (subject–verb–direct object)

Roots (S) prevent (V) erosion (O).

The roots (S) of trees often prevent (V) erosion (O) of the soil.

**PATTERN 3:** S-V-I-O (subject–verb–indirect object–direct object)

Aunt May (S) sends (V) me (I) postcards (O).

My Aunt May (S) frequently sends (V) me (I) postcards (O) from Idaho.

**PATTERN 4:** S-V-N (subject–verb–predicate nominative)

Dogs (S) are (V) friends (N).

Dogs (S) of all sizes usually are (V) excellent friends (N).

**PATTERN 5:** S-V-A (subject–verb–predicate adjective)

Books (S) are (V) expensive (A).

Books (S) about art are (V) often quite expensive (A).

To find the pattern of a certain sentence, drop all the modifiers and prepositional phrases.

S V O
~~My~~ grandparents own ~~a small~~ farm ~~in Nebraska~~.

### ***EXERCISE 12*** *Determining Sentence Patterns*

Number your paper 1 to 10. Then write the sentence pattern that each sentence follows.

1. The branches of the old tree swayed in the wind.
2. Everyone in the audience grew very restless.
3. A hen often turns its eggs.
4. One of my neighbors is a farmer.
5. The small kitten raced around the room.
6. Some Chinese typewriters have 5,700 keys.
7. The blacksmith gave the black horse a new shoe.
8. The evening air suddenly felt very cold.
9. The secretary in the office gave me an application.
10. That album is this week's top record.

### ***EXERCISE 13*** *Expanding Sentence Patterns*

Expand each sentence by adding modifiers or prepositional phrases or both.

1. (S-V) Eagles fly.
2. (S-V-O) Judges presented medals.
3. (S-V-I-O) Friends gave us presents.
4. (S-V-N) Neighbors are students.
5. (S-V-A) Photographs are old.
6. (S-V) Jake studies.
7. (S-V-O) Ms. Ubach reads stories.
8. (S-V-I-O) Mom sent Dad flowers.
9. (S-V-N) We have been friends.
10. (S-V-A) Hikers were weary.

# Chapter Review

**A Identifying Direct and Indirect Objects.** Number your paper 1 to 10. Write each complement. Then label each one *direct object* or *indirect object.*

1. Christopher Columbus brought cattle to America on his second voyage.
2. The director gave the actors their scripts for the new play.
3. The United States once issued a five-cent bill.
4. I have the key to the apartment.
5. Mr. Davis gave Marita and me an appointment with the guidance counselor.
6. Jonathan showed me the entrance to the football stadium.
7. The guide handed each eager tourist a map of the ancient castle.
8. No one has discovered two snowflakes with exactly the same pattern.
9. Please pass me a fork and a knife.
10. The sun gives the sea a blue tint.

**B Identifying Subject Complements.** Number your paper 1 to 10. Write each complement. Then label each one *predicate nominative* or *predicate adjective.*

1. The honeydew melons seem ripe.
2. That sweater looks comfortable.
3. Paper money is an invention from China.
4. The down comforter felt soft and warm.
5. Pure seawater is colorless.
6. Corn is one of the largest farm crops in the United States.
7. Willis was captain of the soccer team last year.
8. My baseball cap is old but comfortable.
9. The salad dressing tasted very bitter.
10. My best friends are Cheryl and Teresa.

**C Identifying Complements.** Number your paper 1 to 10. Write each complement. Then label each one *direct object, indirect object, predicate nominative,* or *predicate adjective.*

ncle Sam

1. Samuel Wilson was only a boy in 1775.
2. Nevertheless, he played an important role in the American Revolution.
3. Immediately after Paul Revere's ride through town, Sam told the people in each house the bad news.
4. His father and brother were minutemen.
5. Years later the government gave Sam the job of meat inspector.
6. Uncle Sam became his nickname.
7. Someone drew a picture of Sam.
8. This picture eventually became a new symbol of the United States.
9. "Uncle Sam" was famous overnight.
10. The workers in the meat plant were proud of their old friend with the white pointed beard.

# Mastery Test

Number your paper 1 to 10. Then label each underlined complement *direct object, indirect object, predicate nominative,* or *predicate adjective.*

1. All bulls are <u>colorblind</u>.
2. The class bought <u>Mrs. Peterson</u> a desk clock.
3. I have seen that <u>movie</u> three times already.
4. Alaska has a <u>desert</u> with dunes over 100 feet high.
5. Those redwood trees are so <u>tall</u>.
6. Did you ride the <u>bus</u> to school?
7. Evan is the best <u>artist</u> in the class.
8. Are the dogs in the window of the pet store <u>beagles</u>?
9. Mom gave <u>everyone</u> some fruit for dessert.
10. The party decorations were very <u>colorful</u>.

8

# Simple and Compound Sentences

## Diagnostic Test

Number your paper 1 to 10. If a sentence is a simple sentence, write *simple*. If a sentence is a compound sentence, write *compound*.

1. In ancient China children played with kites and tops, but hoops and boats were favorite toys in ancient Rome.
2. Carrie is working at the computer or is reading a book.
3. The Monteros family painted their kitchen and wallpapered their living room.
4. I cleaned the fish, and my brother cooked them over the campfire.
5. Kara buys each new stamp and pastes it in a notebook.
6. The river rose above its banks, and the park flooded.
7. Tumbleweeds break off at the base and blow across open spaces.
8. Each rolling tumbleweed drops seeds, and many new plants take hold.
9. Some female birds have dull colors, but their mates are quite colorful.
10. Clouds and fog are formed from water particles in the air.

# Simple Sentences

In the previous chapters in this book, you have worked with simple sentences.

8a A **simple sentence** is a sentence that has one subject and one verb.

In the following examples, the subjects are underlined once, and the verbs are underlined twice.

ONE SUBJECT, ONE VERB Amelia Earhart was a pioneer in the field of flying.

In a simple sentence, either the subject or the verb, or both, can be compound.

COMPOUND SUBJECT Amelia and her crew flew nonstop from Mexico City to New York City.

COMPOUND VERB Amelia flew alone across the Atlantic and made the first solo flight from California to Hawaii.

COMPOUND SUBJECT, COMPOUND VERB Amelia Earhart and Fred Noonan flew along the equator and attempted a transworld flight.

## EXERCISE 1 Writing Sentences

Number your paper 1 to 10. Write ten sentences that use the following compound subjects and compound verbs.

EXAMPLE students and teachers
ANSWER Many students and teachers attended the play.

1. pen and pencil
2. baseball and soccer
3. Paloma or Carl
4. cars, buses, and trucks
5. coach and team
6. washed and polished
7. yawned and stretched
8. will draw or paint
9. kicked and sprinted
10. clapped and cheered

# Compound Sentences

There are other kinds of sentences besides simple sentences. For example, two or more related simple sentences can be placed together to make a *compound sentence.*

8b A **compound sentence** is made up of two or more simple sentences, usually joined by a comma and the coordinating conjunction *and, but, or,* or *yet.*

If the comma and the conjunction are dropped from a compound sentence, two simple sentences will remain.

COMPOUND SENTENCE The picnic will begin at noon, but the buses will leave at nine o'clock.

SIMPLE SENTENCES The picnic will begin at noon. The buses will leave at nine o'clock.

COMPOUND SENTENCE I had forgotten about the spaghetti, and our dinner burned.

SIMPLE SENTENCES I had forgotten about the spaghetti. Our dinner burned.

### EXERCISE 2 *Understanding Compound Sentences*

Number your paper 1 to 10. Copy each compound sentence. Draw one line under each subject and two lines under each verb. Then circle the conjunction that joins the two simple sentences.

EXAMPLE The sun is shining, but rain is falling.
ANSWER The sun is shining, (but) rain is falling.

1. Many hares turn white in winter, but rabbits always stay the same color.
2. Robin Hood escaped with his prize, and the sheriff of Nottingham wanted revenge.
3. The swing went higher and higher, but my little sister was enjoying the ride.

4. The crickets were chirping, and an owl hooted from the woods.
5. Lee will bake the bread today, or I can bake it tomorrow night.
6. My bicycle is blue, but Kevin's bicycle is silver.
7. The music grew louder and louder, and then the band marched around the corner.
8. We will walk to the library, but we will ride home on the bus.
9. I can wait for you at school, or we can meet at the library.
10. I waited for two hours, but nobody came.

### EXERCISE 3 Understanding Compound Sentences

Number your paper 1 to 10. Copy each compound sentence. Draw one line under each subject and two lines under each verb. Then circle the conjunction that joins the two simple sentences.

1. I filled my bicycle tire with air last night, but by morning the tire was flat again.
2. The band is practicing today, and on Saturday it will march in the town parade.
3. You can come to my house, or we can meet halfway between your house and mine.
4. At birth a flounder looks like an ordinary fish, but later its eyes move to one side of its head.
5. Veins bring blood to the heart, and arteries carry blood away from the heart.
6. My sister sorted the seeds, and we planted them.
7. Cotton burns easily, but wool has more resistance to fire.
8. You must arrive on time, or the show will start without you.
9. I read *The Call of the Wild,* but Cindy read a different book.
10. A light rain was falling, yet the players barely noticed it during the football game.

## Compound Sentence or Compound Verb?

If you write quickly, you may easily mistake a compound sentence for a simple sentence that has a compound verb. To find out if a sentence is a compound sentence, see if you can make two complete sentences out of it.

| | |
|---|---|
| COMPOUND SENTENCE | Roy stepped forward, and his opponent swiftly served a deadly curveball. |
| SIMPLE SENTENCES | Roy stepped forward. His opponent swiftly served a deadly curveball. |

The first sentence is a compound sentence because it is made up of two complete simple sentences that are closely related. The sentences are joined by a comma and a conjunction. Each verb has its own subject. Now try the same test on another sentence.

| | |
|---|---|
| COMPOUND VERB | Roy stepped forward and served the ball. |
| | Roy stepped forward. Served the ball. |

You cannot make two complete sentences out of this example. It is a simple sentence with a compound verb. Both verbs share the same subject. In a compound sentence, each verb must have its own subject.

### EXERCISE 4 Recognizing Compound Sentences

Number your paper 1 to 10. Then label each sentence *simple* or *compound.*

Softball versus Baseball

1. Softball began in Chicago in 1887 and became popular as an indoor version of baseball.
2. Softball requires less space and demands fewer pieces of equipment than baseball.
3. A game of softball is similar to a game of baseball, but the bases are closer together in softball.
4. Softball bases are 60 feet apart, but baseball requires 90 feet between bases.

5. A softball pitcher stands 40 to 46 feet from home plate, but the distance in baseball is 60½ feet.
6. The circumference of a softball usually measures 12 inches and is larger than a baseball's circumference.
7. A baseball is 9 inches in circumference or measures 9¼ inches at most.
8. Baseball players sometimes leave the base before the pitch, but softball players always wait for the pitch.
9. Baseball allows a choice of pitches, but softball pitchers always throw underhand.
10. A softball team has 9 or 10 players and plays only 7 innings.

### EXERCISE 5 Recognizing Compound Sentences

Number your paper 1 to 10. Then label each sentence *simple* or *compound*.

1. Yogurt, cheese, and dark green vegetables are all good sources of calcium.
2. With the advice of the Wampanoag Indians, the Pilgrims planted and cultivated corn.
3. Sharon gave me a sweater for my birthday, but it didn't fit me.
4. After the drama club meeting, Joe or Susan will turn off the lights and lock the door.
5. The bodies of insects have three main parts, but the bodies of spiders have only two.
6. Can you walk home from soccer practice, or do you need a ride?
7. Immigrants have come to the United States, and their cultures have enriched American life.
8. The weather report calls for sunshine, yet it looks like rain.
9. Jennifer and Douglas bought yellow kites and flew them in the park.
10. Ken is joining the computer club and will pay his dues today.

### Punctuating Compound Sentences

A compound sentence and a simple sentence that has a compound verb are not punctuated the same way. In most compound sentences, a comma comes before the conjunction that connects the two simple sentences.

| | |
|---|---|
| COMMA WITH A COMPOUND SENTENCE | We went to Greenwood**, but** our friends were waiting for us in Greenville. |

No comma comes between the parts of a compound verb.

| | |
|---|---|
| NO COMMA WITH A COMPOUND VERB | I looked for my science book but couldn't find it. |

## EXERCISE 6 *Punctuating Compound Sentences*

Number your paper 1 to 10. If a sentence needs a comma, write the sentence and add the comma. If a sentence does not need a comma, write *none* after the number.

1. The full moon rose over the mountain and flooded the campsite with moonlight.
2. At the party Judy was dressed as a clown but Carlos came as Abraham Lincoln.
3. I'll ask my sister Carla and you can ask your cousin Connie.
4. The baby owl blinked and trembled in the bright sunlight.
5. Yuma's horse suddenly bucked and threw her off.
6. We hiked along Dawson River and ate lunch at the waterfall.
7. Thunder roared and lightning flashed across the sky all during the night.
8. The shortstop's throw was wild and Burt reached second base safely.
9. Beth arrived early but José came 20 minutes late.
10. The train pulled into the station and many commuters got off.

## EXERCISE 7 Writing Sentences

Write three compound sentences about your home. Use the conjunctions *and, but,* and *or.* Remember to use a comma before the conjunction.

## TIME-OUT FOR REVIEW • • • • •

Number your paper 1 to 15. Then label each sentence *simple* or *compound.*

Hans Christian Andersen

1. Hans Christian Andersen was born in 1805 and died almost 70 years later.
2. He wrote 156 fairy tales, but his most famous tale was "The Ugly Duckling."
3. Andersen grew up in Denmark and lived in a one-room house.
4. His father was a shoemaker but could not afford leather shoes for his own children.
5. As a boy Andersen was tall and lanky, and his hands and feet were large.
6. His eyes were small and very close together, and his nose was too big for his face.
7. People made jokes about him or ignored him.
8. Consequently, he carved a tiny theater and played by himself most of the time.
9. He made up short plays and acted out all the parts.
10. At age seven he saw a real play and for years longed for the stage.
11. At 14 he went to Copenhagen, but no theater there would hire him.
12. Three years later Andersen went back to school and earned good grades.
13. He then gave up the idea of acting and became a writer.
14. At 30 he wrote his first fairy tale, but he never expected success.
15. People all over the world loved his stories, and they still read them—more than 100 years later.

# Diagraming Compound Sentences

A compound sentence is diagramed like two simple sentences, but the two diagrams are connected by a broken line. The broken line joins the two verbs. The conjunction that joins the two sentences is written on this line.

You prepare the salad, and I will cook the stew.

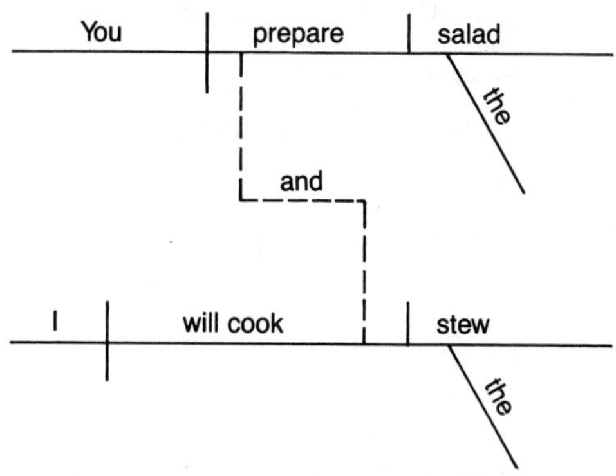


### Exercise 8 Diagraming Compound Sentences

Diagram the following sentences or copy them. If your teacher tells you to copy them, draw one line under each subject and two lines under each verb.

1. I played the violin, and it had a wonderful tone.
2. The storm broke suddenly, and nobody had an umbrella.
3. Charles tossed the ball, and Jennifer caught it.
4. Terry likes mysteries, but her brother prefers westerns.
5. The newspaper arrived, and I read the sports section.
6. We can swim, or I can row us to the island.
7. Chickens have wishbones, but parrots do not have wishbones.
8. The bus reached our street, and we boarded it.
9. I dropped the box, and two plates broke.
10. I will water the garden, and Jane will cut the grass.

## Application to Writing

By combining sentences, you can vary the length and the structure of your sentences.

Two sentences with the same subject should usually be combined into a simple sentence with a compound verb.

| | |
|---|---|
| TWO SIMPLE SENTENCES | Some animals hibernate in the winter. These animals sleep under heavy snow. |
| COMPOUND VERB | Some animals hibernate in the winter and sleep under heavy snow. |

Two closely related simple sentences with different subjects should usually be combined in a compound sentence. Use a comma and a conjunction.

| | |
|---|---|
| TWO SIMPLE SENTENCES | Paul found his shoes. His socks are still missing. |
| COMPOUND SENTENCE | Paul found his shoes, but his socks are still missing. |

### *EXERCISE 9 Combining Sentences*

Combine each of the following pairs of sentences in one of two ways. (1) Write a simple sentence with a compound verb, or (2) write a compound sentence.

1. Robinson Crusoe survived a shipwreck. Crusoe lived alone for a long time on a desert island.
2. I painted my room yellow. Red is my favorite color.
3. We can have lunch now. We can wait for Raphael.
4. Cats have about 30 ear muscles. People have only 6.
5. We went to the roller-skating rink. We saw a movie later.
6. Will opened the old chest. It was empty.
7. I saw the special on TV. I enjoyed the acting.
8. Francis arrived at noon. The others came much later.
9. Ted wrote the letter. Ted hasn't mailed it yet.
10. Hummingbirds beat their wings nearly 1,200 times a minute. Hummingbirds can fly backward.

# Chapter Review

**A** **Identifying Simple and Compound Sentences.** Number your paper 1 to 10. Then label each sentence *simple* or *compound.*

Life in 2050

1. Recently some students talked about the future, and many of their predictions were fascinating.
2. Great advances in medicine will occur, and the normal life span will be 120 years.
3. Factories will spring up everywhere and will produce such items as food pills and rubber cars.
4. Robot servants will clean the yard and will do all the chores around the house.
5. Robots will appear instantly and will disappear at the touch of a button.
6. Some people will live in space colonies, and others will live underwater.
7. Children will no longer go to school but will learn from robot teachers at home.
8. Sidewalks will disappear, and people will fly by means of jet packs on their backs.
9. A machine will make the bed and will put the bed up into the wall.
10. The Olympics will be huge, and people from all over the galaxy will attend.

**B** **Punctuating Compound Sentences.** Number your paper 1 to 10. If a sentence needs a comma, write the sentence and add the comma. If a sentence does not need a comma, write *none* after the number.

1. The car looked old but its engine purred smoothly.
2. A strong gust of wind came up suddenly and the small sailboat nearly overturned.
3. The Memorial Day Parade starts at the fire station and ends at the courthouse.

4. Most leaves are green but some maple leaves are red.
5. Yano told about China and her sister showed slides.
6. The child played with her ball and then took a nap.
7. Huge rocks rolled down the mountainside and a major highway was blocked.
8. Last Saturday Sue and I swam in the lake and had a picnic.
9. Hawaii exports orchids and black coral but pineapples are its most famous export.
10. The House of Representatives has 435 members and the Senate has 100 members.

## Mastery Test

Number your paper 1 to 10. If a sentence is a simple sentence, write *simple.* If a sentence is a compound sentence, write *compound.*

1. Two raccoons found our lunch and ate all of it.
2. Both a dog and a pig can swim, but a pig can swim faster.
3. Matt will wash the car this noon, or I will wash it later.
4. Our dog barked at the ocean and raced up and down the beach.
5. Vince adjusted the television dials, but the picture remained blurry.
6. An elephant looks flatfooted but actually walks on its toes.
7. The wind howled and blew over the large oak tree near our house.
8. Ray dived off the board, and the judges gave him an almost perfect score.
9. The gull tore at a piece of fish and offered some to her young.
10. Corey hit the ball to left field and rounded first base.

9

# Sound Sentences

## Diagnostic Test

Number your paper 1 to 10. Then label each group of words *sentence, fragment,* or *run-on*.

EXAMPLE From my house to the school.
ANSWER fragment

1. A floppy-eared puppy with large, sad eyes.
2. On the top shelf of my closet.
3. Watermelon is 97 percent water.
4. A baseball has a cork center and layers of rubber and woolen yarn, strips of cowhide cover the ball.
5. My ear is sore, I'll visit the clinic.
6. Alvin sawed the log into two-foot pieces then Earl split those pieces into quarters.
7. Waited for the subway.
8. A tasty dinner of tortillas and beans.
9. Mia stayed home.
10. Frogs have ears, and their hearing is quite good.

# Sentence Fragments

Suppose someone said to you, "In the deserted mine." You would expect that person to go on. What happened in the deserted mine? Who or what was in it? The words "in the deserted mine" are a *sentence fragment*. They do not express a complete thought.

9a A **sentence fragment** is a group of words that does not express a complete thought.

Most fragments are missing at least one basic part of a sentence—a subject or a verb.

| | |
|---|---|
| NO SUBJECT | Spoke to the team after the game. [Who spoke to the team?] |
| SENTENCE | The coach spoke to the team after the game. |
| NO VERB | Kim's uncle from Seattle. [What did he do?] |
| SENTENCE | Kim's uncle from Seattle arrived today. |
| NO SUBJECT OR VERB | At the corner near the school. [Who or what was at the corner? What happened there?] |
| SENTENCE | We waited at the corner near the school. |

### EXERCISE 1 Recognizing Sentence Fragments

Number your paper 1 to 10. Then label each group of words *sentence* or *fragment*.

1. Walked down a crowded street at rush hour.
2. Saturn has a moon larger than the planet Mercury.
3. At the edge of the steep cliff.
4. The cucumber plants in the garden.
5. In the basement we found an old bicycle.
6. Wore a sombrero in the hot sun.
7. A letter from a friend at camp.
8. A trout can live for four years.
9. At the end of the final song on the album.
10. Brazil was named after a tree.

## Ways to Correct Sentence Fragments

There are two basic ways to correct a sentence fragment. First, you can attach it to a nearby sentence. Second, you can make the fragment a separate sentence by adding words to make it a complete thought.

| | |
|---|---|
| SENTENCE AND FRAGMENT | I visited the National Baseball Museum. In Cooperstown, New York. |
| ATTACHED | I visited the National Baseball Museum **in Cooperstown, New York.** |
| SEPARATE SENTENCES | I visited the National Baseball Museum. **It is located in Cooperstown, New York.** |

### EXERCISE 2 *Writing Sentences*

Number your paper 1 to 10. Then correct each fragment by writing one complete sentence.

EXAMPLE Wes gripped the bat tightly. And swung at the ball.

ANSWER Wes gripped the bat tightly and swung at the ball.

1. Meteorites were the only source of iron. During the Bronze Age.
2. Several paintings at the art fair.
3. We visited many relatives. At a reunion in Texas.
4. Many students at the bus stop.
5. Tooth enamel is the hardest substance. In the human body.
6. Junk food contains many calories. But has very few vitamins.
7. Will you travel by subway? Or take a bus?
8. Often phones his best friend every evening.
9. The scouts hiked energetically. Up the mountain to the top.
10. The bicycle rims and the tool kit on that table in the garage.

# Run-on Sentences

Another kind of sentence error occurs when two or more sentences run together as one sentence. This kind of sentence error is called a *run-on sentence.* Run-on sentences are often confusing to read because a reader is not sure where one idea ends and another begins.

9b A **run-on sentence** is two or more sentences that are written as one sentence. They are separated by a comma or no mark of punctuation at all.

When you write, avoid separating two or more sentences with only a comma.

RUN-ON SENTENCE Chinese food is tasty, Lee often makes some for dinner.

Also avoid joining two or more sentences without using any punctuation.

RUN-ON SENTENCE A frog got into the garage Stanley chased it for ten minutes.

### EXERCISE 3 Recognizing Run-on Sentences

Number your paper 1 to 10. Then label each group of words *sentence* or *run-on*.

1. Tornadoes and hurricanes differ in size both usually cause much damage.
2. I enjoyed our visit to Colorado with its huge mountain peaks and beautiful valleys.
3. Bruce entered his ant colony in the science contest.
4. Bears climb trees like cats, they sink their claws into the bark.
5. Birds use their bills for many purposes.
6. Did you hear the weather report, will the rain stop soon?

7. Locusts can travel 300 miles nonstop their average air speed can reach 8 miles per hour.
8. Don't tell me the answer to the puzzle I will solve it.
9. Paris has one of the most beautiful boulevards in the world.
10. Virginia protested the Stamp Act, did other colonies follow its example immediately?

## Ways to Correct Run-on Sentences

There are two basic ways to correct a run-on sentence. First, you can make a run-on sentence into separate sentences. Second, you can create a compound sentence by adding a comma and a conjunction such as *and, but, or,* or *yet.*

| | |
|---|---|
| RUN-ON SENTENCE | We rushed into the terminal the bus for Chicago had already left. |
| SEPARATE SENTENCES | We rushed into the terminal**. The** bus for Chicago had already left. |
| COMPOUND SENTENCE | We rushed into the terminal**, but** the bus for Chicago had already left. |

NOTE: If the run-on sentence already has a comma, simply add the proper conjunction.

### EXERCISE 4 Writing Sentences

Number your paper 1 to 10. Correct each run-on sentence (1) by writing two separate sentences, or (2) by writing a compound sentence. Remember to use capital letters, commas, and end marks correctly.

1. Tom washed the dishes Martha will dry them.
2. The sun was shining a minute ago, now it's pouring!
3. Christopher left his bicycle outside in the rain, the fender rusted.
4. Isaac Newton was born in 1642, Galileo died that same year.

5. Ted plays ice hockey his brother isn't interested in any sport.
6. A lightning bolt is about a half mile long, over 100 lightning flashes occur each second.
7. Some centipedes have 28 legs others have as many as 354 legs.
8. Last year I had a paper route now I baby-sit every afternoon instead.
9. Petunias grow well in a sunny garden, they need plenty of water.
10. The original movie *Frankenstein* was released in 1920 it was produced by Thomas Edison.

## TIME-OUT FOR REVIEW • • • • •

Number your paper 1 to 10. Then correct each sentence fragment or run-on sentence. Add capital letters, commas, conjunctions, and end marks where needed.

Subways

1. The first subway in the world opened in London. On January 10, 1863.
2. A trench was dug then a pavement was laid over it.
3. The trains were powered by steam engines, the smoke from the engines filled the tunnels with terrible fumes.
4. Ten feet of water once filled the tunnels the subway shut down briefly.
5. About 30 years later, London's first "tube tunnel" was built. And instantly became a success.
6. In a tube line, a tunnel is actually bored through the ground. Under the foundations of buildings.
7. The first tube line used electric power. And still runs today.
8. In 1897, Boston completed the first subway system. In the United States.
9. It ran only 1½ miles. And used trolley cars on the subway tracks.
10. New York's subway finally opened in 1904, over two billion people now ride it every year.

## Application to Writing

A good habit you can develop is to read aloud everything you write. Reading aloud is an easy way to find any sentence fragments or run-on sentences that you may have included in your first draft. Your natural voice rhythms will help you find these errors.

If you find errors, take the time to correct them. When you edit, try to use different ways of correcting sentence errors. If you turn each run-on sentence into separate sentences, for example, you may have too many short, choppy sentences. Good writing, after all, includes different kinds of sentences.

### EXERCISE 5 *Editing for Sentence Errors*

Rewrite the following paragraphs, correcting each sentence fragment or run-on sentence. Remember to use capital letters, commas, and end marks correctly and to vary the lengths of your sentences.

Bats

Bats come out at night. And look for food. Bats are expert fliers. In total darkness. For centuries people couldn't understand this skill now scientists can explain the bats' unusual abilities. Bats use their ears and vocal cords for navigation, not their eyes.

In the 1780s, an Italian scientist did an important experiment. He blindfolded some bats. And released them into a room. The room was crisscrossed with silk threads not a single thread was touched. Then he plugged their ears, the bats became imprisoned in the threads. A bat's ears, not its eyes, are responsible. For the bats' perfect flight patterns.

In 1920, a scientist made another discovery. Bats make high-pitched squeaks these sounds cannot be heard by humans. The sounds bounce off things. And create an echo. A bat locates things in the dark. With these echoes.

# Chapter Review

**A** **Correcting Sentence Fragments.** Number your paper 1 to 10. Then correct each sentence fragment.

1. The house wren sometimes builds its nest. In the pocket of an old coat.
2. Can't find today's newspaper.
3. The parade with bands and floats.
4. Pulled over to the side of the road.
5. Someone in the stands suddenly jumped up. And ran onto the field.
6. A large school of fish beneath the boat.
7. Chipmunks are really rock squirrels. With black stripes on their backs.
8. The limb of the spruce tree.
9. Owned a red Corvette with white stripes.
10. The apples are just turning red. On the trees at the farm.

**B** **Correcting Run-on Sentences.** Number your paper 1 to 10. Then correct each run-on sentence.

1. The audience enjoyed the acrobats, they were swinging through the air without any net beneath them.
2. Janice swam ten laps then it was time for dinner.
3. Desert oases are far apart, how do camels travel long distances without any water?
4. Franklin D. Roosevelt was president of the United States he was elected four times.
5. Insects are the world's greatest fliers they can twist their wings in different directions.
6. The first Thanksgiving took place in 1621 about 140 people, including 90 Indians, attended.
7. The sun is still shining, rain is forecast.
8. Andrea went to the theater with her friends her mother drove everyone home.

9. The giant oyster weighs 500 to 1,000 pounds its pearl is the size of a golf ball.
10. Monticello is the name of Thomas Jefferson's home, you can see it in Charlottesville, Virginia.

**C** **Correcting Sentence Errors.** Rewrite the following paragraphs, correcting the sentence fragments and run-on sentences.

The First Woman Doctor

In 1844, young Elizabeth Blackwell wanted to become a doctor, medical schools did not accept women students at that time. Blackwell was very determined, however. For a while she studied. With private teachers. Then in 1846, a medical school in New York. Finally admitted her as a student. After she finished her studies, she could not find a job at any established hospital. Therefore, she founded her own hospital. For women and children. Today the Blackwell medal is awarded to women physicians it recognizes their achievements as doctors.

## Mastery Test

Number your paper 1 to 10. Then label each group of words *sentence, fragment,* or *run-on.*

1. Robert Louis Stevenson wrote many books, one of them was *Treasure Island.*
2. The warmth of a wool poncho on a cold day.
3. Benjamin Franklin wanted the wild turkey for our national bird.
4. Through the front door of the Masons' apartment.
5. Mavis and her sister earned their lifesaving certificates last year.
6. Corey bowed, the audience stood and cheered.
7. The horseshoe crab has two pairs of eyes.
8. Enjoyed a salad of bananas, oranges, and papayas.
9. Ostriches cannot fly they have small, weak wings.
10. The display of Indian art at the Boswell Museum.

# Standardized Test

## GRAMMAR

**Directions:** Decide which description best fits each group of words. In the appropriate row on your answer sheet, fill in the circle containing the same letter as your answer.

SAMPLE At the zoo with Martin.

**A** fragment **B** run-on **C** sentence

ANSWER Ⓐ Ⓑ Ⓒ

1. The view from the hill.

   **A** fragment **B** run-on **C** sentence

2. The stairway is dark.

   **A** fragment **B** run-on **C** sentence

3. Gilbert laughed.

   **A** fragment **B** run-on **C** sentence

4. It was almost six o'clock, Adam set the table.

   **A** fragment **B** run-on **C** sentence

5. In the middle of the night.

   **A** fragment **B** run-on **C** sentence

6. Josie was the pitcher, and I was the catcher.

   **A** fragment **B** run-on **C** sentence

7. Sat in the first row of the balcony.

   **A** fragment **B** run-on **C** sentence

8. The computer beeped, nothing else happened.

   **A** fragment **B** run-on **C** sentence

9. Sherlock Holmes is a detective in over fifty stories.

   **A** fragment **B** run-on **C** sentence

10. A purple sweater with red and pink stripes on the front.

    **A** fragment **B** run-on **C** sentence

**Directions:** Decide which underlined part is the subject in each sentence. On your answer sheet, fill in the circle containing the same letter as your answer.

SAMPLE The horses returned to their stalls.
A B C

ANSWER Ⓐ Ⓑ Ⓒ

11. The guitar played the melody.
A B C

12. Two paintings hung over the sofa.
A B C

13. Is Max coming with us?
A B C

14. On the bench sat a dark-haired young girl.
A B C

15. A picture of the ocean won first prize.
A B C

**Directions:** Decide which underlined part is the verb in each sentence. On your answer sheet, fill in the circle containing the same letter as your answer.

SAMPLE Leona left early.
A B C

ANSWER Ⓐ Ⓑ Ⓒ

16. The balloon floated away.
A B C

17. She is an excellent swimmer.
A B C

18. I have seen a salmon ladder.
A B C

19. The best player usually wins.
A B C

20. Across the sky streaked the comet.
A B C

UNIT 2

# Usage

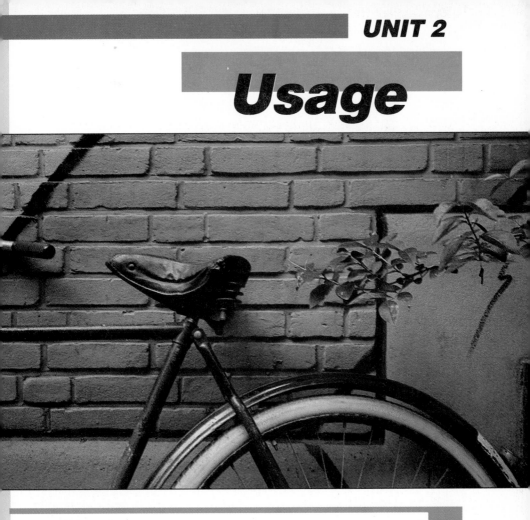

# 10

# Using Verbs

## Diagnostic Test

Number your paper 1 to 10. Then write the correct verb form for each sentence.

EXAMPLE I (saw, seen) Rob at the baseball game.
ANSWER saw

1. The last search party (came, come) back at noon.
2. They shouldn't have (went, gone) out in the boat during the storm.
3. We (blew, blown) up three dozen balloons for the party.
4. Tim (did, done) the math problem in 60 seconds.
5. I have already (rang, rung) the doorbell twice.
6. Who was (chose, chosen) for the leading role?
7. Several people have (swam, swum) the English Channel.
8. Bryan (threw, throwed) the ball to third base.
9. Lou has (wrote, written) an excellent poem.
10. Ellen and Kim have (sang, sung) duets in concerts.

# The Principal Parts of Verbs

You know that a verb shows action or makes a statement about the subject. A verb also tells when the action happens.

| | |
|---|---|
| PRESENT ACTION | Each day I **run** a mile. |
| PAST ACTION | Yesterday I **ran** a mile. |
| FUTURE ACTION | Tomorrow I **will run** a mile. |

Notice that a verb changes its form to show the time of the action. The different forms of a verb are made from the basic parts of a verb, called *principal parts.*

10a Three of the **principal parts** of a verb are the *present,* the *past,* and the *past participle.*

## Regular Verbs

There are hundreds of verbs, but learning their principal parts is easy. Most verbs form their past and past participle the same way. These verbs are called *regular verbs.*

10b A **regular verb** forms its past and past participle by adding *-ed* or *-d* to the present.

Following are the principal parts of the regular verbs *call, bake, drop* and *expel*. Notice that the *p* and the *l* are doubled when *-ed* is added to *drop* and *expel.*

| **PRESENT** | **PAST** | **PAST PARTICIPLE** |
|---|---|---|
| call | call**ed** | (have) call**ed** |
| bake | bake**d** | (has) bake**d** |
| drop | drop**ped** | (had) drop**ped** |
| expel | expel**led** | (had) expel**led** |

NOTE: The past participle is always used with a helping verb such as *have, has,* or *had.*

### EXERCISE 1 Writing Principal Parts of Regular Verbs

Make three columns on your paper. Label them *present, past,* and *past participle.* Then write the three principal parts of each of the following regular verbs. Use *have* when you write the past participle.

| | | | | |
|---|---|---|---|---|
| 1. climb | 3. suppose | 5. wish | 7. use | 9. skip |
| 2. drag | 4. paint | 6. stop | 8. earn | 10. move |

## Irregular Verbs

Although most verbs form their past and past participle by adding *-ed* or *-d,* a few verbs do not. These verbs are called *irregular verbs.*

10c An **irregular verb** does not form its past and past participle by adding *-ed* or *-d* to the present.

Irregular verbs can be divided into groups according to the way they form their past and past participles.

**Group 1**

These irregular verbs have the same form for the present, the past, and the past participle.

| PRESENT | PAST | PAST PARTICIPLE |
|---|---|---|
| burst | burst | (have) burst |
| put | put | (have) put |
| let | let | (have) let |

**Group 2**

These irregular verbs have the same form for the past and the past participle.

| PRESENT | PAST | PAST PARTICIPLE |
|---|---|---|
| bring | brought | (have) brought |
| make | made | (have) made |
| say | said | (have) said |
| leave | left | (have) left |
| teach | taught | (have) taught |

## EXERCISE 2 Using the Correct Verb Form

Number your paper 1 to 10. Then label each underlined verb form *past* or *past participle*.

1. Yesterday no one in the stadium left before the end of the game.
2. Jimmy's old football uniform has burst its seams.
3. Who made the second speech last night?
4. Has everyone brought a book to study hall?
5. She has said that many times before.
6. You should have put the film with the camera.
7. Mrs. Lopez has taught us to use the computer.
8. I let my sister use my bicycle last week.
9. Danny brought us each a bushel of apples last fall from his father's orchard.
10. I have made party favors for everyone.

### Group 3

These irregular verbs form the past participle by adding -*n* to the past.

| PRESENT | PAST | PAST PARTICIPLE |
|---|---|---|
| break | broke | (have) broken |
| choose | chose | (have) chosen |
| freeze | froze | (have) frozen |
| speak | spoke | (have) spoken |
| steal | stole | (have) stolen |

### Group 4

These irregular verbs form the past participle by adding -*n* to the present.

| PRESENT | PAST | PAST PARTICIPLE |
|---|---|---|
| blow | blew | (have) blown |
| drive | drove | (have) driven |
| give | gave | (have) given |
| grow | grew | (have) grown |
| know | knew | (have) known |
| see | saw | (have) seen |
| take | took | (have) taken |
| throw | threw | (have) thrown |

### EXERCISE 3 Determining the Correct Verb Form

Number your paper 1 to 10. Then write the correct verb form for each sentence. Remember that *have, has,* or *had* is used with the past participle.

EXAMPLE I have (grew, grown) six inches this year.
ANSWER grown

1. Has anyone (saw, seen) my blue sweater with the white reindeer design?
2. Ned has (broke, broken) our school record for the high jump.
3. By six in the evening, we had (drove, driven) nearly 500 miles through the mountains.
4. I have (froze, frozen) many of the vegetables from our garden.
5. My brother Leon has (stole, stolen) three bases so far in this game.
6. Much to our relief, the hurricane (blew, blowed) itself out to sea.
7. I have (took, taken) a raincoat with me.
8. By accident the quarterback (threw, throwed) the ball to a player on the other team.
9. I have (spoke, spoken) to Lucy twice today about the plans for the dance.
10. I once (knew, knowed) the name of that song.

### EXERCISE 4 Using the Correct Verb Form

Number your paper 1 to 10. Write the past or the past participle of each verb in parentheses. Remember that *have, has,* or *had* is used with the past participle.

EXAMPLE I have (choose) those jeans.
ANSWER chosen

1. Uncle Mel (drive) a school bus during the winter last year.
2. Who (break) the record at last night's game?

3. Ms. Tracy has (choose) the best runner on the track team for the marathon.
4. Yesterday Mr. Kane (give) us two trout from his fishing trip.
5. Had Kevin (see) the smoke coming from the window of the apartment?
6. The population in our city has (grow) steadily for five years.
7. The puppy has (steal) the last two bites of the cat's dinner.
8. Frank (choose) the first song at the dance last Friday.
9. I should have (know) that answer.
10. No one (take) the last piece of cheese at lunch yesterday.

## Group 5

These irregular verbs form the past and past participle by changing a vowel.

| PRESENT | PAST | PAST PARTICIPLE |
|---|---|---|
| begin | began | (have) begun |
| drink | drank | (have) drunk |
| ring | rang | (have) rung |
| sing | sang | (have) sung |
| swim | swam | (have) swum |

NOTE: In these verbs the *i* in the present changes to an *a* in the past and a *u* in the past participle.

## Group 6

These irregular verbs form the past and past participle in other ways.

| PRESENT | PAST | PAST PARTICIPLE |
|---|---|---|
| come | came | (have) come |
| do | did | (have) done |
| eat | ate | (have) eaten |
| go | went | (have) gone |
| ride | rode | (have) ridden |
| run | ran | (have) run |
| wear | wore | (have) worn |
| write | wrote | (have) written |

## Exercise 5 Determining the Correct Verb Form

Number your paper 1 to 10. Then write the correct verb form for each sentence. Remember that *have, has,* or *had* is used with the past participle.

1. Has John ever (did, done) this kind of work?
2. The deer (ran, run) into the clearing.
3. Have you ever (went, gone) to a rodeo?
4. I (began, begun) the chore after dinner.
5. The first bell (rang, rung) three minutes ago.
6. Has Nick ever (wore, worn) that shirt?
7. Jessica (drank, drunk) three glasses of water after the race.
8. Who (sang, sung) the solo in the musical?
9. Have you (wrote, written) a thank-you note?
10. Several porpoises (swam, swum) close to the boat.

## Exercise 6 Using the Correct Verb Form

Number your paper 1 to 10. Write the past or the past participle of each verb in parentheses. Remember that *have, has,* or *had* is used with the past participle.

1. George (do) a second ballot count after the election last Tuesday.
2. Have you ever (sing) in the school choir?
3. I have never (eat) such tasty meat loaf as yours.
4. Michael must have (ride) to school with Lucía.
5. The mail (come) an hour ago.
6. Rehearsal has (begin) without us.
7. I (wear) my heavy jacket to last Tuesday's meeting.
8. Who (write) the Gettysburg Address?
9. Karen has (swim) across the lake several times.
10. The bells have (ring) announcing the new year.

## Exercise 7 Writing Sentences

Write sentences using each principal part of the irregular verbs *put, break, leave, know,* and *sing.*

## TIME-OUT FOR REVIEW • • • • •

Number your paper 1 to 15. Write the past or the past participle of each verb in parentheses. (This exercise includes regular and irregular verbs.)

EXAMPLE After the American Revolution, the United States (need) a capital city.

ANSWER needed

The Nation's Capital

1. People (write) and (say) why their city should be the nation's capital.
2. Congress finally (decide) to create a new city.
3. Congress (pass) a bill in 1790 giving permission to the President to choose a site.
4. George Washington (go) to several places and finally (choose) the place where the city now stands.
5. He (know) it was a good location because the Potomac River (run) deep enough for ships.
6. Maryland and Virginia (give) the land to the federal government.
7. President Washington then (bring) in a French architect to design the new city.
8. The architect (begin) to draw plans with broad avenues.
9. He (divide) the city into four sections, with the Capitol Building in the center.
10. He then (make) designs of beautiful government buildings and monuments.
11. The name of this ten-mile-square area, the District of Columbia, (come) from the name Christopher Columbus.
12. The architect and a planning commission (name) the city Washington, in honor of the country's first president.
13. By 1800, builders had nearly (complete) the President's house.
14. President John Adams and his wife (ride) to their new home.
15. Soon other members of the government also (move) to Washington, D.C.

# Problem Verbs

*Lie/lay* and *sit/set* are problem verbs because people sometimes confuse *lie* with *lay* and *sit* with *set*.

## Lie *and* Lay

*Lie* means "to recline or rest." This verb is never followed by a direct object. Its principal parts are *lie, lay,* and *(have) lain.*

| | |
|---|---|
| PRESENT | Each afternoon I **lie** down for a rest. |
| PAST | Yesterday Dan **lay** down for half an hour. |
| PAST PARTICIPLE | My cousin has **lain** in the shade of the oak tree all afternoon. |

*Lay* means "to put or place (something) down." This verb is usually followed by a direct object. Its principal parts are *lay, laid,* and *(have) laid.*

| | |
|---|---|
| PRESENT | The coaches **lay** the mats on the gym floor every morning. |
| PAST | I **laid** the mail beside the telephone. |
| PAST PARTICIPLE | Bill has **laid** the bag of groceries on the wet paint. |

### EXERCISE 8 Using Lie *and* Lay

Number your paper 1 to 10. Then write the correct form of *lie* or *lay.*

1. The clerk (lay, laid) the books on the shelf.
2. Rover usually (lies, lays) by the door.
3. The Smiths (lay, laid) blue carpeting in their hall.
4. That book has (lain, laid) there for weeks.
5. Yesterday I (lay, laid) in the tall grass.
6. Holly (lay, laid) in the hammock for an hour.
7. Victor has (lain, laid) your books beside his.

8. Three newborn kittens (lay, laid) in the box.
9. I usually (lie, lay) my clean wash on my bed.
10. I have (lain, laid) awake for two hours.

## Sit *and* Set

*Sit* means "to occupy a seat" or "to rest in a seated position." This verb is never followed by a direct object. Its principal parts are *sit, sat,* and *(have) sat.*

| | |
|---|---|
| PRESENT | I often **sit** on the dock. |
| PAST | Barry **sat** in the car while it warmed up. |
| PAST PARTICIPLE | For years no one has **sat** in those old chairs on the front porch. |

*Set* means "to put or place (something) down" and is usually followed by a direct object. Its principal parts are *set, set,* and *(have) set.*

| | |
|---|---|
| PRESENT | Don't **set** any disks on top of the computer. |
| PAST | We **set** the cups on the saucers. |
| PAST PARTICIPLE | He has **set** the hamburgers and hot dogs on the grill. |

### *EXERCISE 9* *Using* Sit *and* Set

Number your paper 1 to 10. Then write the correct form of *sit* or *set.*

1. I often (sit, set) in that big old rocking chair.
2. Joanna has (sat, set) the hammer on the workbench.
3. Our dog always (sits, sets) by my brother Leon.
4. Kim has (sat, set) the books back on the shelf.
5. Laverne (sat, set) the tray of glasses on the table.
6. We have (sat, set) here for about an hour.
7. Allison (sat, set) the new candlesticks next to the vase.
8. Luis (sat, set) on the steps and waited for us.
9. If you don't (sit, set) still, the bees may sting you.
10. Who (sat, set) the newspapers on the toaster?

# Verb Tense

*Tense* is the form a verb takes to show time. The principal parts of a verb are used to form the tenses.

| | |
|---|---|
| PRESENT | I **paint** pictures. |
| PAST | I **painted** a picture yesterday. |
| FUTURE | I **will paint** another picture today. |
| PRESENT PERFECT | I **have painted** pictures for a year. |
| PAST PERFECT | I **had painted** pictures before I attended nursery school. |
| FUTURE PERFECT | I **will have painted** 15 pictures by June. |

## Conjugation of a Verb

A *conjugation* is a list of all the singular and plural forms of a verb in its six tenses.

### Conjugation of *Fall*

**PRINCIPAL PARTS**

| Present | Past | Past Participle |
|---|---|---|
| fall | fell | fallen |

**Present**

This tense expresses action that is going on now.

| SINGULAR | PLURAL |
|---|---|
| I fall | we fall |
| you fall | you fall |
| he, she, it falls | they fall |

**Past**

This tense expresses action that took place in the past.

| SINGULAR | PLURAL |
|---|---|
| I fell | we fell |
| you fell | you fell |
| he, she, it fell | they fell |

### Future

This tense expresses action that will take place in the future. It is formed by adding *shall* or *will* to the present.

| SINGULAR | PLURAL |
|---|---|
| I shall/will fall | we shall/will fall |
| you will fall | you will fall |
| he, she, it will fall | they will fall |

### Present Perfect

This tense expresses action that was completed at some indefinite time in the past or action that started in the past and is still going on. It is formed by adding *has* or *have* to the past participle.

| SINGULAR | PLURAL |
|---|---|
| I have fallen | we have fallen |
| you have fallen | you have fallen |
| he, she, it has fallen | they have fallen |

### Past Perfect

This tense expresses action that took place before some other past action. It is formed by adding *had* to the past participle.

| SINGULAR | PLURAL |
|---|---|
| I had fallen | we had fallen |
| you had fallen | you had fallen |
| he, she, it had fallen | they had fallen |

### Future Perfect

This tense expresses action that will be completed by some given time in the future. It is formed by adding *shall have* or *will have* to the past participle. (This tense is seldom used.)

| SINGULAR | PLURAL |
|---|---|
| I shall/will have fallen | we shall/will have fallen |
| you will have fallen | you will have fallen |
| he, she, it will have fallen | they will have fallen |

## EXERCISE 10 *Conjugating a Verb*

Write the conjugation of the verb *wear*.

## EXERCISE 11 Identifying Verb Tenses

Number your paper 1 to 10. Decide whether the tense of each underlined verb is *present, past, future, present perfect, past perfect,* or *future perfect.* Then write the tense.

EXAMPLE Maria will choose her favorite poem.
ANSWER future

1. A filly becomes a mare at the age of five.
2. Debbie suddenly realized that she had left her flippers on the dock.
3. I think I have met you before.
4. Mom and Dad will meet you at the airport.
5. Roger Bannister broke the four-minute mile in 1954.
6. After Alex had raked the leaves, he put them in large plastic bags.
7. Dolphins sleep with one eye open at all times.
8. I will ride Brown Beauty tomorrow after school.
9. My cousin has lived in Omaha for three years.
10. The first wristwatch appeared as early as 1790.

## EXERCISE 12 Writing Sentences

Read the examples of the six tenses on page 144. Then write a sentence for each tense of the verb *play.*

## TIME-OUT FOR REVIEW • • • • •

Number your paper 1 to 10. Then write each underlined verb in the tense that is indicated in parentheses.

EXAMPLE I run *(past)* as fast as I could.
ANSWER ran

1. In a few hours, snow cover *(present perfect)* all the landscape within sight.
2. By the end of the summer, Kate earn *(past perfect)* enough money for a new bicycle.
3. I enjoy *(present perfect)* the weather this fall.

4. Jackie Robinson play *(past)* for the Brooklyn Dodgers.
5. Next semester I take *(future)* art, gymnastics, and computer science.
6. At the close of school, I discovered that I drop *(past perfect)* my glasses somewhere in the hall.
7. Last summer we visit *(past)* the Black Hills in South Dakota.
8. The language in Iceland remain *(present perfect)* unchanged since the twelfth century.
9. Today's heavy rains end *(future)* the recent drought.
10. The crew paint *(past)* the house in ten days.

## Application to Writing

Good writers are not finished when they place their final period on a piece of paper. They always revise and edit their work, whether that work is a short letter or a long report.

Looking for verb errors should be part of the editing stage of your writing. One way to find some verb errors is to read your work aloud. If you find any errors, always take the time to correct them.

### EXERCISE 13 Editing for Verb Errors

Read the following paragraph. Then write the paragraph, correcting each incorrect verb.

A Small Loan

Henry Ford begun his motor company in 1903 with only $28,000. He employed 12 workers and maked his cars in a factory that was only 50 feet wide. Soon, however, Ford run out of money. He then went to the Dodge brothers for a loan. In 1908, the first Model T was ready, but Ford had once again came close to bankruptcy. He ask a friend's sister for $100 to launch his new car. That $100 was eventually worth $260,000!

# Chapter Review

**A** **Using the Correct Verb Form.** Number your paper 1 to 10. Write the past or the past participle of each verb in parentheses.

1. Allen has (ride) horses for ten years.
2. Last weekend we (drive) to Salem.
3. My baby sister has (lie) happily in her crib for over an hour.
4. Who (make) this fruit salad for lunch?
5. Pam (run) into the house after she spilled paint on her clothes.
6. Who (teach) you to water-ski last summer?
7. He (say) that his speech was a success.
8. No one (know) the name of the visitor when he arrived.
9. My brother has (give) me his catcher's mitt.
10. Everyone (bring) a swimsuit and a towel to last Sunday's picnic.

**B** **Using the Correct Verb Form.** Number your paper 1 to 10. Find and correct each verb form that is incorrectly used in the following sentences. If the verb form is correct, write *C* after the number.

1. Julio has accidentally broke the light bulb.
2. My cousin has often sang solos with the choir.
3. I have drunk the last glass of milk.
4. They have chose Connie as the captain of the softball team.
5. We swum at the town beach yesterday morning.
6. Matthew done everything on the list.
7. The lake had nearly frozen by morning.
8. Who throwed the ball into our court?
9. The wind has blown the leaves around the yard.
10. The grass has already growed another inch.

**C Using the Correct Verb Form.** Number your paper 1 to 10. Then write each underlined verb in the tense that is indicated in parentheses.

1. In 1985, Pete Rose break (*past*) Ty Cobb's record of 4,191 base hits.
2. Linda live (*past perfect*) in Ohio before she moved here.
3. Most bats sleep (*present*) upside down.
4. I write (*present perfect*) for a free catalog.
5. Tomorrow the sun rise (*future*) over those mountains.
6. Brian said that he mail (*past perfect*) only half of the invitations.
7. Nancy save (*present perfect*) enough money for a new bicycle.
8. One thousand bees make (*present*) only one pound of honey during their entire lives.
9. Who carry (*future*) the flag in tomorrow's parade?
10. Elephants, lions, and camels roam (*past*) across Alaska 12,000 years ago.

## Mastery Test

Number your paper 1 to 10. Then write the correct verb form for each sentence.

1. Ellie has (went, gone) to the park.
2. I have never (saw, seen) a more beautiful sunset!
3. The clock (began, begun) to strike at midnight.
4. The first settlers (came, come) to Oak Corners over 100 years ago.
5. I (lay, laid) down for a short nap after dinner.
6. Have you (took, taken) the meat out of the freezer?
7. The bells in the church steeple (rang, rung) after the wedding.
8. Has the elephant (ate, eaten) all your peanuts?
9. I have (spoke, spoken) to Mr. Lee about extra help.
10. Brenda has (wrote, written) her report.

# 11

# Using Pronouns

## Diagnostic Test

Number your paper 1 to 10. Then write the correct word in parentheses.

EXAMPLE Evan will sing with Carol and (I, me).
ANSWER me

1. Rebecca and (they, them) are going to camp.
2. That's (he, him) on the school bus.
3. Swimmers like (they, them) are needed on the county team.
4. The Oak Street bus took Marty and (I, me) directly to the carnival.
5. Were Tim and (he, him) at the mall on Saturday?
6. John gave Lynn and (I, me) his tickets to the concert.
7. Several of the girls have had (her, their) eye tests.
8. The seat beside Mike and (she, her) is empty.
9. Is this (your, you're) locker?
10. Dawn and (we, us) are working at a garden center on weekends.

# The Cases of Personal Pronouns

The personal pronouns *he, him,* and *his* can all refer to the same person because pronouns have case.

Jerry said **he** would take **his** brother with **him** to the baseball game.

11a **Case** is the form of a noun or a pronoun that indicates its use in a sentence.

In English there are three cases: the *nominative case,* the *objective case,* and the *possessive case.*

**Nominative Case**

(used for subjects and predicate nominatives)

| | Singular | Plural |
|---|---|---|
| FIRST PERSON | I | we |
| SECOND PERSON | you | you |
| THIRD PERSON | he, she, it | they |

**Objective Case**

(used for direct objects, indirect objects, and objects of prepositions)

| | Singular | Plural |
|---|---|---|
| FIRST PERSON | me | us |
| SECOND PERSON | you | you |
| THIRD PERSON | him, her, it | them |

**Possessive Case**

(used to show ownership or possession)

| | Singular | Plural |
|---|---|---|
| FIRST PERSON | my, mine | our, ours |
| SECOND PERSON | your, yours | your, yours |
| THIRD PERSON | his, her, hers, its | their, theirs |

## The Nominative Case

The following list shows all the personal pronouns in the nominative case. (*See page 31 for a review of person.*)

**Nominative Case**

| | Singular | Plural |
|---|---|---|
| FIRST PERSON | I | we |
| SECOND PERSON | you | you |
| THIRD PERSON | he, she, it | they |

Pronouns in the nominative case are used two ways in sentences.

11b The **nominative case** is used for subjects and predicate nominatives.

SUBJECT **They** discovered buried treasure.

PREDICATE NOMINATIVE The lady in the red coat is **she.**

***Pronouns Used as Subjects.*** A subject names the person, place, or thing the sentence is about. A pronoun used as a subject is in the nominative case.

SUBJECTS **He** joined the track team.
Did **they** drive? [**They** did drive.]

Sometimes a sentence has more than one subject.

COMPOUND SUBJECT Ann and (I, me) swim daily.

To find the correct pronoun, say the sentence as if the pronoun stood alone.

CORRECT **I** swim daily.
INCORRECT **Me** swim daily.
CORRECT Anna and **I** swim daily.

### *EXERCISE 1 Using Pronouns in the Nominative Case*

Number your paper 1 to 10. Then write the correct personal pronoun in parentheses.

EXAMPLE Robert and (they, them) are leaving.
ANSWER they

1. Last night Fred and (I, me) studied at the library.
2. The Riveras and (we, us) are going to the rally.
3. Are Beth and (he, him) school reporters for the *Town Crier?*
4. Chuck and (she, her) are working together on their history projects.
5. The Roys and (they, them) are having a barbecue.
6. Brendan and (I, me) saddled the horses.
7. After school Andrew and (he, him) helped Mr. Bennett.
8. Have Chung and (she, her) joined the math team?
9. Shannon and (I, me) won the table-tennis game.
10. My parents and (they, them) are good friends.

***Pronouns Used as Predicate Nominatives.*** A predicate nominative is a word that follows a linking verb and identifies or renames the subject. (*See pages 41 and 42 for lists of common linking verbs.*) A pronoun used as a predicate nominative is in the nominative case.

PREDICATE NOMINATIVE My modern dance coach is **she**.

In a compound predicate nominative, there is an easy way to choose the correct pronoun. Turn the sentence around. Use each pronoun as a subject. Then say the sentence as if the pronoun stood alone.

The boys in line are Tim and (he, him).
Tim and (he, him) are the boys in line.

CORRECT **He** is in line.
INCORRECT **Him** is in line.
CORRECT The boys in line are Tim and **he.**

NOTE: Expressions like *It's me* or *That's him* are becoming acceptable for informal use. When you write, however, the correct expressions to use are *It is I* and *That is he.*

### EXERCISE 2 Using Pronouns in the Nominative Case

Number your paper 1 to 10. Then write the correct personal pronoun in parentheses.

EXAMPLE Was that (they, them) on the bobsled?
ANSWER they

1. In my opinion the best candidate is (she, her).
2. That's (he, him) in the blue shirt.
3. The two people next to Senator Jensen are Mr. Ricker and (she, her).
4. Yes, it's (I, me) in the newspaper photo.
5. The PTA president will be Mrs. Lee or (she, her).
6. The tour guides will be the teachers or (we, us).
7. Was that (she, her) in the gorilla costume?
8. The two finalists were Carlos and (I, me).
9. The winners of the contest are Tara and (he, him).
10. That was (they, them) in the blue truck.

### EXERCISE 3 Using Pronouns in the Nominative Case

Number your paper 1 to 10. Then complete each sentence by writing an appropriate pronoun for each blank. (Do not use *you* or *it*.)

1. Sandra and ______ are riding the bus.
2. It's ______ in the blue station wagon.
3. Last night Dad and ______ couldn't sleep.
4. Laura and ______ just got a new dog.
5. When did Wade and ______ leave?
6. The drivers will be the Bentleys and ______.
7. The announcers at the game will be Judy and ______.
8. Haven't the teachers and ______ met yet?
9. Was the runner-up Sarah or ______?
10. Did the Parkses and ______ meet outside the stadium?

### EXERCISE 4 Finding Errors in Case

Number your paper 1 to 10. If an underlined pronoun is in the wrong case, write it correctly. If it is in the correct case, write *C* after the number.

1. The cooks tonight are Grace and her.
2. Is that he on stage?
3. Was that him on the telephone?
4. The Cases and we are making plans for lunch.
5. The actors and us are selling tickets to the play.
6. Bob and me often fly remote-control airplanes.
7. At dawn the scouts and they will eat breakfast.
8. Will Mrs. Ming and them take care of Mittens?
9. May Alice and me go for a swim after lunch?
10. Rico and him live on the same street.

### EXERCISE 5 Writing Sentences

Write sentences that follow the directions below.

1. Use *she* as a subject.
2. Use *Patrick and I* as a compound subject.
3. Use *neighbors and I* as a compound subject.
4. Use *they* as a predicate nominative.
5. Use *Ken and he* as a compound predicate nominative.

## The Objective Case

The following list shows all the personal pronouns in the objective case.

**Objective Case**

| | Singular | Plural |
|---|---|---|
| FIRST PERSON | me | us |
| SECOND PERSON | you | you |
| THIRD PERSON | him, her, it | them |

Pronouns in the objective case are used in three ways in sentences.

**11c** The **objective case** is used for direct objects, indirect objects, and objects of prepositions.

| | |
|---|---|
| DIRECT OBJECT | Barry will call **her** tonight after basketball practice. |
| INDIRECT OBJECT | The teachers gave **us** homework in math and science. |
| OBJECT OF A PREPOSITION | Is Corey going with **them** to the art museum? |

***Pronouns Used as Direct and Indirect Objects.*** A pronoun used as a direct object or an indirect object is in the objective case. A direct object follows an action verb and answers the question *Whom?* or *What?*

| | |
|---|---|
| DIRECT OBJECT | Dad took **us** to the Ice Capades. [Dad took whom? *Us* is the direct object.] |

An indirect object comes before a direct object and answers the question *To or for whom?* or *To or for what?*

| | |
|---|---|
| INDIRECT OBJECT | Ron gave **her** a ticket. [Ron gave a ticket to whom? *Her* is the indirect object.] |

To choose the correct pronoun for a compound object, just say the sentence as if the pronoun stood alone.

| | |
|---|---|
| DIRECT OBJECT | Mom called Marty and (I, me). |
| INCORRECT | Mom called **I.** |
| CORRECT | Mom called **me.** |
| CORRECT | Mom called Marty and **me.** |
| INDIRECT OBJECT | Gail gave Emma and (she, her) a pen. |
| INCORRECT | Gail gave **she** a pen. |
| CORRECT | Gail gave **her** a pen. |
| CORRECT | Gail gave Emma and **her** a pen. |

### EXERCISE 6 Using Pronouns in the Objective Case

Number your paper 1 to 10. Then write the correct personal pronoun in parentheses.

EXAMPLE The principal called Braden and (he, him) to the office.

ANSWER him

1. Give the club officers or (we, us) your membership dues.
2. Grandpa told Pepe and (I, me) stories about his childhood.
3. Did you see the Wilsons or (they, them) at the home show?
4. You should have called (we, us) for help at the science fair.
5. Will you drive Aretha and (I, me) to the store?
6. Mr. Sims promised Pedro and (I, me) a summer job at a hockey camp.
7. Show Earl and (he, him) the pictures from the dance.
8. Did you find Aaron and (she, her) in the crafts museum?
9. The audience applauded Shelley and (he, him) at the end of the show.
10. Evelyn sent Alma and (they, them) a postcard.

***Pronouns Used as Objects of Prepositions.*** A prepositional phrase begins with a preposition, such as *to, for, near,* or *by.* (*See page 67 for a list of common prepositions.*) A prepositional phrase ends with the object of a preposition. A pronoun used as the object of a preposition is in the objective case.

OBJECTS OF PREPOSITIONS Are the ice skates for **me?** [*For me* is the prepositional phrase.]

The story was about **him.** [*About him* is the prepositional phrase.]

An easy way to choose the correct pronoun in a compound object of a preposition is to say the sentence as if the pronoun stood alone.

| | |
|---|---|
| OBJECT OF A PREPOSITION | The party was planned by Ian and (she, her). |
| INCORRECT | The party was planned by **she.** |
| CORRECT | The party was planned by **her.** |
| CORRECT | The party was planned by Ian and **her.** |

## EXERCISE 7 *Using Pronouns in the Objective Case*

Number your paper 1 to 10. Then write the correct personal pronoun in parentheses.

1. The vegetable soup is for Tony and (he, him).
2. Ginger always barks at Glen and (I, me).
3. This present is from Keith and (she, her).
4. The bill will be paid by the Morrisons and (we, us).
5. Is that orange juice for Barney or (he, him)?
6. Hard workers like (they, them) should be invited.
7. I will share my umbrella with you and (she, her).
8. Send these photos to the Smiths and (they, them).
9. Who wants to go hiking with Ben and (I, me)?
10. This is a photograph of the Millers and (we, us).

## EXERCISE 8 *Using Pronouns in the Objective Case*

Number your paper 1 to 10. Then complete each sentence by writing an appropriate pronoun for each blank. (Do not use *you* or *it.*)

1. Mr. Porter asked Maureen and _____ to be guides for International Day at our school.
2. Has Justin written to David and _____?
3. Will you give Carrie and _____ a pencil?
4. Rags ran across the street after Rona and _____.
5. The Langs invited Cora and _____ to lunch.
6. My sister always beats Carlos and _____ at checkers.
7. Jeffrey won't go without Ronnie and _____.
8. Mom offered Joyce and _____ a snack.
9. Rico just received this package from Rob and _____.
10. Dad bought Liz and _____ a record.

### EXERCISE 9 *Finding Errors in Case*

Number your paper 1 to 10. If an underlined pronoun is in the wrong case, write it correctly. If it is in the correct case, write *C* after the number.

1. Mr. Daniels drove Doris and I to the library.
2. There are books for the new students and he.
3. Has Jamie given Douglas and her directions yet?
4. Please give Amanda and he some advice.
5. A sandwich is enough for Sharon and me.
6. The money was intended for Bonnie and she.
7. Arthur's musical ability amazed us and the judges.
8. Mom told Megan and he the good news.
9. Joyce went canoeing with Ginnie and I.
10. Did Darcy remember the O'Briens and we?

### EXERCISE 10 *Writing Sentences*

Write sentences that follow the directions below.

1. Use *him* as a direct object.
2. Use *James or her* as a compound direct object.
3. Use *us* as an indirect object.
4. Use *Carrie and me* as a compound indirect object.
5. Use *me* as the object of the preposition *about*.

## The Possessive Case

The following list shows all the personal pronouns in the possessive case.

**Possessive Case**

| | Singular | Plural |
|---|---|---|
| FIRST PERSON | my, mine | our, ours |
| SECOND PERSON | your, yours | your, yours |
| THIRD PERSON | his, her, hers, its | their, theirs |

**11d** The **possessive case** is used to show ownership or possession.

A possessive pronoun can be used before a noun or by itself.

BEFORE A NOUN **My** coat is red.
BY ITSELF The red coat is **mine.**

The possessive forms of personal pronouns should always be written without an apostrophe.

POSSESSIVE PRONOUN The hat is **hers.** [not *"her's"*]

Sometimes people confuse possessive pronouns with contractions. *Its, your, their,* and *theirs* are possessive pronouns. *It's* (it is), *you're* (you are), *they're* (they are), and *there's* (there is) are contractions.

POSSESSIVE PRONOUN **Your** turn is next.
CONTRACTION **You're** (you are) my best friend.

## EXERCISE 11 Using Pronouns in the Possessive Case

Number your paper 1 to 10. Then write the correct word in parentheses.

1. Where is (your, you're) apartment?
2. (Its, It's) going to rain tomorrow.
3. (Hers, Her's) is the best poem in the class.
4. (Their, They're) car just drove up.
5. (Your, You're) the perfect person for this job!
6. (Theirs, There's) a surprise for you in the den.
7. The car with the rusty fender is (ours, our's).
8. We should join them at (their, they're) house.
9. My cat doesn't like (its, it's) new bed.
10. (Theirs, There's) is the only house on the street.

## EXERCISE 12 Writing Sentences

Write a separate sentence for each possessive pronoun.

1. mine 2. hers 3. its 4. your 5. his

## TIME-OUT FOR REVIEW • • • • •

Number your paper 1 to 25. Then write each sentence, correcting any error. If a sentence is correct, write *C* after the number.

EXAMPLE Barry and me are camping this weekend.
ANSWER Barry and I are camping this weekend.

1. Perry and us pitched the tent.
2. Will you please bring Laura and I a glass of milk before bedtime?
3. Can the photographer see us in the back row?
4. The dog can't go out without it's leash.
5. Theirs an empty seat in the seventh row behind her and Louise.
6. Was it they in the red truck?
7. The sudden light blinded Terry and I.
8. You're turn is next.
9. Kim sang in a trio with Donato and she.
10. That's she playing the violin.
11. Have you seen Joel and he anywhere?
12. Without a doubt your the most popular candidate for class president.
13. That lawn mower is our's.
14. A small dog followed Lee and me to the library yesterday.
15. Kara and me carried the packages inside.
16. Did you elect Sally and him at the class meeting?
17. The bus didn't wait for Larry and them.
18. Are you and him brothers?
19. Mom made the twins and them wool scarves.
20. Is Lynn they're cousin?
21. Everyone except Chris and she rode the Ferris wheel.
22. Leslie told the Howards and they the good news about the swim meet.
23. Could that be them in the TV commercial?
24. Mr. Wilson and us are planning a class outing.
25. The collie watched Dennis and we.

# Pronouns and Their Antecedents

The word or group of words that a pronoun refers to, or replaces, is called the pronoun's *antecedent.* In the following sentences, *Ruth* is the antecedent of *her,* and *McGanns* is the antecedent of *their.*

PRONOUNS AND ANTECEDENTS **Ruth** left **her** gloves at the house.

The **McGanns** are selling **their** car.

A pronoun and its antecedent should agree, since they refer to the same person, place, or thing.

11e A pronoun must agree in number and gender with its antecedent.

*Number* is the term that indicates whether a noun or a pronoun is singular (one) or plural (more than one). A pronoun must be singular if its antecedent is singular. It must be plural if its antecedent is plural.

SINGULAR **James** can't find **his** catcher's mitt.

PLURAL The **boys** can't find **their** catcher's mitts.

A pronoun must also agree with its antecedent in gender. *Gender* is the term that indicates whether a noun or a pronoun is masculine, feminine, or neuter. *He, him,* and *his* are masculine. *She, her,* and *hers* are feminine. *It* and *its* are neuter.

MASCULINE **Andrew** said that **he** wasn't feeling well.

FEMININE **Judy** finished **her** test early.

NEUTER The maple **tree** shed **its** leaves.

Plural pronouns such as *them* and *their* can refer to masculine, feminine, or neuter antecedents.

## EXERCISE 13 Making Pronouns and Antecedents Agree

Number your paper 1 to 10. Then write the personal pronoun that correctly completes each sentence.

1. Janice is giving a birthday party for ______ best friend.
2. Mom and Dad packed ______ bags for the trip.
3. Thomas gave ______ report yesterday.
4. Susan forgot to dry ______ bathing suit.
5. Band members should bring ______ instruments to the football field on Friday.
6. Did the boys have ______ physical exams?
7. A squirrel dropped ______ acorn on the front porch.
8. Ellen signed ______ name on the card for Mr. Lee.
9. Peter took ______ lunch to school today.
10. Do the actors know ______ lines?

## Indefinite Pronouns as Antecedents

Sometimes an indefinite pronoun can be the antecedent of a personal pronoun. Some indefinite pronouns are singular and some are plural.

| | Common Indefinite Pronouns |
|---|---|
| SINGULAR | anybody, anyone, another, anything, each, either, everybody, everyone, everything, neither, nobody, nothing, no one, one, somebody, someone, something |
| PLURAL | both, few, many, several |

A personal pronoun must be singular if its antecedent is one of the singular indefinite pronouns.

SINGULAR **One** of the girls can't find **her** coat.

**Somebody** in the boys' gym lost **his** sneakers.

NOTE: When the gender of a singular indefinite pronoun has not been indicated, use *his* or *his or her* to refer to the indefinite pronoun.

Everyone must wash **his** dishes.
Everyone must wash **his or her** dishes.

A personal pronoun must be plural if its antecedent is one of the plural indefinite pronouns.

PLURAL **Several** of the girls can't find **their** coats in the locker room.

**Many** of the boys forgot **their** towels.

### EXERCISE 14 Making Pronouns Agree

Number your paper 1 to 10. Then write the personal pronoun that correctly completes each sentence.

1. Each of the girls on the track team wore ______ school sweater to the game.
2. Only one of the collie puppies has had ______ distemper shots.
3. Both of my uncles like ______ jobs at the foundry very much.
4. Neither of my sisters remembered ______ bus ticket today.
5. Several of the science books in that bookcase do not have ______ covers.
6. Everyone in the boys' choir wore ______ robe in honor of the graduating class.
7. Someone on the girls' basketball team left ______ locker open.
8. Many of the men on my street take ______ children to school in the morning.
9. Either of my brothers will give you ______ baseball glove.
10. Few of the boys on the team have taken ______ physical examinations yet.

## TIME-OUT FOR REVIEW • • • • •

Number your paper 1 to 10. Then complete each sentence with the personal pronoun that agrees with its antecedent.

EXAMPLE Mindy donated ______ wages to food relief.
ANSWER her

1. Everybody in the girls' chorus sang ______ best.
2. Many of the tourists brought ______ cameras.
3. Someone in the Girl Scout troop has lost ______ hat.
4. The city has improved ______ subway system.
5. Clarence repaired an old bicycle for ______ sister.
6. The Browns are selling ______ farm.
7. Did anyone on the boys' soccer team lose ______ key?
8. Several of the parents offered ______ help.
9. Each of the brothers has ______ own paper route.
10. Mrs. Tomkins gave ______ nephew a pair of skis.

## Application to Writing

When you edit your writing, check to see if you have used the correct form of each pronoun. Then make sure that each pronoun agrees with its antecedent.

### EXERCISE 15 Editing for Pronoun Errors

Read the following paragraph and find the five pronoun errors. Then write the paragraph correctly.

Penguins

The science teachers and us recently saw a film about penguins. Them are such comical birds. Each of the penguins had their own funny waddle. Karen and me were surprised that penguins cannot fly. Penguins, however, are good swimmers and can swim up to 22 miles per hour. Sometimes they ride on ice. Often it will climb onto a floating piece of ice, ride along for a while, and then dive off and swim home.

# Chapter Review

**A Using Pronouns in the Correct Case.** Number your paper 1 to 10. Then write the correct personal pronoun in parentheses.

1. The coach put James and (I, me) in the game in the last quarter.
2. Michael went to the basketball game with Rebecca and (she, her).
3. Did Eli or (he, him) make this bread?
4. Joan snapped a picture of Lana and (I, me).
5. Will you give Christopher and (they, them) the invitation to the party?
6. Uncle George told Dad and (we, us) some good jokes.
7. That climb won't be hard for Sam and (she, her).
8. It must be (they, them) on the dock.
9. Did (he, him) and Rudy study their Spanish notes at the library today?
10. Before dinner Brett and (I, me) went to the store for potatoes.

**B Correcting Pronoun Errors.** Number your paper 1 to 10. Then write and correct any error. If a sentence is correct, write *C* after the number.

1. Mr. Daniels drove Doris and I to the stadium.
2. The cooks tonight are Grace and her.
3. The money was intended for Bonnie and him.
4. Mom gave Megan and he the good news.
5. The Wongs and us are having a barbecue on the Fourth of July weekend.
6. That could be he in the plaid shirt.
7. Joyce went canoeing down the Concord River with Ginnie and we.
8. May Allie and me go for a swim after lunch?
9. The invitation is for Martha and me.
10. Rico and him live on the same street.

**C** **Making Pronouns Agree with Antecedents.** Number your paper 1 to 10. Then write the personal pronoun that correctly completes each sentence.

1. Neither of the boys could finish ______ dinner.
2. Julie hasn't found ______ glasses yet.
3. Many of the members have paid ______ club dues.
4. Somebody on the men's football team has left the lights on in ______ car.
5. A few of the fathers played soccer with ______ daughters.
6. Should Carlos bring ______ sunscreen to the beach?
7. Each of my sisters is looking for a job during ______ summer vacation.
8. A turtle must carry ______ home all the time.
9. One of the girls on the field trip left ______ sweater on the bus.
10. The students in Mr. Rogers' math class must turn in ______ homework at the beginning of the period.

## Mastery Test

Number your paper 1 to 10. Then write the correct word in parentheses.

1. Mom passed Ellie and (she, her) the scrambled eggs and toast.
2. Haven't Laurel and (he, him) arrived yet?
3. Doug steered his rowboat toward Dad and (I, me).
4. Was that (she, her) on the corner?
5. (Their, They're) car is for sale.
6. Later Leila and (they, them) are going to a movie at the Circle Cinema.
7. Joy and (we, us) went to the crafts fair.
8. Both of my brothers worked hard on (his, their) math projects.
9. Deborah saw Roy and (he, him) at the soccer game on Saturday afternoon.
10. The story was about my dog and (I, me).

# 12

# Subject and Verb Agreement

## *Diagnostic Test*

Number your paper 1 to 10. Then write the form of the verb in parentheses that agrees with each subject.

EXAMPLE Where (is, are) the pens and pencils?
ANSWER are

1. The opossum and the kangaroo (is, are) related.
2. One of those girls (is, are) my sister.
3. A string of beads (has, have) been found.
4. Near the trail (was, were) the footprints of a fox.
5. Film and flashbulbs (comes, come) with the camera.
6. Neither Ted nor his brothers (is, are) going to the fair.
7. Where (was, were) you during the tryouts?
8. There (is, are) many nicknames for *Elizabeth*.
9. The clocks in our school (doesn't, don't) always work.
10. Mercury and Venus (is, are) smaller than Earth.

# Agreement of Subjects and Verbs

He don't like spaghetti.
Is you taking Spanish this year?

Something is wrong with these sentences. Read the sentences below. This time the form of the verb has been changed in each sentence.

He **does**n't like spaghetti.
**Are** you **taking** Spanish this year?

Now the sentences are correct because there is *agreement* between each verb and its subject. One basic agreement rule applies to all subjects and verbs.

12a A verb must agree with its subject in number.

## Number

*Number* is the term used to indicate whether a word is singular or plural. In this chapter you will see that nouns, pronouns, and verbs all have number and that the number of a subject and a verb must agree.

***Number of Nouns and Pronouns.*** The plural of most nouns is formed by adding *-s* or *-es* to the singular form.

| | | |
|---|---|---|
| SINGULAR | truck | potato |
| PLURAL | truck**s** | potato**es** |

A few nouns, however, form their plurals in other ways. A dictionary always lists an irregular plural.

| | | |
|---|---|---|
| SINGULAR | mouse | child |
| PLURAL | **mice** | **children** |

Pronouns also can be singular or plural. *I, he, she,* and *it* are singular, and *we* and *they* are plural. *You* can be singular or plural.

## EXERCISE 1 Determining the Number of Nouns and Pronouns

Number your paper 1 to 20. Then label each word *singular* or *plural.*

| | | | |
|---|---|---|---|
| 1. Ohio | 6. lamps | 11. we | 16. car |
| 2. test | 7. shoe | 12. horse | 17. Mike |
| 3. boxes | 8. men | 13. flower | 18. he |
| 4. glasses | 9. glove | 14. it | 19. clocks |
| 5. they | 10. she | 15. flags | 20. sisters |

***Number of Verbs.*** In the present tense, most verbs add *-s* or *-es* to form the singular. Plural forms in the present tense do not end in *-s* or *-es*.

| SINGULAR | | PLURAL | |
|---|---|---|---|
| The boy | sing**s.** | The boys | sing. |
| | laugh**s.** | | laugh. |
| | catch**es.** | | catch. |

*Be, have,* and *do,* however, have special singular and plural forms in the present tense. *Be* also has special forms in the past tense.

**Forms of *Be, Have,* and *Do***

| | Singular | Plural |
|---|---|---|
| ***be*** | is (present) | are (present) |
| | was (past) | were (past) |
| ***have*** | has | have |
| ***do*** | does | do |

In the following examples, each subject is underlined once, and each verb is underlined twice.

SINGULAR She is my best friend.
Lance has a new bicycle.

PLURAL They are here also.
The Morrisons have a nice apartment.

### EXERCISE 2 Determining the Number of Verbs

Number your paper 1 to 10. Then label each item *singular* or *plural.*

1. Alvin enjoys
2. twins have
3. students play
4. he was
5. truck has
6. we do
7. it is
8. they dive
9. albums are
10. Pauline does

## Singular and Plural Subjects

The number of a verb must agree with the number of its noun or pronoun subject.

**12b** A singular subject takes a singular verb.

**12c** A plural subject takes a plural verb.

To make a verb agree with its subject, ask yourself two questions: *What is the subject?* and *Is the subject singular or plural?* Then choose the correct verb form.

SINGULAR She dances gracefully.
PLURAL They dance gracefully.

SINGULAR He was in a hurry.
PLURAL They were in a hurry.

### EXERCISE 3 Making Subjects and Verbs Agree

Number your paper 1 to 10. If the item is singular, write it in the plural form. If the item is plural, write it in the singular form.

1. car travels
2. pen writes
3. telephone rings
4. clown does
5. apartment has
6. boats sail
7. boys laugh
8. candles melt
9. movies delight
10. flowers grow

### EXERCISE 4 Making Subjects and Verbs Agree

Number your paper 1 to 10. Write each subject and label it *singular* or *plural.* Then write the form of the verb in parentheses that agrees with the subject.

About Birds

EXAMPLE A robin (likes, like) earthworms.
ANSWER robin, singular—likes

1. Brown pelicans (dives, dive) for fish.
2. A white pelican (scoops, scoop) fish out of the water just below the surface.
3. Mockingbirds (eats, eat) insects.
4. Owls (flies, fly) almost noiselessly.
5. The short-eared owl (helps, help) control rodents.
6. All birds (has, have) special colors and songs.
7. Male blue jays (is, are) a different color from female blue jays.
8. An average condor (has, have) a wingspan of over nine feet.
9. A duck's webbed feet (acts, act) as paddles.
10. The trumpeter swan (is, are) the largest of all water birds.

## You *and* I *as Subjects*

The singular pronouns *you* and *I* are exceptions to the two rules for agreement between subjects and verbs. *You* is *always* used with a plural verb.

PLURAL VERBS
Anne, you are always very thoughtful.
Boys, you work very hard.

*I* usually takes a plural verb.

PLURAL VERBS
I build models of ships.
I have a new alarm clock.

The only exceptions are the verbs *am* and *was.*

SINGULAR VERBS
I am ready to go.
I was sick yesterday.

### EXERCISE 5 *Making Verbs Agree with You and I*

Number your paper 1 to 10. Then write the form of the verb in parentheses that agrees with each subject.

1. I (likes, like) mystery stories.
2. You (is, are) a good friend.
3. I (has, have) some homework.
4. You (has, have) another turn.
5. We (was, were) in the gym.
6. You (needs, need) a weekend of relaxation with your family and friends.
7. You (was, were) very amusing in the play.
8. This year you (looks, look) much taller.
9. I always (wears, wear) bright colors.
10. You (has, have) a good sense of humor.

## Verb Phrases

In a verb phrase, the helping verb must agree in number with the subject.

**12d** The helping verb must agree in number with its subject.

SINGULAR Chris **was** looking for you.
PLURAL They **were** waiting for us.

Following is a list of singular and plural forms of common helping verbs.

**Common Helping Verbs**

| Singular | Plural |
| --- | --- |
| am, is, was, has, does | are, were, have, do |

SINGULAR The baby **is** sleeping now.
PLURAL Many students **are** going on the field trip.

## EXERCISE 6 *Making Subjects and Verb Phrases Agree*

Number your paper 1 to 10. Write each subject and label it *singular* or *plural.* Then write the helping verb in parentheses that agrees with the subject.

1. The first football game (was, were) played between Rutgers and Princeton.
2. Dad (has, have) put hamburgers on the grill.
3. The red cardinal (is, are) known for its cheerful song.
4. Downhill skiers (has, have) raced at over 120 miles per hour.
5. That old house (does, do) have a lot of charm.
6. The first cheese (was, were) made about 4,000 years ago by tribes in Asia.
7. The kite (is, are) tugging at its strings.
8. Helmets (was, were) introduced to the major baseball leagues in 1941.
9. This puzzle (does, do) require patience.
10. The Great Smoky Mountains (is, are) located in North Carolina and Tennessee.

## TIME-OUT FOR REVIEW • • • • •

Number your paper 1 to 20. Write each subject. Then write the form of the verb in parentheses that agrees with each subject.

1. Fresh raspberries (makes, make) a tasty snack.
2. In the morning I always (takes, take) the bus.
3. Certain South American spiders (grows, grow) to a length of three or more inches.
4. I (was, were) prepared for class.
5. You (has, have) been very brave.
6. I often (reads, read) on Saturday night.
7. You (was, were) talking on the telephone for half an hour.
8. The new members (is, are) meeting this afternoon.

9. You (has, have) made a delicious meal.
10. I (does, do) wonder about the future.
11. Douglas (enjoys, enjoy) a cool swim.
12. After breakfast Lauren usually (walks, walk) to school with her brother.
13. Today the subway (is, are) making extra stops because of the parade.
14. I (visits, visit) the dentist regularly.
15. You (plays, play) the piano very well.
16. My brothers often (catches, catch) trout for dinner.
17. This flannel shirt (does, do) press easily.
18. You (has, have) written an excellent essay.
19. I (sees, see) my grandmother almost every day.
20. Yellow tulips (was, were) blooming next to a stone wall at the end of the garden.

## Interrupting Words

Words, such as a prepositional phrase, can come between a subject and its verb. When this happens, people sometimes make a mistake in agreement. They make the verb agree with a word that is closer to it, rather than with the subject.

**12e** The agreement of a verb with its subject is not changed by any interrupting words.

In the following examples, the subject and the verb in each sentence agree in number—in spite of the words that come between them.

INTERRUPTING WORDS A list (of new books) is available. [*Is* agrees with the subject *list,* not with the object of the preposition *books.*]

The students (in that room) are juniors. [*Are* agrees with the subject *students,* not with the object of the preposition *room.*]

### EXERCISE 7 Making Interrupted Subjects and Verbs Agree

Number your paper 1 to 10. Write each subject and label it *singular* or *plural.* Then write the form of the verb in parentheses that agrees with the subject.

1. The farm with six acres (sits, sit) high on a hill.
2. The new students at our school (seems, seem) friendly.
3. The girls' friendship throughout the years (has, have) remained strong.
4. The two deer by the pond (is, are) quite tame.
5. The boy with the two horses (is, are) my cousin.
6. The singer in the striped shirt (was, were) nervous.
7. People like Julie (appears, appear) self-confident.
8. My relatives from Mexico (is, are) visiting.
9. The jewels in the Queen's crown (was, were) priceless.
10. A basket of daisies (decorates, decorate) the piano.

## Inverted Order

In most sentences the subject comes before the verb. This is a sentence's natural order. In some sentences, however, the verb or part of a verb phrase comes before the subject. Such a sentence has *inverted order.* A verb always agrees with its subject, whether the sentence is in its natural order or in inverted order.

**12f** The subject and the verb of an inverted sentence must agree in number.

There are several types of inverted sentences. When you are looking for the subject in an inverted sentence, turn the sentence around to its natural order.

| | |
|---|---|
| INVERTED ORDER | In the supply closet is some glue. |
| NATURAL ORDER | Some glue is in the supply closet. |
| QUESTION | Has he answered your letter? |
| NATURAL ORDER | He has answered your letter. |

| | |
|---|---|
| SENTENCE BEGINNING WITH *HERE* | Here is my favorite science magazine. |
| NATURAL ORDER | My favorite science magazine is here. |
| SENTENCE BEGINNING WITH *THERE* | There were six members present at the meeting. |
| NATURAL ORDER | Six members were present at the meeting. [Sometimes *here* or *there* must be dropped for the sentence to make sense.] |

NOTE: The words *here* and *there* are never the subject of a sentence.

## EXERCISE 8 *Making Verbs Agree with Subjects in Inverted Order*

Number your paper 1 to 10. Write each subject and label it *singular* or *plural*. Then write the form of the verb in parentheses that agrees with the subject.

1. There (is, are) only one baseball game after school this week.
2. When (does, do) your sister Maria graduate from high school?
3. (Has, Have) your classes in computer programming been challenging this year?
4. Here (is, are) my laboratory report for the science experiments.
5. By the dock there (was, were) two canoes full of camping gear.
6. Where (was, were) Ray at four o'clock?
7. At the bottom of the world's oceans (lies, lie) many buried treasures.
8. (Does, Do) Tim and his brother work after school at the local supermarket?
9. Here (is, are) some apples from our tree.
10. (Was, Were) there any mosquitoes in your tent after the rainstorm last night?

## TIME-OUT FOR REVIEW • • • • •

Number your paper 1 to 20. Write each subject. Then write the form of the verb in parentheses that agrees with the subject.

1. The largest cat in the Americas (is, are) the jaguar.
2. Elephants in Africa (has, have) large ears and flat heads.
3. (Was, Were) you in the elevator during the power failure last week?
4. In the jungle (roams, roam) many wild animals.
5. A hiker in the woods (has, have) found the lost child sleeping under a tree.
6. There (is, are) sand dunes in Colorado over 500 feet high.
7. Pieces of chalk (was, were) formed originally from tiny shells.
8. (Does, Do) the flashlight need batteries?
9. Queen ants in a colony (lives, live) about 10 to 20 years.
10. Here (stands, stand) the oldest oak tree in town.
11. The highest city in the United States (is, are) Leadville, Colorado.
12. Many reporters from the newspaper (does, do) have a degree in English.
13. In the garage (is, are) many garden tools belonging to my grandfather.
14. The fenders on the new car (shines, shine) in the bright sunlight.
15. There (was, were) two alligators in the mud at the edge of the lake.
16. The body of a jellyfish (has, have) little or no color.
17. Beyond the cottages (was, were) a huge lake with a small island in the center.
18. Several kinds of seaweed (is, are) used for food.
19. There (is, are) many underground streams in the Sahara Desert.
20. The dry deserts of Saudi Arabia (contains, contain) rich oil deposits.

# Common Agreement Problems

Some subjects and verbs frequently create agreement problems. In this section you will learn how to make compound subjects and indefinite pronouns agree with verbs and how to make a subject and a contraction agree.

## Compound Subjects

A compound subject is two or more subjects that have the same verb. A compound subject is usually joined by a single conjunction such as *and* or *or,* or by a pair of conjunctions such as *either/or* or *neither/nor*.

12g When subjects are joined by *and,* the verb is usually plural.

When a subject is more than one, it is plural. The verb, therefore, must also be plural to agree with the subject.

PLURAL VERBS Cathy **and** Beth take the bus.
This trunk **and** those suitcases **have** traveled many miles.

Agreement between the subject and the verb follows a different rule, however, when a compound subject is joined by *or, either/or,* or *neither/nor.*

12h When subjects are joined by *or, either/or,* or *neither/nor,* the verb agrees with the closer subject.

SINGULAR VERB **Either** Janice **or** Susan is her best friend. [The verb is singular because *Susan,* the subject closer to it, is singular.]

PLURAL VERB **Neither** the terns **nor** the gulls **have** returned yet. [The verb is plural because *gulls,* the subject closer to it, is plural.]

This rule applies even when one subject is singular and the other is plural.

SINGULAR VERB **Either** those high bushes **or** that tree **is** blocking the sunlight. [The verb is singular because *tree,* the subject closer to it, is singular.]

PLURAL VERB **Either** that tree **or** those bushes **are** blocking the sunlight. [The verb is plural because *bushes,* the subject closer to it, is plural.]

### EXERCISE 9 *Making Verbs Agree with Compound Subjects*

Number your paper 1 to 10. Then write the correct form of the verb in parentheses.

1. The sun and the moon (seems, seem) almost the same size in the sky.
2. Strawberries and blueberries often (grows, grow) wild.
3. The scallop and the oyster (is, are) found from Maine to Florida.
4. Sandra or Frank (has, have) set the table.
5. Saturn and Jupiter (has, have) moons.
6. Neither Meredith nor her dog (is, are) here.
7. The McAdams twins or John (has, have) a telescope.
8. A pen or two pencils (is, are) needed.
9. The trains and the buses (runs, run) until midnight.
10. Neither my aunt nor my uncle (owns, own) a car.

### EXERCISE 10 *Writing Sentences*

Number your paper 1 to 5. Choose the correct form of the verb in parentheses. Then complete each sentence.

1. Juan and his brothers (was, were) . . .
2. The dog or the cat (has, have) . . .
3. The phone and the doorbell often (rings, ring) . . .
4. That truck or those old cars (was, were) . . .
5. Oranges and grapefruit (is, are) . . .

## Indefinite Pronouns

An indefinite pronoun—such as *someone, many,* and *all*—can be the subject of a sentence. Indefinite pronouns have number. Some are singular and some are plural.

**12i** A verb must agree in number with an indefinite pronoun used as a subject.

Following is a list of common indefinite pronouns according to their number.

| Common Indefinite Pronouns | |
|---|---|
| SINGULAR | anybody, anyone, each, either, everybody, everyone, neither, nobody, no one, one, somebody, someone |
| PLURAL | both, few, many, several |

Singular indefinite pronouns used as subjects always take a singular verb. Plural indefinite pronouns used as subjects always take a plural verb. Interrupting words do not affect this agreement.

SINGULAR Everyone is ready. [*Is* agrees with the singular indefinite pronoun *everyone.*]

One of my sisters was there. [*Was* agrees with the singular indefinite pronoun *one,* not with the object of the preposition *sisters.*]

PLURAL Many shop at this mall each day. [*Shop* agrees with the plural indefinite pronoun *many.*]

Several in the group go to camp each summer. [*Go* agrees with the plural indefinite pronoun *several,* not with the object of the preposition *group.*]

## EXERCISE 11 Making Verbs Agree with Indefinite Pronouns

Number your paper 1 to 10. Write each subject and label it *singular* or *plural*. Then write the correct form of the verb in parentheses that agrees with the subject.

1. Many of the candles (has, have) burned down.
2. Each of our soccer players (is, are) wearing green shorts.
3. A few of the uniforms (was, were) the wrong size.
4. One of those stamps (is, are) worth a fortune.
5. Somebody in one of the music classes (plays, play) the flute.
6. Either of the two plans (is, are) workable.
7. Several in the club (has, have) worked very hard.
8. Everybody within 20 miles (does, do) farm work.
9. Many in the chorus (has, have) soprano voices.
10. No one at the relay races (was, were) from the middle school.

## EXERCISE 12 Making Verbs Agree with Indefinite Pronouns

Number your paper 1 to 10. Write each subject and label it *singular* or *plural*. Then write the form of the verb in parentheses that agrees with the subject.

1. One of the apples (has, have) a worm in it.
2. Each of the ducks (has, have) eaten some bread.
3. Several of my friends (watches, watch) the news.
4. (Has, Have) everyone studied hard?
5. Neither of the twins (has, have) gone to the beach this summer.
6. Both of these records (has, have) been ordered.
7. Nobody (was, were) waiting at the train station.
8. Many of the members of the hockey team (skates, skate) in the county tournament.
9. Everybody in the bleachers (cheers, cheer) for the home team.
10. Somebody in the apartment building (is, are) a pianist.

# Doesn't *and* Don't

When contractions are used, agreement with a subject can be confusing. When you check for agreement, always say the individual words of a contraction.

12j The verb part of a contraction must agree in number with the subject.

INCORRECT The lamp **do**n't look good on the table.
CORRECT The lamp **does** not look good on the table.
The lamp **does**n't look good on the table.

INCORRECT Tim and his father **does**n't want any squash.
CORRECT Tim and his father **do** not want any squash.
Tim and his father **do**n't want any squash.

The previous rule applies to all other contractions as well. Keep in mind which contractions are singular and which are plural.

SINGULAR **does**n't, **has**n't, **is**n't, **was**n't
PLURAL **do**n't, **have**n't, **are**n't, **were**n't

### EXERCISE 13 *Making Subjects and Contractions Agree*

Number your paper 1 to 10. Write each subject. Then write the contraction in parentheses that agrees with the subject.

1. James (doesn't, don't) care much about soccer.
2. (Wasn't, Weren't) you set for that broad jump?
3. Our cousins in Ohio (doesn't, don't) often visit us.
4. (Wasn't, Weren't) those birds unusual?
5. There (isn't, aren't) many prizes left.
6. Some of the guests (isn't, aren't) coming tonight.
7. (Hasn't, Haven't) anyone seen my sunglasses?
8. Eddie and Ellis (hasn't, haven't) arrived.
9. (Isn't, Aren't) one of the forks missing?
10. Julie and Joan (doesn't, don't) know our address.

### EXERCISE 14 Writing Sentences

Number your paper 1 to 5. Choose the correct form of the verb in parentheses. Then complete each sentence.

1. The girls and their aunt (wasn't, weren't) . . .
2. Many of the floats (was, were) . . .
3. (Doesn't, Don't) the music . . . ?
4. Each of the monkeys (is, are) . . .
5. Either Terry or Beth (has, have) . . .

## TIME-OUT FOR REVIEW • • • • •

Number your paper 1 to 20. Then write the form of the verb in parentheses that agrees with each subject.

Coins to Collect

1. Coins (has, have) been around for over 2,500 years.
2. Once only kings and rich people (was, were) collectors.
3. Now over five million people throughout the world (takes, take) part in this hobby.
4. Many of the collectors (does, do) it as an investment.
5. This hobby (is, are) often begun with just pennies.
6. There (is, are) a few pennies with a value of $115.
7. A Jefferson nickel or a Roosevelt dime (is, are) also a good addition to a collection.
8. The condition of coins (is, are) very important.
9. Collectors (doesn't, don't) hold coins in their hands.
10. The moisture from hands (has, have) stained many coins.
11. Coin dealers across the country (rates, rate) coins.
12. One of the best ratings (is, are) "extremely fine."
13. The surface of these coins (shows, show) little wear.
14. Pennies in "extremely fine" condition (is, are) worth twenty-five cents.
15. (Has, Have) you ever wanted a coin collection?
16. Here (is, are) some advice for new collectors.
17. Coins of pure silver (is, are) worth more than others.
18. Pre-1965 dimes and quarters (is, are) very valuable.
19. There (is, are) many books about coins.
20. The books often (gives, give) the value of each coin.

## Application to Writing

A very important part of your editing should include looking for correct subject and verb agreement. When you finish writing, always take time to check the agreement of each subject and verb.

### ***Exercise 15*** Editing for Subject and Verb Agreement

Read the following paragraphs and find the 15 verbs that do not agree with their subjects. Then rewrite the paragraphs, correcting each error.

Fingerprints

There are something unique about you. Your fingerprints are different from those of everyone else. What is fingerprints? Why are they different for every person?

The skin on your fingers consist of two layers of tissue. One of the layers are a thick, deep layer. Over this layer are a delicate membrane called the *epidermis*. This membrane in cold-blooded animals fit smoothly. There is no ridges and no prints.

In mammals, however, these two layers of skin is joined very closely. The under layer buckles underneath the upper layer. Part of the lower tissue project into the upper layer.

Among the lower animals, projections or pegs of this kind is scattered. There are no uniform pattern to them. For example, these pegs in an ape is arranged in rows. All apes have these parallel rows. As a result, fingerprints of all apes are much the same.

The rows of ridges on the fingers of a human being forms definite patterns. In fact, the classification of human fingerprints was developed by studying these patterns. An Englishman named Sir Edward Henry developed this system of classifying fingerprints. Authorities all over the world uses this system. By the way, the chance of identical patterns are 1 in 24 million!

# Chapter Review

**A** **Making Subjects and Verbs Agree.** Number your paper 1 to 10. Then write the form of the verb in parentheses that agrees with each subject.

1. The canals on Mars (is, are) probably dry riverbeds.
2. Many of my friends (was, were) at the mall today.
3. Here (is, are) five quarters from my allowance.
4. (Does, Do) a normal caterpillar have 16 legs?
5. A trumpeter and a drummer (is, are) needed tonight.
6. In the small pond (was, were) several goldfish.
7. One of those oranges (is, are) enough for me.
8. (Has, Have) you noticed the school's new flag?
9. A boxer or a collie (is, are) a good pet.
10. Eleven letters of the alphabet (is, are) identical to their mirror images.

**B** **Making Subjects and Verbs Agree.** Number your paper 1 to 10. Find and write the verbs that do not agree with their subjects. Then write each sentence correctly. If a sentence is correct, write *C* after the number.

EXAMPLE Are Marty or Jake the leader?
ANSWER are—Is Marty or Jake the leader?

1. The crickets in that field chirp loudest on warm nights.
2. One of the books have a funny title.
3. Haven't Lou or Max mowed the lawn yet?
4. There is many tiny creatures in a drop of water.
5. The first shots of the American Revolution was fired in Lexington, Massachusetts.
6. Behind the garage is three grapevines.
7. Was you afraid of that Doberman?
8. Stacy and I have been friends since fifth grade.
9. Each of those flowers have its own special scent.
10. Doesn't the eagle and the crow belong to the same family?

**C** **Editing for Subject and Verb Agreement.** Write the following paragraphs, correcting each verb that does not agree with its subject.

The Great Sphinx

One of the world's greatest masterpieces are the Great Sphinx at Giza, Egypt. A sphinx is a mythical animal with the head of a human and the body of a lion. Many sphinxes were built in Egypt, but the Great Sphinx is the oldest of its kind. The features of the sphinx resembles King Khafre, the king at that time.

The body and the head is carved from a natural cliff in the center of a large stone quarry. However, the outstretched paws of the sphinx was added. The figure was originally covered with painted plaster, and there is still some traces of the plaster. The Great Sphinx is 66 feet high and 240 feet long. Its nose alone measures 5 feet 7 inches.

## Mastery Test

Number your paper 1 to 10. Then write the form of the verb in parentheses that agrees with each subject.

1. Temperatures in Siberia (has, have) reached 93 degrees below zero.
2. (Wasn't, Weren't) you the winner of the art contest?
3. Each of those trees (is, are) an evergreen.
4. Dan and his dad (has, have) restored an old car.
5. There (is, are) a statue in honor of sea gulls in Salt Lake City.
6. The bowl of strawberries (was, were) for dessert.
7. None of the watermelon (was, were) eaten.
8. Either these magazines or that book (includes, include) information for your report.
9. My aunt and three cousins (visits, visit) often.
10. (Is, Are) the heaviest organ in the human body the brain or the liver?

# 13

# Using Adjectives and Adverbs

## Diagnostic Test

Number your paper 1 to 10. Then write the correct word in parentheses.

EXAMPLE This is the (longer, longest) of the two books.
ANSWER longer

1. Of my three brothers, Kevin is (taller, tallest).
2. Which do you like (better, best), music or art?
3. In class no one works (harder, more harder) than Clarence.
4. Which do you like to read (more, most), fiction or nonfiction?
5. There weren't (no, any) instructions in the kit.
6. After only two lessons, Brian drives (good, well).
7. Haven't you (never, ever) taken a canoe ride?
8. The (most brightest, brightest) planet is Venus.
9. Which can run (faster, fastest), a cheetah or an impala?
10. Your spaghetti sauce tastes so (good, well).

# Comparison of Adjectives and Adverbs

Adjectives and adverbs usually change form when they are used to compare two or more people or things. Most adjectives and adverbs have three forms to show differences in the degree of comparison.

13a Most adjectives and adverbs have three degrees of comparison: the *positive,* the *comparative,* and the *superlative.*

The *positive* degree is used when no comparison is being made.

ADJECTIVE This box is **light.**
ADVERB Kim works **quickly.**

The *comparative* degree is used when two people, things, or actions are being compared.

ADJECTIVE This box is **lighter** than the last one.
ADVERB Kim works **more quickly** than Tad.

The *superlative* degree is used when more than two people, things, or actions are being compared.

ADJECTIVE This box is the **lightest** box on the shelf.
ADVERB Of all the clerks, Kim works **most quickly.**

## Regular Comparison

Almost all adjectives and adverbs form the comparative and superlative degrees in a regular manner. These forms depend on the number of syllables in the modifier.

13b Add *-er* to form the comparative degree and *-est* to form the superlative degree of one-syllable modifiers.

| | POSITIVE | COMPARATIVE | SUPERLATIVE |
|---|---|---|---|
| ADJECTIVE | smart | smart**er** | smart**est** |
| | hot | hott**er** | hott**est** |
| ADVERB | near | near**er** | near**est** |

NOTE: A spelling change sometimes occurs when *-er* or *-est* is added to certain modifiers, such as *hot.*

Many two-syllable modifiers are formed exactly like one-syllable modifiers. There are some two-syllable modifiers, however, that would be difficult to say with *-er* or *-est.* For such two-syllable modifiers, *more* and *most* should be used to form the comparative and superlative degrees. *More* and *most* are generally used with adverbs that end in *-ly.*

**13c** Use *-er* or *more* to form the comparative degree and *-est* or *most* to form the superlative degree of two-syllable modifiers.

| | POSITIVE | COMPARATIVE | SUPERLATIVE |
|---|---|---|---|
| ADJECTIVE | narrow | narrow**er** | narrow**est** |
| | happy | happi**er** | happi**est** |
| | helpless | **more** helpless | **most** helpless |
| ADVERB | slowly | **more** slowly | **most** slowly |
| | soon | soon**er** | soon**est** |

NOTE: A spelling change occurs in many modifiers that end in *y,* such as *happy.* The *y* changes to *i* before *-er* or *-est* is added.

All modifiers with three or more syllables form their comparative and superlative degrees by using *more* and *most.*

**13d** Use *more* to form the comparative degree and *most* to form the superlative degree of modifiers with three or more syllables.

| | POSITIVE | COMPARATIVE | SUPERLATIVE |
|---|---|---|---|
| ADJECTIVE | horrible | **more** horrible | **most** horrible |
| ADVERB | eagerly | **more** eagerly | **most** eagerly |

## EXERCISE 1 Forming the Regular Comparison of Modifiers

Number your paper 1 to 20. Copy each modifier. Then write its comparative and superlative forms.

EXAMPLE frosty
ANSWER frosty, frostier, frostiest

1. quick
2. quiet
3. slowly
4. great
5. witty
6. merrily
7. dangerous
8. rapidly
9. dry
10. steadily
11. cold
12. neatly
13. careful
14. big
15. thin
16. curious
17. early
18. weakly
19. pretty
20. long

## EXERCISE 2 Using the Correct Form of Modifiers

Number your paper 1 to 10. Then write the correct modifier in parentheses.

1. Mary wasn't sure which was (easier, easiest), rowing or paddling.
2. Which day was the (colder, coldest), Monday, Thursday, or Friday?
3. Of the ten books I've read this year, *Light in the Forest* was the (more enjoyable, most enjoyable) because of the plot and characters.
4. Paul is the (taller, tallest) member of the basketball team.
5. Does the horse or the donkey run (faster, fastest)?
6. Juan faced the situation (more bravely, most bravely) than I did.
7. A cat can move (more quickly, most quickly) than a dog.
8. Of the two suitcases, which one do you think is (bigger, biggest)?
9. Of the five piano players, Barry performs the (more skillfully, most skillfully).
10. Which of the two telescopes is (more powerful, most powerful)?

## Irregular Comparison

A few adjectives and adverbs are compared in an irregular manner.

**Irregularly Compared Modifiers**

| Positive | Comparative | Superlative |
|---|---|---|
| bad/badly | worse | worst |
| good/well | better | best |
| little | less | least |
| much/many | more | most |

POSITIVE The salad was **good.**
COMPARATIVE It was **better** than yesterday's salad.
SUPERLATIVE It was the **best** salad we've ever had.

### EXERCISE 3 *Using the Correct Form of Modifiers*

Number your paper 1 to 5. Read the first sentence in each group. Then write the comparative and superlative forms of the underlined modifier.

1. I feel bad today.
   I felt ______ yesterday.
   On Monday, however, I felt the ______.
2. Many people in my apartment house walk to work.
   ______ people drive their cars.
   However, ______ people take the subway.
3. The news this week is good.
   I think it is ______ than last week's news.
   In fact, it is the ______ news so far this month.
4. You skate quite well.
   You skate ______ than my sister.
   You skate the ______ of all the skaters on the pond.
5. I have little interest in science fiction.
   I have even ______ interest in fables.
   I have the ______ interest in biographies.

## TIME-OUT FOR REVIEW • • • • •

Number your paper 1 to 20. Find and write each incorrect modifier. Then write it correctly. If a sentence is correct, write *C* after the number.

EXAMPLE Of the four seasons, I like spring better.
ANSWER better—best

1. Which do you like best, animal stories or science fiction stories?
2. Of the three bats, this one looks stronger.
3. Is German, French, or Spanish the harder to learn?
4. Who works most carefully, Ana or Paul?
5. Your thighbones are the biggest bones in your entire body.
6. That song was the worse I've heard all year!
7. Which runs most quietly, a diesel engine or a gasoline engine?
8. Of all the cars my family has owned, I've enjoyed the last one least.
9. Of my four aunts, I have seen Aunt Sarah the more recently.
10. Which should be planted earliest in the season, peas or tomatoes?
11. I am less eager to see that movie than Cynthia is.
12. He couldn't decide which he liked most, the green or the blue shirt.
13. Which is tastier, a peach or a plum?
14. Which sweater do you think would be warmest, this one or that one?
15. Of all the magician's tricks, I think the first one was better.
16. Eggplant is my least favorite vegetable.
17. Which has the largest population, France or Germany?
18. Who is the more reliable, Willie, Pedro, or Emma?
19. Among the five Great Lakes, which one is larger?
20. Which is most abundant on the earth's surface, water or land?

# Problems with Modifiers

You need to be aware of a few special problems when you use modifiers in your writing.

## Double Comparisons

You should use only one method of forming the comparative or the superlative form of a modifier. Using both methods—for example, *-er* and *more* together—results in a *double comparison.*

13e Do not use both *-er* and *more* to form the comparative degree, or both *-est* and *most* to form the superlative degree.

| | |
|---|---|
| DOUBLE COMPARISON | Our morning newspaper comes **more earlier** than yours. |
| CORRECT | Our morning newspaper comes **earlier** than yours. |
| DOUBLE COMPARISON | We drove through the **most foggiest** area in the valley. |
| CORRECT | We drove through the **foggiest** area in the valley. |

### Exercise 4 Correcting Double Comparisons

Number your paper 1 to 10. Then write the following sentences, correcting each error.

1. Surprisingly, this August was more drier than July.
2. King Solomon was more wiser than most rulers of ancient times.
3. Beyond the reef the water becomes more deeper.
4. Rebecca's train from Chicago arrived more later than her grandparents had expected.
5. I can swim more faster than Robin.
6. The berries are the most juiciest I have ever seen.

7. Your chili is more tastier than mine.
8. He jumped more farther than anyone else on the track team.
9. The Olivetti family lives in the most oldest house on Elm Street.
10. Today's weather seems more drearier than yesterday's.

## Double Negatives

Following is a list of common negative words. Notice that all of these words begin with *n*.

**Common Negatives**

| | |
|---|---|
| never | none |
| no | not (and its contraction *n't*) |
| no one | nothing |

Two of these words should not be used together to express the same idea. When they are, the result is a *double negative.*

13f Avoid using a double negative.

DOUBLE NEGATIVE Ken does**n't** know **nothing** about sailing.

CORRECT Ken does**n't** know anything about sailing.

CORRECT Ken knows **nothing** about sailing.

### EXERCISE 5 *Correcting Double Negatives*

Number your paper 1 to 10. Then write the following sentences, correcting each error.

1. Our wrestling team hasn't never won a match.
2. Porpoises don't have no gills.
3. I haven't done none of my homework yet.

4. David didn't know nothing about the missing cat.
5. There wasn't no way to reach the camp except through the woods.
6. Haven't you never seen that picture before?
7. I have not done nothing about the hole in the tent's window flap.
8. Janice didn't let no one know about the plans.
9. Some salamanders don't have no lungs; they breathe through their skin.
10. Dad can't never find his glasses.

## Good *and* Well

*Good* is always an adjective. *Well* can be used as an adverb. When *well* means "in good health," it is used as an adjective.

| | |
|---|---|
| ADJECTIVE | The milk tasted **good.** [*Good* is a predicate adjective that describes *milk.*] |
| ADVERB | He always plays **well.** [*Well* tells how he played.] |
| ADJECTIVE | He doesn't feel **well** today. [*Well* means "in good health."] |

### EXERCISE 6 *Using* Good *and* Well

Number your paper 1 to 20. Then write *good* or *well* to correctly fill each blank.

1. Vacuum the rug ____.
2. Janice dances ____.
3. I feel quite ____.
4. The steak looks ____.
5. It's running ____.
6. The sun feels ____.
7. He windsurfs ____.
8. Does he write ____?
9. I'm ____ again.
10. He draws rather ____.
11. The lunch tasted ____.
12. The Lions played ____.
13. That rain feels ____.
14. Sandra dives ____.
15. Tim's voice is ____.
16. The soup tastes ____.
17. What smells so ____?
18. They're growing ____.
19. The flute sounds ____.
20. The trick worked ____.

## *Time-out for Review* • • • • •

Number your paper 1 to 20. Then write the following sentences, correcting each error. If a sentence is correct, write *C* after the number.

1. The umpire handled the argument about the foul ball very well.
2. I didn't have nothing to do during the afternoon while it rained.
3. Which is largest, an elephant or a whale?
4. Everyone in the choir sang good today.
5. Who is more younger, Betsy or Melba?
6. Mom and Dad don't have no objections to our plans for the barbecue.
7. His old car runs quite well.
8. Which team has the best record—the White Sox, the Royals, or the Giants?
9. Of all the new members in our club, Kari is the most friendliest I know.
10. Mom really looks well in that dress.
11. Sharks don't have no real bones; their skeleton is made up of a flexible material called cartilage.
12. Which piano in the auditorium sounds best, the grand piano or the spinet?
13. An adult's broken bone may take four times more longer to heal than a child's.
14. Suzanne doesn't knit very good.
15. No one shouldn't stay in the sun without using a good sunscreen.
16. This dinosaur bone is the most oldest fossil in the collection.
17. Move the lamp more closer to the sofa.
18. Sean won't tell no one about his secret project.
19. Some flowers in our gardens are more fragrant than others.
20. Which usually causes more damage, a hurricane or a tornado?

## Application to Writing

Throughout your school years, you will often be asked to write reports that include comparisons. You might, for example, be asked to compare two authors or two periods of history. When you write comparisons, always edit your work to make sure you have used the correct forms of comparison. Also check to see if you have avoided all problems with modifiers.

### *Exercise 7 Editing for the Correct Use of Modifiers*

Read the following paragraphs and find the ten errors. Then write the paragraphs correctly.

Rabbits and Hares

Which is most famous, a rabbit or a hare? There's no question about it. Rabbits win every time. After all, who hasn't never read about Bugs Bunny, Peter Rabbit, or Brer Rabbit?

A rabbit is different from a hare. Of the two animals, the rabbit is smallest. A rabbit has more shorter ears and legs than a hare. Rabbits build warm nests in burrows. Their young are born blind. A newly born hare, on the other hand, has fully opened eyes. In addition, a rabbit doesn't have no hair when it is born, but a newborn hare has a full coat of hair. Newborn hares are able to hop more earlier than baby rabbits. Young hares are born in an open field. As a result they can take better care of themselves sooner than young rabbits.

All rabbits and hares run and jump good. A running jackrabbit takes a more higher leap every sixth stride. By doing this, it is able to look around for any possible danger. The strong hind legs of rabbits make them fast runners.

Both kinds of animals are more activer at night than in the day. Rabbits and hares eat plants, but they don't eat no meat.

# Chapter Review

**A Using the Correct Form of Modifiers.** Number your paper 1 to 10. Then write the correct modifier in parentheses.

1. This is the (heavier, heaviest) crate I have ever lifted.
2. Of my two uncles, I think Uncle Pete is (older, oldest).
3. Our young chickens are coming along (good, well).
4. Of all the people at the play tryouts, Ned was the (more, most) talented.
5. Sandy types (more, most) accurately than Eric.
6. Both pieces of meat look good, but this piece is (more, most) tender.
7. There aren't (no, any) erasers for the chalkboard in homeroom.
8. Because Ricco didn't sing (good, well) at rehearsal, he is nervous about the concert.
9. Your skates are (newer, more newer) than mine.
10. Mr. Lyons looks (good, well) in a three-piece suit.

**B Correcting Errors with Modifiers.** Number your paper 1 to 10. Then write the following sentences, correcting each error. If a sentence is correct, write *C* after the number.

1. This bread is more fresher than those rolls.
2. Doesn't no one have a flashlight?
3. I think a panther looks more fiercer than a tiger.
4. He learned his lesson good.
5. I play basketball more better than soccer.
6. Which do you like better, swimming in the ocean or swimming in a lake?
7. We didn't have no practice for three days.
8. Tim's was the most biggest trout caught today.
9. You can't ever depend on the weather in New England.
10. The lost notebook doesn't have no name on it.

**C** **Forming the Comparison of Modifiers.** Write the correct form of each modifier indicated below. Then use each word in a sentence.

1. the comparative of *quickly*
2. the superlative of *long*
3. the comparative of *little*
4. the superlative of *fast*
5. the comparative of *bad*
6. the comparative of *energetic*
7. the superlative of *helpful*
8. the superlative of *good*
9. the comparative of *clear*
10. the comparative of *bravely*

## Mastery Test

Number your paper 1 to 10. Then write the correct word in parentheses.

1. Of the three candidates, who do you think is (better, best)?
2. Red is gentle, so he wouldn't bite (no one, anyone).
3. This is the (biggest, most biggest) fish I've ever caught.
4. Which is (larger, largest), Tennessee or Kentucky?
5. Jim plays the French horn very (good, well).
6. That is the (loveliest, most loveliest) rose I've ever seen.
7. Which do you like (better, best), fresh strawberries or blueberries?
8. My walk to school is (more longer, longer) than yours.
9. Don't you have (no, any) plans for Saturday?
10. The new stereo sounds very (good, well).

# Standardized Test

## USAGE

**Directions:** Choose the word or words that best complete each sentence. In the appropriate row on your answer sheet, fill in the circle containing the same letter as your answer.

SAMPLE The sparrow ______ some string for its nest.

**A** stealed **B** stolen **C** stole

ANSWER Ⓐ Ⓑ ●

1. Norman has ______ Mrs. Sanchez all his life.

   **A** knowed **B** known **C** know

2. Mr. Li ______ to us about the organization of the library.

   **A** spoke **B** spoken **C** speaked

3. The air felt ______ after the rain.

   **A** cooler **B** more cooler **C** more cool

4. Of the three suitcases, which is ______?

   **A** most heaviest **B** heavier **C** heaviest

5. After much thought we ______ the gray and white kitten.

   **A** choosed **B** chose **C** chosen

6. Toby ______ down to rest at two o'clock this afternoon.

   **A** laid **B** lay **C** lain

7. The football team is playing ______ than ever.

   **A** more good **B** more better **C** better

8. Has band practice ______ yet?

   **A** begun **B** began **C** beginned

9. It actually feels ______ today than yesterday.

   **A** hotter **B** hoter **C** more hot

10. The whole family ______ and watched the program.

    **A** set **B** sitted **C** sat

**Directions:** Decide which underlined part in each sentence contains an error in usage. On your answer sheet, fill in the circle containing the same letter as the incorrect part. If there is no error, fill in *D*.

SAMPLE He (A) don't (B) have his key with him (C). No error (D)

ANSWER Ⓐ Ⓑ Ⓒ Ⓓ

11. I (A) doesn't (B) know her (C). No error (D)

12. Have (A) you spoken (B) to they (C) about the party? No error (D)

13. Planes is (A) sometimes delayed (B) even in good (C) weather. No error (D)

14. All of the girls have (A) played (B) good (C) this year. No error (D)

15. David and I (A) are (B) getting ready for our (C) meeting tomorrow afternoon. No error (D)

16. They (A) don't (B) have no (C) more copies of *Born Free.* No error (D)

17. Which one of your (A) two sisters is more (B) older (C)? No error (D)

18. Everyone on the boys' baseball team is (A) doing (B) his (C) best to win this game. No error (D)

19. Her (A) and Monica have (B) better (C) seats than we do. No error (D)

20. That police officer and his (A) horse has (B) been (C) stationed in this park for years. No error (D)

## UNIT 3

# Mechanics

# 14

# Capital Letters

## Diagnostic Test

Number your paper 1 to 10. Then write each word that should begin with a capital letter.

EXAMPLE kim was born in mobile, alabama.
ANSWER Kim, Mobile, Alabama

1. pam and i will march in the parade on columbus day.
2. my brother works for the wellesley company.
3. which is the largest country in africa?
4. have you ever read the story "the legend of sleepy hollow"?
5. is hawthorne middle school going to get a new gym?
6. the great lakes were filled by melting glaciers.
7. my favorite subjects are spanish and social studies.
8. the maynard library is on trent highway and route 4.
9. there are 50,000 characters in the chinese system of writing.
10. last summer we visited several towns in the midwest.

# First Words and the Word I

Capital letters and punctuation marks were not used when writing first began. They were developed over the years to make written communication easier for the reader to read and understand.

Without capital letters and end marks, one sentence would run into another. A capital letter is a clear signal that a new sentence is beginning. It is also the usual signal for a new line of poetry.

**14a** Capitalize the first word in a sentence or a line of poetry.

SENTENCE **L**ast night's frost killed our tomatoes.

LINES OF POETRY **B**y day the bat is cousin to the mouse.
**H**e likes the attic of an aging house.
—*Theodore Roethke*

The pronoun *I* is always capitalized when it stands alone and when it is part of a contraction.

**14b** Capitalize the pronoun *I*, both alone and in contractions.

ALONE Did you see what **I** just did?

CONTRACTION Next year **I**'d like a part-time job.

### Exercise 1 Capitalizing First Words and I

Number your paper 1 to 10. Then write each word that should begin with a capital letter.

At the Airport

my class went to the airport yesterday. that's when i saw my first helicopter. oh, i'd seen helicopters in movies and on television. i just hadn't ever been close to one before. no other aircraft can stand still in the air or go straight up and down. i think i'll get a helicopter pilot's license when i'm older.

# Proper Nouns

A noun is the name of a person, a place, a thing, or an idea. A *proper noun* is the name of a particular person, place, thing, or idea.

14c Capitalize proper nouns and their abbreviations.

Study the following groups of rules for capitalizing proper nouns. Refer to them when you edit your writing.

***Names of Persons and Animals.*** Capitalize the names of particular persons and animals.

| | |
|---|---|
| PERSONS | **L**inda; **R**. **B**. **T**aylor; **C**arl **R**obertson, **J**r. |
| ANIMALS | **R**anger, **S**camp, **D**ancer, **P**rince, **M**ittens |

***Geographical Names.*** Capitalize the names of particular places and bodies of water.

| | |
|---|---|
| STREETS, HIGHWAYS | **W**indsor **R**oad (**R**d.), **M**ann **T**urnpike, **F**orty-third **S**treet (**S**t.), **R**oute 2 (**R**t.) |
| CITIES, STATES | **A**ustin, **T**exas; **A**kron, **O**hio |
| COUNTRIES | **F**rance, **M**exico, **G**reece, **I**taly |
| CONTINENTS | **A**ustralia, **S**outh **A**merica, **E**urope |
| MOUNTAINS | **R**ocky **M**ountains, **M**ount (**M**t.) **H**ood |
| PARKS | **Y**ellowstone **N**ational **P**ark |
| ISLANDS | **B**ahama **I**slands, **G**alveston **I**sland |
| BODIES OF WATER | **R**ed **R**iver, **L**ake **E**rie, the **A**tlantic **O**cean, **B**antry **B**ay, **N**iagara **F**alls |

Sections of the United States—such as the *Midwest,* the *Northeast,* and the *West*—are also capitalized. (The word *the* usually comes before a section of the country.) Simple compass directions, however, are not capitalized.

| | |
|---|---|
| SECTION OF THE COUNTRY | We moved to *the* **S**outh during the summer. |
| COMPASS DIRECTION | We turned **s**outh on Route 34. |

***Planets and Stars.*** Capitalize the names of the planets, stars, constellations, and galaxies. Do not capitalize *sun* and *moon*.

| | |
|---|---|
| PLANETS | **J**upiter, **V**enus, **P**luto, **M**ars |
| STARS | **V**ega, the **N**orth **S**tar, **S**irius |
| CONSTELLATIONS | **O**rion's **B**elt, the **G**reat **B**ear |
| GALAXY | the **M**ilky **W**ay |

NOTE: Do not capitalize *earth* if the word *the* comes in front of it.

| | |
|---|---|
| CAPITAL | My report compared Mars with **E**arth. |
| NO CAPITAL | How many times does the **e**arth travel around the sun in one year? |

## EXERCISE 2 Using Capital Letters

Number your paper 1 to 10. Then write each word that should begin with a capital letter.

1. almost a quarter of california is desert.
2. we named our miniature terrier skye.
3. the caspian sea links the soviet union with iran.
4. vegetables are an export of the southwest.
5. our cousins in sweden plan to visit new york city.
6. two miles west on route 7 is ocala parkway.
7. the structure of mars is probably most like that of earth.
8. we visited harpers ferry national historic park in west virginia.
9. how many moons does jupiter have?
10. we took a cruise of the islands in boston harbor.

## EXERCISE 3 Using Capital Letters

Number your paper 1 to 10. Then write each word that should begin with a capital letter.

1. hodgenville, kentucky, was the birthplace of abraham lincoln.
2. mount rainier is in the state of washington.
3. iceland is about the same size as virginia.

4. marco polo gave europe its first detailed account of china.
5. it takes 243 days on earth for venus to turn once on its axis.
6. new rochelle, a city in new york, was named after a city in france.
7. carolyn called her new dog pal.
8. many craters on the moon were formed by meteorites.
9. the panama canal was opened in 1914.
10. my father pointed to lake itasca on the map.

### EXERCISE 4 Writing Sentences

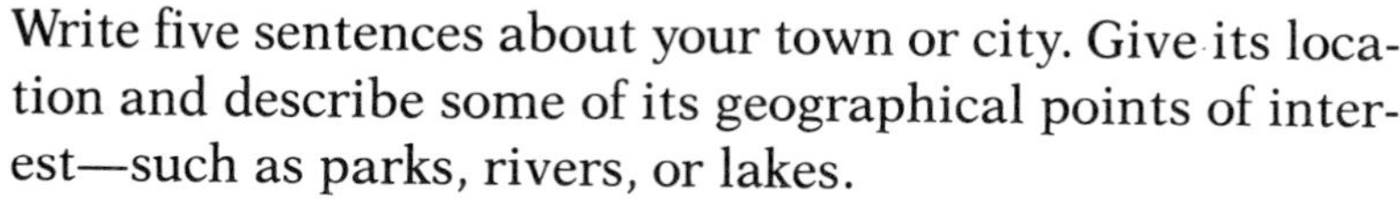

Write five sentences about your town or city. Give its location and describe some of its geographical points of interest—such as parks, rivers, or lakes.

***Nouns of Historical Importance.*** Capitalize the names of historical events, periods, and documents.

| | |
|---|---|
| EVENTS | the **B**oston **T**ea **P**arty, the **B**attle of **S**an **J**uan **H**ill, the **S**eneca **F**alls **C**onvention |
| PERIODS OF TIME | the **I**ndustrial **R**evolution, the **M**iddle **A**ges, the **C**olonial **P**eriod, the **J**azz **A**ge |
| DOCUMENTS | the **C**onstitution, the **B**ill of **R**ights, the **E**mancipation **P**roclamation |

NOTE: Prepositions, such as the *of* in *Bill of Rights,* are not capitalized.

***Names of Groups and Businesses.*** Capitalize the names of groups—such as organizations, businesses, institutions, and government bodies.

| | |
|---|---|
| ORGANIZATIONS | the **U**nited **W**ay, the **R**ed **C**ross |
| BUSINESSES | **R**aytheon **C**ompany, **S**tate **S**treet **B**ank |
| INSTITUTIONS | **R**eed **C**ollege, **O**akland **H**ospital |
| GOVERNMENT BODIES | the **H**ouse of **R**epresentatives, the **F**ederal **B**ureau of **I**nvestigation |

***Specific Time Periods and Events.*** Capitalize the days of the week, the months of the year, civil and religious holidays, and special events. Also capitalize the abbreviations A.D., B.C., A.M., and P.M.

| | |
|---|---|
| DAYS, MONTHS | **S**unday, **S**aturday, **J**anuary, **M**ay |
| HOLIDAYS | **F**ourth of **J**uly, **W**ashington's **B**irthday |
| SPECIAL EVENTS | **R**ose **B**owl **P**arade, **O**lympics |
| CERTAIN ABBREVIATIONS | Confucius lived during the years 551 to 487 **B.C.** |

NOTE: Do *not* capitalize the seasons of the year unless they are part of a specific name.

| | |
|---|---|
| NO CAPITAL | We will plant the corn in the **s**pring. |
| CAPITAL | Are you coming to the **S**pring **C**oncert? |

## EXERCISE 5 *Capitalizing Proper Nouns*

Number your paper 1 to 10. Then write each word that should begin with a capital letter.

1. all 50 states officially observe six holidays, including thanksgiving and labor day.
2. the early 1920s are sometimes called the jazz age.
3. the justice department gave support to the civil rights act.
4. we should leave the house by 6:30 a.m. in order to reach the ferry by noon.
5. the orange bowl parade is held in miami, florida, every new year's day.
6. on the first arbor day in nebraska, april 10, 1872, over one million trees were planted.
7. on december 3, 1967, christiaan barnard performed the first human heart transplant.
8. the peace corps was founded in 1961.
9. in which month does winter officially begin, november or december?
10. delegates from georgia did not attend the continental congress in philadelphia.

### **EXERCISE 6** *Capitalizing Proper Nouns*

Number your paper 1 to 10. Then write each word that should begin with a capital letter.

1. the hudson's bay company was founded in canada.
2. on our trip to washington, we visited the senate.
3. the battle of bunker hill was a costly victory for great britain.
4. in 1966, betty friedan founded the national organization for women.
5. who was the founder of harvard college?
6. the gary memorial hospital is adding a new wing.
7. the united nations was formed after world war II.
8. carthage in africa was founded in 814 b.c.
9. when did thanksgiving become a legal holiday?
10. the red cross offers help during emergencies.

### **EXERCISE 7** *Writing Sentences* 

Write four or five related facts about an event in history. Capitalize each proper noun.

***Nationalities, Races, and Languages.*** Capitalize the names of nationalities, races, and languages.

| | |
|---|---|
| NATIONALITIES | a **S**paniard, an **A**merican, a **G**erman |
| RACES | **C**aucasian, **O**riental, **A**frican |
| LANGUAGES | **E**nglish, **S**panish, **F**rench, **R**ussian |

***Religions and Religious References.*** Capitalize the names of religions. Capitalize religious references.

| | |
|---|---|
| RELIGIONS | **C**hristianity, **J**udaism, **B**uddhism, **I**slam |
| RELIGIOUS REFERENCES | **G**od, the **L**ord, the **C**reator, the **B**ible, the **T**orah, the **K**oran, the **N**ew **T**estament |

NOTE: The word *god* is not capitalized when it refers to mythological gods. Do capitalize their names, however.

The Vikings said **T**hor was the **g**od of thunder.

***Specific School Courses.*** Capitalize the names of courses that are followed by a number.

NUMBERED COURSES **A**rt II, **C**reative **W**riting I, **S**hop II

NOTE: Except for language courses, course names without a number—such as *history, math, science,* and *physical education*—are not capitalized.

***Other Proper Nouns.*** Capitalize all other proper nouns.

| | |
|---|---|
| AWARDS | the **A**cademy **A**ward, the **H**eisman **T**rophy |
| BRAND NAMES | **D**ove soap, **K**raft cheese, **P**erdue chicken [The product itself—such as *soap, cheese,* or *chicken*—is not capitalized.] |
| BUILDINGS | the **F**argo **B**uilding, the **T**ower of **L**ondon |
| MONUMENTS, MEMORIALS | the **W**ashington **M**onument, the **J**efferson **M**emorial, the **S**tatue of **L**iberty |
| VEHICLES | *Apollo 17*, the ***C**olumbia*, ***O**ld **I**ronsides* |

### EXERCISE 8 *Capitalizing Proper Nouns*

Number your paper 1 to 10. Then write each word that should begin with a capital letter.

1. there are 132 rooms in the white house.
2. in the early years of this country's growth, many chinese helped build the central pacific railroad.
3. john paul jones's ship during the american revolution was called the *bonhomme richard.*
4. her favorite subjects are music I, history, and math.
5. sinclair lewis, an american, won the nobel prize.
6. at the meeting were protestants, catholics, and jews.
7. the world trade center in new york city is 100 feet higher than the empire state building.
8. in 1929, gerber baby food was first produced.
9. did you enjoy woodworking II better than art?
10. have you ever visited the wright brothers national monument in north carolina?

### EXERCISE 9 Capitalizing Proper Nouns

Number your paper 1 to 15. Then write each word that should begin with a capital letter.

1. you bought green giant corn instead of the store brand.
2. the arch of triumph and the eiffel tower are famous monuments in paris.
3. every year the nation's best lineman in college football is given the lombardi award.
4. of the 102 passengers on the *mayflower,* only 41 were puritans.
5. many explorers of the territories of north america were spaniards.
6. the first time kleenex tissues were used was during world war I.
7. which do you prefer, nabisco shredded wheat or sunshine shredded wheat?
8. if my brother takes german next year, he won't be able to take two courses in math.
9. around 1828, mexicans living in what is now texas invented chili con carne.
10. my brother matthew launched his sailboat, the *captain nemo,* on sebago lake in maine on july 4, 1985.
11. did more germans or scandinavians settle in the midwest?
12. instead of gymnastics I, i'm going to take archery.
13. kennedy high school offers several language courses such as latin, spanish, and french.
14. how many books are there in the old testament?
15. the greeks believed that a god named prometheus lived on the earth before people were created.

### EXERCISE 10 Writing Sentences 

In an atlas or an encyclopedia, find information about a famous building, monument, or memorial. Then write five sentences that describe your choice. Remember to use capital letters correctly.

## TIME-OUT FOR REVIEW • • • • •

Number your paper 1 to 20. Then write each word that should begin with a capital letter.

Who's Who?

1. who was the first person to sign the declaration of independence?
2. who used a middle initial that did not stand for a middle name, ulysses s. grant or harry s truman?
3. who built their empire first, the mayas or the aztecs?
4. who was raised in the midwest, jefferson or lincoln?
5. who, little orphan annie or mickey mouse, owned a dog named pluto?
6. who was the first person to walk on the moon, michael collins or neil armstrong?
7. who sold louisiana to the americans in 1803, the english or the french?
8. who was the captain of *starship enterprise,* james kirk or alan shepard?
9. who warned the colonists that the british were coming by land?
10. who was the mythological god who held the world on his shoulders, zeus or atlas?
11. who was the englishman who first sailed around the world, drake or magellan?
12. who delivered the gettysburg address on november 19, 1863?
13. who lived at 221 baker street in london, england?
14. who in the bible was the lawgiver who received commandments on mount sinai?
15. who is honored on the second sunday in may?
16. who won an oscar, marlon brando or tom seaver?
17. who was visited by ghosts on christmas eve?
18. who founded islam in the seventh century a.d., buddha or muhammad?
19. who lived in sherwood forest with his band of men?
20. who painted the ceiling of the sistine chapel in rome, bernini or michelangelo?

# Other Uses for Capital Letters

You have learned the most common uses for capital letters. There are, however, a few other uses that you need to know.

## Proper Adjectives

You just finished reviewing proper nouns, words that name specific people, places, and things. Like proper nouns, most proper adjectives begin with a capital letter.

**14d** Capitalize most proper adjectives.

| PROPER NOUNS | PROPER ADJECTIVES |
|---|---|
| Europe | **E**uropean history |
| North American | **N**orth **A**merican countries |
| the South | **S**outhern states |

### EXERCISE 11 Capitalizing Proper Adjectives

Number your paper 1 to 10. Then write the following items, adding capital letters only where needed.

1. the finnish language
2. australian cities
3. a big mexican hat
4. the canadian border
5. african folktales
6. scottish dances
7. american history
8. a swedish recipe
9. celtic legends
10. italian cooking

### EXERCISE 12 Writing Sentences

Number your paper 1 to 5. Use each proper adjective in a sentence.

1. Korean
2. Irish
3. Asian
4. Cuban
5. Egyptian

# Titles

Capital letters are used in the titles of people, of written works, and of other works of art.

**14e** Capitalize the titles of people and works of art.

***Titles Used with Names of People.*** Capitalize a title showing office, rank, or profession when it comes before a person's name. The same title is usually not capitalized when it follows a name.

| | |
|---|---|
| BEFORE A NAME | Have you ever met **S**enator Mason? [capital letter] |
| AFTER A NAME | Is Rachel Mason a **s**enator from your state? [no capital letter] |
| BEFORE A NAME | Did you consult **C**hairman Brooks? [capital letter] |
| AFTER A NAME | Adam Brooks is **c**hairman of that special committee. [no capital letter] |

Other titles or their abbreviations—such as *Mrs.*, *Dr.*, and *Lt.*—should be capitalized when they come before a person's name.

This package is for **M**r. Jordan.
A letter from the company that supplies uniforms has arrived for **S**gt. Samuelson.

***Titles Used in Direct Address.*** A noun of *direct address* is used to call someone by name. Capitalize a title used alone, instead of a name, in direct address.

| | |
|---|---|
| DIRECT ADDRESS | When will you be free, **D**octor, to take off the cast on my arm? |
| | I think, **G**overnor, that we must consider this issue carefully. |

***Titles Showing Family Relationships.*** Capitalize titles showing family relationships when the titles come before people's names. Capitalize the titles also when they are used instead of names or in direct address.

| | |
|---|---|
| BEFORE A NAME | Is **A**unt Mary coming to dinner? |
| USED AS A NAME | Tell **M**om that we'll be home soon. |
| IN DIRECT ADDRESS | How are you feeling, **S**is? |

Do not capitalize a title showing a family relationship when it is preceded by a possessive noun or pronoun—unless it is considered part of a person's name.

| | |
|---|---|
| NO CAPITAL | Are you Cathy's **s**ister? [the word *sister* is preceded by a possessive noun, *Cathy's*.] |
| | My **d**ad works at the hospital. [The word *dad* is preceded by a possessive pronoun, *my*.] |
| CAPITAL | I saw your **U**ncle **L**eon yesterday. [In this sentence *Uncle* is considered part of the person's name.] |

### EXERCISE 13 Capitalizing Titles of People

Number your paper 1 to 10. Then write each word that should begin with a capital letter. If a sentence is correct, write *C* after the number.

1. My grandmother will visit us soon.
2. Yes, dad, I have already cleaned my room.
3. Does Daniel's brother work at the gas station every afternoon after school?
4. May I ask you one question, professor?
5. How long have you known rabbi brenner?
6. Is dad the person in charge of that committee?
7. Sally wants to be a doctor.
8. The speaker at the assembly about the town's new sports complex will be mayor willis.
9. My uncle richard was a senator from our state.
10. Will mayor mann run for office this fall?

***Titles of Written Works and Other Works of Art.*** Capitalize the first word, the last word, and all important words in the titles of books, newspapers, magazines, stories, poems, movies, plays, musical compositions, and other works of art. Do not capitalize a preposition, a coordinating conjunction, or an article *(a, an,* or *the)* unless it is the first or last word in a title.

| | |
|---|---|
| WRITTEN WORKS | Have you read the chapter "**T**he **G**rowth of **R**ussia" in our book ***H**istory in **R**eview?* |
| | Did you read the article "**T**urntable of **T**unes" in the ***N**ew **Y**ork **D**aily **N**ews*? [Generally the word *the* before the first word of a newspaper or magazine title is not capitalized.] |
| MUSICAL COMPOSITIONS | I like the song "**L**eaving for the **P**romised **L**and" from George Gershwin's musical ***P**orgy and **B**ess.* |

## EXERCISE 14 Capitalizing Titles

Number your paper 1 to 10. Then write each word that should begin with a capital letter.

1. Katharine Lee Bates wrote the words to "america the beautiful" at the top of Pikes Peak.
2. I enjoyed the article "a season of winners" in *sports illustrated.*
3. I saw the painting *portrait of a peasant.*
4. The movie *tender mercies* won an award.
5. The article "computers in the future" in the *nashville banner* was very interesting.
6. I thoroughly enjoyed James Thurber's modern fable "the tortoise and the hare."
7. The song "maria" is from the musical *west side story.*
8. Tonight read the poem "mama is sunrise."
9. Did you cover your book *mysteries of the universe*?
10. Tony played dr. Baird in *flight into danger.*

## TIME-OUT FOR REVIEW • • • • •

Number your paper 1 to 20. Then write each word that should begin with a capital letter.

What's What?

1. what planet is closer to the sun, mercury or venus?
2. what is the name of clark kent's newspaper, the *daily news* or the *daily planet*?
3. what river begins in new hampshire but is named for another state, the connecticut or the delaware?
4. what famous indian princess rescued john smith from death?
5. in what year did columbus sight land in what is now the bahamas?
6. what group first recorded the song "with a little help from my friends"?
7. what is the first monday in september called?
8. what was another name for cape canaveral in florida?
9. what is the name of the state directly north of oregon?
10. what city is sacred to jews, christians, and muslims?
11. what was the name of the girl who hid from the nazis in an attic in amsterdam?
12. what is the name of the world's highest mountain, mount everest or mount rainier?
13. what is the name of the author of *alice's adventures in wonderland,* lewis carroll or carol lewis?
14. what president issued the emancipation proclamation on january 1, 1863?
15. in 1959, alaska and what other state were admitted to the united states?
16. what award does the best actor in a movie get, an oscar or an emmy?
17. what is the name of a south american country that starts with the letter *e*?
18. in what state is mount rainier, colorado or washington?
19. what holiday besides veterans day falls in november?
20. what city is closer to walt disney world in florida, tampa or orlando?

## Application to Writing

Before you write the final draft of something you have written, always reread your work. Check to see if you have included all necessary capital letters.

### **EXERCISE 15** *Editing for Proper Capitalization*

Read the following paragraphs and find the 33 items that should begin with a capital letter. (Do not include words that are already capitalized.) Then rewrite the paragraphs correctly.

The Incas

More than 350 years ago, the inca indians of south america controlled an empire of almost 2,500 miles from colombia to chile. In approximately 1400 a.d., this tribe conquered some 10 million inhabitants of the present nations of peru, ecuador, bolivia, western argentina, and the northern part of chile.

Across the many miles of the empire, the incas built a network of roads. The roads, however, had to run through and around the andes mountains. This feat would be difficult even for modern engineers.

Often the incas tunneled through mountain cliffs, but they also built bridges. The longest of the inca bridges was the basis for thornton wilder's novel *the bridge of san luis rey*. This 148-foot suspension bridge crossed a deep ravine of the apurimac river. Until the bridge fell earlier in this century, it had been in use longer than any other bridge in south america.

Because of an internal civil war in their empire, these mighty indians were conquered by a handful of spaniards led by francis pizarro. Information about their art, culture, and village life is contained in spanish chronicles.

# Chapter Review

**A** **Using Capital Letters.** Number your paper 1 to 10. Then write each word that should begin with a capital letter.

1. five states border the gulf of mexico.
2. for more than 150 years, american colonists lived under british rule.
3. i love the poem "the road not taken."
4. the capital of arkansas is little rock.
5. a painting titled *lady musician and young girl* was painted in the first century b.c.
6. which is larger, jupiter or earth?
7. after moving to the east from oregon, my brother settled in connecticut.
8. get onto venton road and go north for two miles.
9. my favorite aunt and uncle will visit us soon.
10. president lyndon b. johnson signed a document called the education bill.

**B** **Using Capital Letters.** Number your paper 1 to 10. Then write each word that should begin with a capital letter.

1. is the sun farther from earth in summer or in winter?
2. is your computer an apple or a commodore?
3. every morning my mom reads the *washington post.*
4. the last of the 13 english colonies to be settled was georgia.
5. my uncle david is president of the ridley golf league.
6. one american signed the declaration of independence in very large letters.
7. tell us, officer, were there any witnesses?
8. which do you enjoy more, science or european history?
9. the name of the first space shuttle was *columbia.*
10. have you ever been to walker lake in nevada?

**C Editing for Proper Capitalization.** Number your paper 1 to 25. Read the following paragraphs, finding the 25 words that should begin with a capital letter. Then rewrite the paragraphs correctly.

When News Traveled Slowly

the battle of new orleans was one of the greatest victories in united states history. leading a force of frontiersmen, general andrew jackson of tennessee confronted troops of british soldiers who had just defeated napoleon's great french army.

the battle took place on january 8, 1815—just 15 days after a treaty ending the war of 1812 had been signed in europe. unfortunately, the news of the treaty had not reached andrew jackson or the british. in fact, jackson's superiors in washington were unaware of either the battle or the treaty.

## Mastery Test

Number your paper 1 to 10. Then write each word that should begin with a capital letter.

1. the log cabin was introduced to america by swedish settlers in delaware.
2. when will our school open in the fall?
3. is algeria the largest country in africa?
4. which countries did not attend the 1984 olympics in los angeles?
5. the largest painting in the world, *the battle of gettysburg,* weighs 11,792 pounds.
6. my uncle enjoyed his trip to the west.
7. the first mail-order catalog, issued by montgomery ward, was only one sheet of paper.
8. which soccer team won the world cup last year?
9. on a sunday in 1941, the united states entered world war II.
10. we visited the superdome in new orleans.

# 15

# End Marks and Commas

## Diagnostic Test

Number your paper 1 to 10. Write each sentence, adding a comma or commas where needed. Then write an appropriate end mark.

EXAMPLE Well how do you like my new sweater
ANSWER Well, how do you like my new sweater?

1. Stop that grounder Wes
2. The lock is jammed or we have the wrong key
3. Sharks however rarely attack human beings
4. On September 9 1850 California was admitted to the Union
5. Do you want an apple a pear or a banana
6. After the severe snowstorm all schools were closed for three days
7. The tour guide for the United Nations was polite attractive and witty
8. Oh was that a flash of lightning
9. The raccoon a cousin of the bear usually washes its food
10. We visited Paul Revere's house at 19 North Square Boston Massachusetts last summer

# End Marks

End marks and capital letters signal to a reader that one sentence has ended and another has started. Different kinds of sentences end with different end marks. (*See page 3 for a review of kinds of sentences.*)

**15a** Place a **period** after a statement, after an opinion, and after a command or request made in a normal tone of voice.

PERIODS I own a cocker spaniel. [statement]
Dogs make the best pets. [opinion]
Give the dog a bath. [command]

**15b** Place a **question mark** after a sentence that asks a question.

QUESTION MARK Is that your cocker spaniel?

**15c** Place an **exclamation point** after a sentence that states strong feeling and after a command or request that expresses great excitement.

EXCLAMATION POINTS My cocker spaniel won the blue ribbon!
Close the gate before the dog escapes!
[command said with great excitement]

NOTE: An exclamation point also follows an interjection.

Wow! Did you see the size of that Great Dane?

### *EXERCISE 1 Using End Marks*

Number your paper 1 to 10. Then write the correct end mark for each sentence.

1. Today is a terrific day for a picnic
2. Should we go to Kenney Park or Rosewood Park
3. Pack two kinds of sandwiches
4. I'll make some lemonade

5. Call Jan and Peter and invite them
6. What's splashing against the windows
7. The forecast mentioned occasional showers
8. Does this look like just a shower
9. We'll take a rain check for the picnic
10. What exactly is a rain check

## Periods with Abbreviations

Abbreviations are brief ways of writing words. Most abbreviations, however, do not belong in formal writing like letters or reports.

**15d** Use a period with most abbreviations.

Following is a list of some abbreviations that are acceptable in formal writing.

| | | | | | |
|---|---|---|---|---|---|
| TITLES WITH NAMES | Mr. | Ms. | Rev. | Sgt. | Jr. |
| | Mrs. | Dr. | Gen. | Lt. | Sr. |
| TIMES WITH NUMBERS | 2:30 A.M. | 7:00 P.M. | | | |
| | 47 B.C. | A.D. 200 | | | |

When an abbreviation is the last word in a sentence, only one period is used to end the sentence.

The train arrives at 7:30 P.M.

### EXERCISE 2 Writing Abbreviations

Number your paper 1 to 10. Then write the abbreviations that stand for the following items. If necessary, consult a dictionary for the spelling of a particular abbreviation.

1. Saturday
2. Doctor
3. yard
4. Avenue
5. pound
6. Senior
7. teaspoon
8. December
9. before Christ
10. Captain

# Commas That Separate

Basically, a comma is used in two ways. One of those ways is to separate items. Just as an end mark keeps sentences from running together, a comma keeps items within a sentence from running together.

## Items in a Series

A series is three or more similar items listed one after another. When words and groups of words are written in a series, commas should separate them.

**15e** Use commas to separate items in a series.

**WORDS**

NOUNS Paper, paint, and brushes are the supplies we'll need.

VERBS We danced, talked, and laughed all evening at the block party.

ADJECTIVES The newborn kitten was small, thin, and weak.

**GROUPS OF WORDS**

COMPLETE SUBJECTS My older sister, our cousin Ted, and one of our neighbors went hiking.

COMPLETE PREDICATES We washed the car, cleaned its windows, and vacuumed its rugs.

PREPOSITIONAL PHRASES We walked down the road, across the bridge, and through the tunnel.

If a conjunction such as *and* or *or* connects *all* the items in a series, no commas are needed.

We ran **and** ran **and** ran around the track until the coach told us to stop. [no commas]

### EXERCISE 3 Using Commas in a Series

Number your paper 1 to 10. Then write each sentence, adding commas where needed. If a sentence does not need any commas, write *C* after the number.

1. Last year my grandfather grew lettuce tomatoes and beets in his backyard.
2. The crew sanded painted and papered the kitchen.
3. The story about his vacation was short humorous and descriptive.
4. We arrived in Atlanta at noon left our suitcases at the motel and went sightseeing.
5. The children ran down the lane through the field and into the barn.
6. Prince picked up the newspaper brought it into the house and then chewed it to bits.
7. Some words that come from the Latin word *porto* are *portable import* and *reporter.*
8. Educated people are always needed in government and in industry and in education.
9. The Chinese rug was large thick and colorful.
10. The chipmunk ran through the living room down the hall and into the bedroom.

## Compound Sentences

A *compound sentence* is made up of two or more simple sentences. When the parts of a compound sentence are joined by a coordinating conjunction *(and, but, or, yet),* a comma is usually placed before the conjunction. (*See pages 112–119 for a review of compound sentences.*)

**15f** Use a comma before a coordinating conjunction that joins the parts of a compound sentence.

You can make the salad, and I will set the table.
Three horses jumped the fence, but we caught them within half an hour.

Do not confuse a compound sentence with a simple sentence that has a compound verb.

| | |
|---|---|
| COMPOUND SENTENCE | Kate swims well, and everyone wants her for team captain. [A comma is needed.] |
| COMPOUND VERB | Kate swims well and dives excellently. [No comma is needed.] |

## EXERCISE 4 *Using Commas with Compound Sentences*

Number your paper 1 to 15. Then write each sentence, adding a comma where needed. If a sentence does not need a comma, write *C* after the number.

A Greek Legend

1. King Midas loved gold very much and a god granted him the "golden touch."
2. Midas touched his throne and it turned to gold.
3. He was very happy with his new power and soon almost everything in his palace became gold.
4. One day the king called for his dinner and a delicious meal was set before him.
5. He picked up a goblet and raised it to his lips.
6. His drink instantly hardened to gold and he could not drink it.
7. Then Midas quickly crammed a piece of potato into his mouth but it turned into a lump of hot gold.
8. Sometime later he walked through his garden and forgot about his power.
9. The roses made the air sweet and Midas loved them.
10. He touched one red rose and it instantly turned to gold.
11. Just then the king's daughter entered the garden and Midas drew back in horror.
12. The little girl put her hand on his arm and at once she became a golden statue.
13. Midas prayed very hard and finally the god heard him.
14. The king followed the god's instructions and soon the golden touch was gone.
15. Midas threw his arms around his daughter and thanked the god for bringing her back to life.

## Introductory Elements

A comma follows certain words and groups of words when they introduce, or begin, a sentence.

**15g** Use a comma after certain introductory elements.

Usually a comma follows words such as *no, oh, well,* or *yes* when they begin a sentence.

WORDS Oh, I didn't see you standing there.
Well, the weather turned warm after all.

Two or more prepositional phrases or one that is four words or longer should also be followed by a comma.

PREPOSITIONAL PHRASES From the ceiling of the kitchen, we hung a colorful mobile.
Throughout the long play, all the children sat quietly.

### EXERCISE 5 Using Commas with Introductory Elements

Number your paper 1 to 10. Then write each sentence, adding a comma where needed. If a sentence does not need a comma, write *C* after the number.

1. No bats do not fly into people's hair.
2. From our seats in the bleachers we could hardly see that last play.
3. Well we can get something to eat at the stadium.
4. After tomorrow Dad will take us to school.
5. Why I think I know him.
6. On our trip from Ohio to Kansas we both drove.
7. With their help we can win.
8. Near the large tree we could see a squirrel.
9. Yes let's sit down and calmly discuss our vacation plans.
10. During the first lap of the race Leon ran faster than anyone else.

## Dates and Addresses

Use commas to separate different parts of a date or an address.

15h Use commas to separate elements in dates and addresses.

A comma is also used to separate a date or an address from the rest of the sentence.

DATE On Monday, May 3, 1986, my parents celebrated their wedding anniversary.

ADDRESS I lived at 40 Elm Street, Boise, Idaho 06103, for two years.

NOTE: A comma is not used between the name of a state and a ZIP code.

### EXERCISE 6 Using Commas in Dates and Addresses

Number your paper 1 to 10. Then write each sentence, adding commas where needed.

1. Lombard Illinois is known for its lilacs.
2. On Monday April 1 1985 my brother was born in University Hospital Chapel Hill North Carolina 27514.
3. Sandy moved to 89 Southard Avenue Rockville Center New York 11570 a year ago.
4. John Glenn orbited in space on February 20 1962.
5. Is 47 Main Street Clearwater Florida 33515 his address?
6. On May 29 1917 President John F. Kennedy was born in Brookline Massachusetts.
7. On October 8 1956 New York Yankee Don Larsen pitched the first perfect game in a World Series.
8. I drove to 6 Lee Court Mills Iowa with my aunt.
9. Send a letter to Daniel Davidson Marchand Brothers Oakland Highway Nashua New Hampshire 03062.
10. My parents have lived at 476 Pioneer Drive Lansing Michigan 48910 for 45 years.

## Exercise 7 Writing Sentences

Number your paper 1 to 5. Then write sentences that follow the directions below, adding a comma or commas where needed.

1. Write a sentence that includes a series of nouns.
2. Write a compound sentence with the conjunction *but.*
3. Begin a sentence with *After gymnastics practice on Friday.*
4. Write a sentence that includes the month, date, and year of someone's birth.
5. Write a sentence that includes all the elements in your current address.

## Time-out for Review • • • • •

Number your paper 1 to 10. Then write each sentence, adding a comma or commas where needed.

Amelia Earhart

1. Amelia Earhart was born on July 24 1898 in Atchison Kansas.
2. She worked hard to pay for flying lessons a small plane and travel expenses.
3. Well in 1928 she was a passenger in a flight across the Atlantic.
4. After the Atlantic crossing she yearned to fly the Atlantic alone.
5. For the next four years she flew as much as she could and made plans.
6. On Friday May 20 1932 she put on a silk shirt a leather flying suit and a helmet.
7. She took off from Harbour Grace Newfoundland before the sun set.
8. During her flight her instruments failed and she was forced to drop to a dangerously low altitude.
9. After 14 hours and 56 minutes she landed in a pasture in Ireland.
10. Yes she was the first woman to pilot a plane alone across the Atlantic.

# Commas That Enclose

Commas are also used to enclose some words that interrupt the main idea of a sentence.

## Interrupting Expressions

Following is a list of common interrupting expressions. These words are usually enclosed by commas.

**Common Interrupting Expressions**

| | | |
|---|---|---|
| after all | for instance | of course |
| at any rate | generally speaking | on the contrary |
| by the way | I believe (guess, hope, know) | on the other hand |
| consequently | | moreover |
| however | in fact | nevertheless |
| for example | in my opinion | to tell the truth |

15i Use commas to set off interrupting expressions.

A spider has eight legs, **for example,** not six.

Only one comma is needed when this kind of expression comes at the beginning or at the end of the sentence.

**In fact,** a spider is not an insect.
A spider is often called an insect, **nevertheless.**

### EXERCISE 8 Using Commas with Interrupters

Number your paper 1 to 10. Then write each sentence, adding a comma or commas where needed.

1. The porpoise however is not a fish.
2. September for example is a hot month in Florida.
3. On the other hand I liked the movie.
4. Everyone is welcome of course.

5. Moreover we have a golden retriever.
6. *Black Beauty* after all is considered a classic.
7. The math test in my opinion was not too difficult.
8. Blue is his best color I think.
9. Generally speaking owls hunt at night.
10. The coach on the contrary agreed with the referee.

## Direct Address

Sometimes when you talk, you call another person by name. This kind of sentence interrupter is called a noun of *direct address.*

15j Use commas to set off nouns of direct address.

Please**, Mr. Curtis,** give me the recipe.

In the following examples, only one comma is needed because the noun of direct address comes at the beginning or at the end of the sentence.

**Mr. Curtis,** your barbecue sauce is wonderful!
I will give you the recipe**, Arlene.**

### EXERCISE 9 Using Commas with Direct Address

Number your paper 1 to 10. Then write each sentence, adding a comma or commas where needed.

1. Quick Karen I need your help!
2. Chris didn't you know I was an Orioles fan?
3. On your way home Carla please buy some stamps.
4. Do you want another ear of corn Fred?
5. Look over there Scott at the shooting star.
6. José one of the tires on your bicycle is flat.
7. Yes Jim a rainbow has seven bands.
8. When is your doctor's appointment Lionel?
9. Cora diagram this sentence on the board.
10. You're wanted on the phone Mother.

## Appositives

Another interrupter, the *appositive,* renames or explains a noun or pronoun in the sentence. Most appositives have one or more modifiers. Usually an appositive comes immediately after the word it renames or explains and is enclosed in commas.

15k Use commas to set off most appositives and their modifiers.

TWO COMMAS Alaska**, the largest state,** was once owned by Russia.

Only one comma is needed when the appositive comes at the end of the sentence. Sometimes commas are not used if an appositive is a name.

ONE COMMA Have you met Paula**, my cousin from Denver**?

NO COMMAS My sister **Pat** is a nurse.
Have you read the book ***Oliver Twist***?

### EXERCISE 10 *Using Commas with Appositives*

Number your paper 1 to 10. Then write each sentence, adding a comma or commas where needed. If a sentence does not need any commas, write *C* after the number.

Paul Bunyan

1. Over the years the legend of Paul Bunyan the most famous lumberjack of all grew and grew.
2. Paul Bunyan a huge man towered above the trees.
3. His voice once caused a landslide near Pikes Peak a mountain in Colorado.
4. His mighty blue ox Babe straightened the course of the Whistling River.
5. The cook Hot Biscuit Slim was an important member of his logging crew.
6. Cream puffs the favorite dessert of the crew were baked by the camp cook.

7. Big Swede one of Paul's workers was known for getting into accidents.
8. Johnny Inkslinger the first bookkeeper in legend did all the figuring for Paul.
9. It took a bucket brigade of 30 men to fill Johnny's pen a giant rubber hose.
10. The Paul Bunyan legends stories about life in the forest are a big part of American folklore.

### EXERCISE 11 Writing Sentences

Number your paper 1 to 3. Then write sentences that follow the directions below, adding a comma or commas where needed.

1. Include *however* as an interrupting expression.
2. Include *Mom* as a noun of direct address.
3. Include *a holiday in February* as an appositive.

### TIME-OUT FOR REVIEW • • • • •

Number your paper 1 to 10. Then write each sentence, adding a comma or commas where needed.

The Death of Poirot

1. Melissa did you read this unusual story?
2. Years ago *The New York Times* a very important newspaper ran a front-page story about a death.
3. This was no ordinary story however.
4. It reported the death of Hercule Poirot a Belgian detective.
5. Poirot of course never really lived.
6. Agatha Christie the famous writer of detective stories created him in 1920.
7. Yes Melissa Mrs. Christie wrote 42 novels about Monsieur Poirot.
8. In 1975 however Hercule Poirot died in the book *Curtain*.
9. Mrs. Christie's fans nevertheless refused to accept Poirot's death.
10. Consequently she brought Poirot back to life.

## Application to Writing

As you edit your written work for the correct use of capital letters and end marks, also make sure that you have used commas correctly. One of the best ways to check for end marks and commas is to read your work aloud. Be careful, moreover, that you do not include unnecessary commas.

### ***Exercise 12*** *Editing for the Correct Use of Commas*

Write the following paragraphs, adding commas where needed.

Figure Skating

The first ice skates were made of animal bones tied with leather straps to shoes. People in Norway Sweden and Finland were skating over 2,000 years ago. Holland however is the country that really made skating popular. During the long winters in Holland people skated to work to church and to school on the many frozen canals.

Animal-bone skates soon were replaced with wooden skates and these were followed by all-metal skates with steel blades. Steel blades were eventually screwed on a boot and the modern skate was invented. There was finally a skate that was fast sturdy and safe.

Early skaters performed simple routines with stiff movements. Then Jackson Hines an American ballet teacher changed figure skating forever. Hines glided jumped and spun gracefully across the ice. Moreover he wore colorful costumes and included music in his routines.

More than 20 million Americans now skate. For more facts about skating you can write to the United States Figure Skating Association 20 First Street Colorado Springs Colorado 80906 and include a stamped envelope with your name and address on it.

# Chapter Review

**A** **Using Commas Correctly.** Number your paper 1 to 10. Then write each sentence, adding a comma or commas where needed.

1. Springfield is the name of cities in Massachusetts Illinois and several other states.
2. Please Peter help me deliver the newspapers.
3. On August 20 1975 *Viking I* made a trip to Mars.
4. Paul Revere a colonial silversmith made the bolts and spikes for the hull of the *Constitution.*
5. Today the sun rose at 7:12 but I got up at 6:30.
6. On the computer screen we saw some strange letters.
7. The cat stopped quickly arched its back and hissed.
8. From October to May my grandparents live in Florida.
9. Bread of course stays fresh in a freezer for weeks.
10. Yes people used water faucets about 2,000 years ago.

**B** **Using Commas Correctly.** Number your paper 1 to 10. Then write each sentence, adding a comma or commas where needed. If a sentence does not need any commas, write *C* after the number.

1. My neighbor Ellen Klerman is home from college.
2. The trunk in our attic is old large and heavy.
3. Greenland the largest island on this planet is about 1,600 miles in length.
4. For an hour all the lights were out.
5. Your dental appointment David is on Monday.
6. The magician's first trick is good but you haven't seen anything yet.
7. We walked for two miles and then took a rest.
8. The ladybird on the other hand is actually a beetle.
9. We hunted for a present for Dad in a department store in smaller stores and in catalogs.
10. The Rose Bowl a large football stadium is in Pasadena California.

**C** **Using Commas Correctly.** Write the following paragraphs, adding commas where needed.

What Should I Read?

Are you interested in athletics animals or science? There are magazines about each of these subjects. *Young Athlete* for example tells you about events in the sports world. The articles will keep you up-to-date on all the latest news and each issue includes an interview with a big star. For more information about this magazine write to *Young Athlete* P.O. Box 246 Mt. Morris Illinois 61054 and send a stamped envelope with your name and address.

*Three-Two-One Contact* a magazine about science covers interesting topics from hiccups to *Star Trek.* Each month there is a new experiment and each issue has some regular columns. One column for instance gives helpful facts about your health. For information write to *Three-Two-One Contact* P. O. Box 2934 Boulder CO 80321.

## Mastery Test

Number your paper 1 to 10. Write each sentence, adding a comma or commas where needed. Then write an appropriate end mark.

1. On Friday the city traffic is heavy slow and noisy
2. At tonight's Honor Society meeting I will speak about scholarships
3. We moved to Minnesota on February 18 1985
4. Marty watch out for that tree
5. Gold in fact is even found in seawater
6. The rooster crowed at five o'clock but Daniel didn't hear it
7. The area has flat land straight roads and many fields
8. What a beautiful name you have Melanie
9. Is Boise the capital of Idaho near Twin Falls
10. The first American presidential mansion was at 1 Cherry Street New York New York

16

# Underlining and Quotation Marks

## Diagnostic Test

Number your paper 1 to 10. Then write each direct quotation, adding quotation marks, other punctuation marks, and capital letters where needed.

EXAMPLE do you think we're lost Lee asked
ANSWER "Do you think we're lost?" Lee asked.

1. Julie asked did you notice a brilliant morning star before sunrise
2. everyone is up and ready to go Mom announced
3. have you seen the film in science class yet Kara inquired
4. do you have a pen Matthew asked
5. today declared Bryan proudly I made the track team
6. I just finished my book report Jane told us
7. it's a great day Jennifer said to go to the beach
8. is there any more milk Dan asked
9. I'll add another log to the fire Dad offered it's beginning to die down
10. those rocks Amy warned are slippery

# Underlining

Italics is a type of print that slants to the right *like this*. You can substitute underlining for italics when you are writing certain kinds of titles.

16a Underline the titles of long written or musical works that are published as a single unit. Also underline titles of paintings, sculptures, vehicles, and radio and television series.

Long written works include books, magazines, newspapers, full-length plays, movies, and very long poems. Long musical works include operas, symphonies, ballets, and albums. Vehicles include airplanes, ships, trains, and spacecraft.

| | |
|---|---|
| BOOKS | Tom Sawyer, Old Yeller |
| NEWSPAPERS | the Daily News, the Boston Globe [In general, do not underline *the* before newspaper titles.] |
| VEHICLES | Orient Express, Titanic |
| RADIO AND TV SERIES | Nova, Smithsonian World |

### EXERCISE 1 Underlining Titles

Number your paper 1 to 10. Then write and underline each title that should be printed in italics.

1. President Kennedy wrote the book Profiles in Courage.
2. Robert Fulton called his steamboat the Clermont.
3. A famous painting by Vincent Van Gogh is Sunflowers.
4. Our daily newspaper is the Nashville Banner.
5. The last episode of M*A*S*H aired in 1983.
6. One sculpture by Henry Moore is The Archer.
7. I bought Dad the magazine Business Week.
8. Annie is a musical based on a comic strip.
9. We saw the light opera The Pirates of Penzance.
10. I enjoyed Steven Spielberg's film E.T.

# Quotation Marks

You can improve your writing if you use quotation marks correctly. Your stories, for example, will be more realistic if you include conversations among your characters. Your reports will be read with greater interest if they include quoted statements.

## Quotation Marks with Titles

Not all titles are underlined. The titles of smaller parts of long works are enclosed in quotation marks.

**16b** Use quotation marks to enclose the titles of chapters, articles, stories, one-act plays, short poems, and songs.

"Shipwrecked and Alone" is the title of the first chapter of the book The Swiss Family Robinson.
"The Star-Spangled Banner" was first published on September 20, 1814.

### EXERCISE 2 Using Quotation Marks with Titles

Number your paper 1 to 10. Then write each sentence, adding underlining and quotation marks where needed.

1. The song Guinevere is from the musical Camelot.
2. I read the poem Paul Revere's Ride in speech class.
3. The Buck in the Hills is a short story about hunting.
4. Have you read the chapter The Colonies Win Freedom in this history book, The Heritage of America?
5. The article A Lost Son Is Found was in Newsweek.
6. The Ugly Duckling is a one-act play.
7. I copied Helen Hunt Jackson's poem September.
8. Julie loves the song Tomorrow from the musical Annie.
9. Sponges is a chapter in our textbook Life Science.
10. We read the article India Today in this week's Time.

## Quotation Marks with Direct Quotations

A person's exact words are quoted in a *direct quotation.* Quotation marks are used before and after any words the person says.

**16c** Use quotation marks to enclose a person's exact words.

| | |
|---|---|
| EXACT WORDS | Mike said, "I have a meeting after school." |
| | He added, "It will probably last until six o'clock." |

A person's exact words are not directly quoted in an *indirect quotation.* Quotation marks, therefore, are not used.

| | |
|---|---|
| INDIRECT QUOTATIONS | Mike said he had band practice after school at three o'clock. |
| | He added that he would probably finish by six o'clock. |

NOTE: The word *that* is often used with an indirect quotation. In the first example, *that* is understood: *He said (that) he had band practice after school at three o'clock.*

A one-sentence direct quotation can be written in several ways. It can be placed before or after a speaker tag such as *she said* or *he asked.* A direct quotation can also be interrupted by a speaker tag. In all cases quotation marks enclose only the person's exact words, not the speaker tag.

| | |
|---|---|
| BEFORE | "Your temperature is high," said the nurse. |
| AFTER | The nurse said, "Your temperature is high." |
| INTERRUPTED | "Your temperature," the nurse said, "is high." [Two sets of quotation marks are needed because the speaker tag interrupts the direct quotation.] |

***Capital Letters with Direct Quotations.*** A capital letter begins a direct quotation.

16d Capitalize the first word of a direct quotation.

"**T**he meeting will be held in the gym," she said.

She said, "**T**he meeting will be held in the gym."

"**T**he meeting," she said, "**w**ill be held in the gym." [*Will* does not begin with a capital letter because it is in the middle of a one-sentence direct quotation.]

"**T**he meeting will be held in the gym," she said. "**I**t begins at four." [*It* starts a new sentence.]

### EXERCISE 3 Using Quotation Marks and Capital Letters

Number your paper 1 to 10. Then write each direct quotation, adding quotation marks and capital letters where needed. In this exercise, the comma or the end mark goes *inside* the closing quotation marks.

EXAMPLE we'll eat dinner at six, she said.
ANSWER "We'll eat dinner at six," she said.

1. without a doubt the statue of liberty is the most famous statue in the world, Leon remarked.
2. our house is advertised in today's real-estate section, announced Mom.
3. she stated, today my family is celebrating my grandmother's 80th birthday.
4. that, she exclaimed, is a wonderful bargain!
5. from the mountaintop, she said, you can see all the way to the Pacific Ocean.
6. she replied, my dog is a golden retriever.
7. the fastest fish is a wahoo, he explained.
8. he added, it can swim 60 miles per hour.
9. the ear, the teacher explained, is the most complicated organ in the human body.
10. the plane from Seattle is late, he told us.

## EXERCISE 4 Using Quotation Marks and Capital Letters

Number your paper 1 to 10. Then write each direct quotation, adding quotation marks and capital letters where needed. In this exercise, the comma or the end mark goes *inside* the closing quotation marks.

EXAMPLE chuckwallas live in the desert, said Ms. Poe.
ANSWER "Chuckwallas live in the desert," said Ms. Poe.

Fun in the Desert

1. chuckwallas are playful lizards, she said.
2. she continued, chuckwallas play hide-and-seek.
3. they run and hide, she explained, and then peep out to spy on the others.
4. Ms. Poe went on, sometimes a chuckwalla will jump out and grab another's tail just for fun.
5. does a chuckwalla have any enemies? Susan asked.
6. snakes and birds, Ms. Poe answered, attack them.
7. she added, a chuckwalla can easily protect itself.
8. it crawls in between rocks, she explained, and blows up like a balloon.
9. she added, an enemy cannot pull it loose.
10. the attacker soon gives up, she concluded. then the chuckwalla lets out the air and scurries off.

**Commas with Direct Quotations.** A comma belongs between a direct quotation and the speaker tag.

16e Use a comma to separate a direct quotation from a speaker tag. Place the comma inside the closing quotation marks.

"The first contestant may begin**,**" the judge said.

The judge said**,** "The first contestant may begin." [The comma comes *before* the quotation marks.]

"The first contestant**,**" the judge said**,** "may begin." [Two commas are needed to separate the speaker tag from the direct quotation. The first comma goes *inside* the closing quotation marks.]

***End Marks with Direct Quotations.*** When a quotation ends with a period, the period goes *inside* the closing quotation marks.

**16f** Place a period inside the closing quotation marks when the end of the quotation comes at the end of the sentence.

He said, "Class begins in two minutes."
"Class begins," he said, "in two minutes."

The same is true of question marks and exclamation points that end a quotation.

She yelled, "Watch out!" [The exclamation point belongs *inside* the closing quotation marks.]

"When," he asked, "did you find time to decorate the living room?" [The question mark goes *inside* the closing quotation marks.]

NOTE: When a question or an exclamation comes before a speaker tag, the question mark or the exclamation point is still placed *inside* the closing quotation marks in place of the usual comma.

"Please hurry!" Margo pleaded.
"Do you want a peanut-butter sandwich?" Peg asked.

### EXERCISE 5 *Using Commas and End Marks with Direct Quotations*

Number your paper 1 to 10. Then write each direct quotation, adding commas and end marks where needed.

EXAMPLE Kevin shouted "I got an A on the test"
ANSWER Kevin shouted, "I got an A on the test!"

1. "Meet me in the library in the reference room in ten minutes" Mr. Thomas directed
2. David announced "The soccer game begins at four o'clock at the Wayland Junior High field"
3. Mom asked "Have you set the table for dinner"

4. "Yes" he answered "I will volunteer to help on Tuesday and Thursday afternoons"
5. He yelled "Don't go near that fire"
6. Mrs. Myers explained "The king cobra is the largest poisonous snake on Earth"
7. "The ice is very thin" she screamed to the boys at the edge of the lake
8. Tim said "Asia is about four times the area of Europe"
9. "What was the patient's temperature immediately after lunch" the doctor asked
10. "The elevators in the Sears Tower" the guide announced "travel at 20 miles per hour"

### ***EXERCISE 6 Using Commas and End Marks with Direct Quotations***

Number your paper 1 to 10. Then write each direct quotation, adding commas and end marks where needed.

EXAMPLE "Have you ever hunted for pearls" asked Linda
ANSWER "Have you ever hunted for pearls?" asked Linda.

Finding Pearls

1. "No" Mr. Quinn answered "but I would like to find one sometime"
2. Linda asked "Do pearl divers know which oysters contain pearls"
3. "They can't tell" Mr. Quinn replied "until they look inside the shell"
4. "What happens to the oyster once the pearl is removed" she asked
5. He explained "A diver returns the oyster to the water"
6. "The diver hopes" Mr. Quinn continued "that the same oyster will make another pearl"
7. "Is diving for pearls dangerous" Linda asked
8. "It can be extremely dangerous" Mr. Quinn exclaimed
9. She finally asked "Are all pearls valuable"
10. "The most valuable pearls" Mr. Quinn stated "are perfectly round"

## TIME-OUT FOR REVIEW • • • • •

Number your paper 1 to 15. Then write each direct quotation, adding quotation marks, other punctuation marks, and capital letters where needed.

EXAMPLE the crow is here to stay Mr. Adams stated
ANSWER "The crow is here to stay," Mr. Adams stated.

The Clever Crow

1. many people do not realize that the crow is an extremely smart bird he said
2. he added a crow can outwit hawks and most human beings
3. does putting a scarecrow in a cornfield really help andrea asked
4. most crows Mr. Adams explained use scarecrows as lookout posts
5. one crow he continued will act as a guard for a flock of crows in a cornfield
6. Billy asked what does the crow do if it becomes aware of any danger
7. it caws a danger signal to the others Mr. Adams said and they all fly away
8. Mr. Adams went on a team of three crows will also work together to get food from an animal
9. would you please give us an example of how they do that Beth asked
10. a crow lands on each side of the animal Mr. Adams stated and pretends to steal the animal's food
11. then the third crow he stated swoops down and snatches the food
12. I'm amazed to learn that crows really are smart birds Jeff exclaimed
13. these smart birds also like to have fun Mr. Adams said
14. he explained one will quietly land next to a sleeping animal and peck it on the head
15. the crow then flies away Mr. Adams concluded cawing with delight as the animal leaps up

## Quotation Marks with Dialogue

A conversation between two or more persons is called a *dialogue*. The way a dialogue is written shows the reader who is speaking.

**16g** When writing dialogue, begin a new paragraph each time the speaker changes.

In the following dialogue between Gina and Connie, a new paragraph begins each time the speaker changes.

> "What time is it?" Gina asked Connie, who was sitting beside her in study hall.
>
> "It's quarter of two," Connie answered. "The bell will ring in five minutes."

### EXERCISE 7 Writing Dialogue

Correctly write the following dialogue between Gina and Connie. Add any needed punctuation and indent each time there is a change of speaker.

Gina asked do you want to come to my house after school to finish your homework? That's a great idea Connie answered and we can work on our science reports. When is your report due Gina asked. I have to finish it by Friday Connie said.

### Application to Writing

If you write a story that includes dialogue, always edit the dialogue for the correct use of quotation marks.

### EXERCISE 8 Writing Dialogue

200 words

Write a short imaginary dialogue between an athlete and a reporter. Punctuate the dialogue correctly.

# Chapter Review

**A** **Punctuating Titles.** Number your paper 1 to 10. Then write each sentence, adding quotation marks or underlining to the titles. (These sentences are *not* direct quotations.)

1. The Honeymooners once was a popular TV series.
2. Catalogue is a delightful short poem about cats.
3. Tracy Austin was featured on the cover of World Tennis at the age of four.
4. I finished reading the short story The Pacing Goose.
5. The painting Twittering Machine is by Paul Klee.
6. I loved the movie Planet of the Apes.
7. Charles Lindbergh flew the Spirit of St. Louis on the first nonstop solo flight from New York to Paris.
8. Education in America was an article in Newsweek.
9. The American troops marched to Yankee Doodle at Yorktown.
10. Read the chapter Animal Behavior in Science Today.

**B** **Punctuating Direct Quotations.** Number your paper 1 to 10. Then write each quotation, adding capital letters, quotation marks, and other punctuation marks where needed.

1. the Yukon is the largest river in Alaska he stated
2. why are you leaving so early Mandy asked
3. Vickie remarked fish is a good source of protein
4. the travel guide asked have you ever been to Spain
5. wow he exclaimed look at that wave
6. an earthquake can create huge sea waves she stated
7. you can't have everything Steven Wright said
8. watch out for that falling ladder she screamed
9. the earth he explained is made up of several layers
10. Kerry repeated a dragon supposedly had a snake's body and a bat's wings

**C** **Writing Dialogue.** Correctly rewrite the following dialogue between Kenneth and Shirley. Add capital letters, quotation marks, and other punctuation marks where needed.

ooking for Spices

Kenneth began our report is about the discovery of America. Shirley added as everyone knows, Columbus discovered America by accident, since he was really looking for a faster route to the Far East. Why was a faster route so important Kenneth asked. A shipload of spices Shirley replied could make a person rich for life. Kenneth continued the nation that controlled the spice trade to a great extent controlled the commerce of Europe. Why were spices so important in the fifteenth and sixteenth centuries Shirley asked. They were needed for everyday life Kenneth replied. In the days before refrigeration, spices were needed to preserve food and make medicines.

# Mastery Test

Number your paper 1 to 10. Then write each sentence adding quotation marks, other punctuation marks, and capital letters where needed.

1. be home by nine o'clock Dad told us
2. Tracy said I saw that adventure film twice
3. did you have a swim Jamie asked
4. at first Mr. Reynolds explained many Americans didn't want to join the League of Nations
5. Hannah exclaimed I am so pleased to see you
6. this isn't the road Dad insisted we missed our turn
7. here's a perfect place Mark said for a picnic
8. is dinner ready yet Martin asked
9. won't the dog eat Mom asked maybe he's sick
10. has everyone read the rules Mrs. Grant asked

17

# Other Punctuation

## Diagnostic Test

Number your paper 1 to 10. Then write each sentence, adding apostrophes, semicolons, colons, and hyphens where needed.

EXAMPLE Are Mrs. Murphys students in the library?
ANSWER Are Mrs. Murphy's students in the library?

1. The earths orbit is not a perfect circle.
2. Does the bus schedule say 6 20 A.M. or P.M.?
3. The television character Howdy Doody had a twin brother his name was Double Doody.
4. To win the scavenger hunt, we must find the following a nail, a balloon, and a red pencil.
5. Dan can join us after school, but Ellie cant.
6. The lowest state is Delaware the highest one is Colorado.
7. Thirty two new apartments will be created in the old building.
8. Mr. Thompson takes childrens portraits.
9. I have lived in three states Nebraska, Michigan, and Arizona.
10. Most of the students band instruments are new.

# Apostrophes

Two uses of the apostrophe will be covered in this section. An apostrophe is used to show ownership or possession. It is also used in contractions.

## Apostrophes with Possessive Nouns

The possessive form of a noun shows that someone or something owns something else. This form is used when an *of* phrase could be substituted for the noun.

Richard**'s** book = the book of Richard
the dinosaur**s'** bones = the bones of dinosaurs

***The Possessive Form of Singular Nouns.*** Before writing the possessive form of a singular noun, write just the noun itself. Then add an apostrophe and an *s*.

17a Add 's to form the possessive of a singular noun.

| | |
|---|---|
| Jess + **'s** = Jess's | Is this Jess**'s** coat? |
| car + **'s** = car's | What is the car**'s** problem? |

### EXERCISE 1 Forming the Possessive of Singular Nouns

Number your paper 1 to 10. Then rewrite each expression, using the possessive form.

EXAMPLE life of a dog
ANSWER a dog's life

1. fields of the farmer
2. tires of the tractor
3. whiskers of the cat
4. skill of the typist
5. role of the actor
6. muffins of Sue
7. end of the day
8. job of my mother
9. hum of the motor
10. rays of the sun

### *Exercise 2 Writing Sentences*

Number your paper 1 to 5. Then write sentences that use five of the answers from Exercise 1.

***The Possessive Forms of Plural Nouns.*** Most plural nouns end in *s: tomatoes, papers, slippers.* A few plural nouns, such as *children* and *mice,* do not end in *s.* How the possessive form of a plural noun is written depends on the ending of the noun.

17b Add only an apostrophe to form the possessive of a plural noun that ends in *s.*

| | |
|---|---|
| chairs + **'** = chairs**'** | The chairs**'** arms are worn. |
| girls + **'** = girls**'** | Is this the girls**'** gym? |

17c Add *'s* to form the possessive of a plural noun that does not end in *s.*

| | |
|---|---|
| men + **'s** = men**'s** | This is the men**'s** department. |
| geese + **'s** = geese**'s** | The geese**'s** refuge is nearby. |

When you write the possessive of a plural noun, take two steps. First, write the plural of the noun. Second, look at the ending of the word. If the word ends in *s,* add only an apostrophe. If it does not end in *s,* add an apostrophe and an *s.*

| PLURAL | ENDING | ADD | | POSSESSIVE |
|---|---|---|---|---|
| lawyers | *s* | **'** | = | lawyers' office |
| children | no *s* | **'s** | = | children's toys |

NOTE: The possessive forms of the personal pronouns are written without an apostrophe.

| | |
|---|---|
| POSSESSIVE PRONOUNS | my, mine |
| | your, yours |
| | his, her, hers, its |
| | our, ours |
| | their, theirs |

## EXERCISE 3 Forming the Possessive of Plural Nouns

Number your paper 1 to 10. Then rewrite each expression, using the possessive form.

1. playground of the children
2. feathers of the turkeys
3. meeting of the teachers
4. mealtime of the puppies
5. howls of the wolves
6. nest of the birds
7. tails of the mice
8. sizes of the shoes
9. suits of the women
10. claws of the tigers

## EXERCISE 4 Writing Sentences

Number your paper 1 to 5. Then write sentences that use five of the answers from Exercise 3.

## EXERCISE 5 Forming the Possessive of Nouns

Number your paper 1 to 10. Then write the singular or plural possessive form of each underlined word.

EXAMPLE Bud ice skates are on Henry porch.
ANSWER Bud's, Henry's

1. By the day end, I had earned ten dollars for shoveling snow.
2. Many clouds shapes remind me of castles.
3. A fox weight seldom exceeds 12 to 14 pounds.
4. Car mechanics fees can be very high for certain types of repairs.
5. Many artists paintings were on display in the lobby of the new hotel.
6. Our aunt sells women coats at a small boutique in the mall.
7. Last night a sudden and severe frost killed my uncle orange crop.
8. Tuesday fog caused an hour delay in our flight to San Francisco for the convention.
9. A shipment of boys and men boots has just arrived at the Barn Sport Shop.
10. A moment hesitation might cost a pilot life.

## Apostrophes with Contractions

A contraction is formed by combining two or more words. An apostrophe replaces one or more missing letters.

**17d** Use an apostrophe in a contraction to show where one or more letters have been omitted.

The following examples show how some contractions are formed.

| | |
|---|---|
| does + not = doesn't | let + us = let's |
| he + would = he'd | that + is = that's |
| who + is = who's | of + the + clock = o'clock |

When a contraction is written, no letters should be added or moved around. There is only one common exception to this rule: *will* + *not* = *won't*.

***Contraction or Possessive Pronoun?*** Do not confuse a contraction with a pronoun.

| | | | | | |
|---|---|---|---|---|---|
| CONTRACTIONS | it's | you're | they're | there's | who's |
| PRONOUNS | its | your | their | theirs | whose |

To avoid any confusion, always say the individual words of a contraction separately.

It's *(It is)* a lovely day today.

### EXERCISE 6 *Using Apostrophes with Contractions*

Number your paper 1 to 20. Then write the contractions for each pair of words.

1. there is
2. would not
3. they are
4. will not
5. could not
6. we have
7. were not
8. had not
9. do not
10. what is
11. who is
12. are not
13. let us
14. you are
15. he will
16. I have
17. I am
18. I will
19. it is
20. was not

## Exercise 7 Distinguishing between Contractions and Possessive Pronouns

Number your paper 1 to 10. Then write the correct word in parentheses.

1. (There's, Theirs) a snake!
2. Did (you're your) team place second or third in the play-offs?
3. (They're, Their) arriving at 6:30 to spend the weekend with our family.
4. The cat is chasing (it's, its) tail again.
5. (Who's, Whose) playing third base?
6. I think (you're, your) right.
7. (It's, Its) going to be a good movie.
8. Where did you see (they're, their) car?
9. I don't know (who's, whose) gloves these are.
10. (There's, Theirs) are on the kitchen table.

## Time-Out for Review • • • • •

Number your paper 1 to 10. Then correctly write each word that needs an apostrophe.

1. Collecting antique radios has been my brother Allens hobby for many years.
2. Twenty-four students havent arrived yet.
3. Hang these posters in the students cafeteria and in the lobby.
4. Why arent mens shoes on sale also?
5. Lets make a bookcase because well need one soon in the career office.
6. Mr. Johnsons window was filled with babies clothes, toys, and furniture.
7. Thirty-six members of the parents committee will meet tomorrow night.
8. Two days rest isnt going to help.
9. Dont you know when the womens movement started?
10. Last Sundays parade wasnt very enjoyable.

# Semicolons and Colons

A semicolon (;) and a colon (:) are both used to create a pause in a sentence. These two punctuation marks, however, are used for different purposes.

## Semicolons

A compound sentence is two or more sentences that are joined together. The parts of a compound sentence can be joined by a comma and a conjunction. They can also be joined by a semicolon if there is no conjunction. (*See Chapter 8 for a review of compound sentences.*)

| | |
|---|---|
| COMMA AND CONJUNCTION | The tornado struck suddenly**,** and several buildings and houses were damaged. |
| SEMICOLON | The tornado struck suddenly**;** several buildings and houses were damaged. |

17e Use a semicolon between the parts of a compound sentence that are not joined by a conjunction.

A semicolon signals a pause**;** a period signals a full stop.

### EXERCISE 8 Punctuating Compound Sentences

Number your paper 1 to 10. Then write each sentence, adding a semicolon or a comma where needed.

1. There really is a national groundhog it lives in Pennsylvania.
2. Ransom Olds invented the assembly line Henry Ford just developed the idea.
3. The pitcher threw wild and Johnny raced toward home.
4. Bulls don't see the color red they are color-blind.

5. Skiing on water is easy but I can't ski well on snow.
6. We have cans of soup but we don't have a can opener.
7. Snakes have no eyelids their eyes are always open.
8. An ant can lift 50 times its own weight a bee can carry 300 times its own weight.
9. Insects gather around bright lights but they usually avoid yellow lights.
10. Sarah swam in the meet she placed third.

## Colons

A colon is used mainly to introduce a list of items.

17f Use a colon before most lists of items, especially when the list comes after an expression like *the following.*

We have packed the following items**:** first-aid kit, sunscreen lotion, and mosquito repellent.

The bouquet included three kinds of flowers**:** roses, carnations, and daisies.

NOTE: Commas separate the items in the series.

A colon is not needed between a verb and its complements or directly after a preposition.

INCORRECT Three good friends of mine are**:** Mary, Bob, and Tad.
CORRECT I have three good friends**:** Mary, Bob, and Tad.

INCORRECT On our vacation we will be going to**:** Houston, Dallas, and Austin.
CORRECT On our vacation we will be going to the following cities**:** Houston, Dallas, and Austin.

Also use a colon between hours and minutes.

The plane should arrive at 7**:**10 P.M.

## EXERCISE 9 Using Colons

Number your paper 1 to 10. Then write each sentence, adding a colon where needed. If a sentence is correct, write *C* after the number.

1. The following animals have only one toe on each foot the horse, the donkey, and the zebra.
2. In the drawer the detective found the following items a gold pen, a lady's glove, and a button.
3. I will work with Willy, Sandra, and Mavis on the stage crew.
4. The town committee will discuss the following problems potholes, traffic, and pollution.
5. I usually get up at 6 30 A.M. and go to sleep around 10 30 P.M.
6. Most lizards live on insects, spiders, and other small creatures.
7. In third-century China, kites were used for many things toys, weapons, and parachutes.
8. The first five American generals were Prebel, Ward, Pomeroy, Thomas, and Heath.
9. If we have dinner at 6 00 or 6 30, will we have time for a movie?
10. There are four basic types of clouds cirrus, cumulus, stratus, and nimbus.

## EXERCISE 10 Writing Sentences

Number your paper 1 to 5. Then write sentences that follow the directions below.

1. Write a sentence that includes the contraction *there's*.
2. Write a sentence that includes the possessive pronoun *theirs*.
3. Write a compound sentence using a conjunction and a comma.
4. Write a compound sentence using a semicolon.
5. Write a sentence that uses a colon before a series.

# Hyphens

A hyphen is used most often to divide a word at the end of a line. You should avoid dividing words whenever possible, however. Divided words slow a reader down and can cause misunderstanding. When you must divide a word at the end of a line to keep your margin even, remember to include a hyphen.

**17g** Use a hyphen to divide a word at the end of a line.

Following are several guidelines for dividing a word at the end of a line. If you are not certain about where each syllable in a word ends, look the word up in a dictionary. Each entry word is divided into syllables.

**Dividing Words**

1. Divide words only between syllables.
   gym nas tics: gym-nastics or gymnas-tics
2. Never divide a one-syllable word.
   DO NOT BREAK stay laugh call
3. Do not divide a word so that one letter stands alone.
   DO NOT BREAK around emit obey sleepy

A hyphen is also used when numbers above 20 are written out.

**17h** Use a hyphen when writing out the numbers *twenty-one* through *ninety-nine*.

Twenty-one rooms in our school have computers.
He counted fifty-six seagulls.

### EXERCISE 11 Using Hyphens

Number your paper 1 to 15. Then add a hyphen or hyphens to show where each word can be correctly divided. If a word should not be divided, write *no* after the number.

1. hamster
2. among
3. make
4. galaxy
5. about
6. liquid
7. item
8. single
9. surprise
10. strong
11. captain
12. build
13. action
14. opal
15. trespass

## Application to Writing

As you edit your work for correct end marks and commas, make sure that you check for the proper use of other punctuation marks as well.

### EXERCISE 12 Editing for Proper Punctuation

Write the following paragraphs, adding apostrophes, semicolons, and colons where needed.

Cats as Hunters

Morris and other domestic cats belong to the animal family that includes the following large cats tigers, lions, and leopards. Cats are very different in size they are very alike in other respects. All have bodies adapted for hunting all are highly specialized beasts of prey.

A cats eyes help it to be a good hunter. Its eyes are adapted for seeing in the dark. The backs of the eyes are coated with a substance like polished silver. Its this substance that reflects every bit of light that comes into the eye. Thats why a cats eyes seem to glow in the dark.

The whiskers of a cat help it know whats around it. Cats also have four long, pointed teeth in the front of their mouths these teeth are deadly weapons. Other features that make cats good hunters are the following sharp claws, soft pads on their feet, and extremely keen senses.

# Chapter Review

**A** **Punctuating Correctly.** Number your paper 1 to 10. Then write each sentence, adding apostrophes, semicolons, colons, and hyphens where needed.

1. Pineapples are not native to Hawaii they were first planted there in 1790.
2. A mosquitos wings can move 1,000 times a second.
3. Well meet you for lunch at 12 30.
4. New York Citys population is greater than that of the following countries Denmark, Austria, and Norway.
5. Six photographers studios are on the sixth floor.
6. Thirty six members were present at the meeting.
7. Why havent you cleaned the hamsters cages?
8. Texas has 154 counties Alaska has none.
9. Why isnt the Browns dog inside tonight?
10. Blackboard chalk is not made from chalk it is made from plaster of paris.

**B** **Punctuating Correctly.** Number your paper 1 to 10. Then write each sentence, adding apostrophes, semicolons, colons, and hyphens where needed.

1. The lunch includes the following an appetizer, the main course, dessert, and a beverage.
2. The Pentagon is the worlds largest office building.
3. Eighty four people entered the contest.
4. That brand of mens sweaters runs small.
5. There are three small eyes on the top of a bees head two larger ones are in the front.
6. Didnt you enjoy your two weeks vacation?
7. In 1841, the United States had three presidents Martin Van Buren, William Harrison, and John Tyler.
8. Im late because the mall was crowded.
9. The cucumber is not a vegetable it is a fruit.
10. Eleanor owned two dachshunds both were named Jennie.

**C** **Punctuating Correctly.** Number your paper 1 to 10. Then write each sentence, adding apostrophes, semicolons, colons, and hyphens where needed. If a sentence is correct, write *C* after the number.

The Nearest Star

1. The sun is an average star it is not a huge one.
2. Because its so close to Earth, the sun seems much brighter than other stars.
3. Seventy five percent of the sun consists of hydrogen.
4. The suns interior temperature is about 27 million degrees Fahrenheit.
5. Its energy comes from nuclear reactions.
6. The following are all caused by the suns energy plant growth, ocean currents, and tides.
7. Without the sun there wouldnt be any life on Earth.
8. The sun is the center of the solar system there are nine planets orbiting the sun.
9. The planets orbits are determined by gravity.
10. The sun rotates on its axis each rotation takes a month.

# Mastery Test

Number your paper 1 to 10. Then write each sentence, adding apostrophes, semicolons, colons, and hyphens where needed.

1. Kilts are not native to Scotland they came from France.
2. Does this store sell womens jogging shoes?
3. I have several pets a dog, a cat, and two hamsters.
4. Are the guests arriving at 5 30?
5. Most of the earths surface is underwater.
6. Lets not make the same kind of mistake again.
7. The two teams rivalry has been going on for years.
8. Sixty six signatures were written on the petition.
9. *Old Ironsides* did not have iron sides its sides were made of wood.
10. He has four sisters Ann, Emily, Dale, and Tara.

# Standardized Test

## MECHANICS

**Directions:** Decide which numbered part in each sentence contains an error in capitalization or punctuation. In the appropriate row on your answer sheet, fill in the circle containing the same number as the incorrect part. If there is no error, fill in *4*.

SAMPLE The capital of | New York state | is Albany. | None
1 2 3 4

ANSWER ① ② ③ ④

1. May i see | your drawing | of Helen? | None
1 2 3 4
2. One glove and | three socks were | lost | None
1 2 3 4
3. The French Club | met on april | 4, 11, and 25. | None
1 2 3 4
4. At 2:30 | in the afternoon, | the mayor will speak. | None
1 2 3 4
5. The childrens' | toys, however, | were not there. | None
1 2 3 4
6. Oscar shouted, | "There are | the gorillas! | None
1 2 3 4
7. Isabel | was in the show | "The Sound of Music." | None
1 2 3 4
8. They're show is at | the Shubert Theater | at 7:45. | None
1 2 3 4
9. I'll be responsible | for the following plates, cups, |
1 2
napkins, and spoons. | None
3 4
10. Wasn't Marconi, | the inventor of the radio, | Italian? | None
1 2 3 4
11. The *Bedford news* | is our | town's newspaper. | None
1 2 3 4
12. Whose is that | cookbook, yours | or your boss's? | None
1 2 3 4
13. John is writing | about India; but | she chose China. | None
1 2 3 4

14. Is that | Rhonda's copy of | *Great Expectations*? | None
1 2 3 4

15. "I'm | positive!" exclaimed | governor Ellis. | None
1 2 3 4

**Directions:** Choose the answer that shows the correct way to write the underlined part in each sentence. On your answer sheet, fill in the circle containing the same number as your answer.

SAMPLE Have you met Mrs Packer?
1. Mrs Packer?
2. Mrs. Packer.
3. Mrs. Packer?

ANSWER ① ② ③

16. The sun rose at 5 37.
    1. 5 37.
    2. 5:37.
    3. 5:37

17. Have you seen the World Trade Center?
    1. World Trade Center?
    2. World trade center?
    3. World trade Center?

18. This afternoon Ronald studied history, science and math.
    1. history, science and math.
    2. history science and math.
    3. history, science, and math.

19. Hilda screamed "be careful!"
    1. screamed "be
    2. screamed, "Be
    3. screamed "Be

20. We sang America the Beautiful.
    1. America the Beautiful.
    2. "America the Beautiful."
    3. America the Beautiful.

UNIT 4

# Composition

## Part One

# 18

# Words

Precise, vivid words provide the charge that lights up good writing. In the paragraph below, notice how the colorful words spark the scene of the winter woodlands.

| | |
|---|---|
| VIVID SIGHTS | In the woods there are tracks of deer and snowshoe rabbits and long streaks where partridges slide to alight. Chipmunks make tiny footprints on the limbs, and one can hear |
| VIVID SOUNDS | squirrels busy in hollow trees, sorting acorns. Soft lake waves wash the shores, and sunsets burst each evening over the lakes and make |
| VIVID COLORS | them look as if they were afire. —THOMAS S. WHITECLOUD, "BLUE WINDS DANCING" |

This chapter will show you how to choose words that make your writing bright and clear.

## Your Writer's Notebook

Keeping a notebook, or journal, is a good way to strengthen your word power and discover ideas to write about. Every day for a week, write a short description of a person, scene, or object that struck you as interesting or unusual. Try to use vivid words. Be sure to include the day and the date of each entry.

# Specific Words

Weak words, like those in the following sentence, make writing dull and provide little information.

WEAK Near the water stood a tree, some flowers, and a stone.

The sentence springs to life, however, with specific, colorful words.

SPECIFIC Near the waterfall stood a crooked birch, daffodils in bloom, and a boulder the size of a bear.

The chart below shows general and specific words for different parts of speech. When you write, always choose precise nouns, lively verbs, colorful adjectives, and specific adverbs.

| | **General** | **Specific** | |
|---|---|---|---|
| NOUNS | road | path<br>lane<br>trail<br>alley | avenue<br>boulevard<br>highway<br>turnpike |
| VERBS | said | mumbled<br>muttered<br>urged<br>whispered | boasted<br>demanded<br>snapped<br>blurted |
| ADJECTIVES | big | lofty<br>thick<br>bulky<br>roomy | bottomless<br>towering<br>massive<br>important |
| ADVERBS | slowly | gradually<br>cautiously<br>hesitantly<br>leisurely | gently<br>lazily<br>reluctantly<br>sluggishly |

18a Use specific nouns, verbs, adjectives, and adverbs to help your readers picture exactly what you mean.

### EXERCISE 1 Writing Specific Nouns

Number your paper 1 to 20. For each general noun, write one specific noun.

EXAMPLE sports
POSSIBLE ANSWER lacrosse

| | | | |
|---|---|---|---|
| 1. animal | 6. vehicle | 11. place | 16. clothing |
| 2. plant | 7. leader | 12. job | 17. appliance |
| 3. person | 8. name | 13. store | 18. entertainment |
| 4. food | 9. object | 14. sound | 19. furniture |
| 5. pet | 10. tool | 15. event | 20. equipment |

### EXERCISE 2 Writing Specific Verbs

Number your paper 1 to 10. Then write a specific verb that replaces the underlined verb in each sentence.

EXAMPLE I <u>saw</u> the answer in Chapter 9.
POSSIBLE ANSWER found

1. From the top of the Sears Tower, we <u>saw</u> the whole city of Chicago.
2. Suddenly Ben <u>saw</u> his sister in the crowd.
3. I <u>saw</u> the mother cat's hiding place.
4. "Help! Help! The house is on fire!" <u>said</u> Jo.
5. "I don't know what happened to my homework assignment," <u>said</u> Mark.
6. "We always have to wait for Mark," <u>said</u> Gail.
7. Ray <u>went</u> home, arriving breathless and just minutes too late.
8. The horse <u>went</u> down the trail.
9. The ambulance driver <u>went</u> through city traffic with great skill.
10. "You won't believe what I just <u>saw</u>," <u>said</u> Mariel.

### EXERCISE 3 Writing Specific Adjectives

Number your paper 1 to 20. Then write a specific adjective that replaces the underlined adjective in each phrase.

EXAMPLE a good dog
POSSIBLE ANSWER obedient

1. a big book
2. a pretty face
3. a good dancer
4. a new bicycle
5. a tall building
6. a small tree
7. a small child
8. a good story
9. a pretty scarf
10. an awful room
11. little toys
12. a high hill
13. a good student
14. an ugly car
15. a nice person
16. a funny joke
17. a pretty model
18. a good friend
19. a nice house
20. an interesting painting

### EXERCISE 4 Writing Specific Adverbs

Number your paper 1 to 10. Then write two specific adverbs that might be used to complete each sentence.

EXAMPLE The plane flew ______ from Miami to Brasília.
POSSIBLE ANSWERS directly, nonstop

1. Mosquitoes sang ______ outside the tent.
2. Dirt bikers raced ______ around the track.
3. We looked ______ down the shadowy path.
4. Through all nine innings, he pitched ______.
5. The sun shone ______ all day.
6. That's Sarah riding ______ down South Street.
7. Skiers sped ______ past the markers.
8. Rain fell ______ on the crowd in the bleachers.
9. Uncle Henry called ______ when he saw our family arriving at last.
10. The experienced divers swam ______ toward the coral reef.

## EXERCISE 5 On Your Own

Write five sentences about the picture of the beach above. Use as many specific words as possible.

POSSIBLE ANSWER: The blazing white sand scorched the tender pads of a young girl's feet as she dashed into the cool blue water.

## Writing Extra

Tom Swift was a character in books written by Edward Stratemeyer early in the twentieth century. Tom never just *did* things; he did them with an adverb—swiftly, thoughtfully, fearlessly.

Recently Tom Swift's name has returned in a game called Tom Swifties. To write Tom Swifties, match your adverb to the action of the verb or the meaning of the noun, like this:

"I'll mow the lawn," Tom said cuttingly.
"I like hot dogs," Tom said frankly.
"Watch out for the broken glass," Sally said sharply.

Number your paper 1 to 5. Then write five Tom Swifties. Your best ones could be made into posters with illustrations or drawings to be shared with the class.

# Appealing to the Senses

You experience the world mainly through your five senses—sight, hearing, touch, smell, and taste. You can share your experiences with readers by using words that appeal to their five senses.

**18b** Create vivid pictures by using words that appeal to your readers' senses.

## Sight

Writers try to capture the mood and feeling of a subject by painting a picture with words. Following are some words you can use to help your readers see what you see.

**Sight Words**

| Colors | Movements | Shapes | Sizes |
|---|---|---|---|
| beige | twisted | round | tiny |
| rust | raced | craggy | large |
| tawny | sauntered | curved | enormous |
| drab | sped | pointed | deep |
| scarlet | bent | angled | high |
| rosy | dangled | tilted | shallow |
| emerald | slid | lanky | slim |

### EXERCISE 6 Describing Sights

Answer each question about the photograph on page 272. Save your work for Exercise 7.

1. What colors do you see in this picture?
2. What objects do you see in this picture?
3. What shapes are in this picture?
4. What words describe the movements in this picture?
5. How would you describe the sizes in this picture?

### EXERCISE 7 Writing Sentences with Sight Words

Write five sentences describing the scene in the photograph above. Use the words you thought of in Exercise 6 to paint a vivid picture of the scene.

## Sound

All the details in the following paragraph are sounds. Notice how well they can help you picture the scene.

| | |
|---|---|
| SOUND OF GLIDER<br><br>SOUND OF CRICKETS<br><br>SOUND OF FARAWAY TRUCK | The glider on the front porch creaked to the slow rhythm of my grandmother's rocking. From all around the farm came the sounds of the crickets in a faster tempo. *"Chick chuck, chick chuck,"* they sang in metallic voices. Every now and then the muffled roar of a distant truck would break the soothing monotony of those summer nights. |

You may want to use some of the following words to communicate sounds to your reader.

| Sound Words | | | |
|---|---|---|---|
| clang | purr | moan | ring |
| crash | tap | roar | pluck |
| bang | drip | splash | chatter |
| thump | swish | patter | laugh |
| hiss | crackle | thud | cluck |
| sizzle | sigh | giggle | crack |
| rumble | whisper | twitter | rustle |
| murmur | shout | cough | squish |

Before you can write about the sounds in a scene, you must be able to hear or imagine them yourself. Whenever possible, practice listening with care.

### EXERCISE 8 *Describing Sounds*

Number your paper 1 to 10. Try to imagine *yourself* in the picture below. Then write ten sounds that you might hear from the marching bands.

### EXERCISE 9 *Writing Sentences with Sound Words*

Write five sentences describing the sounds you might hear in the scene below. Use the sound words from Exercise 8 to bring the picture to life.

# Touch

Your sense of touch tells you many things. It can tell you whether something is smooth or rough, hot or cold. It can also tell you about things that your hands themselves cannot touch. When your skin feels clammy, for example, your sense of touch is recording dampness and cold. When your cheeks feel flushed, you may be embarrassed or you might have a fever. All of these sensations come under the sense of touch.

The following words will help you appeal to your reader's sense of touch.

**Touch Words**

| | | | |
|---|---|---|---|
| silky | furry | windy | gooey |
| smooth | downy | gusty | oozy |
| cool | soft | coarse | sticky |
| gritty | clammy | glassy | frozen |
| rough | arid | wiry | steamy |
| grainy | damp | sandy | glossy |
| sharp | slimy | icy | slippery |

Notice all of the details of touch in the following paragraph about two children and Wilbur, a young pig.

| | |
|---|---|
| FEEL OF SUN'S WARMTH | One warm afternoon, Fern and Avery put on bathing suits and went down to the brook for a swim. Wilbur tagged along at Fern's heels. |
| FEEL OF COLD WATER | When she waded in the brook, Wilbur waded in with her. He found the water quite cold—too cold for his liking. So while the children |
| FEEL OF SPLASHING | swam and played and splashed water at each other, Wilbur amused himself in the mud along the edge of the brook, where it was warm and |
| FEEL OF MUD | moist and delightfully sticky and oozy. |

—E. B. WHITE, *CHARLOTTE'S WEB*

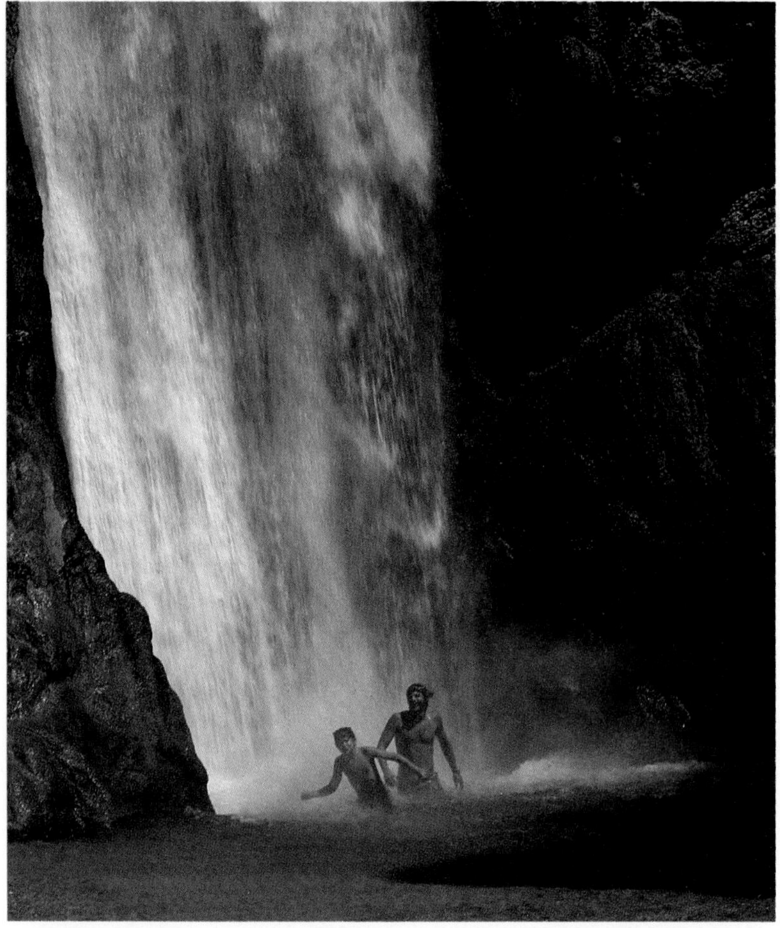

### EXERCISE 10 Writing Sentences with Touch Words

Try to imagine *yourself* in the picture above. Then write five sentences describing this scene. Be sure to use words that appeal to the sense of touch.

### EXERCISE 11 Describing with Touch Words

Think of a favorite place. It could be a garden, a park bench, your bedroom, or a friend's backyard. Then write five sentences describing that place. Instead of describing its appearance, however, use details that will appeal to your reader's sense of touch.

## Smell

A smell will sometimes bring back a flood of memories. The sense of smell is very powerful in recreating a scene in writing. The following words will appeal to your reader's sense of smell.

**Smell Words**

| | | | |
|---|---|---|---|
| musty | fishy | fragrant | piny |
| burnt | stale | pungent | smoky |
| oily | fresh | moldy | mildewed |
| stuffy | lemony | sour | floral |

### EXERCISE 12 Sharpening Your Sense of Smell

Number your paper 1 to 10. Then write ten words that describe smells you might experience in the scene pictured below.

### EXERCISE 13 Describing with Smell Words

Write five sentences describing the scene in the picture. Use at least two smell words from the list above.

## Taste

How many different things can you taste in the following paragraph?

TASTE WORDS

When they had eaten the soft maple candy until they could eat no more of it, then they helped themselves from the long table loaded with pumpkin pies and dried berry pies and cookies and cakes. There was salt-rising bread, too, and cold boiled pork, and pickles. Oo, how sour the pickles were! —LAURA INGALLS WILDER, *LITTLE HOUSE IN THE BIG WOODS*

Besides naming specific foods, you can also use any of the following taste words to whet your reader's appetite.

**Taste Words**

| | | | |
|---|---|---|---|
| spicy | bland | sharp | savory |
| bitter | caramel | smooth | lumpy |
| sweet | sugary | creamy | chewy |
| doughy | tender | gooey | moist |

### EXERCISE 14 *Describing with Taste Words*

Write five sentences describing your favorite food. Help your reader really taste it by using precise taste words.

### EXERCISE 15 *On Your Own*

Choose one of the following items. Then write 10 sentences to describe it, using words that appeal to all five senses.

1. apple picking
2. the school cafeteria
3. an amusement park
4. fishing
5. a city street

# Spotlight on Writing

**A** **Replacing General Words with Specific Words.** In the following fable, 20 general words and phrases have been underlined. Number your paper 1 to 20. Then write a specific noun, verb, adjective, or adverb to replace each general word or phrase.

The Grasshopper and the Ants

A grasshopper lived in a (1) place near an anthill. Every day the ants worked (2) without stopping. They built (3) things, and they collected (4) things. They were preparing for winter. The grasshopper, on the other hand, said, "I'd rather (5) have fun."

One day the ants (6) said, "What will you eat and where will you sleep when the (7) bad weather comes in (8) a few months and you have no (9) place to go?"

The grasshopper laughed and said, "I'd rather (10) have fun."

In (11) a few months, the wind brought snow and cold. The ants lived (12) well inside their (13) nice (14) place, but the grasshopper was outside, hungry and cold.

"Please let me share your (15) warm (16) place," (17) said the grasshopper.

"We (18) were busy while you played," said the ants. "Now you are hungry and cold, but we have food and a (19) nice (20) place. You must learn to plan ahead."

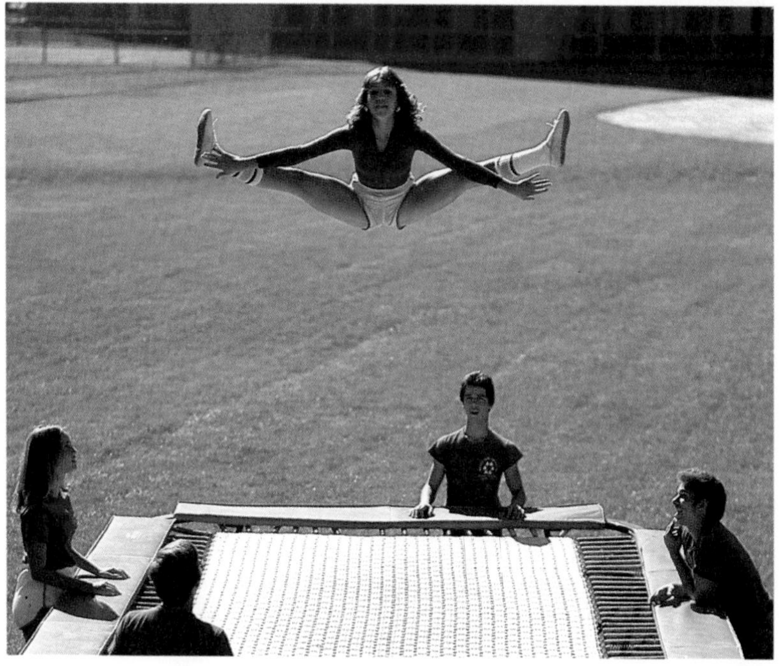

**B** **Writing Sentences with Specific Verbs.** Write five sentences about a gymnast on a trampoline. Use specific verbs. Then underline the verbs in your sentences.

**C** **Writing Sentences with Specific Adjectives.** Write five sentences that describe a prized possession. Use colorful adjectives to make your nouns more specific. Then underline your adjectives.

**D** **Listing Sensory Words.** Write the following five headings on your paper. Then add ten sensory words to each list.

| SIGHT | SOUND | TOUCH | SMELL | TASTE |
|---|---|---|---|---|
| pale | swish | spongy | musty | vanilla |
| hazy | crackle | slimy | rotten | salty |

**E** **Using Words That Appeal to the Senses.** Number your paper 1 to 20. Then complete each sentence with a word or phrase that appeals to the senses.

The Four Seasons

Every season has its sights, smells, tastes, and sounds. In the autumn I see (1) ______ and (2) ______. The sounds of autumn include (3) ______ and (4) ______. The taste that suggests autumn to me most is (5) ______.

The sights and sounds of winter are different from those of fall. In winter I see (6) ______, (7) ______, and (8) ______. The winter sounds of (9) ______ and (10) ______ are everywhere. The sky looks like (11) ______, and the air feels like (12) ______.

Spring is the time of bright colors. The flowers are (13) ______, (14) ______, and (15) ______. The blue sky looks like (16) ______. The breeze feels like (17) ______. The sounds of (18) ______ remind me that summer will soon be here.

Summer is a time capsule full of happy moments. It smells like (19) ______ and tastes like (20) ______. The days pass too quickly. The signs of autumn soon return.

**F** **Writing Sentences Using Sensory Words.** All of the following were actual last names of people, as recorded in the census of 1790. Choose one name that has special appeal. Think of a first name to go with it. Then write five sentences describing the person who had that name. Use your imagination and your five senses for ideas.

| | |
|---|---|
| Grog | Toogood |
| Pancake | Buttery |
| Gravy | Fryover |
| Pettyfool | Spitsnoggle |

**G** **Writing from Your Writer's Notebook.** Choose one of the people, scenes, or objects that you wrote about in your writer's notebook. Then describe your choice using specific words and words that appeal to the senses. (*See the model on page 266.*) Exchange papers with a partner. Use the Chapter Summary on page 281 to help you revise your partner's sentences.

# Chapter Summary
# Words

### Specific Words

1. Use specific nouns, verbs, adjectives, and adverbs to help your reader picture exactly what you mean. (*See pages 267–268.*)

### Words That Appeal to the Senses

2. Create vivid pictures by using words that appeal to your reader's senses. (*See pages 271–277.*)

# Sentences

Writing is a process of making choices. Choosing words carefully is one secret to good writing. Arranging those words into varied and concise sentences is another. This chapter will help you improve your sentences.

## Your Writer's Notebook

Memories of childhood are good sources for writing ideas. Read the following childhood memory by Lorraine Hansberry. Then every day for two weeks, write a childhood memory in your journal. Try to record sights, sounds, and other sense impressions that you remember from the events.

Memories

Evenings were spent mainly on the back porches where screen doors slammed in the darkness with those really very special summertime sounds. And, sometimes, when Chicago nights got too steamy, the whole family got into the car and went to the park to sleep out in the open on blankets. Those were, of course, the best times of all because the grownups were invariably reminded of having been children in the South and told the best stories then. It was also cool and sweet to be on the grass, and there was usually the scent of freshly cut lemons or melons in the air.

—LORRAINE HANSBERRY, *TO BE YOUNG, GIFTED, AND BLACK*

# Sentence Combining

One short sentence is clear and forceful. Too many in a row, however, are hard to read. Sentence combining is one way to vary the length of your sentences and add interest to your writing.

**19a** Combine short sentences into longer, more interesting ones.

## Combining Specific Details

Specific details help readers picture exactly what you are explaining or describing. Often the details in several separate sentences can be combined to form one longer sentence. Read the following short, choppy sentences.

CHOPPY SENTENCES
The kite bobbed.
The kite was **huge.**
It bobbed **gently.**
It moved **in the wind.**

These sentences can be combined by adding the descriptive words and phrase to the first sentence.

COMBINED SENTENCE The **huge** kite bobbed **gently in the wind.**

When you combine sentences to include two or more adjectives in a row, a comma is often needed to separate them. (*Review the rules for using commas on page 225.*) Study the following example.

CHOPPY SENTENCES The **long** string tugged against my hand. The string was **thin.**

COMBINED SENTENCE The **long, thin** string tugged against my hand.

### EXERCISE 1 Combining with Prepositional Phrases

Number your paper 1 to 10. Then combine each pair of short sentences into one longer one. Use the underlined prepositional phrases.

EXAMPLE A jumping bean is really a seed. It is the seed <u>of a Mexican shrub</u>.

ANSWER A jumping bean is really the seed of a Mexican shrub.

Jumping Beans

1. The Mexican jumping bean is famous. It is well-known <u>for its quick, jumping movements</u>.
2. These movements are caused by a caterpillar. The caterpillar is <u>inside the seed</u>.
3. Moths deposit their eggs. They leave them <u>in a shrub's flowers</u>.
4. After the eggs hatch, the caterpillars burrow. They dig <u>into the seeds</u> <u>of the shrub</u>.
5. The caterpillar eats the inside of the seed so it can build a web. It builds the web <u>along the inner wall</u>.
6. The seed jumps when the caterpillar grasps the web and snaps its body. It holds the web <u>with its feet</u>.
7. According to research the jumping helps scare away birds that try to eat the seeds. The research has been done <u>by scientists</u>.
8. The jumping bean is active until the caterpillar cuts a hole through the seed wall. It stays active <u>for several months</u>.
9. Later the caterpillar forms a cocoon and begins to change. It turns <u>into a moth</u>.
10. The adult moth finally leaves the seed. It goes <u>through the hole</u> <u>in the seed wall</u>.

### EXERCISE 2 Combining with Adjectives and Adverbs

Number your paper 1 to 10. Then combine each group of short sentences into one longer one.

Super Heroes

1. Popeye is a character in a comic strip. He is strong. He is also odd-looking.
2. He eats spinach. It is canned. He eats it often.
3. This vegetable always gives him strength. It gives him strength immediately. It gives him tremendous strength.
4. Olive Oyl is his girlfriend. She is tall. She is thin.
5. In 1980, this couple starred in a movie. They are an unusual couple. It was a popular movie.
6. Another superhero is a visitor from a planet. The visitor is powerful. He comes from a distant planet.
7. Superman arrived on Earth after the destruction of the planet Krypton. Superman arrived mysteriously. Krypton is an imaginary planet.
8. He pretends to be a newspaper reporter. The reporter is timid. The reporter is mild-mannered.
9. In this disguise Superman can investigate crimes. His disguise is clever. He investigates crimes openly.
10. At the last moment, the hero stops the criminals. They are dangerous. He stops them effortlessly.

## Combining Sentence Parts

Another way to combine sentences is to join equal sentence parts to form compounds. Use *and, but,* or *or* to form compound subjects and compound verbs. You may want to review compound subjects and compound verbs on pages 17, 18, 114, and 179.

COMPOUND SUBJECT
The **fish** was fresh.
The **vegetables** were fresh.
The **fish and vegetables** were fresh.

COMPOUND VERB
I **can bake** the chicken.
I **can barbecue** the chicken.
I **can bake or barbecue** the chicken.

If you combine three or more subjects and verbs, remember to use commas. (*See page 225.*)

COMPOUND VERB On our vacation in Wyoming, we **hiked.** We **swam.** We also **canoed.**
On our vacation in Wyoming, we **hiked, swam, and canoed.**

## EXERCISE 3 Combining Sentence Parts

Number your paper 1 to 10. Then combine each group of sentences, using a compound subject or a compound verb. Use the conjunction *and, but,* or *or.* Use commas where needed.

EXAMPLE Frank left his locker key at home yesterday. He forgot it again today.
ANSWER Frank left his locker key at home yesterday and forgot it again today.

1. Sheila can have my extra ticket to the concert. Gary can have it.
2. We'll broil the hamburgers in the oven. We'll barbecue them on the grill.
3. Luke finished his science project on time. He left it at home.
4. Phil and Sarah ran a road race on Saturday. They couldn't finish it.
5. Gerard's surprise party will be on Saturday. My first soccer game will be on Saturday too.
6. Kathy skates during the winter. She runs five miles a day in the spring.
7. Willie was named rookie of the year. He became an NBA All-Star.
8. Over the weekend I mowed the lawn. I weeded the garden. I also planted some vegetables.
9. The terrier growled at the visitors. He bared his teeth.
10. Penguins cannot fly. They can swim very well, even in ice-cold water.

## Combining Simple Sentences

You have learned that a *simple sentence* is a sentence that has one subject and one verb.

| | |
|---|---|
| SIMPLE SENTENCES | A **bolt** of lightning **flashed.**<br>The **tree exploded** into flames. |

If two simple sentences contain related ideas, they can be combined to form a compound sentence. The two simple sentences above may be combined by using the conjunction *and* preceded by a comma.

| | |
|---|---|
| COMPOUND SENTENCES | A bolt of lightning flashed**, and** the tree exploded into flames. |

In addition to *and,* the conjunctions *but* and *or* may be used to form compound sentences. When combining simple sentences, choose the conjunction that makes the relationship between the two ideas clear.

| | |
|---|---|
| SIMILAR IDEAS | Anthony was elected class president.<br>His twin brother was elected treasurer.<br><br>Anthony was elected class president**, and** his twin brother was elected treasurer. |
| CONTRASTING IDEAS | Dana hit two home runs.<br>Her team still lost the game.<br><br>Dana hit two home runs**, but** her team still lost the game. |
| CHOICE BETWEEN IDEAS | I can finish the posters after school today.<br>Nate can finish them on Saturday afternoon.<br><br>I can finish the posters after school today**, or** Nate can finish them on Saturday afternoon. |

You may want to review simple sentences and compound sentences on pages 111–116.

## EXERCISE 4 Combining with Compound Sentences

Number your paper 1 to 10. Then use the conjunctions in brackets to combine each pair of sentences into one compound sentence. Remember to use commas.

Space Camp

1. Many people dream about outer space. These dreams become a reality for students at Space Camp. [but]
2. Space Camp is located in Huntsville, Alabama, at the Space and Rocket Center. The staff runs programs there from March to September. [and]
3. Students can request information by letter. The staff at Space Camp will send them an application form and brochures. [and]
4. Many students from across the United States apply to Space Camp. Each year only 3,000 are accepted. [but]
5. Students in grades 5 through 7 are in the Level I program. Students in grades 8 through 10 are placed in Level II. [and]
6. The students take imitation flights. Information about previous NASA missions is provided. [and]
7. NASA donates equipment to the program. Real astronauts visit and talk with the campers. [and]
8. After Space Camp students may want a career as a scientist. Perhaps they would like to work for NASA as an engineer. [or]
9. Space Camp lasts for only one week. The campers will remember the experience for a lifetime. [but]
10. Three-day programs are now available for adults. Two-week advanced courses are being developed for college students. [and]

## EXERCISE 5 Combining with Compound Sentences

Number your paper 1 to 10. Then use *and, but,* or *or* to combine each pair of sentences into one compound sentence.

1. We could leave now. Dad could give us a ride later.
2. Kara wrote a poem for English class. It was printed in the school newspaper.
3. We could hear the music. No one could see the band.
4. My birthday is Thursday. My friends are taking me to an amusement park.
5. I can ride my bicycle to David's house. He could get a ride over here.
6. Jerry planted corn and squash in the garden. Leslie planted some tomatoes.
7. Terry's outfit looked great. His socks didn't match.
8. Jeff can mow the Pinellas' lawn on Monday. Fred could mow it on Tuesday.
9. Pat raced after the downtown bus. It left without her.
10. The game went into overtime. We won by one point.

## EXERCISE 6 On Your Own

Write ten simple sentences (one subject, one verb) about the picture below. Then combine those that are related.

## Writing Extra

Another way to avoid short, choppy sentences is to expand them by adding interesting details. Adding adjectives, adverbs, or prepositional phrases is one way to expand sentences and supply lively, specific information. Compare the sentences below.

CHOPPY SENTENCE I swam in a pool.

EXPANDED SENTENCE **Yesterday** (adv.) I swam in the **new** (adj.) pool **at the YMCA.** (prep. phrase)

Following is an advertisement for a new fruit drink. Expand the sentences by adding descriptive details and sensory words that would make a customer want to buy it.

Introducing SunSips! They're ___(adj.)___ fruit drinks with a ___(adj.)___ taste. SunSips are 100% natural and are ___(adv.)___ thirst-quenching. They're the perfect refreshment for ___(adj.),___ ___(adj.)___ summer days. SunSips come in four ___(adj.)___ flavors: ___(adj.)___ orange, ___(adj.)___ grape, ___(adj.)___ strawberry, and ___(adj.)___ pineapple. SunSips are available ___(adv.),___ so look for them ___(prep. phr.).___ The cans have a ___(adj.)___ and ___(adj.)___ label with a ___(adj.),___ ___(adj.)___ sun ___(prep. phr.).___ You can't miss 'em! Pick up some SunSips ___(adv.)___ and join the growing number of people who are ___(adv.)___ enjoying ___(adj.)___ sips of the sun!

Most companies use catchy sayings called slogans to help advertise a new product. For example, the company that makes SunSips might use the slogan *SunSips make anytime summertime!* Write a slogan for the new fruit drink SunSips that you described in the advertisement above. Then create an attractive poster displaying the slogan or draw a colorful design for the can.

# Sentence Variety

When all of the sentences in a passage sound the same, the writing seems dull and difficult to read. Study the example below.

| | |
|---|---|
| LACK OF SENTENCE VARIETY | Sailboats rocked in the cove. Bell buoys bobbed up and down. There were flags on the boats. They fluttered in the breeze. Children were on the beach. They called to the sailors. The wind carried their voices. |

Add variety to your writing by varying the length and structure of your sentences. Notice that the passage below is more interesting and easier to read.

| | |
|---|---|
| SENTENCE VARIETY | Sailboats rocked in the cove, and bell buoys bobbed up and down. The flags on the boats fluttered in the breeze. On the beach children called to the sailors, and the wind carried their voices. |

## Varying Sentence Beginnings

You have learned how to use sentence combining to vary the length and structure of your sentences. Another way to add variety to your sentences is to begin them in different ways. Instead of starting all of your sentences with a subject, start some of them with an adverb or a prepositional phrase.

| | |
|---|---|
| SUBJECT | The **raft** floated slowly down the river. |
| ADVERB | **Slowly** the raft floated down the river. |

| | |
|---|---|
| SUBJECT | A souvenir **banner** hung on the wall. |
| PHRASE | **On the wall** hung a souvenir banner. |

**19b** Vary the beginnings of your sentences.

## EXERCISE 7 *Varying Sentence Beginnings*

Number your paper 1 to 10. Then add variety to each sentence by moving either an adverb or a prepositional phrase to the beginning of the sentence. (*See page 67 for a list of prepositions.*)

Hot Spots

1. Volcanoes have frightened people for centuries.
2. Smoke and steam escape during active times.
3. The liquid rock and gases below the earth's surface gain strength.
4. Liquid rock suddenly pours out.
5. The liquid rock becomes lava after the eruption.
6. The clouds above the volcano turn red.
7. The lava slowly chokes the opening.
8. The fiery blasts gradually die down.
9. The liquid rock and gases again begin to build pressure.
10. The sleeping giant will repeat its cycle soon.

## EXERCISE 8 *Writing Sentence Beginnings*

Number your paper 1 to 10. Write a sentence beginning for each of the following. Use either an adverb or a prepositional phrase as shown in brackets. (*Review the rules for commas on page 228.*)

1. ______ the lights in the house went out. [adverb]
2. ______ the field was too muddy for the soccer game. [prepositional phrase]
3. ______ Jim slammed the door to his room. [adverb]
4. ______ Angela asked us to turn down the stereo. [adverb]
5. ______ there was bumper-to-bumper traffic. [prepositional phrase]
6. ______ the mosquitoes were really bothering us. [prepositional phrase]
7. ______ my sister tripped over my model of the solar system. [adverb]
8. ______ the ballerina twirled across the stage. [adverb]

9. ______ Sam burst into laughter for no reason. [prepositional phrase]
10. ______ the quarterback threw the ball to his favorite receiver. [adverb]

### EXERCISE 9 On Your Own

Write ten sentences about the picture below. Then revise your sentences by beginning each one with an adverb or a prepositional phrase.

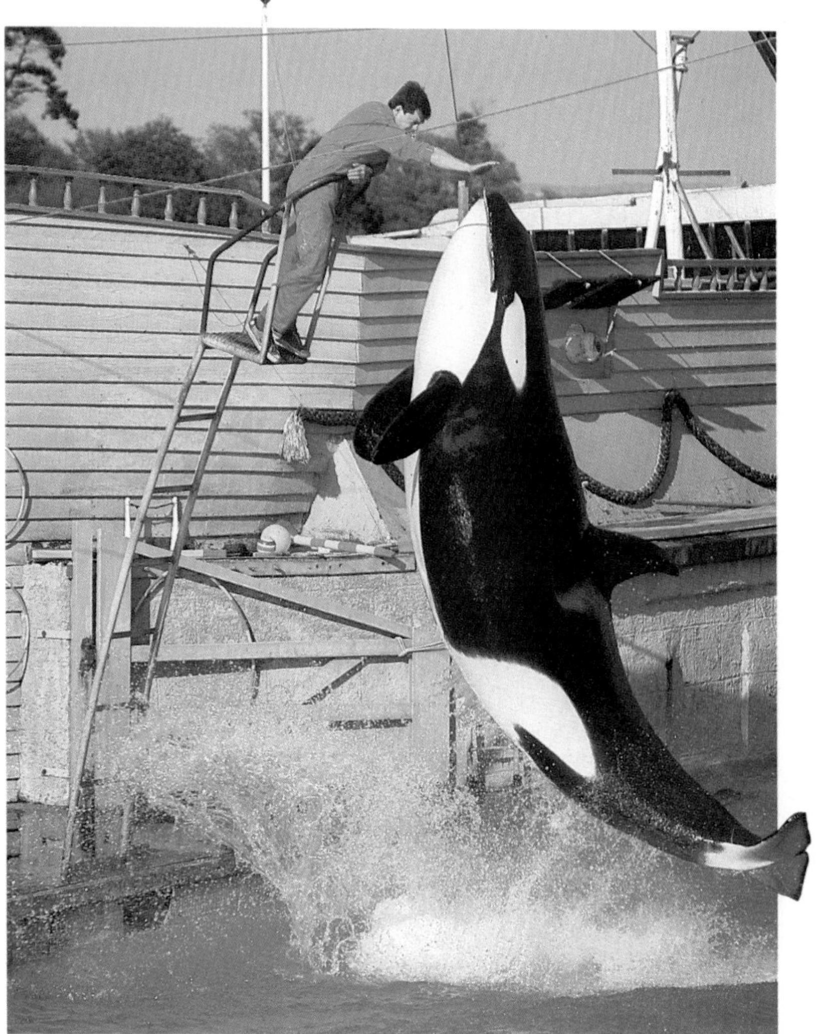

# Concise Sentences

Wrestlers always watch their weight and trim off extra pounds before a meet. When you write, trim off extra words that add no meaning to your sentences.

19c Express your meaning in as few words as possible.

## Rambling Sentences

Needlessly long sentences are as hard to read as short, choppy ones. In the following paragraph, too many ideas are strung together.

RAMBLING Our Frisbee landed on the Marshalls' roof, **and** Ted climbed the tree beside the house **and** jumped onto the roof. He picked up the Frisbee, **but** then he was afraid to climb back down, **and** I got a tall ladder from the house next-door, **but** Ted still wouldn't budge. I decided to ask Mr. Marshall to help us. He climbed the ladder, **and** soon Ted was safely on the ground, **and** we smiled with relief, **but** then we realized Ted had left the Frisbee on the roof!

A paragraph is easier to read if you break up rambling sentences by removing some of the conjunctions.

REVISED Our Frisbee landed on the Marshalls' roof. Ted climbed the tree beside the house and jumped onto the roof. He picked up the Frisbee, but then he was afraid to climb back down. I got a tall ladder from the house next-door, but Ted still wouldn't budge. I decided to ask Mr. Marshall to help us. He climbed the ladder, and soon Ted was safely on the ground. We smiled with relief. Then we realized Ted had left the Frisbee on the roof!

### EXERCISE 10 Revising Rambling Sentences

Revise the paragraph to eliminate rambling sentences.

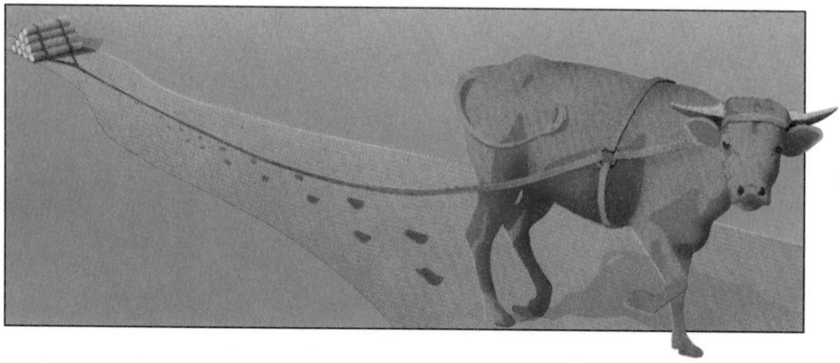

Babe Hauls the Lumber

Paul Bunyan had a mighty blue ox named Babe, and Babe often hauled logs to the lumber camp for Paul, but one rainy morning Babe arrived in camp without the logs. The rain had soaked into the leather straps of the harness, and the straps had been stretching for miles, and the lumber was somewhere back in the forest, but Paul wasn't worried. Soon the sun came out, and the leather straps started to shrink, and in no time at all, the shrinking straps pulled the load of logs right into camp.

## Repetition

When you write, make every word count. Avoid wordiness, or unnecessary repetition of words or ideas.

WORDY Because of the storm, the principal dismissed us at noon and said we could go home. [*Dismissed us* and *said we could go home* mean the same thing.]

CONCISE Because of the storm, the principal dismissed us at noon.

WORDY Tired, the weary travelers returned home. [*Tired* and *weary* mean the same thing.]

CONCISE The weary travelers returned home.

### EXERCISE 11 Eliminating Repetition

Number your paper 1 to 10. Then revise each sentence by taking out words that repeat ideas.

1. She whispered to me quietly.
2. Through the mist, we could see the sight of the runway.
3. Stay in the surrounding area near the school.
4. I looked around in the bakery called Abe's Bakery.
5. I have a tiny little scar on my arm.
6. The teacher has an extra book that he doesn't need.
7. Ron lost over 50 pounds in weight.
8. Some deadly diseases are fatal.
9. A great big bridge crosses into Canada.
10. They ate every single apple and didn't leave any.

## Empty Expressions

Empty expressions are another kind of wordiness. They add nothing to the meaning of a sentence, and they slow the reader down.

WORDY As a matter of fact, the bus left an hour ago.
CONCISE The bus left an hour ago.

WORDY Because of the fact that I jumped into the pile of leaves, I had to rake them again.
CONCISE Because I jumped into the pile of leaves, I had to rake them again.

Following is a list of common empty expressions.

**Empty Expressions**

| | |
|---|---|
| I think that | the thing that |
| on account of | what I mean is |
| the point is that | there is/there was |
| the reason is that | as a matter of fact |
| the reason being | because of the fact that |

## EXERCISE 12 Eliminating Empty Expressions

Number your paper 1 to 10. Then revise each sentence by taking out the empty expression.

1. There was a dirt road that led to our house in Montana.
2. As a matter of fact, I'd like to join the swim team.
3. I think that whales have become an endangered species.
4. The thing that everyone noticed was his height.
5. There were four long tables set up for the banquet.
6. It's a fact that bikers should wear safety helmets.
7. I stayed after school because of the fact that I had band practice.
8. There was a great wave that came crashing down on the boardwalk at Seaside Heights.
9. What I mean is I'd like to go to the party.
10. The reason that many people visit Yellowstone National Park is to see the geysers.

## EXERCISE 13 On Your Own

Write ten sentences about the picture below. Then revise your sentences to be sure you have omitted rambling sentences and needless words.

# Spotlight on Writing

**A** **Combining Sentences.** Combine each group of short sentences into one longer one by using *and, but,* or *or.* Ten of the following should be combined to form simple sentences with compound subjects or compound verbs. The other ten should be combined to form compound sentences. Use commas where needed.

1. We want to go to the concert. The tickets are all sold out. The concert is in the city.
2. Ali left my English book on the bus. I have a test on Chapter 12. The test is tomorrow.
3. Last night we went to the observatory. We did some stargazing. The observatory was at the university.
4. Our class went to the aquarium. It was our science class. We saw the dolphin show.
5. My brother plans to drive cross-country. He is going after graduation. He'll have to earn the money first.
6. Lisa will be elected class president. Perhaps Dennis will be elected. The election is this Tuesday.
7. We had three tickets for the game tonight. The game is against the Detroit Tigers. Jerry lost one of them.
8. Nancy invited us over for pizza. We had a great time. The pizza was homemade.
9. We can eat lunch now. We can go for a swim first. We can swim at Crystal Lake.
10. We visited the John F. Kennedy Museum. We learned so much about our 35th president. The museum is in Boston.
11. Mark's family is looking for a new apartment. They are looking near his father's office. No apartments are available until spring.
12. This month Mr. Garubo's class raised money. They raised money for Children's Hospital. Last month his class collected money for the Salvation Army.

13. Lou can ride to Point Pleasant, New Jersey, with us. We are leaving tonight. The Kozars can take him tomorrow morning.
14. Our team played very well in the basketball tournament. We lost in the semifinals. We lost to Springfield High School.
15. Business will be Joan's major at college. English may be Joan's major. Nursing may be her major. She is going to Elon College.
16. Last night there was a thunderstorm. All the lights in the house went out. The storm was terrible.
17. Over the weekend I rode my bicycle. I rode 17 miles. I finished my English homework. I cleaned my room.
18. Alex wanted to run the five-mile race. The race was on Saturday. His brother Keith forgot to send in the entry form.
19. Anita and Anthony took the subway. They took it to Madison Square Garden. They got off at the wrong station.
20. Bats were flying around the barn. They were flying during the night. In the morning they were gone.

**B** **Revising for Sentence Variety.** The following paragraph contains 20 short, choppy sentences. Revise the paragraph by combining sentences and varying sentence beginnings. Use the Chapter Summary on page 301 to help you. Then make a neat copy of the revised paragraph.

Water Colors

I went to the beach. The beach was near our cottage. I waded into the water. I waded eagerly. The water was warm. I pulled a pair of goggles over my eyes. The new goggles fit securely. I ducked my head into the ocean. I could see the rocks. The rocks were green and silver. There were fish under the water. They were everywhere. I could watch the fish in the water. The water was clear. Fish swam among the rocks. The fish were red, orange, brown, and yellow. Some fish were striped. Others had strange shapes. I had discovered a colorful new world. It was under the sea.

**C** **Writing Concise Sentences.** Revise the following sentences by correcting the weakness shown in brackets.

Men and Sharks

1. Jacques Cousteau has taken many underwater pictures with a camera. [repetition]
2. During one dive a shark came suddenly into view, but this wasn't as alarming to Cousteau as it would have been to most of us because he has had so much experience underwater, and he knows how to stay calm and think of the best plan of action. [rambling]
3. Suddenly more sharks appeared instantly. [repetition]
4. He did not want to swim to the surface, the reason being that the sharks might attack if he did. [empty expression]
5. If he had stayed below, however, it's a fact that he would have run out of air. [empty expression]
6. There was one shark that came so close that its nose touched his camera. [empty expression]
7. The sharks were finally scared away when he waved his arms and shouted loudly, and they were afraid to attack this dangerous human, so they swam off. [rambling]
8. Cautiously Cousteau swam to the surface, but his ship was far away in the distance. [repetition]
9. The thing was that the sharks might have attacked him at any moment. [empty expression]
10. Finally he was picked up by a small boat from his ship, which arrived and rescued him. [repetition]

**D** **Writing from Your Writer's Notebook.** Choose one childhood memory from your writer's notebook. Then describe it, using complete sentences. (*See the model on page 282.*) Exchange papers with a partner. Use the Chapter Summary on page 301 to revise your partner's sentences.

# Chapter Summary
# Sentences

## Sentence Combining

1. Combine short sentences into longer, more interesting ones. (*See pages 283–287.*)
2. Use the conjunctions *and, but,* or *or* to join sentence parts. (*See pages 285–286.*)
3. Use the conjunctions *and, but,* or *or* to join simple sentences. Use a comma before each conjunction. (*See page 287.*)

## Sentence Variety

4. Use sentence combining to vary the lengths of your sentences. (*See page 291.*)
5. Vary the beginnings of your sentences. (*See page 291.*)

## Concise Sentences

6. Break up long, rambling sentences into shorter ones. (*See page 294.*)
7. Avoid unnecessary repetition, or wordiness. (*See page 295.*)
8. Eliminate empty expressions. (*See page 296.*)

# 20 Paragraph Structure

A paragraph is a block of thought. Writers present their thoughts in blocks so that readers can easily follow them. The indented line at the beginning of a paragraph tells the reader that a new idea is being presented.

Paragraphs may be short or long, comic or serious. Their purpose may be to tell a story, explain, describe, or persuade. Despite their differences, however, all paragraphs have one important similarity. They all focus on a single main idea.

20a A **paragraph** is a group of sentences that present and develop one main idea.

Most paragraphs that stand alone have three kinds of sentences within them. The following chart shows the job each type of sentence performs in a paragraph.

20b

**Paragraph Structure**

| | |
|---|---|
| topic sentence | states the main idea |
| supporting sentences | expand on the main idea with specific facts, examples, details, or reasons |
| concluding sentence | provides a strong ending |

As you read the following paragraph, notice how the sentences work together to make the main idea clear.

The Chosen

TOPIC SENTENCE — My dog selected me, not the other way around.

SUPPORTING SENTENCES — As I looked carefully at the batch of Great Dane puppies, one puppy separated himself from the mob. He took several steps before his skin started moving along with the rest of him. He galloped over, sat down heavily on my feet, and looked me over carefully. He was obviously admiring me. His next step was to take my pant leg in his mouth and shake it, possibly to test the material. Then he gave several pleased body wiggles, attempted to climb on me, and washed my hand thoroughly with a salmon pink tongue.

CONCLUDING SENTENCE — I had been chosen.

—JACK ALAN, *"HOW TO RAISE A DOG"* (ADAPTED)

## Your Writer's Notebook

A journal is a good place to express your thoughts and feelings. For the next two weeks, write a personal message to yourself in your journal. The following questions may give you ideas.

1. What things about myself would I like to change?
2. What hopes and wishes do I have for my future?
3. What things are hard for me to understand?

# Topic Sentence

In most paragraphs the main idea is stated in one sentence. This sentence is the topic sentence. In many paragraphs the topic sentence is the first sentence. It may also, however, be the last sentence or any middle sentence. Wherever it falls, its purpose is the same.

20c A **topic sentence** states the main idea of the paragraph.

The topic sentence is more general than the other sentences. Notice how the main idea of the following paragraph is expressed in the general statement at the beginning.

Pele

TOPIC SENTENCE

The man who made soccer an important sport in the United States is a Brazilian named Pele.

SUPPORTING SENTENCES

Three times Pele was on the winning team that Brazil sent to the World Cup in Sweden. When he retired from soccer in 1974, the manager of the New York Cosmos persuaded Pele to come to New York. Pele signed a contract to play 100 games in 3 years. He made appearances on TV and was photographed with famous people. Whenever he played, the stadiums were filled.

CONCLUDING SENTENCE

Wherever he went in the United States, he won friends for himself and for soccer.

### Exercise 1 Identifying the Topic Sentence

Number your paper 1 to 5. Read each paragraph to determine the main idea. Then write each topic sentence.

1. A Real Character

Sherlock Holmes, the fictional British detective, is one of the best-known figures in English literature. Many people used to think he was real. The London post office handled much mail addressed to him at "221B Baker Street." There is even a Sherlock Holmes fan club with members all over the world. The members, who call themselves the Baker Street Irregulars, do research on Holmes's life. When Sherlock died in "The Final Problem," the outcry was so great that Holmes's creator had to bring the famous detective back to life. Even though he never answers his mail, Sherlock Holmes is still a much-loved character.

2. Edison's Contributions

The first phonograph was invented in 1877. It was developed by Thomas Edison. Two years later he also invented the first light bulb for home use. Edison improved or invented hundreds of useful machines. The stock ticker, the storage battery, the cement mixer, the Dictaphone, and the duplicating machine are only a few. Edison, a man of practical genius, left his mark on many items.

3. Mark Twain's Search

Mark Twain, like many writers, had a hard time deciding what he wanted to do. He started his career as a printer in the East and Midwest. Then he decided to seek his fortune in South America. No one knows how this venture would have turned out because he gave it up to become a steamboat pilot on the Mississippi River. Later he turned to soldiering.

Since he found his job not at all to his liking, he headed west. There he became a miner, and then finally a journalist. He won immediate popularity with his short, amusing sketch "The Celebrated Jumping Frog of Calaveras County." From that time on, he was a writer.

4. Small but Serene

The southern European country of San Marino, all 24 square miles of it, has a population of only 21,000. Its army has a grand total of 180 soldiers. The manufacture of postage stamps is considered one of its major industries. With the exception of its official name, The Most Serene Republic of San Marino, nearly everything about this little country is small.

5. Steps into Space

Like other frontiers the last frontier of space is being explored step by step. The space age began in 1957, when the first satellite was launched into space. Soon after, many satellites were launched to perform useful tasks. Today satellites forecast weather, take photographs of the earth, and transmit radio and TV signals. Lunar probes gather information about the moon. *Mariner* and *Viking* probes have orbited Mars and sent out landing craft to unlock some of the planet's secrets. We are even beginning to learn the uses of space shuttles and space stations. Though much remains to be explored, our first step into the space age opened a new frontier.

## EXERCISE 2 Choosing a Topic Sentence

Number your paper 1 to 4. Read each paragraph and the sentences that follow it. Then write the sentence that would be the best topic sentence for the paragraph.

1. Saving Energy

During the winter months, close outside doors quickly when you or your pets go in or out of the house. Cover unused electrical outlets with plastic plugs to keep cold air from seeping in. Place insulating patches behind the wall plates for all light switches, and seal window frames with caulking. Every little bit helps when you're trying to keep the warmth inside and the cold outside.

a. Following a few simple rules will keep your home safer and more comfortable.
b. A few changes around the house can keep you warmer and lower your heating bills.
c. The work of a skilled professional can pay for itself in lower heating costs.

2. Nature's Sonar

As it travels through the water, a dolphin makes very high-pitched sounds. When a sound hits an object, it sends back an echo. By listening carefully to the echoes, the dolphin avoids objects in its path. To a dolphin, *hearing* is believing!

a. A dolphin is an amusing mammal.
b. A dolphin can travel tremendous distances.
c. A dolphin uses its eyes *and* its ears to "see."

3. A Long-standing Record

Johnny Weissmuller held the record for national swimming titles until 1982. Weissmuller, who played Tarzan in the movies, held a total of 36 national swimming titles during the 1930s. Tracy Caulkins from the University of Florida broke his record. Her four victories in the 1982 short-course championships gave her a total of 39 titles and a new record to be challenged.

a. A half century went by before the record number of national swimming titles was broken.
b. Tracy Caulkins was an outstanding student at the University of Florida.
c. Johnny Weissmuller starred in many Tarzan movies.

4. The Dinosaur Dash

A flash flood in Texas washed away soil that had covered the tracks of a dinosaur. James Farlow, a scientist, studied the uncovered tracks and said the dinosaur had been running at a rate of nearly 25 miles per hour. Until then scientists had believed that the top speed of a dinosaur was only about 7 miles per hour. This dinosaur could have beaten the Olympic record for the 100-meter dash.

a. Scientists study fossil remains to learn facts about many prehistoric animals.
b. The fastest dinosaur on record left tracks in Texas.
c. Recently uncovered dinosaur tracks indicate that a relative of ancient dinosaurs is still living.

## EXERCISE 3 *On Your Own*

Write one other possible topic sentence for each of the paragraphs in Exercise 2.

# Supporting Sentences

Supporting sentences provide specific details that back up the main idea stated in the topic sentence. The supporting sentences form the *body* of the paragraph.

20d **Supporting sentences** explain or prove the topic sentence with specific details, facts, examples, or reasons.

Most topic sentences raise questions in readers' minds. Consider the following topic sentence.

| | |
|---|---|
| TOPIC SENTENCE | The number of grizzly bears has decreased so seriously that the bears may soon be wiped out. |

Readers might be prodded to ask, "How many grizzlies are left? What has caused the number of grizzlies to decline? Why is helping grizzly bears an urgent issue?" The job of the supporting sentences is to answer those questions with specific information.

In the following paragraph, the supporting sentences provide facts to explain the topic sentence. Notice that all the supporting sentences relate directly to the main idea.

Grizzly Bears in Danger

| | |
|---|---|
| TOPIC SENTENCE | The number of grizzly bears has decreased so seriously that the bears may soon be wiped out. |
| SUPPORTING SENTENCES | The number of grizzly bears in Yellowstone Park dropped 40 percent between the early 1970s and the early 1980s. In colonial times grizzlies west of the Mississippi numbered 50,000. Now only 1,000 remain. Land development has rapidly deprived these bears of places where they can live, roam, and find food. |
| CONCLUDING SENTENCE | Grizzly bears must be helped soon if they are to be saved. |

### EXERCISE 4 *Identifying Supporting Details*

Number your paper 1 to 4. Read the list of details under each topic sentence. Then write the letters of the three details that directly support each topic sentence.

1. The Cost of Owning a Horse

TOPIC SENTENCE Owning a horse is expensive.

DETAILS
a. Horses usually cost between $500 and $800.
b. Owners spend as much as six hours a day with their horses.
c. Riding equipment and supplies cost from $500 to $1,000 a year.
d. Horses are mature at the age of five.
e. Veterinary expenses usually range from $100 to $300 a year.

2. Cars Threaten Bicycle Riders

TOPIC SENTENCE The greatest dangers to bicycle riders are cars and their drivers.

DETAILS
a. Drivers may not see bicyclists.
b. Drivers may open doors and hit bicyclists.
c. Drivers must pass driving tests.
d. Parked cars may pull out suddenly.
e. Some of the cars on the road are new.

3. Huge Shipwreck

TOPIC SENTENCE The sinking of the *Titanic* was one of the biggest shipwrecks of all time.

DETAILS
a. *Titan* is one of the moons of Saturn.
b. The *Titanic* was the largest ship in the world.
c. Experts called it unsinkable.
d. Another big ship that sank was the *Eastland.*
e. On its first trip, the *Titanic* hit an iceberg and sank.

4. Finding the *Pinta*

TOPIC SENTENCE Scientists may have found the *Pinta,* one of the ships that crossed the ocean with Columbus.

DETAILS
a. The wreck of a Spanish ship from the fifteenth century has been found.
b. Treasure hunters look for sunken ships.
c. The *Pinta* sank on July 6, 1500.
d. The ship that was wrecked was the same kind of ship as the *Pinta.*
e. Columbus was born in 1451.

## EXERCISE 5 *Writing Supporting Sentences*

Write each topic sentence. Then write three sentences that could support each one.

1. It's easy to relax and be yourself around pets.
2. Anyone swimming in pools or at beaches should follow a few safety rules.
3. In most zoos people seem to gather around a few particularly interesting attractions.
4. Certain days in my childhood will always stand out in my memory.
5. Popular television shows often take place in the characters' workplace.

## EXERCISE 6 *On Your Own*

Study the picture on page 312. Then choose one of the following topic sentences and write it on your paper. Underneath it write at least five supporting sentences that could be used in a paragraph. Save your paper for Exercise 8.

1. The sights and sounds of autumn tell of colder days to come.
2. Autumn is my favorite season.
3. Like other living things, humans change their activities in autumn.
4. I'll never forget the autumn when I changed schools.

## Writing Extra!

_____ The ancients named the star pattern shown below Orion the Hunter. They saw the three stars in the middle as the belt of Orion. Pretend you are entering a contest to rename the constellation. What figure do you see in the star pattern currently called Orion? Write a paragraph explaining what you see. Complete the following sentence and use it as the topic sentence of your paragraph.

The constellation Orion should be renamed _____.

In your supporting sentences, refer to specific stars and explain how they help create the figure you see. End your paragraph with a sentence that ties the whole paragraph together.

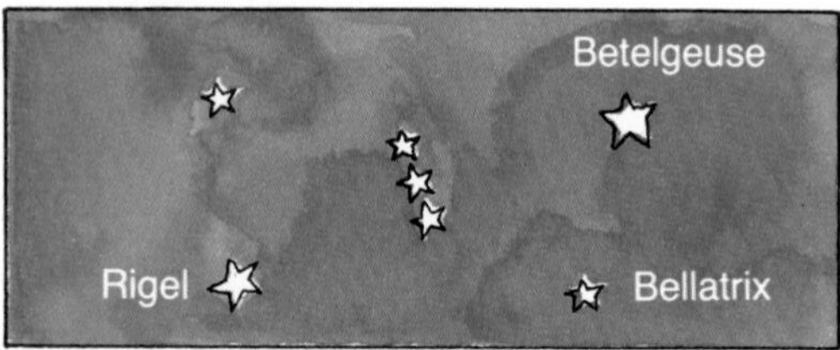

# Concluding Sentence

If someone hung up the telephone without saying good-bye, you would probably feel that you were cut off short. In the same way, a paragraph without a strong concluding sentence leaves the reader feeling cut off.

20e A **concluding sentence** adds a strong ending to a paragraph.

Following are several good ways to end a paragraph.

20f

**Concluding Sentences**

A concluding sentence may

1. summarize the paragraph.
2. state the point of the paragraph.
3. restate the main idea using different words.
4. add an insight about the main idea.

When you write, avoid using a concluding sentence that doesn't add some meaning to the paragraph. Notice how weak the concluding sentence is in the following paragraph. It simply repeats the words in the topic sentence.

Jupiter's Moon

A Chinese astronomer saw one of Jupiter's moons 2,000 years before the astronomer Galileo reported it. An ancient record dated from 364 B.C. says, "In the year of Chan Yan, Jupiter was very large and bright. A small reddish star was attached to it." This star was most likely the moon called Ganymede. As you can see, a Chinese astronomer reported one of Jupiter's moons before Galileo did.

WEAK CONCLUSION

The following concluding sentence is also weak. It adds new information that does not relate directly to the paragraph's main idea.

| | |
|---|---|
| WEAK CONCLUSION | Ganymede was known as the cupbearer in early cultures. |

Either of the following sentences would add a strong ending. Both add real meaning that relates directly to the main idea.

| | |
|---|---|
| STRONG CONCLUSIONS | After 2,400 years this Chinese astronomer is finally receiving credit for his observations. |
| | This observation is only one of many that shows the surprising skill of ancient stargazers. |

### EXERCISE 7 *Choosing Concluding Sentences*

Read each paragraph. Then write the better concluding sentence.

1. First at Indy

Janet Guthrie broke into oval-track racing, but not easily. She drove racing cars for 13 years. Then she finally had a chance to qualify for the Indianapolis Speedway Race, the Indy 500. Car trouble, however, kept her from qualifying. The next year she qualified and drove at Indy, even though some drivers were angry that a woman was allowed to enter. She finally had to drop out because of car trouble. The following year she didn't have a sponsor. With time running out, she appeared on television. That very day a sponsor provided a million dollars for her to buy a car, hire a crew, and enter the race. She finished in the top ten and won $25,000.

a. She was the first woman to finish the Indy 500, and she was a star.
b. Janet is also the first woman to race in the stock car superspeedway race in Charlotte, North Carolina.

2. One Kind of Robot

Some robots have been around for hundreds of years. One kind is called an android. An android is a machine that looks and acts like a person. Most androids have been used as toys. Chinese emperors had mechanical musicians that entertained them. Japanese homes had dolls that could carry a tray and serve tea. One family in Switzerland had a "boy" android that could sit at a writing desk and write messages. Today androids are being used as patients in the training of young doctors. Sim One is the name of one mechanical patient used by medical students at the University of Southern California.

a. A robot flagman has even been invented to direct traffic.
b. Modern androids, no longer playthings, can help people learn how to save lives.

## EXERCISE 8 On Your Own

Review your work from Exercise 6. Then write two possible concluding sentences that would add a strong ending to your paragraph about autumn.

# Spotlight on Writing

**A** **Writing a Topic Sentence.** Write a topic sentence for the following paragraph.

Indian Names

Some rivers have Indian names with colorful meanings. *Susquehanna,* for example, means "crooked water." *Ohio* means "beautiful river." *Merrimack* means "swift water." Some states have Indian names too. *Massachusetts* means "people of the great hills." *Michigan* means "great water," and *Kentucky* means "meadowland." Cities also have Indian names. *Chicago* means "onion place." *Tulsa* means "old city." Indian names all around us remind us of our land's first people.

**B** **Writing Supporting Sentences.** Write each topic sentence. Then write three sentences that could support each one.

1. The continental United States is bounded by two oceans and two countries.
2. Some of my most memorable school-day experiences were field trips.
3. The career that interests me the most is ______.
4. The pace around my house changes on the weekends.

**C** **Writing a Concluding Sentence.** Write a concluding sentence for the following paragraph.

Deadly Tomato?

In 1830 Colonel Robert Gibbon Johnson of Salem, New Jersey, proved that the tomato is safe to eat. Until then most Americans considered the tomato a pretty ornament but a deadly poison. The colonel's own doctor told him he would die instantly if he ate a tomato. Johnson, however, believed that the tomato was good for eating. To prove it, he called a public meeting. At noon he stood before his nervous neighbors and took one bite of a tomato, then another and another. Some people screamed. Some fainted. The colonel chewed on, proving that the tomato was harmless.

**D** **Revising a Paragraph.** The following paragraph has several weaknesses. Read the paragraph carefully and then complete the activities that follow it.

Artist of the Familiar

Three times Grant Wood went to Europe and tried to paint. Each time he came home to his native Iowa to paint what he knew about. Another American painter working at the same time was James Whistler. Wood's most famous painting is called *American Gothic.* In it a couple stands in front of a tall Iowa farmhouse. Every detail in the painting is perfect, even the braid and pin on the woman's dress. Wood encouraged other painters to paint scenes of home and the people they knew. Wood certainly was a great painter.

1. Which is the better topic sentence for this paragraph?
   a. Beauty is in the eye of the beholder.
   b. Grant Wood greatly influenced American art by painting the people and places of his Midwestern home.
2. Write the sentence in the paragraph body that does not relate directly to the main idea.
3. Which is the stronger concluding sentence?
   a. Grant Wood believed that art is found in the things the artist knows best.
   b. Grant Wood taught school in his hometown and later at the university.
4. Write the paragraph on your paper. Begin by writing the topic sentence you chose in number 1. Remember to indent. Then write the body of the paragraph. Leave out the sentence that does not relate to the main idea. Replace the concluding sentence with the one you chose in number 3.

# Chapter Summary
# Paragraph Structure

1. A paragraph is a group of related sentences that present and develop one main idea. (*See pages 302–303.*)
2. The topic sentence states the main idea of the paragraph. (*See page 304.*)
3. The supporting sentences back up the main idea with specific details and form the body of the paragraph. (*See page 309.*)
4. The concluding sentence adds a strong ending to the paragraph. (*See pages 313–314.*)

# Standardized Test

## COMPOSITION

**Directions:** Decide which of the rewritten sentences follows the directions. In the appropriate row on your answer sheet, fill in the circle containing the letter of your answer.

SAMPLE The art books were placed on the top shelf.
Begin with a prepositional phrase.
**A** The art books on the top shelf were placed.
**B** On the top shelf were placed the art books.
**C** Were placed on the top shelf the art books.

ANSWER Ⓐ Ⓑ Ⓒ

1. The band marched around the stadium.
   Begin with a prepositional phrase.
   **A** Marched the band around the stadium.
   **B** The band around the stadium marched.
   **C** Around the stadium marched the band.

2. Katya molded the piece of clay carefully.
   Begin with an adverb.
   **A** Carefully Katya molded the piece of clay.
   **B** The piece of clay Katya molded carefully.
   **C** Katya carefully molded the piece of clay.

3. The electricity went off without any warning.
   Begin with a prepositional phrase.
   **A** The electricity without any warning went off.
   **B** Went off the electricity without any warning.
   **C** Without any warning the electricity went off.

4. Luke moved along the ledge slowly.
   Begin with an adverb.
   **A** Along the ledge moved Luke slowly.
   **B** Slowly Luke moved along the ledge.
   **C** Luke moved slowly along the ledge.

5. The sky gradually turned red above the cliffs.
   Begin with a prepositional phrase.
   **A** Gradually the sky turned red above the cliffs.
   **B** Above the cliffs the sky gradually turned red.
   **C** The sky above the cliffs gradually turned red.

**Directions:** Decide which sentence best combines the underlined sentences. In the appropriate row on your answer sheet, fill in the circle containing the letter of your answer.

SAMPLE The Lees rented a house. It is on the beach. It is small.

**A** The Lees rented a house, and it is on the beach, and it is small.
**B** On the beach the Lees rented a house, and it is small.
**C** The Lees rented a small house on the beach.

ANSWER Ⓐ Ⓑ Ⓒ

6. The passengers moved. They went up the aisle.
   **A** The passengers moved up the aisle.
   **B** The passengers moved, but they went up the aisle.
   **C** Up the aisle the passengers moved and went.

7. Don makes a spaghetti dish. It is spicy. He makes it often.
   **A** Don makes a spaghetti dish, and it is spicy, and he makes it often.
   **B** Don makes a spicy spaghetti dish, and it is often.
   **C** Don often makes a spicy spaghetti dish.

8. The heavy rain made driving difficult. So did the strong wind.
   **A** The heavy rain made driving difficult, and the strong wind did.
   **B** The heavy rain made driving and the strong wind difficult.
   **C** The heavy rain and the strong wind made driving difficult.

9. The floors creak. They groan. The floors are in the old house.
   **A** The floors creak and groan, and they are in the old house.
   **B** The floors in the old house creak and groan.
   **C** The floors creak and groan and in the old house.

10. One engine was sputtering. The pilot landed the plane safely.
   **A** One engine was sputtering but landed the plane safely.
   **B** One engine was sputtering, but the pilot landed the plane safely.
   **C** One engine and the pilot landed the plane safely.

# UNIT 5

# Composition

## Part Two

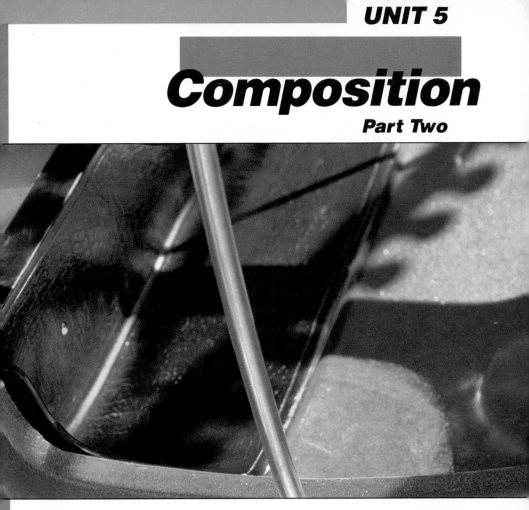

# 21

# The Writing Process

Good writing is easy to read. It may be so smooth and flowing that it seems as though the writer simply sat down and wrote it all out in complete form. Chances are, however, that the writing took time and effort. Good writing only *appears* effortless.

Think about your own writing. Do you spend time thinking of a good subject to write about? Do you plan, scratch out, erase, start over, and sometimes just give up for a while? If so, you are like most writers. Writing is a back-and-forth process of thinking, writing, rewriting, thinking again, and always improving.

Most writers tend to go through four main stages during the writing process. This chapter will take you through those stages.

## Your Writer's Notebook

How do you feel about writing? Explore your attitudes in your journal. Complete the following statement and write freely for about five minutes.

When I think about writing, I feel like . . .

# Prewriting

The first stage of the writing process is called prewriting. During this stage you let your mind bubble and brew with ideas. To focus your thoughts, you think about your *purpose* in writing. You also think about your *audience*—people who will read your work.

21a **Prewriting** is the first stage of the writing process. It includes all the planning steps that come before writing the first draft.

## Exploring Your Interests

Much of what you write about will come from your own experience. When you write about something you know or care about, your writing will be bouncy and fresh.

### EXERCISE 1 Getting to Know Yourself

Using pictures from magazines or other sources, make a poster about yourself. Include pictures that show your special interests and hobbies. Also include pictures or designs that reveal your personality traits.

## Freewriting

Writing freely without stopping can also help you think of ideas. Do not worry about spelling or grammar. If you hit a block, write, "I do not know what to say" until you think of another idea. Your ideas will soon flow again.

### EXERCISE 2 Freewriting

Write freely for three minutes. Answer the following question, adding everything that comes to mind.

How am I different from everyone else?

## Brainstorming

Once you have a general subject of interest, you can brainstorm for details to develop it. *Brainstorming* means writing down everything that comes to mind when you think of a subject. One idea will lead to another, and then to still another.

### EXERCISE 3 Brainstorming

Write down everything that comes to mind when you look at the picture below.

## Organizing Your Ideas

When you brainstorm or freewrite, you put things down in the order in which you think of them. Once you have your ideas, you need to organize them logically for your readers.

### EXERCISE 4 Using Logical Order

Write an explanation of how to build a campfire. Use the illustrations below as a guide. Be sure to list the steps in the proper order.

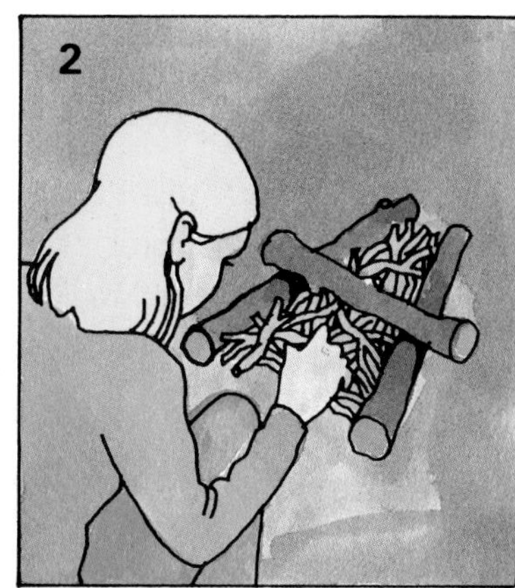

### EXERCISE 5 On Your Own

Brainstorm a list of first names you would like to have if you could name yourself. Write brief notes about why you like each one. Choose three that are your special favorites and rank them as your first choice, second choice, and third choice. Save your work for Exercise 7.

# Writing the First Draft

Once you have found and organized your ideas, you can write the first draft of your composition. During this stage of the writing process, try to put your ideas down on paper as quickly and smoothly as possible.

21b **Writing the first draft** is the second stage of the writing process. Use your prewriting notes to write complete, flowing sentences that would make sense to a reader.

## EXERCISE 6 Writing a First Draft from Notes

Use the prewriting notes that follow to write the first draft of a paragraph-long story. The first and last sentences are given.

**First sentence:** Sometimes your luck is so good you can hardly believe it.

NOTES
- on vacation in Florida five years ago
- family was in a store buying suntan lotion
- my brother and I saw beach ball we wanted
- asked our parents if we could have it
- they asked us how much it was and we told them five dollars
- they said no; five dollars is not easy to come by
- left the store, disappointed
- brother and I found five-dollar bill on sidewalk right outside store

**Last sentence:** My parents recognized a stroke of great luck and laughingly let us buy the ball.

## EXERCISE 7 On Your Own

Write the first draft of a paragraph about names you would choose if you could change your name. Use your work from Exercise 5. Save your work for Exercise 8.

# Revising

After writing your first draft, set it aside. When you read it later, you will be able to see what parts are strong and what parts need work. When you revise, concentrate on the following points.

21c

**Revision Checklist**

1. Does your paper state your main idea?
2. Do any of your sentences wander off the subject?
3. Are your ideas presented in a logical order?
4. Does your composition have a strong ending?
5. Is the purpose of your composition clear?
6. Is your composition suited for your audience?
7. Did you vary your sentences?
8. Did you use specific, lively words?

Study the revised paragraph below.

*My Exercise Program*

*I have a regular exercise schedule that helps me stay in shape. On Mondays, Wednesdays, and Fridays, I jog. Then I usually run for about 25 minutes. I can cover about 3 three miles during that time. I always cool down after running a by doing stretching exercises. I start by warming up with calm, easy stretching exercises. On Tuesdays and Thursdays, I lift weights. The days in between give my muscles a chance to recover from the strain. ~~I save weekends for relaxing.~~ This exercise program takes much time and effort. The good feeling it gives me, though, makes it worth the trouble.*

21d **Revising** is the third stage of the writing process. Revise your draft as often as needed until you are satisfied that it is the best you can make it.

## Sharing Your Work

If you work alone on revising, you may not catch all the parts that are unclear or confusing. For this reason, having someone else read your draft is a good idea. A classmate, friend, or family member can give you a reader's reaction to your work. You can use the comments of your reader to make improvements. When you are reading someone else's work, always remember to comment about both strong and weak points.

### Writing Extra

Do you have a favorite expression that you use often? Sometimes these overused words and phrases can cloud your meaning. As you revise your work, replace tired words with fresh, exact ones.

Practice improving your word choice by replacing the underlined word in each sentence with as many fresh, exact words as you can think of.

1. My Aunt Graciela has a <u>nice</u> personality.
2. I feel <u>bad</u> about what happened.
3. I saw a <u>fine</u> dog in the Gormans' front yard.
4. Soren's car looks <u>terrible</u>.
5. My dad is always a <u>good</u> host when company comes.

### EXERCISE 8 On Your Own

Exchange papers from Exercise 7 with a classmate and comment on both the strong and the weak parts in your partner's work. Then use the checklist on page 327 to revise your paragraph. Save your work for Exercise 9.

# Editing

Writing requires concentration. For this reason, most writers wait until the editing stage to correct errors in usage, capitalization, punctuation, and spelling.

21e **Editing** is the final stage of the writing process. Polish your work by correcting errors and making a neat copy.

Following is an example of a paragraph that has been edited before recopying.

*Cardinel Watch*

*Last summer a cardinel built a nest in a honeysuckle vine right outside our window. Soon we noticed three speckled eggs in the nest. It was visable only when the mother cardinel left the nest. During most of the day she sat pateintly on the eggs, warming them with her body. To help them hatch. Finally the time came. one morning we seen three little birds with their heads tilted straight back and their beaks wide open waiting for food. There mother returned right away and fed her tiny helpless babys. As they growed, our family spent more time watching out that window than watching television*

## Exercise 9 On Your Own

Edit your work from Exercise 8. Look carefully for errors in usage, capitalization, punctuation, and spelling.

# Spotlight on Writing

**A** **Prewriting: Exploring Your Interests.** Copy and complete the following personal profile. List as many items as you can think of. Keep the profile in your writing folder for future use in thinking of subjects.

---

MY FAVORITES
Subjects in school:
Books:
Characters in books:
Animals:
Songs:
Sports and games:

---

EXPERIENCES
Funniest:
Proudest:
Most embarrassing:
Scariest:

---

PEOPLE
Most unusual people I know:
Oldest people I know:
Famous people I admire:

---

HOBBIES AND INTERESTS
Lessons I've taken:
Lessons I'd like to take:
Talents:

---

OPINIONS
About school:
About teens:
About adults:
About society:

**B** **Prewriting: Brainstorming.** Brainstorm a list of details you could use to describe the clown in the picture below. Jot down everything you see in the picture.

**C Prewriting: Organizing Your Ideas.** Arrange your brainstorming notes about the clown in the order of head to toe.

**D Writing a First Draft.** Use your prewriting notes about the clown to write the first draft of a description. Keep the following purpose and audience in mind as you write.

PURPOSE To describe a clown
AUDIENCE A younger brother or sister

**E Revising by Sharing Your Work.** Exchange descriptions of the clown with a classmate. As you read your partner's description, pretend that you are a young child. Ask yourself the following questions.

- If I were a young child, would I be able to understand everything?
- Are any words too hard for a child?
- Would I be able to picture the clown from the description if I had not seen the picture?

Tell your partner what was good about the writing. Also tell what could be improved.

**F Revising Based on a Reader's Reaction.** If your partner suggested changes that you think would improve your description, revise your work to reflect them.

**G Using the Revision Checklist.** Use the Checklist on page 327 to revise your description.

**H Editing Your Work.** Check your description for errors in usage, capitalization, punctuation, and spelling.

**I Peer Editing.** Exchange descriptions with a classmate. See if you can find any errors your partner may have missed.

**J Making a Final Copy.** Copy your description neatly. Be sure to indent your paragraph and leave even margins.

# Steps for Writing
# The Writing Process

### Prewriting

1. Think of ideas to write about by
   - exploring your interests. (*See page 323.*)
   - freewriting. (*See page 323.*)
2. Brainstorm for details that you can use to develop your subject. (*See page 324.*)
3. Organize your ideas in a logical order. (*See page 324.*)

### Writing

4. Use your prewriting notes to write a first draft. Use complete, flowing sentences that would make sense to your readers. (*See page 326.*)

### Revising

5. Look at your first draft with a fresh eye. Also, share your writing with a reader.
6. Use your reader's comments and the Revision Checklist on page 327 to improve your first draft.
7. Revise your draft as often as needed to make your subject clear to your readers.

### Editing

8. Polish your work by correcting any errors in usage, capitalization, punctuation, and spelling.
9. Make a neat final copy.

# 22 Narrative Paragraphs

Before putting any words on paper, writers take time to think about their *audience*—the people who will read their work. They try to determine what their readers need to know in order to understand their message. Writers also take time to determine their *purpose* for writing. One common purpose for writing is to tell a story. Paragraphs that tell a story, either true or imaginary, are called narrative paragraphs.

22a A **narrative paragraph** tells a real or an imaginary story with a clear beginning, middle, and ending.

Following is an example of a narrative paragraph. It tells a true story about three abandoned bear cubs—Rusty, Dusty, and Scratch—and the man who adopted them.

Unspoken Friendship

**TOPIC SENTENCE:** STATES THE MAIN IDEA

**BODY:** TELLS EVENTS IN THE ORDER THAT THEY HAPPENED

**CONCLUDING SENTENCE:** SUMS UP THE STORY

On the ninth evening, I learned what little bears require beyond food, shelter, and protection. Supper was over, dishes were put away, and I was reading in front of a crackling fire. From his rug near the hearth, Rusty looked up at me. After a while he strolled cautiously to my chair and placed both front paws on my knee. I was surprised at the roughness of his tongue when he licked my fingers. I ran my hand across his neck and shoulders. It was the first time I had touched one of the cubs. As I scratched his puppylike head, the little fellow pulled himself up into my lap, where he turned around several times and then finally lay down. Soon Dusty ambled over to the chair, climbed my leg like a monkey, and staked her claim on one third of my lap. Before long Scratch joined his siblings, knocking my book to the floor. As we studied each other's expressions, I became certain of one thing. No matter what time might bring, all of our lives were from that moment on affected by the unspoken pact of friendship that night.

—ROBERT FRANKLIN LESLIE,
*THE BEARS AND I* (ADAPTED)

You have probably already written many narrative paragraphs in letters to friends and relatives and in school. This chapter will help you sharpen your ability to write narrative paragraphs. It will take you step by step through the writing process.

## Your Writer's Notebook

Use your journal to record what happens during each day for the next two weeks. Note anything of special interest that happens during the morning, afternoon, and evening.

# Prewriting

Instead of wondering what to write about, many writers simply begin to write. They jot down any ideas that come to mind. One idea leads to another, and then to still another. Before long they have found a good subject.

The stage in the writing process in which you select a subject and gather ideas is called *prewriting*. It includes all the planning steps that come before writing the first draft. The first goal of prewriting is to start your ideas flowing. The following exercise will help you recall some events that you could tell about in a narrative paragraph.

## EXERCISE 1 Thinking of Subjects for Narrative Paragraphs

Read each question. Think about your past experiences. Then write one or two sentences to answer each question.

1. Which birthday holds special memories for you? Why?
2. Which school vacation do you remember best? What happened?
3. Have you ever been caught in a storm? What happened?
4. What holidays stand out in your memory? Why?
5. How did you meet your best friend?
6. What was the funniest experience of your life?
7. Have you ever been extremely nervous before an event? Describe the event.

8. Have you ever been in danger or had a mishap? What happened?
9. What were some important experiences in your life (first time on a bicycle, first time at a computer, first day at a new school, and so on)? What happened?
10. What experiences have taught you some kind of lesson?

## Choosing a Subject

The next step in writing a narrative paragraph is to choose one subject from your list. The following guidelines will help you make your choice.

22b

**Choosing a Subject**

1. Choose an event that interests you.
2. Choose an event that will interest your audience.
3. Choose an event that has a high point of action and an interesting outcome.

Your own judgment will help you follow the first guideline. To follow the second guideline, think about who will be reading your paragraph. Will your readers find the event interesting? To follow the third guideline, consider whether the event is unusual and dramatic, or whether it is merely an everyday event. Events that are out of the ordinary usually make the best stories.

### EXERCISE 2 Choosing a Subject

a. Number your paper 1 to 3. After each number write a possible subject for a narrative paragraph. You may use ideas from Exercise 1.
b. Review the guidelines above for choosing a subject. Then circle the subject that comes closest to following all three guidelines.

## Limiting a Subject

Occasionally a subject is broad enough to fill a whole book. A slightly more specific subject may take up a whole chapter. A subject for a single-paragraph story, however, must be very specific. Read the following examples.

| BOOK LENGTH | CHAPTER LENGTH | ONE PARAGRAPH |
|---|---|---|
| my travels | one summer vacation | my first case of poison ivy |
| holidays | Thanksgiving | our dog eating the turkey |
| memories | moving to a new city | the day I forgot where I lived |

22c Limit your subject so that it can be adequately covered in one paragraph.

### EXERCISE 3 *Identifying Limited Subjects*

Number your paper 1 to 10. Then decide whether each subject is limited enough for a one-paragraph narrative. Indicate your answer by writing either *limited* or *too broad* after the proper number.

EXAMPLE my childhood
ANSWER too broad

1. my fishing vacation
2. catching the prize trout at the fishing contest
3. when I thought I heard a burglar
4. sixth grade
5. my week in Washington
6. when I lost my cat on moving day
7. when I met a TV star
8. helping out at home
9. giving my sister an unusual present
10. my paper route

## EXERCISE 4 Limiting Subjects That Are Too Broad

The following subjects are too broad for a one-paragraph narrative. Select five subjects. For each one write two events limited enough to be covered in one paragraph.

EXAMPLE playing baseball

POSSIBLE ANSWERS my first home run
quick thinking on the play

1. entering a new school
2. trying something new
3. meeting new friends
4. belonging to a club
5. performing for an audience
6. seeing old friends
7. getting lost
8. making home movies
9. entering a contest
10. receiving an award

## Listing Details

Once you have chosen and limited a subject, you are ready to list all the events and details that make up the story. Brainstorming is one way to help you remember all the details. Brainstorming means writing down everything that comes to mind when you think about your subject. To prod your memory, ask yourself the following questions about your subject.

**Brainstorming Questions**

- Who besides you is involved in the story?
- Where did the event take place?
- When did the event take place?
- How did you feel?
- What happened to start things rolling?
- What happened next?
- What is the high point of the story?
- What is the outcome?
- What did you learn from the experience?

22d **Brainstorm** a list of details to use in your story.

If you had decided to write about the time you took pictures of a dog and her newborn pups, your notes might look like the following.

| | |
|---|---|
| Who is in the story? | Rags, her puppies, and I |
| Where did it happen? | my neighbor's basement |
| When did it happen? | last week |
| How did you feel? | eager to get good pictures |
| What happened first? | I went next door to take pictures of Rags and her puppies. |
| What happened next? | I walked close to get a good shot. |
| What is the high point? | Rags charged at me. |
| What is the outcome? | I dropped my camera and left. |
| What did you learn? | Rags was protective of her pups. |

### EXERCISE 5 *Listing Details for a Narrative Paragraph*

Write one of the following subjects on your paper. Then under it brainstorm a list of details. Use the questions on page 339 to help you think of ideas.

1. the day I lost something valuable
2. my first dance
3. the time I met a friend through a computer
4. the day I made a promise I could not keep
5. how I got my first pet

Newspaper reporters ask themselves five questions when they are gathering information for a story. These are *Who? What? Where? When?* and *Why?* These questions can help you think of supporting details for a story. They can also help you write a five-line poem.

Read the following examples of five-line poems. Then write two poems of your own. Start with *Who?* End with *Why?* Remember to give each poem a title.

Remembering

WHO? A white-haired man
WHAT? Stops to watch the kids shoot baskets
WHERE? At the corner playground
WHEN? When school is out for the day.
WHY? Memories now fill his life.

Hurry Up

WHO? A freckle-faced ten-year-old
WHAT? Races into the waves
WHERE? At the shore
WHEN? Every August day.
WHY? September is coming soon.

## Arranging Details in Chronological Order

To help readers follow your story easily, you should present the events in the order in which they happened. This type of order is called chronological order, or time order.

Read the following narrative paragraph. Notice that several things happen in this story. The writer tells about each one in the order that it happened.

Applause from the Cabbage Patch

BEFORE RECITAL

On the day of my first piano recital, I became more and more nervous. To help me calm down, my piano teacher told me to place several heads of cabbage in the room where I practiced. If I could play for them, he said, I could play for a real audience. I was so eager to get over my nerves that I was willing to try anything. For the next few hours, I played to an audience of

BEGINNING OF RECITAL

cabbage heads. When the time of the recital finally arrived, I was still a wreck. I waited, sick with fear, for my turn. My hands felt like

DURING RECITAL

ice. When I finally walked across the stage, I looked out into the dark audience. I could not

HIGH POINT

see anyone! All those people out there could just as easily have been cabbage heads! As I sat down to play, my hands relaxed. Before I knew

OUTCOME

it, I had played all my pieces without a mistake. For the first time, the cabbage heads applauded!

**22e** Check your list of details to make sure that the events are in **chronological order.**

### EXERCISE 6 *Arranging Details in Chronological Order*

Number your paper 1 to 3. Write the subject. Then write the details under each subject in chronological order.

1. SUBJECT the surprise party for me last year
   DETAILS
   - turning on the lights
   - noticing that lights in house were out
   - everyone shouting, "Surprise!"
   - opening door carefully
2. SUBJECT the time I won the race
   DETAILS
   - crossing the finish line
   - gasping for breath toward the end
   - lying exhausted on the grass
   - crouching at the chalk line

3. SUBJECT losing a homework assignment on the computer

DETAILS
- rewriting the whole report the night before it was due
- working for two weeks writing a report on the computer
- being careful after each day's work to remove the disk and store it carefully
- chasing my dog and seeing his foot catch on the cord and unplug the computer
- playing with my dog to celebrate having finished the report
- turning the computer back on and finding the whole report had been erased
- watching the computer screen go black

### EXERCISE 7 On Your Own

Review what you have learned about prewriting on pages 336–342. Then use the picture below to help you choose and limit a subject for a narrative paragraph. Brainstorm a list of details and arrange them in chronological order. Save your work for Exercise 11.

# Writing

With your prewriting notes handy, you are ready to begin the first draft of your paragraph. As you write, keep your readers in mind.

## Writing a Topic Sentence

In Chapter 20, you learned that a topic sentence states the main idea of a paragraph. (*See page 304.*) In a narrative paragraph, the main idea is the event you plan to write about. Follow the steps outlined below for writing a topic sentence.

22f

**Steps for Writing a Topic Sentence**

1. Look over your prewriting notes.
2. Try to express your main idea in one sentence.
3. Rewrite that sentence until it covers all the supporting details you listed in your notes.

If you were writing a paragraph about the time you tried to take pictures of Rags and her newborn pups (*see page 340*), you might write the following topic sentence.

TOPIC SENTENCE Rags was a protective mother.

If you were to look over your prewriting notes again, however, you would notice that this sentence does not clearly set the stage for the story to follow. Your readers would not know who Rags is, and they would not know what to expect in the rest of the paragraph. The following topic sentence does a better job.

TOPIC SENTENCE Photographing pets can sometimes be a dangerous and expensive hobby.

This topic sentence is strong because it focuses attention on the subject and prepares the reader for what is to follow. Avoid openings such as "This paragraph will be about . . ." or "In this paragraph I will . . ." These phrases focus attention on the writer rather than on the story.

### EXERCISE 8 *Writing Topic Sentences*

Read the five lists of details for narrative paragraphs. Then, after the proper number on your paper, write a topic sentence for each list. Save your work for Exercise 9.

1. (your topic sentence)
   - rained all day
   - lights went out
   - went to basement for candles
   - basement flooded
   - spent all evening drying things out

2. (your topic sentence)
   - left at 4:00 A.M. on a fishing trip
   - drove for two hours
   - rented a boat
   - rowed out into lake
   - discovered I'd left fishing gear home

3. (your topic sentence)
   - decided to paint a picture of my dog
   - bought paints and brushes
   - paint spilled on the rug
   - everyone thought the dog looked like a seal
   - dog ran off with the picture

4. (your topic sentence)
   - decided to do my homework early
   - decided to make dinner when my mother was late
   - neighbors were locked out, and I helped them by crawling through a window
   - grandparents arrived a day early
   - began homework at 11:00 P.M.

5. (your topic sentence)
   - wanted to try my new computer game
   - waited for my birthday party to be over
   - had to eat dinner first
   - helped with the dishes
   - electricity went off

## Writing the Paragraph Body

The *supporting details* that make up the body of a narrative paragraph are the specific events in the story. Presenting these ideas in chronological order will help your readers follow the events. To make sure that the order is clear, use transitional words and phrases.

22g **Transitions** are words and phrases that show how ideas are related. In chronological order transitions point out the passing of time.

In the following first draft about Rags and her puppies, you can see how the prewriting notes have been made into sentences. The transitions are printed in heavy type.

TOPIC SENTENCE

EVENTS IN THE ORDER THAT THEY HAPPENED

Photographing pets can sometimes be a dangerous and expensive hobby. **One day last week** I went next door to take some pictures of Rags and her newborn puppies. **As** I walked close to her and her pups, she charged at me, barking in a wild, high-pitched voice. **Before** I knew it, I was racing to the door, dropping my camera on the way. **Only later** did I learn that all animals are very protective of their young.

Following is a list of transitions often used with chronological order.

**Transitions for Chronological Order**

| | | |
|---|---|---|
| before | finally | meanwhile |
| after | last | after a while |
| first | at last | later that day |
| next | soon | the next day |
| then | when | on Saturday |

The following steps will help you change your prewriting notes into the body of a paragraph.

22h

**Steps for Writing the Body**

1. Review your topic sentence and prewriting notes.
2. Write a complete sentence for each supporting detail.
3. Combine sentences that seem to go together.
4. Add transitions to show the passing of time.

### EXERCISE 9 *Writing the Body of a Narrative Paragraph*

Choose one of the events from Exercise 8. First copy your topic sentence. Then follow the steps above to write the body of the paragraph. Be sure to add transitions where necessary. Save your work for Exercise 10.

## Writing a Concluding Sentence

The last sentence in a narrative paragraph is as important as the punch line in a joke. A strong concluding sentence brings the event to a close and leaves the reader satisfied. (*See pages 313–314.*) Remember that a concluding sentence can serve a variety of purposes.

22i

**Writing a Concluding Sentence**

The concluding sentence may
1. restate the topic sentence in fresh words.
2. summarize the paragraph.
3. pull the supporting sentences together.
4. state an insight or lesson learned from the experience.

Any of the following would be a strong concluding sentence for the paragraph about Rags and her pups.

CONCLUDING SENTENCES

Although my hobby has its risks, the chance to snap good pictures is worth it. [restates an idea from the topic sentence]

Trying to photograph Rags and her pups was an experience I will never forget. [summarizes the paragraph]

Rags may have thought her pups were in danger, but I *knew* I was! [pulls the supporting sentences together]

Next time I will play it safe and wait till the pups are older. [states a lesson learned from the experience]

### ***EXERCISE 10 Writing Concluding Sentences***

Review your work from Exercise 9. Then write two possible concluding sentences for your paragraph.

### ***EXERCISE 11 On Your Own***

Using your work from Exercise 7, write the first draft of your narrative paragraph. Include a topic sentence, a body of supporting sentences, and a concluding sentence. Save your work for Exercise 14.

# Revising

In the revising stage of the writing process, try to read your work as if you were seeing it for the first time. In this way you can spot and correct any confusing or unclear passages.

## Checking for Unity

A paragraph in which all the sentences support the topic sentence is said to have unity. Sentences that wander off the subject make your ideas hard to follow.

In the following paragraph, the crossed-out sentences stray from the story. Read the paragraph twice—once with the sentences that stray and once without them. Notice that the paragraph is clearer and easier to read without the sentences that wander from the main idea.

My Comic Book Collection

Because I am a pack rat, I may be a rich person someday. Ten years ago my aunt gave me a subscription to *Batman*. ~~I once saw the Batmobile in a car show downtown.~~ Since I never throw anything away, I kept all the copies of the old comic books in a carton in my closet. ~~I keep my baseball equipment there too.~~ Just recently I learned that those old comic books are worth money. If I keep them another ten years, they will be worth even more. Maybe I will sell them then and retire before I even start working.

22j Check your paragraph for **unity** by eliminating any sentences that stray from the point.

## Checking for Coherence

A paragraph with coherence is well organized and tightly knit. The ideas are presented in a logical order with clear transitions. The writer of the following paragraph has used chronological order. Notice how the writer has improved the coherence of the paragraph by revising the order and adding a transition.

*An Unexpected Guest*

*My family is large, and we're all used to having neighborhood friends drop in. One summer night, however, a neighborly visitor surprised us all. The next morning even our visitor had a good laugh. We were all sitting in the living room, watching a late movie. During an especially scary part of the movie, one of our neighbors, nine-year-old Timmy, surprised us all by walking right into our house without knocking. Dressed in his pajamas and barefoot, Timmy headed straight for the kitchen without saying a word. He poured himself a glass of milk. Then He left as quickly and silently as he had come. My dad rushed after him to make sure he arrived home safely. Timmy had been sound asleep during the whole visit!*

22k Revise your paragraph for **coherence** by checking the logical order of ideas and adding transitions where needed.

## EXERCISE 12 *Checking for Unity*

Two sentences in the following narrative paragraph wander off the subject. Write the sentences that break the unity of the paragraph.

Skiing Ups and Downs

All skis should read: "Skiing may be hazardous to your health." I should know, because I tried skiing for the first time yesterday. Many of my friends know how to ski. I fell getting onto the chair lift, and I fell getting off the chair lift. Then as soon as I started skiing, my skis crossed. I fell forward, lost my skis, and rolled halfway down the hill. We were skiing in the Green Mountains. Then I had to climb back up again to pick up my skis. After falling several more times and running into another skier, I finally reached the bottom of the hill.

## EXERCISE 13 *Adding Transitions*

The following paragraph lacks transitions. Write the paragraph, adding a transition each time you see a blank space. Choose the transitions from the list below.

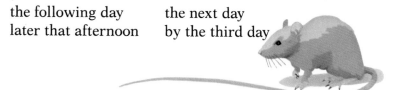

| | |
|---|---|
| the following day | the next day |
| later that afternoon | by the third day |

An Unusual Passenger

When the wood for our fireplace was delivered one afternoon, I stacked it in the garage. ______ Dad noticed the wood and asked me to move it. "If you leave it in the garage," he said, "we will have mice in the garage and in the house too. Stack it between the two birch trees and cover it with plastic." ______ I was too busy with homework to move the wood. ______ our class had a car wash, and the wood still remained in the garage. ______, Dad had waited long enough. "Move that wood!" he commanded. "This morning a mouse tried to catch a ride with me on the hood of the car."

## Using a Revision Checklist

The following checklist will help you revise your paragraph effectively. Work on your paragraph until you can answer yes to all of the following questions.

22l

**Checklist for Revising Narrative Paragraphs**

Checking Your Paragraph

1. Does your topic sentence focus attention on the subject and prepare the reader for what is to follow? (*See pages 344–345.*)
2. Are your supporting details in chronological order? (*See pages 341–342 and 347–348.*)
3. Did you use transitions to give your paragraph coherence? (*See pages 347–348 and 351.*)
4. Does your paragraph have unity? (*See page 350.*)
5. Does your concluding sentence bring the event to a close? (*See pages 348–349.*)

Checking Your Sentences

6. Did you combine related sentences to avoid too many short, choppy sentences in a row? (*See pages 283–287.*)
7. Did you vary the beginnings of your sentences? (*See page 291.*)
8. Did you avoid rambling sentences? (*See page 294.*)
9. Did you avoid repetition? (*See page 295.*)
10. Did you avoid empty expressions and unnecessary wordiness? (*See page 296.*)

Checking Your Words

11. Did you use specific, lively words? (*See pages 267–268.*)
12. Did you use words that appeal to the senses? (*See pages 271–277.*)

### EXERCISE 14 On Your Own

Revise your work from Exercise 11, using the Revision Checklist above. Save your work for Exercise 17.

# Editing

The final stage in the writing process is called *editing.* During this stage you polish your work so that others can read it without being distracted by errors. The following checklist is a good editing guide.

22m

**Editing Checklist**

1. Are your sentences free of errors in grammar and usage?
2. Did you spell each word correctly?
3. Did you use capital letters where needed?
4. Did you punctuate your sentences correctly?
5. Did you indent your paragraph?
6. Are your margins even?
7. Is your handwriting clear and neat?

When you edit, you may want to use proofreading symbols as a shorthand way of showing corrections. Below are some commonly used proofreading symbols.

22n

**Proofreading Symbols**

| Symbol | Meaning | Example |
|---|---|---|
| ∧ | insert | I waited ∧ for you. (an hour) |
| | delete | Tomorrow is my ~~very own~~ birthday. |
| . . . | let it stand | I recognized Sue's lilting voice. |
| # | add space | We made our own icecream. |
| ⁀ | close up | See you to night! |
| ∽ | transpose | The clwon had a red big nose. |
| ≡ | capital letter | I was born in chicago. |
| / | lowercase letter | Chicago is West of Detroit. |

## EXERCISE 15 Using Proofreading Symbols for Editing

Number your paper 1 to 10. Next to the proper number, write the corrected form of the word.

A Lucky Break

I had been staying with my aunt and (1) unlce in California for nearly two months. (2) Id had fun; but at the end of my visit, I (3) could wait to get home. When I arrived at the (4) Air port, though, I was told that too many passengers had been booked and that I might not have (5) aseat. I was (6) extremely upset, and I told the ticket agent about my problem. To my (7) delihgt she found a solution. Although the (8) couch section was full, there was a seat left in (9) First class. I took it gladly and smiled all the way home to (10) philadelphia.

## EXERCISE 16 Editing a Narrative Paragraph

Write the paragraph below, using the Editing Checklist on page 354 to help you correct the errors.

Mountain Lure

Ill never forget the time I allmost became stranded in the mountins. On a beautiful Autumn day last year I decided to veiw the foliage from the mountains near our town. I rushed to catch the bus. In the mountains, the seenry was spectacular. Suddenly I realized it was geting dark i raced to the bus stop but I had missed the last bus back to town? I stood their and wondered how id get home that night? Just than a bus pulled up. The Driver explaned that an extra bus had been skeduled for folaige viewers. As I sank into my seat, I realized just how close Id come to bunking with the bears.

## EXERCISE 17 On Your Own

Edit your work from Exercise 14, using the Editing Checklist on page 354.

# Spotlight on Writing

**A** **Writing a Narrative Paragraph.** The following notes are out of order. First arrange the notes in chronological order. Then use them to write a narrative paragraph that suits the following purpose and audience.

PURPOSE To tell about giving your first oral report
AUDIENCE Someone nervous about giving an oral report

- my mouth's getting very dry as I waited for my turn
- facing the class, my mind a blank
- planning and writing my report
- classmates interested and asking questions afterward
- knocking my books off my desk as I got up to speak
- giving my report
- trying to practice in front of my younger brother
- teacher congratulating me on a good job

**B** **Writing a Narrative Paragraph.** Pretend you are a person in the picture on page 357. Then write a narrative paragraph that suits the following purpose and audience. Use the Steps for Writing a Narrative Paragraph on page 359 as a guide. The following questions may help you brainstorm for ideas.

PURPOSE To entertain by telling a story with a high point of action and an interesting outcome
AUDIENCE Your classmates

- Who besides you is involved in the story?
- Where did the event take place?
- When did the event take place?
- How did you feel?
- What happened to start things rolling?
- What happened next?
- What is the high point of the story?
- What is the outcome?

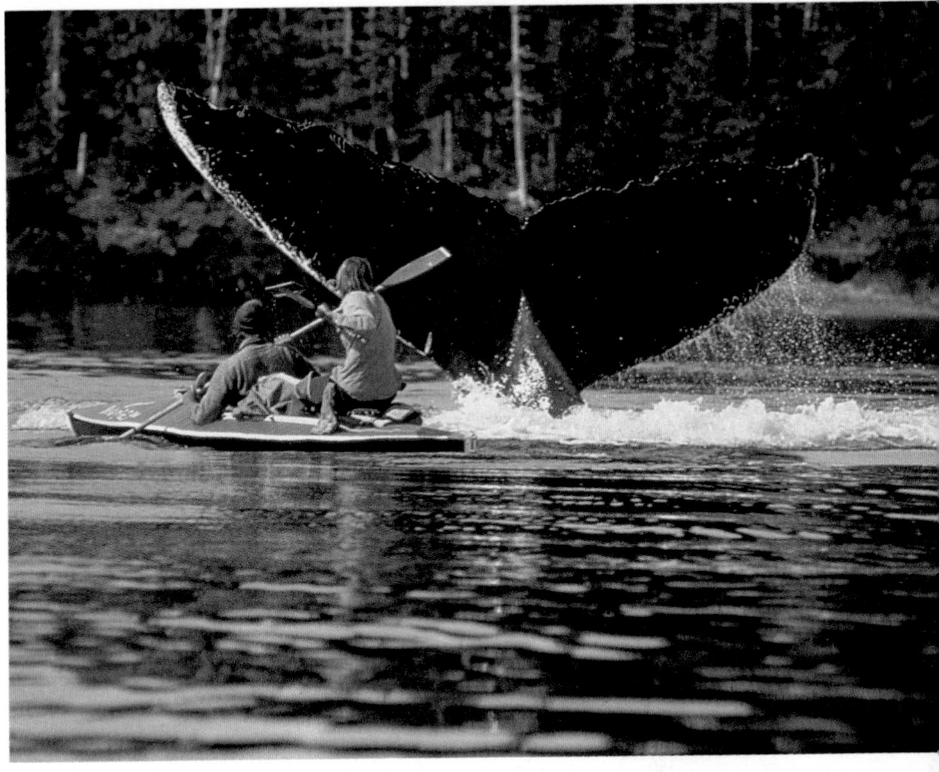

**C** **Writing a True Story.** Write a narrative paragraph to suit the following purpose and audience. Use the Steps for Writing on page 359 as a guide.

| | |
|---|---|
| PURPOSE | To tell a true story from your life about learning an important lesson |
| AUDIENCE | People younger than you who would learn from your experience |

**D** **Revising a Narrative Paragraph.** Revise the following narrative paragraph, using the checklist on page 353 as a guide.

Baby-sitting Brother Brian

Baby-sitting sounded easy. My parents told me that my two-year-old brother Brian would be in bed when they left. His room is upstairs next to mine. I would not have to do anything except stay at home. Sometimes in the evenings, I like to visit my friends. That is not exactly what happened though. Brian woke up three minutes after they left. He was hungry. We had had spaghetti that night for dinner. He was thirsty. He had a stomachache. Every time I tried to put him back to bed, he cried. He finally fell asleep in front of the television set.

E **Editing a Narrative Paragraph.** Edit the following narrative paragraph, using the Editing Checklist on page 354 as a guide.

My parents is not the type to say, "I told you so!"—even when they have a right too. Last year we were on vacation in kentucky. I begged my parents to take me horseback riding. They told me that it is not as easy as it looks. And that you sit very high off the ground. They thought that I might be afriad and not have a good time. I assured them I would enjoy it, and he finely gave in to my pestering. Well they was right. I was petrified the minute the horse went faster then just a walk. after five minutes of panick I gave up and asked to be helped off the horse. Not once did my parent's remind me of there better judgment. Instead, they suggested that I take a few riding lessons when I got home. I am greatful to them for that.

F **Ideas for Writing.** Choose one of the subjects below or one of your own. Then write a narrative paragraph using the Steps for Writing on page 359 as a guide.

1. finding a lost object
2. competing with others
3. alone during a storm
4. training a pet
5. learning to use a computer
6. taking an important test
7. a backpacking or camping experience
8. a rewarding moment
9. making a discovery
10. a struggle with your conscience

# Steps for Writing a Narrative Paragraph

### Prewriting

1. Think about your purpose in writing and consider your audience. (*See page 334.*)
2. Make a list of subjects by jotting down ideas. (*See page 336.*)
3. Choose one subject and limit it. (*See pages 337–338.*)
4. Brainstorm a list of supporting details. (*See pages 339–340.*)
5. Arrange your details in chronological order. (*See pages 341–342.*)

### Writing

6. Write a topic sentence. (*See pages 344–345.*)
7. Write a body of supporting sentences telling the story event by event. Use transitions. (*See pages 347–348.*)
8. Add a concluding sentence. (*See pages 348–349.*)

### Revising

9. Using the Checklist for Revising a Narrative Paragraph on page 353, check your paragraph for structure, unity, coherence, sentences, and word choice.

### Editing

10. Using the Editing Checklist on page 354, check your spelling, capitalization, punctuation, and form.

# Descriptive Paragraphs

When your purpose in writing is to help a reader picture something, you are writing description. You can use descriptive writing in many ways. In everyday life you might need to describe a lost object so that it can be located. In letters to friends, you might want to recreate a pleasant or exciting scene. In school you might be asked to describe a plant or an animal you are studying or a character in a book. Descriptive writing appeals to a reader's senses and brings a scene, a person, or an object to life.

23a A **descriptive paragraph** creates a vivid picture in words of a person, an object, or a scene.

## Your Writer's Notebook

Good descriptive writing requires careful observing. Every day for five days, choose a different place that you know well. Go to each place and observe carefully. Then, in your journal, record your impressions by listing specific details that appeal to your senses. You may want to refer to the lists of sensory words in Chapter 18. Write your details under the following headings.

| SIGHT | SOUND | SMELL | TASTE | TOUCH |
|---|---|---|---|---|

# Developing Descriptive Paragraphs

Every writer is unique. No two writers would use the same words even if they were describing the same subject. Their descriptions, however, would be similar in several ways. The information in this chapter will show you some of the common features of descriptive writing. It will also assist you in writing your own unique descriptions.

## Paragraph Structure

In the following descriptive paragraph, the writer's purpose is to describe a barn. As you read the paragraph, notice how each sentence works to create the picture.

The Old Barn

TOPIC SENTENCE

Their barn was a marvelous, solid structure with a sense of long ago about it. There were a couple of old horse stalls in there. There were even a few oats left in the feed bins and some wisps of old, shiny hay, dark with age. With a little imagination you could hear a gentle ghostly whinny and the restless stirring of ironshod hooves on the wide-board floors. People sometimes tried to buy the barn for lumber, or to haul it away to someplace else and make a house out of it. The owners refused to sell. Barns like this, they said—once they are gone, they do not come back. —MARY STOLZ, *THE EDGE OF NEXT YEAR* (ADAPTED)

SUPPORTING SENTENCES

CONCLUDING SENTENCE

The following chart summarizes the function of each kind of sentence in a descriptive paragraph.

23b

**Structure of a Descriptive Paragraph**

1. The topic sentence introduces the subject and suggests a general impression of it.
2. The supporting sentences provide details that bring the picture to life.
3. The concluding sentence summarizes the overall impression of the subject.

### EXERCISE 1 *Writing Descriptive Topic Sentences*

For each descriptive subject, write a topic sentence that suggests a general impression. The impression may be either positive or negative.

EXAMPLE a cave

POSSIBLE ANSWER The cave was dark and mysterious, full of unexpected sights from another world.

1. a porpoise
2. a city bus
3. a block party
4. a spring day
5. a seashore
6. a path in the woods
7. a pair of new shoes
8. a hockey game
9. an ice, snow, or rain storm
10. a view from a rooftop

## Specific Details and Sensory Words

If a description contains only vague ideas and general words, readers will soon lose interest. Specific details and words that appeal to the senses are the sparks that activate a reader's imagination. (*See pages 266–277.*)

23c

Use **specific details** and **sensory words** to bring your description to life.

Notice the sensory words used to describe the canyon in the following paragraph.

The Saint Elena Canyon

SUGGESTS GENERAL IMPRESSION — Just before dawn one day, I stood at the mouth of the majestic Santa Elena Canyon, watching the sun come up. SIGHTS — The Rio Grande, about 50 feet wide at this point, spilled out of the canyon. As the sun rose, the coloring of the canyon walls, reflected in the slow-moving waters, gradually changed. Faint blacks, browns, and warm, rusty reds faded into grayish white. Before long the sun moved on and left the canyon in shade. I felt dwarfed by the high, massive, sheer walls. SOUNDS — More than anything I remember the sounds. Like a symphony songs of birds and insects flowed from the lower canyon, then vibrated and echoed up and out of the sky. Looking up, following the sounds, I could see black vultures soaring up and down the canyon walls. It looked almost as if they were dancing to the songs. —TOR EIGELAND, *AMERICA'S MAJESTIC CANYONS* (ADAPTED)

### EXERCISE 2 Listing Specific Details

Under each subject list four specific details that appeal to the senses of sight, sound, taste or smell, and touch.

EXAMPLE a roller coaster

POSSIBLE ANSWER
Sight: four orange cars
Sound: squealing of wheels on tracks
Smell: corn being popped far below
Touch: sweaty palms on cold steel safety bar

1. a skating rink
2. an attic
3. a costume party
4. a lake in autumn
5. a pancake breakfast
6. a windy day
7. a hayride
8. a parade
9. a locker room
10. a hospital

## Spatial Order and Transitions

For readers to "see" what you are describing, your details must be arranged in a logical order. The most logical order for descriptions is spatial order.

23d **Spatial order** arranges details according to their location. **Transitions** show the relationship of the details.

The following chart shows several types of spatial order and transitions.

| Spatial Order | Transitions |
|---|---|
| near to far (or reverse) | close by, beyond, around, farther, across, behind, in the distance |
| top to bottom (or reverse) | at the top, in the middle, lower, below, at the bottom, above, higher |
| side to side | at the left (right), in the middle, next to, at one end, to the west |
| inside to outside (or reverse) | within, in the center, on the inside, the next layer, on the outside |

In the paragraph below, the details are arranged from bottom to top.

The Singing Tower

Thousands of people have listened to the music of the bells at the Singing Tower in Lake Wales, Florida. **At the base** of the tower is a clear pool that reflects the entire 205-foot structure. Reaching **from the bottom of the tower to the top** are wide stripes of pink and gray marble. Florida plants and animals are carved in these marble stripes. **At the crown-shaped top** of the tower, a set of bells plays melodies. People from all over the country come to hear the bell chimes ring out over the surrounding park.

## EXERCISE 3 Understanding Spatial Order

Write the paragraph below, filling in the blanks with the appropriate transitions. Choose the transitions from the following list.

| | |
|---|---|
| near the rear window | at the far end of the room |
| on the right wall | to the right of the children |
| on the left wall | in the center of the picture |
| inside the fireplace | in front of the fireplace |

The painting of a colonial home shows the many uses of a single room. ______, two children are busy playing. ______, a woman is rolling pastry dough on a wooden table, while a man is peeling apples. Plates are arranged neatly ______. ______ is a fireplace. Food is cooking in a pot ______. ______, a woman is kneeling to check the food. Another woman ______ is weaving cloth at a loom. ______, through a doorway, a fourth woman is busy churning butter. As in many colonial homes, this one room served as kitchen, dining room, workroom, and playroom.

### EXERCISE 4 On Your Own

In your writer's notebook, jot down answers to the following questions. Your answers will be good subjects for descriptive paragraphs.

1. If you were moving and could take only 12 objects with you, what objects would you take?
2. If you were making a photo album of places to remember in years to come, what 5 places would you include?
3. If you were collecting pictures of places you would like to visit someday, what 5 places would you choose?

## Writing Extra

Shaping your message to suit your readers is an important part of writing. Practice writing for different audiences by doing the following activity.

Imagine that you have lost a suitcase that you have owned since you were a child. The suitcase has been with you on every trip you have ever taken. Write a letter to the lost-and-found department of Mercury Airlines describing the suitcase. Be sure to include details to identify the lost suitcase. Then write a letter to a friend. Describe the suitcase and the personal memories it holds for you. Make your description show the importance the suitcase has had in your life.

# Writing Descriptive Paragraphs

The process of writing moves back and forth between free-flowing ideas and carefully controlled thought. During prewriting, for example, you might try freewriting or brainstorming to start your ideas flowing. Later, however, you must give structure to your ideas by arranging them in an order that readers can easily understand. The following activities will give you practice in the process of writing descriptive paragraphs.

## EXERCISE 5 Describing an Object

**STEP 1: Prewriting**
Look at the picture below. What does it make you think of? How would you describe it? Write freely for five minutes, answering these questions. Then study your notes and make a plan for writing a paragraph describing this sculpture.

**STEP 2: Writing**
Use your plan to write a descriptive paragraph. Be sure to include specific details that will create a clear picture in the mind of your reader.

**STEP 3: Sharing Your Work**
Exchange papers with a classmate. Read your partner's paragraph carefully. Point out the parts that you especially like as well as the parts that could be improved. When your own paper is returned to you, make any revisions that are needed to improve your description.

## EXERCISE 6 *Describing a Person*

**STEP 1: Prewriting**
Imagine that you are writing a science-fiction story about someone living on a distant planet. Give your character a name. Then jot down answers to the following brainstorming questions.

1. What does your character's face look like?
2. What do your character's hands look like?
3. What do your character's feet look like?
4. How does your character move around?
5. What sounds does your character make?

Use your brainstorming notes to create a plan for a descriptive paragraph.

**STEP 2: Writing**
Use your plan to write the first draft of a paragraph describing your character.

**STEP 3: Sharing Your Work**
Exchange papers with a classmate. Draw a picture of the character described in your partner's first draft. Give the picture and the first draft back to your partner. Then look at the picture your partner drew. Does it accurately reflect your character? Revise your paragraph to include anything that brings your written picture into sharper focus.

## EXERCISE 7 *Revising a Descriptive Paragraph*

Choose one of the descriptive paragraphs you wrote in Exercises 5 and 6. Use the Revision Checklist that follows to make a thorough and final revision of the paragraph.

### Checklist for Revising Descriptive Paragraphs

Checking Your Paragraph

1. Does your topic sentence introduce the subject and suggest a general impression of it? (*See pages 361–362.*)
2. Do your supporting sentences provide details that bring your description to life? (*See pages 361–363.*)
3. Does your paragraph have unity? (*See page 350.*)
4. Are your details in either spatial order or another logical order? (*See page 364.*)
5. Did you use transitions to give your paragraph coherence? (*See page 364.*)
6. Does your concluding sentence summarize the overall impression of the subject and provide a strong ending? (*See pages 361–362.*)

Checking Sentences

7. Did you combine related sentences to avoid too many short, choppy sentences in a row? (*See pages 283–287.*)
8. Did you vary the beginnings of your sentences? (*See page 291.*)
9. Did you avoid rambling sentences? (*See page 294.*)
10. Did you avoid repetition and empty expressions? (*See pages 295–296.*)

Checking Words

11. Did you use specific, lively words? (*See pages 267–268.*)
12. Did you use words that appeal to the senses? (*See pages 271–277.*)

## EXERCISE 8 *Editing a Descriptive Paragraph*

Use the Editing Checklist on page 354 to make a final copy of the paragraph you revised for Exercise 7.

# Spotlight on Writing

**A** **Describing an Object.** For each picture below, brainstorm a list of details that could be used in a descriptive paragraph. Then choose one picture and write your description. Use the Steps for Writing on page 373 to help you.

| | |
|---|---|
| PURPOSE | To describe either the scarecrows or the winter decoration using specific details |
| AUDIENCE | Young children |

**B** **Describing a Person.** Write a descriptive paragraph about a famous person without naming your subject. Identify the person's profession in your topic sentence. Then limit your description to the person's *appearance.* When you have finished, read your paragraph to your classmates. See if they can guess the name of the person you have described.

| | |
|---|---|
| PURPOSE | To describe a famous person clearly |
| AUDIENCE | Your classmates |

**C** **Describing a Place.** Use the picture that follows to write a descriptive paragraph for a travel magazine. Use the Steps for Writing on page 373 to help you.

| | |
|---|---|
| PURPOSE | To describe Bryce Canyon in Utah vividly enough to make people want to visit it |
| AUDIENCE | People who want to plan a trip to see some of the natural wonders of the United States |

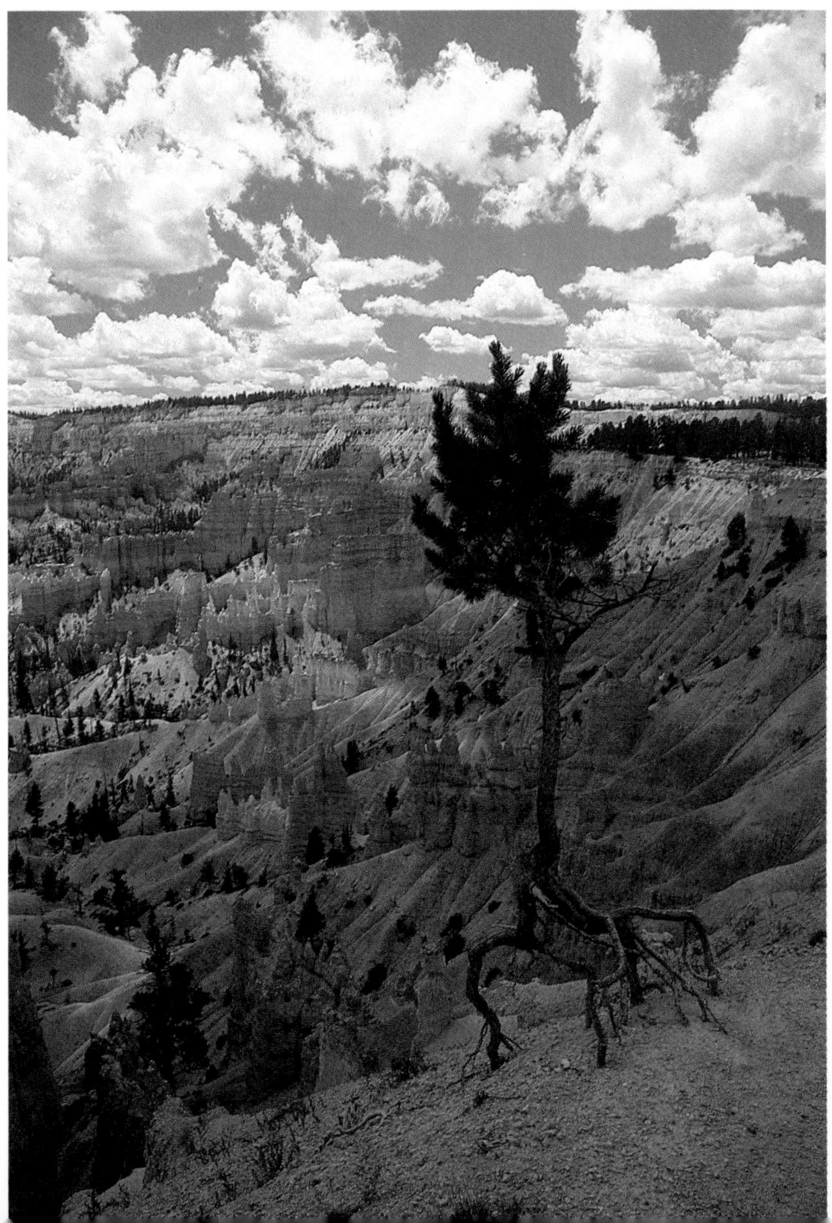

**D** **Describing to Provide Information.** Use the notes that follow to write a descriptive paragraph about a poisonous snake, the water moccasin.

PURPOSE To describe water moccasins so people can recognize and avoid them
AUDIENCE People who fish or use boats

- between three and six feet long
- head shaped like a stone arrowhead
- wide, flat body
- brownish gray color
- no strong pattern of colors
- often looks like a stick hanging from a tree limb
- nicknamed cottonmouth because its open mouth is white

**E** **Writing from Your Writer's Notebook.** Choose one of the places that you wrote about in your writer's notebook. Then describe it, using specific details and words that appeal to the senses. Use the steps for writing on page 373 to help you. Then exchange papers with a partner. Use the checklist for revising on page 369 to help you revise each other's sentences.

**F** **Ideas for Writing Descriptive Paragraphs.** Write a descriptive paragraph on one of the following subjects or on one of your own. Follow the Steps for Writing a Descriptive Paragraph on page 373.

1. a skyscraper
2. a band rehearsal
3. a large cave
4. a farmyard
5. a childhood hero
6. a view at sunset
7. today's weather
8. a pizza
9. a tent
10. a game room
11. a pair of old shoes
12. a hot baked potato
13. the view from a window
14. an old sweater
15. a veterinarian's office
16. your cafeteria at lunchtime
17. a school corridor
18. a clown's face
19. a city street
20. a night sky with a full moon

# Steps for Writing a Descriptive Paragraph

## Prewriting

1. Determine your purpose and audience.
2. Make a list of possible subjects, including scenes, objects, and persons. (*See Your Writer's Notebook, page 360.*)
3. Choose a subject that interests you and suits your purpose and audience.
4. Limit your subject so that it can be adequately covered in one paragraph.
5. Brainstorm a list of sensory details that come to mind when you think about your subject. (*See pages 362–363.*)
6. Arrange your notes in either spatial or some other logical order. (*See page 364.*)

## Writing

7. Write a topic sentence that expresses an overall impression of your subject. (*See pages 361–362.*)
8. Use your prewriting notes to write supporting sentences that bring your description to life. (*See pages 361–362.*)
9. Add a concluding sentence that summarizes the overall impression and provides a strong ending. (*See pages 361–362.*)

## Revising

10. Put your paper aside for a while. Then come back to it with a fresh eye. Use the Checklist for Revising on page 369 to improve your work.

## Editing

11. Use the Editing Checklist on page 354 to prepare a final, polished paragraph.

# 24

# Expository Paragraphs

One of the most common purposes in writing is to explain. Paragraphs that explain are called expository paragraphs. You write expository paragraphs in school whenever you answer essay questions and prepare reports.

An expository paragraph can serve two purposes. One purpose is to provide information. A paragraph on why the moon shines would give factual information. The second purpose is to give directions. A paragraph on how to find the moon through a telescope would give step-by-step instructions.

24a An **expository paragraph** explains with facts and examples or gives directions.

## Your Writer's Notebook

Answer the questions below in your journal to help you explore subjects for expository paragraphs.

1. If I were asked to teach young children, what have I learned that I could explain to them? [List two subjects.]
2. What do I already know about each subject?
3. What more do I need to learn in order to explain each subject clearly?

# Developing Expository Paragraphs

Whether your purpose is to provide information or give directions, the ideas in an expository paragraph must be presented clearly to your readers.

## Paragraph Structure

The purpose of the following paragraph is to explain. Notice the clear structure of the paragraph.

Which Li Wei?

TOPIC SENTENCE STATES MAIN IDEA

SUPPORTING SENTENCES PROVIDE FACTS AND EXAMPLES

CONCLUDING SENTENCE ADDS STRONG ENDING

With the population of China so enormous, the authorities have great trouble keeping track of people with the same name. In one district 4,800 women were found with the same name. In one work unit ten men shared the name Li Wei. To tell one from another, they were called "Big Li Wei," "Li Wei No. 2," "Big Eyes Li Wei," and so forth. To try to reduce the confusion, one government district is supplying parents with a guide to naming babies.

—MILTON MELTZER, *A BOOK ABOUT NAMES*

In the following paragraph, the writer's purpose is to give directions. The same overall structure is used.

How to Lace Your Ice Skates

TOPIC SENTENCE STATES MAIN IDEA

SUPPORTING SENTENCES GIVE STEPS IN ORDER

CONCLUDING SENTENCE SUMMARIZES

Properly laced ice skates should be loose enough to let your toes stay warm, and tight enough to support your ankles. First, remove all laces. Then, starting near the toe, thread the laces loosely through the first two eyelets. Next, slip your foot into the skate. Finally, thread the remaining eyelets very securely over your instep and ankle. Skates laced this way will give your ankles support without pinching your toes.

The following chart shows the role of each sentence in an expository paragraph.

24b

**Structure of an Expository Paragraph**

1. The topic sentence states a main idea based on fact.
2. The supporting sentences provide facts, examples, or steps in a process.
3. The concluding sentence summarizes the main idea and adds a strong ending.

### EXERCISE 1 *Identifying the Purpose in Topic Sentences*

Read each topic sentence. Then write *provide information* or *give directions* to tell the purpose of the paragraph.

EXAMPLE Invisible ink is easy to make.
ANSWER give directions

1. Releasing a bowling ball properly is the key to a high score.
2. The zodiac is made up of 12 constellations.
3. It is important to warm up before exercising.
4. Before taking a picture, follow these steps to make sure the lighting is correct.
5. Dogs and wolves are similar in many ways.

### EXERCISE 2 *Writing Expository Topic Sentences*

Choose two subjects from each list below. Under each subject write a topic sentence that suits the purpose.

| PROVIDING INFORMATION | GIVING DIRECTIONS |
|---|---|
| classes you are taking | how to make friends |
| what a double play is | how to train a pet |
| why pets are popular | how to get to school |
| the meaning of *ROM* | how to load a program disk |
| clubs at school | how to draw a human face |

## Methods of Development

The purpose of your paragraph will help you decide what kind of supporting details you need. If you are explaining a subject to provide information, you will use facts and examples. If you are giving directions, your supporting details will be the steps in the process.

***Facts and Examples.*** Read the following topic sentence. Then ask yourself what kind of supporting details you expect the rest of the paragraph to contain.

TOPIC SENTENCE — In recent years disabled athletes have set new milestones.

The questions probably raised in your mind are these: *Who were these athletes? What did they do to set new milestones?* Facts and examples will answer those questions.

FACTS AND EXAMPLES

- Jack Robertson, an athlete with paralyzed legs, swam most of the English Channel.
- Bruce Jennings, an athlete with only one leg, bicycled 3,000 miles across the United States.
- Two wheelchair athletes in the 1977 Boston Marathon finished in the top third.

**24c** Use **facts** and **examples** to support the main idea of a paragraph that provides information.

### *EXERCISE 3 Listing Facts and Examples*

Write each topic sentence on your paper. Then, under each one, list at least three facts or examples to back it up.

EXAMPLE The Fourth of July is a holiday with many traditions.

POSSIBLE ANSWER People usually set off fireworks.
Many people have barbecues.
Some towns have parades.

1. The parents of my friends have interesting jobs.
2. Most television comedy series have one male and one female lead character.
3. The only way to lose weight is to use more calories than you take in.
4. Dogs express emotion in many ways.
5. The one invention I could never live without is the ______. (*Fill in the blank with your choice.*)

***Steps in a Process.*** The following topic sentence introduces a paragraph that gives directions. What are the questions it raises?

TOPIC SENTENCE You can return tennis balls hit to you if you follow a few important steps.

Readers will wonder what these steps are. The following details give the steps in the process.

STEPS IN A PROCESS
- First decide whether to use your forehand or backhand as the ball approaches.
- Then turn your body to get in position.
- As you turn, bring your racket as far back as possible.
- Bend your knees and swing through with your whole body.
- Follow through on your stroke.

**24d** Use **steps in a process** in the supporting sentences of a paragraph that gives directions.

### *EXERCISE 4 Listing Steps in a Process*

Write each of the following topic sentences on your paper. Then list the steps in the process the reader will have to follow to accomplish the goal in the topic sentence.

EXAMPLE Making scrambled eggs is easy.

POSSIBLE ANSWER
- First melt some butter in a frying pan.
- Then crack open some eggs.
- Beat the eggs.
- Pour the eggs into the hot pan and stir them.

1. Learning how to ride a bicycle requires help at first.
2. Checking a book out of the library is easy.
3. A good way to get downtown from my house is by bus.
4. I have found a way to get up on time every morning.
5. Following these steps can help you prepare for a test.

## *Logical Order and Transitions*

Explanations that are presented in a logical order help readers understand your message. Two kinds of order often used in expository paragraphs are *order of importance or size* and *sequential order.*

***Order of Importance or Size.*** In paragraphs that offer information, details are often arranged in the order of *least to most* or *most to least.* Transitions are used to point out the relationships among the details.

**Transitions Used with Order of Importance or Size**

| | | |
|---|---|---|
| first | larger | equally important |
| next | even larger | more important |
| finally | the largest | most important |

**24e** In paragraphs that provide information, use **order of importance or size** with appropriate **transitions.** Arrange the details in the order of least to most or most to least.

The Great Lakes

TOPIC SENTENCE

ORDER OF SMALLEST TO LARGEST

CONCLUDING SENTENCE

The five Great Lakes in North America vary significantly in size. The smallest is Lake Erie, covering 32,630 square miles. Lake Ontario is slightly larger, with an area of 34,850 square miles. Lake Michigan is the third largest lake. It is as big as Lake Erie and Lake Ontario combined. Next in size is Lake Huron. Its total area is 74,700 square miles. Lake Superior deserves its name as the largest of the Great Lakes. Its total area, in the United States and Canada, is 81,000 square miles. So important have the Great Lakes been to North Americans that even the smallest is great.

## EXERCISE 5 *Arranging Details in Order of Size*

Write each topic sentence. Then under each one, arrange the supporting details in the order of *least to most* or *most to least.*

1. Dogs come in many sizes.
   - Mid-sized dogs, such as retrievers, hounds, setters, and huskies, usually weigh between 40 and 75 pounds.
   - Small dogs, such as the Chihuahua, the Pekingese, and the toy poodle, often weigh between 10 and 40 pounds.
   - Large dogs, such as the Great Dane, the St. Bernard, and the Newfoundland, weigh up to 150 pounds.

2. Some branches of the armed services have many more people on active duty than others.
   - In 1982, the total number of people in the Air Force was 578,822.
   - The 1982 figure for the U.S. Army was 788,026.
   - The Marines had 192,380 people in 1982.
   - The U.S. Navy had 553,000 in 1982.

3. Humans have the longest life span of all mammals, living an average of about 70 years.
   - A rabbit lives an average of 5 years.
   - A leopard lives an average of 12 years.
   - An opossum lives only 1 year.
   - A lion lives an average of 15 years.
   - A gorilla lives 20 years, on average.
   - A hippopotamus lives about 25 years.

***Sequential Order.*** In paragraphs that give directions, the supporting details must be presented in the proper sequence. This kind of order is called sequential order.

In the following paragraph, the directions are clear because the steps are presented in the order that the reader would do them. Notice the transitions printed in heavy type.

How to Make a Magnifying Lens

TOPIC SENTENCE

STEPS IN SEQUENTIAL ORDER

CONCLUDING SENTENCE

A simple magnifying lens can be made from a piece of wire and a drop of water. **First,** partly fill a container with water. **Then,** cut a piece of thin wire about six inches long. Bend one end of the wire, forming a small loop. **Next,** twist the wire at the bottom of the loop to hold it in place. **Now** you are ready to dip the loop into the water. **When** you do, a drop of the water will stay in the loop. **When** you look through the drop of water, you will see things magnified four or five times their real size. With only wire, water, and a little know-how, you have created a magnifying lens.

24f In paragraphs that give directions, use **sequential order** and appropriate **transitions.**

The following chart shows some useful transitions for sequential order.

**Transitions for Sequential Order**

| | | | |
|---|---|---|---|
| first | before | while | finally |
| next | after | as soon as | as a last step |
| then | when | second | now |

### EXERCISE 6 Listing Steps in Sequential Order

The illustrations on page 383 show how to say in sign language, *Please write your name and address.* Using the illustrations, rewrite the directions below in the proper sequence. Save your work for Exercise 7.

- To make the sign for *name,* extend the second and third fingers of both hands while your hands are apart. Then bring the right hand over the left to form a cross.
- You can make the sign for *please* by rubbing in a circular motion on your chest with your right hand.
- The sign for *address* is a combination of two signs that indicate eating and sleeping.
- With all five fingers cupped together, bring your right hand up to your mouth.
- Make the sign for *and* by closing the fingers of your right hand as you move your hand to the left.
- The second part of the sign is the right hand over the ear, signifying sleep.
- *Your* is signed by pushing your open hand outward from the chest.
- In the sign for *write,* your left hand acts as the paper while your right hand slides outward from your palm to your fingers as if it were holding a pencil.

### *EXERCISE 7 Adding Transitions*

Use the following sentences and your work from Exercise 6 to write a well-organized paragraph about sign language. Add transitions where necessary.

| | |
|---|---|
| TOPIC SENTENCE | Learning to sign the sentence *Please write your name and address* is one way to appreciate the sign language used by people who have a hearing impairment. |
| CONCLUDING SENTENCE | By learning to sign this sentence, you can appreciate the clarity of sign language. |

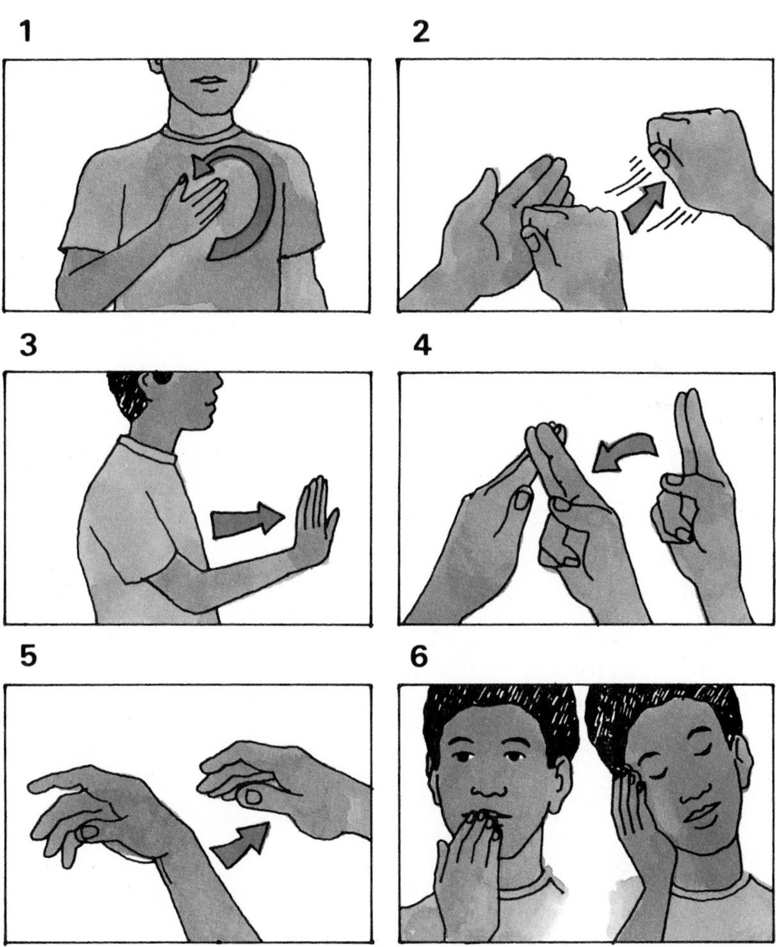

## EXERCISE 8 On Your Own

Use the following ideas to help you think of subjects for expository paragraphs.

1. List two interesting television shows you have watched recently. Next to each one, write an idea or a lesson you learned from watching the show.
2. Browse through the library. Check out and read a few books on a subject that interests you. Write down any new information that you learn from reading these books.
3. Ask family members who are older than you to tell you how their youth was different from yours. Write their responses in note form.

## Writing Extra

Thomas Jefferson wrote his own message for his gravestone. Although he had been president of the United States, he wanted to be remembered for his other accomplishments as well. One was writing the Declaration of Independence. The second was helping to keep the church and state separate. The third was the founding of the University of Virginia.

Think about three things that you would like to be remembered for. They can be small or large accomplishments. They can be things you have already done or things you hope to do in the future. Explain your choices in a paragraph.

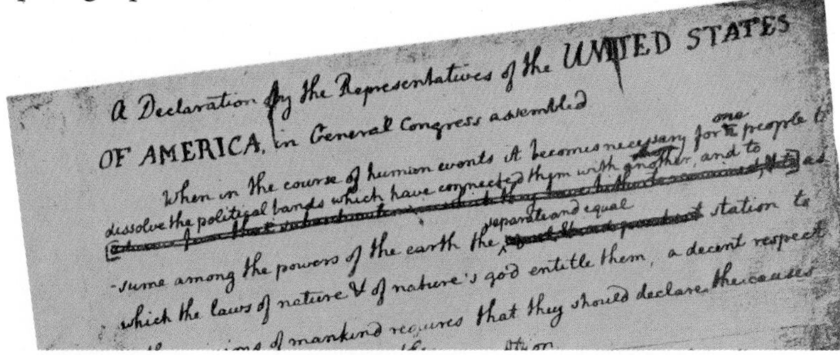
A Declaration by the Representatives of the UNITED STATES OF AMERICA, in General Congress assembled.

When in the course of human events it becomes necessary for one people to dissolve the political bands which have connected them with another, and to ... separate and equal station to ...-sume among the powers of the earth the ... which the laws of nature & of nature's god entitle them, a decent respect to the opinions of mankind requires that they should declare the causes ...

# Writing Expository Paragraphs

Have you ever been upset because directions were hard to follow? If so, you know the importance of clear explanations. As you write your own explanations, keep your readers in mind. Ask yourself, "Would I understand this if I were reading it for the first time?" The following activities will help you write clear expository paragraphs.

## EXERCISE 9 Explaining Symbols

**STEP 1: Prewriting**
You know what all the symbols on the American flag stand for. The stars are for the 50 states. The stripes are for the original 13 colonies. Red, white, and blue are the colors of the British flag. Each shape and color on the flag stands for something.

Now think about yourself. Think about the things that are important to you and that help identify you. Then make a list of some of your interests. On your paper create symbols for these things and interests. When you have created a number of symbols, design your own personal flag. Draw a picture of your flag, using colors that have special meaning for you.

**STEP 2: Writing**
Write an expository paragraph explaining each symbol and color on your flag. Since your readers will already have a picture of your flag, you do not need to describe it in your paragraph.

**STEP 3: Sharing Your Work**
Exchange paragraphs and pictures with a classmate. Read your partner's paragraph carefully as you study the picture. If there are any symbols or colors that are on the flag but are left out of the paragraph, tell your partner about them.

**STEP 4: Revising**

When your own work is returned, make any revisions that would improve your explanation. Use your partner's comments and the following Checklist for Revising to help you.

**Checklist for Revising Expository Paragraphs**

Checking Your Paragraph

1. Does your topic sentence state a main idea based on fact? (*See pages 375–376.*)
2. If your paragraph provides information, do your supporting sentences support the main idea with facts and examples? (*See pages 375, 377–378.*)
3. If your paragraph gives directions, do your supporting sentences provide the steps in the process? (*See pages 375, 378–379.*)
4. Are your details arranged in order of importance or size, in sequential order, or in some other type of logical order? (*See pages 379–382.*)
5. Do you use transitions to give your paragraph coherence? (*See pages 351, 379–382.*)
6. Does your paragraph have unity? (*See page 350.*)
7. Does your concluding sentence summarize the main idea and add a strong ending? (*See pages 375–376.*)

Checking Your Sentences

8. Did you combine related sentences to avoid too many short, choppy sentences in a row? (*See pages 283–287.*)
9. Did you vary the beginnings of your sentences? (*See page 291.*)
10. Did you avoid rambling sentences? (*See page 294.*)
11. Did you avoid repetition and empty expressions? (*See pages 295–296.*)

Checking Your Words

12. Did you use clear, specific words? (*See page 267.*)

**STEP 5: Editing and Publishing**

Check over your paragraph for errors, using the Editing Checklist on page 354. Then make a neat final copy. On a separate sheet of paper, make a fresh picture of your flag. Mount your paragraph and flag on a large sheet of construction paper. Display your finished work in your classroom or at home for others to enjoy.

## EXERCISE 10 *Giving Directions*

**STEP 1: Prewriting**
Think about exercises you know how to do. Toe touches, knee bends, and jumping jacks might be a few. Write them on your paper. Under each one list all the steps you follow to complete that exercise. Then choose the exercise you most like to do. Write a sentence telling why that exercise is your favorite.

**STEP 2: Writing**
Use your notes to write an expository paragraph giving directions on how to do the exercise you chose.

**STEP 3: Sharing Your Work**
Pair off with a partner. Leave room to move around. Have your partner read his or her paragraph to you. Follow the directions as your partner reads them. Let your partner know if any parts of the directions are confusing.

**STEP 4: Revising**
Use your partner's comments and the Checklist for Revising on page 386 to help you revise your directions.

**STEP 5: Editing and Publishing**
Check over your paragraph for errors, using the Editing Checklist on page 354. Then make a neat final copy.

## EXERCISE 11 *On Your Own*

Write an expository paragraph on the meaning of your name. Find the information you need for your paragraph in the library. Use the Steps for Writing an Expository Paragraph on page 391 as a guide.

# Spotlight on Writing

**A** **Developing an Expository Paragraph.** Tell what kind of supporting details you would use with each of the following topic sentences. Give your answer by writing *facts and examples* or *steps in a process* after the proper number on your paper.

1. Learning to drive a stick-shift car may be easier than you think.
2. Many special effects in movies are created by advanced computers.
3. Indian fry bread is delicious and simple to make.
4. Braille is a system of raised dots on heavy paper that blind people read with their fingertips.
5. Do you want to amaze your friends with a simple magic trick?

**B** **Using Logical Order and Transitions.** Use the topic sentence and the notes below to write an expository paragraph. First arrange the details in logical order. Then write the paragraph, using complete sentences and transitions. Add a concluding sentence to complete your paragraph.

TOPIC SENTENCE Saltwater marshes hide many kinds of wildlife, including plants, insects, shellfish, birds, and small animals.

- small animals live on banks of marshes
- birds like the osprey make nests overlooking marshlands
- of first importance, rich plant life in marshes
- shellfish and insects, in turn, form link in food chain for birds and small animals
- insects feed on plant life
- shellfish feed on insects

**C** **Writing a Paragraph to Provide Information.** Use the facts and examples from the information that follows to write an expository paragraph.

PURPOSE To explain how people use personal computers
AUDIENCE People who do not have a personal computer

**Some Leading Uses of Home Computers**
***(Source: Gallup Organization)***

| Uses | Percent of Users |
|---|---|
| video games | 51% |
| learning tool | 46% |
| budgeting | 37% |
| word processing | 18% |
| storing recipes | 9% |
| counting calories | 4% |

**D** **Writing a Paragraph to Give Directions.** Use the map below to write a paragraph that gives directions.

PURPOSE To give directions from the bus station to the stadium
AUDIENCE A person from out of town

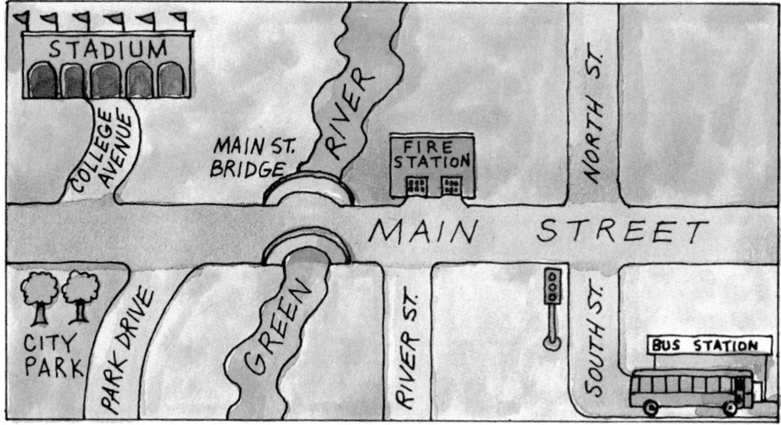

**E** **Writing an Expository Paragraph.** Write an expository paragraph that suits the following purpose and audience. Gather information from the library as necessary.

PURPOSE Imagine that an eclipse of the moon will take place next week. A local television station has asked you to give its viewers a brief explanation of what causes an eclipse.

AUDIENCE Viewers of the six o'clock news who have never seen a lunar eclipse.

**F** **Ideas for Writing Expository Paragraphs.** Write an expository paragraph on one of the following subjects or on one of your own. Follow the Steps for Writing an Expository Paragraph on page 391.

1. what causes an eclipse of the sun
2. how to memorize something
3. what your favorite movies have in common
4. how to get from one city to another city
5. unusual gifts you have received
6. a person you admire
7. how to throw a curveball
8. how to be a good friend
9. how lightning forms
10. your school's rules and regulations

# Steps for Writing an Expository Paragraph

## Prewriting

1. Determine your writing purpose and think about who will be reading your work.
2. Make a list of possible subjects and choose one that interests you the most.
3. Limit your subject so that it can be adequately covered in one paragraph.
4. Write down everything that comes to mind when you think about your subject. If your purpose is to provide information, list facts and examples. If your purpose is to give directions, list steps in the process. (*See pages 377–379.*)
5. Arrange your notes in a logical order. (*See pages 379–381.*)

## Writing

6. Write a topic sentence suited to your purpose. (*See pages 375–376.*)
7. Use your prewriting notes to write the supporting sentences. (*See pages 377–379.*)
8. Add a concluding sentence that summarizes the main idea and adds a strong ending. (*See pages 375–376.*)

## Revising

9. Put your paper aside for a while. Then use the Checklist for Revising Expository Paragraphs on page 386 to make it as clear as possible.

## Editing

10. Use the Editing Checklist on page 354 to prepare a final, polished paragraph.

# 25 Persuasive Paragraphs

Every day, in many ways, people are trying to persuade you. Commercials on television try to persuade you to buy certain products. Friends may try to persuade you to see a certain movie. If the reasons for doing these things are persuasive enough, you will go along with them. If not, you will object.

Learning how to persuade others is a valuable skill. This chapter will help you develop the skill of persuasion.

25a A **persuasive paragraph** states an opinion and uses facts, examples, and reasons to convince readers.

## Your Writer's Notebook

What kinds of things would you like to persuade others about? Use your journal to take an inventory of your opinions. The following questions will help you think of ideas to write about.

1. Do my friends do anything I disapprove of?
2. In what ways could school be better?
3. What have I heard in the news that makes me angry?
4. What are some things I do not like about television?
5. What advice could I give to a younger friend?

# Developing Persuasive Paragraphs

If everyone already agreed with your opinions, you would have no reason to write a persuasive paragraph. Everyone will not always agree with you, however. Many of your readers have views that strongly differ from yours. To convince these readers, you need to use your best techniques of persuasion. A clear, logical structure combined with carefully supported points will help you build a strong case for your opinion.

## Paragraph Structure

Read the following persuasive paragraph twice. The first time you read it, decide whether you agree or disagree with the writer. The second time, notice the structure of the paragraph. Think about the role each sentence plays in persuading the reader.

Year-round School

TOPIC SENTENCE

SUPPORTING SENTENCES

CONCLUDING SENTENCE

Year-round school is a good idea. First of all, the school buildings would be put to good use during the summer instead of just sitting empty. Second, students could complete their schooling at a younger age. They would then have more time to think about what they would like to do with their adult lives. Most important, students would remember more from class to class if there were not a long summer vacation breaking the flow of learning between grades. With short breaks planned along the way, year-round school would provide real benefits economically, personally, and educationally.

The role of each sentence in a persuasive paragraph is summarized in the following chart.

25b

**Structure of a Persuasive Paragraph**

1. The topic sentence states an opinion.
2. The supporting sentences use facts, examples, and reasons to back up the opinion.
3. The concluding sentence makes a final appeal to readers.

### EXERCISE 1 *Writing Persuasive Topic Sentences*

For each of the following subjects, write a topic sentence that states an opinion.

EXAMPLE the school newspaper
POSSIBLE ANSWER The school newspaper should include an advice-to-students column.

1. school rules
2. the value of money
3. your neighborhood
4. bad habits
5. television shows
6. telephones
7. national holidays
8. cars and driving
9. movies
10. UFO's

## Facts and Opinions

Readers who disagree with your opinion need proof before they will consider changing their minds. Facts and examples will help you prove your point. Opinions, on the other hand, will not prove anything.

25c

**Facts** are statements that can be proved. **Opinions** are judgments that vary from person to person.

Advertisers know that opinions can be very persuasive, even though they do not prove anything. Commercials on television and advertisements in newspapers and magazines use opinions heavily to sell products. Try to spot all the opinions in the advertisement on the next page.

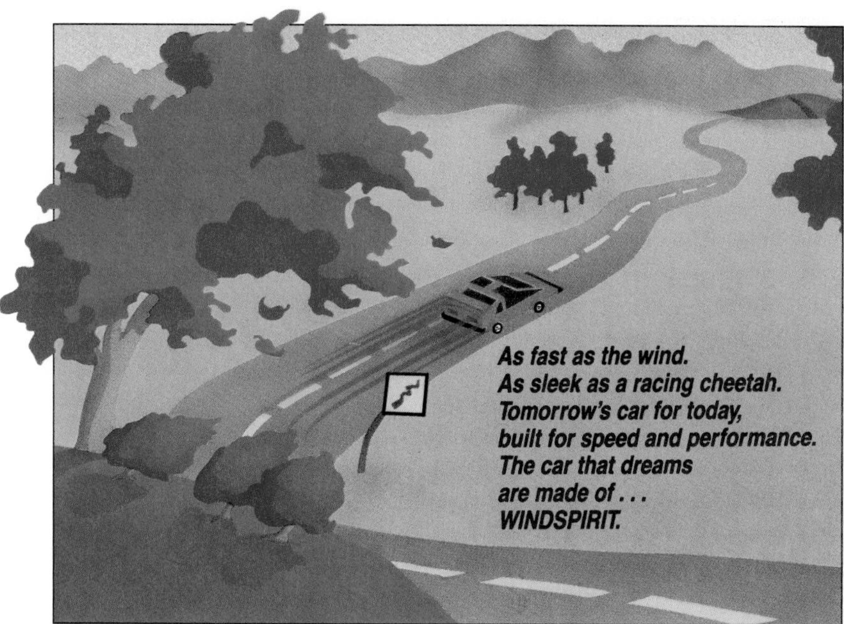

As fast as the wind.
As sleek as a racing cheetah.
Tomorrow's car for today,
built for speed and performance.
The car that dreams
are made of . . .
WINDSPIRIT.


This advertisement appeals to the emotions. It implies that owning a Windspirit will make dreams come true and will give the owner power. Although not a single fact is presented, the advertisement stirs strong feelings and could succeed in selling the Windspirit.

A different approach to selling the Windspirit would be to provide some facts about the car. The facts might include its gas mileage, leg room, trunk space, warranty policy, available colors, and price. Facts like these would help a person compare the features of the Windspirit with those of other cars.

When you develop a persuasive paragraph, rely on facts to prove your point. Although opinions and emotions may often help to sell a product, they alone will not convince serious readers. Watch for words such as the following that signal an opinion.

OPINION WORDS should, must, ought, better, best, worst

**25d** Use **facts** and **examples** to convince your readers. Do not use opinions to support your position.

### EXERCISE 2 *Recognizing Facts and Opinions*

Number your paper 1 to 10. For each statement write *F* if it is a fact or *O* if it is an opinion.

1. Sears Tower in Chicago is the world's tallest building.
2. Illinois passed a seat-belt law in 1985.
3. Cats make better pets than dogs.
4. Nothing tastes better than a glass of cold milk.
5. Milk contains both protein and calcium.
6. All the best movies are comedies.
7. Robert Frost was truly a great poet.
8. Yosemite is America's most beautiful national park.
9. Nathaniel Hawthorne wrote *The Marble Faun*.
10. Weeping-willow trees do not really weep.

### EXERCISE 3 *Designing an Advertisement*

Imagine that friends are found through advertisements. Write an advertisement selling yourself as a good friend. Include an illustration. Appeal to the emotions and use at least five opinions. Save your work for Exercise 4.

### EXERCISE 4 *Writing a Personal Fact Sheet*

Write each opinion you included in your advertisement for yourself. Under each one, list at least one fact or real-life example that backs it up.

EXAMPLE opinion: I am a great student!
fact: I get good grades in all my classes.

## *Order of Importance and Transitions*

Ideas at the beginning or at the end of a paragraph are more likely to stay in a reader's mind than those located in the middle. For this reason, the most important point is usually placed either at the beginning or at the end of a persuasive paragraph. Transitions help to show the order of importance of the ideas presented.

25e Arrange your supporting points in **order of importance.** Use **transitions** to show the connections between ideas.

**Transitions for Order of Importance**

| | | |
|---|---|---|
| also | for example | moreover |
| another | in the first place | furthermore |
| besides | in the second place | in addition |
| finally | in the same way | more important |
| first | likewise | most important |
| second | to begin with | similarly |

Notice the logical order in the following paragraph. The transitions are printed in heavy type.

Preparing for the Worst

TOPIC SENTENCE: OPINION

SUPPORTING POINTS: IN ORDER OF LEAST TO MOST IMPORTANT

CONCLUDING SENTENCE: FINAL APPEAL

Communities along the San Andreas fault should plan ahead in case an earthquake should strike. **First of all,** the risk of an earthquake along the fault is very high. Scientists predict a major earthquake will occur within the next 100 years. **Second,** emergency shelters, food supplies, and fire extinguishers needed for adequate planning are not expensive compared to other town or city costs. **Most important,** conducting earthquake drills, like fire drills, can help people be as calm as possible if an earthquake does occur. Perhaps thousands of lives could be saved with proper planning.

### *EXERCISE 5 Using Transitions*

In the paragraph on the next page, the ideas are arranged in order of least to most important. The transitions, however, are missing. Using the list above, rewrite this paragraph to include transitions.

Bicycle Lanes Are a Good Idea

The city should paint bicycle lanes along Reston Street, Tower Avenue, and Madison Street. Having a safe place to bicycle might encourage more people to take their bikes rather than their cars to work. Fewer cars would mean less pollution. Fewer people would ride their bikes on the sidewalks, where they endanger pedestrians. Bicycle lanes promote safety by keeping cyclists away from cars and by reminding drivers that cyclists are on the road. The cost of having the lanes painted is low compared with the benefits that the bicycle lanes will provide.

## EXERCISE 6 *On Your Own*

Bring to class an advertisement that appeals to you. Be prepared to discuss the opinions and facts it presents and the emotions, if any, it suggests.

## Writing Extra

A rebuttal is an opposing viewpoint. Writing a rebuttal will help you appreciate both sides of an argument. On page 393 you read a paragraph in favor of year-round school. To practice seeing all sides of an argument, write a rebuttal to this argument. Take the side of someone favoring a long summer vacation.

First reread the original paragraph and consider each of the points raised. Then think of good reasons why school should stop for the summer. The following questions will help you think of ideas for your rebuttal.

1. What disadvantages might there be in keeping school buildings open throughout the summer?
2. What disadvantages might there be in graduating at a younger age?
3. What disadvantages to learning might year-round school create?

# Writing Persuasive Paragraphs

When you plan a persuasive paragraph, think about the people who disagree with you. Why do they see things differently? If you were debating with these people, what points would they probably make to support their viewpoint? Having solid arguments to counter opposing viewpoints will help you win your case.

## EXERCISE 7 Persuading with Examples

**STEP 1: Prewriting**
Imagine that you are having a debate with a friend about which television show is best. You think that your favorite show is best because the characters are true to life. As you plan a persuasive paragraph to convince your friend, list all the important characters in your show. Then arrange your list in the order of least to most important. For each character, list several examples that show why he or she is true to life.

**STEP 2: Writing**
Use your notes and the following topic sentence to write a draft of a persuasive paragraph.

TOPIC SENTENCE [*your favorite show*] is the best show on television because its characters are true to life.

**STEP 3: Sharing Your Work**
Exchange papers with a classmate. Read your partner's paper carefully. Does it convince you that his or her choice could be considered the best show on television? Tell your partner what is good about the paragraph and what could be improved. After your paper has been returned, revise your paragraph to make it as convincing as possible. Save your work for Exercise 10.

## EXERCISE 8 Persuading with Facts

**STEP 1: Prewriting**

**A.** A young boy you know often stays up late at night reading adventure stories. When he does, he seems tired and cranky the next day. Think of how to advise this boy. The following facts will help you back up your advice. Arrange the facts in a logical order.

- Heartbeat slows down to about 56 beats per minute during sleep
- Lungs and other organs rest during sleep
- Blood pressure and body temperature fall during sleep
- People who do not dream enough during the night do not perform well during the day

**B.** Now think about how the boy might respond to your advice. Make a list of objections he might have. Prepare yourself to answer his objections with convincing solutions.

**STEP 2: Writing**

Using your notes from Step 1, write a draft of a paragraph advising the boy on the benefits of sufficient sleep. Be sure to include answers to any objections he may have.

**STEP 3: Sharing Your Work**

Exchange papers with a classmate. As you read your partner's paper, pretend you are the boy receiving advice. Would you be convinced? Tell your partner why or why not. When your own paper is returned, revise it as needed to make it more persuasive. Save your work for Exercise 10.

## EXERCISE 9 *Explaining with Reasons*

**STEP 1: Prewriting**

Think of a club you belong to or would like to join. Imagine that you are in charge of recruiting new members for that club. Brainstorm a list of reasons why someone should join. The picture below may give you some ideas. Then design an advertising poster for your club. The poster should include pictures and statements that will persuade new members to join.

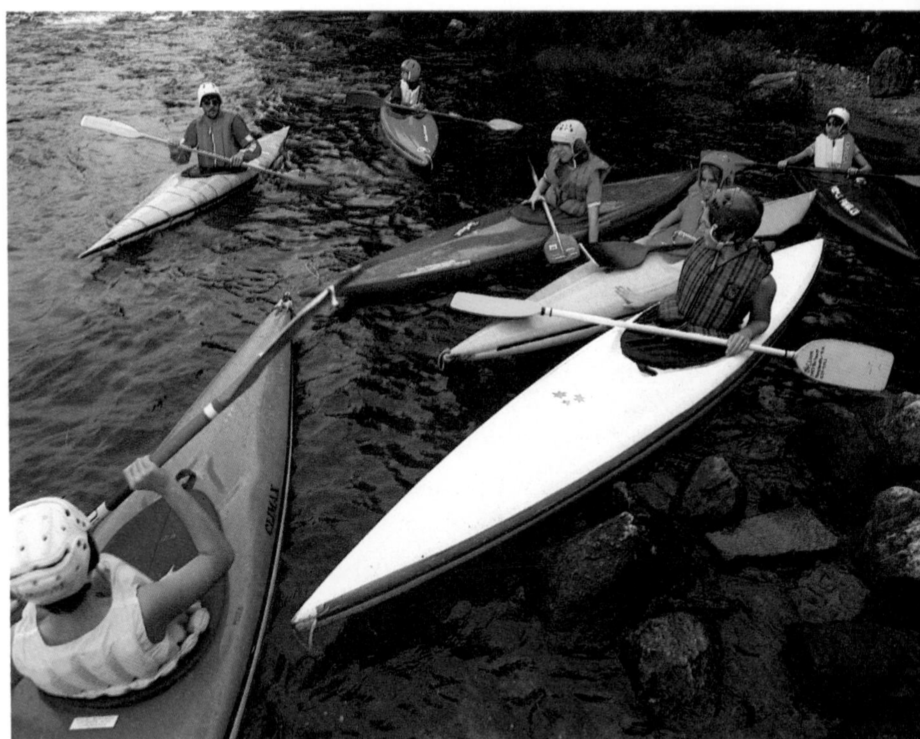

**STEP 2: Writing**

Using your poster and brainstorming notes, write a paragraph to persuade someone to join your club. Be sure to use logical order and transitions.

**STEP 3: Sharing Your Work**

Exchange paragraphs with your partner. Read your partner's paper carefully. Tell your partner whether or not you agree with the order of importance given to each reason. When your own paper is returned, revise it as needed for clarity. Save your work for Exercise 10.

## EXERCISE 10 *Revising a Persuasive Paragraph*

Choose one of the paragraphs you wrote in Exercises 7–9. Use the Revision Checklist that follows to make a thorough and final revision.

### Checklist for Revising Persuasive Paragraphs

Checking Your Paragraph

1. Does your topic sentence state an opinion? (*See pages 393–394.*)
2. Did you use facts, examples, and reasons to support your position? (*See pages 393–395.*)
3. Are your supporting points organized in order of importance? (*See pages 396–397.*)
4. Did you use transitions to give your paragraph coherence? (*See pages 351, 396–397.*)
5. Does your paragraph have unity? (*See page 350.*)
6. Does your concluding sentence make a final appeal? (*See pages 393–394, 397.*)

Checking Your Sentences

7. Do your sentences have varied beginnings and lengths? (*See pages 283–291.*)

Checking Your Words

8. Did you use lively, specific words? (*See pages 267–268.*)

## EXERCISE 11 Editing Practice

Use the Editing Checklist on page 354 to edit the following persuasive paragraph.

Handling Stress

The better way to fight tension and stress are to exercise vigorosly. First of all, physical exercise can relieve tense mucsles, second, Sientists has found that transferring stress from the mind to the body can make you feel better. In addition, the activity will take you're mind off your worrys for a while. Finally, dayly exercise will eliminate the weary, feeling caused by stress. Vigorous exercise will give you more energy throughout the day and your stress will be releived.

## EXERCISE 12 Editing a Persuasive Paragraph

Use the Editing Checklist on page 354 to edit the paragraph you chose for Exercise 10.

## EXERCISE 13 On Your Own

Write freely for five minutes, answering the following question: "In what way would I most like to improve myself?" Then write a persuasive paragraph to yourself, giving reasons why the improvement would be worth the effort.

# Spotlight on Writing

**A** **Recognizing Facts and Opinions.** Some of the following statements are opinions. Others are facts. Write <u>opinion</u> or <u>fact</u> for each statement.

1. Animals that are in danger of becoming extinct should be protected.
2. Several species of animals in the United States are endangered.
3. Ramon will make a better class treasurer than Jesse.
4. The eye of a hurricane is the calm part.
5. Some common garden flowers are poisonous.
6. Keeping important telephone numbers handy will save time in an emergency.
7. The moon is an easy object to find when you are first learning to use a telescope.
8. The teenage years are the most exciting time of life.
9. Doing crossword puzzles is a relaxing pastime.
10. Television shows seem to improve each year.

**B** **Writing a Persuasive Paragraph.** The following notes give information about cats and dogs as pets. Think about which pet would be better for a person who works all day. Use the notes to write a persuasive paragraph.

PURPOSE To recommend a pet
AUDIENCE A person who works all day

| **Cats** | **Dogs** |
|---|---|
| • use a litter box | • must be taken out |
| • quiet | • bark often |
| • shed hair | • shed hair |
| • hard to train | • easy to train |
| • can act aloof | • very dependent |
| • groom themselves | • need to be groomed |
| • love to play | • love to play |
| • cannot protect house | • can protect house |

**C** **Writing to Give Advice.** Imagine that you write an advice column in a newspaper. You have received the following letter. Write a persuasive paragraph suggesting a solution. Be sure to include convincing reasons.

PURPOSE To recommend a course of action
AUDIENCE An unhappy student

Dear Wise Writer:

I have a problem. Last week in school I received a low grade on a test. I did study, but I did not study enough because I had a bad cold. I would like to ask the teacher to let me take the test again now that I feel better. I am not sure, though, whether that would be fair to my classmates who did well on the test. What should I do?

Sincerely,

Unhappy Student

**D** **Writing a Recommendation.** Your friend wants to be a volunteer in a hospital. The hospital needs volunteers who are reliable, friendly, and honest. Write a recommendation for your friend. Use convincing examples.

PURPOSE To show your friend's qualifications
AUDIENCE Hospital volunteer director

**E** **Ideas for Writing.** Write a persuasive paragraph on one of the following subjects or on one of your own. Follow the Steps for Writing on page 406.

1. contributing to charities
2. extra classes your school could offer
3. the best movie of last year
4. how your neighborhood could be improved
5. why littering should be avoided
6. the meaning of certain clothing styles
7. rules your school should or should not have
8. why junk food should be avoided
9. preserving wilderness
10. what you wish people understood about you

# Steps for Writing a Persuasive Paragraph

## Prewriting

1. Determine your purpose and audience.
2. List some opinions on subjects you feel strongly about. (*See Your Writer's Notebook, page 392.*)
3. Choose a subject that interests you especially and that suits your purpose and audience.
4. Limit your subject so that it can be adequately covered in one paragraph.
5. Brainstorm a list of facts, examples, and reasons that could support your opinion. (*See pages 394–395.*)
6. If necessary, find facts and figures in the library. (*See pages 544–558.*)
7. Arrange your notes in order of importance. (*See pages 396–397.*)

## Writing

8. Write a topic sentence that states an opinion. (*See pages 393–394.*)
9. Use your prewriting notes to add supporting sentences with clear transitions. (*See pages 396–397.*)
10. Add a concluding sentence that makes a final appeal. (*See pages 393–394.*)

## Revising

11. Put your paper aside for a while. Then pretend you disagree with your own opinion as you read the paper over. Use the Checklist for Revising Persuasive Paragraphs on page 402 to make your paper more persuasive.

## Editing

12. Use the Editing Checklist on page 354 to prepare a final, polished paragraph.

# Standardized Test

## COMPOSITION

**Directions:** Decide which order is best for the sentences in each group. In the appropriate row on your answer sheet, fill in the circle containing the letter that indicates the best order.

SAMPLE
(1) First we cut the apples and remove the cores.
(2) We cook the pieces until they are very mushy.
(3) Then we throw the pieces in a pot with water.
(4) This is how we make applesauce.

**A** 2 - 4 - 1 - 3 **C** 4 - 1 - 3 - 2
**B** 3 - 1 - 2 - 4 **D** 1 - 4 - 2 - 3

ANSWER Ⓐ Ⓑ Ⓒ Ⓓ

1. (1) Begin by holding the nail below its head with your thumb and forefinger.
(2) Finally remove your fingers and swing the hammer with your whole arm.
(3) Do you really know how to hammer a nail?
(4) Then put it in place and tap it lightly with a hammer.

**A** 2 - 1 - 3 - 4 **C** 4 - 3 - 1 - 2
**B** 3 - 1 - 4 - 2 **D** 1 - 2 - 4 - 3

2. (1) From the hilltop we could see for miles.
(2) In front of the mountains was a checkerboard of farmland.
(3) Farthest away were the purplish shapes of mountains.
(4) Between us and the farmland lay a sparkling blue lake.

**A** 1 - 3 - 2 - 4 **C** 4 - 2 - 3 - 1
**B** 2 - 4 - 1 - 3 **D** 3 - 4 - 1 - 2

3. (1) Three have long been recognized as especially important.
(2) Many useful objects and techniques began in China.
(3) They also were first to develop the art of printing.
(4) Gunpowder and the compass were invented by the Chinese.

**A** 1 - 4 - 3 - 2 **C** 4 - 1 - 2 - 3
**B** 3 - 4 - 1 - 2 **D** 2 - 1 - 4 - 3

**Directions:** Choose the sentence that does not belong in each paragraph. Fill in the appropriate circle on your answer sheet.

SAMPLE (A) All week Owen's had been running ads for its big sale. (B) Nan wanted a silk dress. (C) By 7:30 A.M. on Friday, a long line stood outside. (D) Opening time was not till 9:00 A.M.

ANSWER Ⓐ ● Ⓒ Ⓓ

4. (A) In 1777 the flag had 13 stars and 13 stripes. (B) Betsy Ross probably had nothing to do with it. (C) The stars could be arranged in any way. (D) A circle was the most popular design.

5. (A) Mr. Ricci was not a tall man, yet he appeared large. (B) His body was lean but sturdy. (C) He always wore a jacket and tie. (D) A surprisingly thick neck supported his narrow head.

6. (A) Mexico has had many earthquakes. (B) Giant China has suffered the world's deadliest quakes. (C) Over 830,000 Chinese were killed in a 1556 quake. (D) In a 1976 quake, 242,000 died.

7. (A) A comet is a ball of frozen gases. (B) The sun is a giant ball of very hot gas. (C) It is kept hot by atomic reactions. (D) On its surface the temperature is about 11,000° Fahrenheit.

8. (A) *Fungi* are a kind of plant. (B) They cannot make their own food and live on other plants or animals. (C) Mushrooms are a familiar kind of fungi. (D) Algae are another kind of plant.

9. (A) The umbrella is a popular subject for riddles. (B) I collect riddles. (C) What goes up when the rain comes down? (D) What can go up a chimney down but cannot go down a chimney up?

10. (A) We had planned the picnic weeks ago. (B) Jess and I had made a luscious lunch. (C) Jess is Amy's cousin. (D) At the park we remembered the picnic basket on the kitchen table.

UNIT 6

# Composition

## Part Three

# Essays

Many times in your schooling, you will be asked to write compositions. In social studies you may write a composition describing the landforms of Latin America. In science you may write a composition explaining how to do an experiment. Compositions of three or more paragraphs are called essays.

26a An **essay** is a composition of three or more paragraphs that presents and develops one main idea.

## Your Writer's Notebook

Ideas for essays can come from a number of sources. Most of all, however, they come from your unique viewpoints. Nobody sees the world quite the way you do. Develop an understanding of yourself and the way you see things with the following activity for your journal.

Every day for a week, write out the words to a favorite song. Then answer the following questions.

1. Why do the words appeal to me? What do they say about life?
2. How does the music make me feel? Do the words and music go well together?

# Essay Structure

You learned in earlier chapters that a paragraph has three main parts. These are a topic sentence, a body of supporting sentences, and a concluding sentence. An essay also has three main parts, which function in the same way as the paragraph parts.

26b

| Parts of a Paragraph | Parts of an Essay |
|---|---|
| topic sentence expresses the main idea | introductory paragraph catches the reader's attention and contains a sentence expressing the main idea |
| body of supporting sentences | body contains one or more paragraphs that support the main idea with facts, examples, and other details |
| concluding sentence | concluding paragraph completes the essay and emphasizes the main idea |

As you develop your essay, from prewriting through editing the final draft, your personal ideas will give life to this three-part structure—introduction, body, and conclusion.

Essays have other features in common with paragraphs. Like paragraphs they have a clear *purpose*. That purpose may be to tell a story, to describe, to explain, or to persuade. Essays also must be suited to their *audience*. An essay in your journal, for example, could be personal and poetic. An essay for science class, on the other hand, would be more informative. Finally, good essays and good paragraphs have unity and coherence. The following pages will guide you through the prewriting, writing, revising, and editing stages of writing an essay.

# Prewriting

The process for writing essays is similar to the process for writing paragraphs. The first step is to find ideas. Essays written on subjects of real interest to the writer are usually the most effective.

### Exercise 1 *Thinking of Subjects by Taking Inventory*

Fold a sheet of paper in half. While it is still folded, fold it in half again, and then again. When you open the paper, you will have eight boxes. At the top of each box, write one of the categories below. Then, for each category, list the specific items that interest you most.

EXAMPLE careers
POSSIBLE ANSWERS animal trainer
pilot
teacher

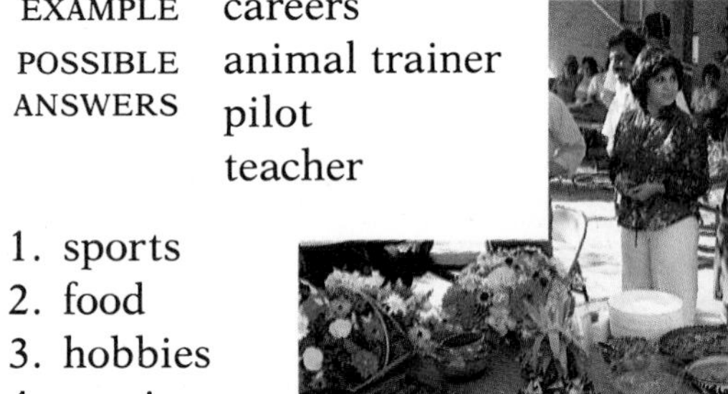

1. sports
2. food
3. hobbies
4. music
5. animals
6. games
7. history
8. science

### Exercise 2 *Thinking of Subjects by Completing Statements*

Complete each sentence with as many items as you can.

1. Scenes, objects, and people that have left a lasting impression in my mind include . . .
2. At home or with friends, I often talk about . . .
3. I could teach my friends how to . . .
4. I like to read about . . .
5. I've always wondered why . . .

## Choosing and Limiting a Subject

The following guidelines will help you choose one subject from your list of essay ideas.

26c

**Choosing an Essay Subject**

1. Choose a subject you are interested in.
2. Choose a subject that will interest your readers.
3. Choose a subject that you know enough about or can learn enough about later to develop well in three paragraphs.

After you have selected one subject, the next step is to limit it, or narrow it down. The first step in limiting your subject is to decide on your writing purpose. Do you want to tell a story, describe, explain, or persuade? Next think about who will be reading your essay—your audience. What information do your readers need to understand your subject?

The final step is to list several possible focus points that would suit your purpose and audience. Focus points are the smaller, more limited topics contained within your general subject. If you had decided to write about gymnastics, for example, you might list the focus points below.

| | |
|---|---|
| SUBJECT | Gymnastics |
| PURPOSE | To explain |
| AUDIENCE | People who enjoy watching gymnastics but do not know much about it |
| FOCUS POINTS | • how women's gymnastics is judged<br>• movements for the floor exercises<br>• safety and training equipment<br>• how the men's events differ from the women's |

Any one of these four focus points would be a suitably limited subject for a short essay.

26d

**Steps for Limiting an Essay Subject**

1. Decide on the purpose of your essay: to tell a story, to describe, to explain, or to persuade.
2. Think about who your audience (readers) will be.
3. List focus points that suit your purpose and audience.
4. Choose one focus point as your limited subject.

### EXERCISE 3 *Limiting a Subject*

Write each subject. Then list three possible focus points for each one.

1. SUBJECT victories in my life
   PURPOSE to tell a story
   AUDIENCE people who want to succeed
2. SUBJECT childhood fears
   PURPOSE to explain
   AUDIENCE young children
3. SUBJECT my neighborhood
   PURPOSE to describe
   AUDIENCE people who have never been there
4. SUBJECT earning money
   PURPOSE to explain
   AUDIENCE teenagers who want to earn money
5. SUBJECT being a teenager
   PURPOSE to explain
   AUDIENCE parents or other adults

## Listing Supporting Details

After you have decided on a focus point for your essay, the next step is to list the details you will use to support your main idea. One way to help you think of ideas is brainstorming. *Brainstorming* means "writing down everything that comes to mind when you think of your limited subject." (*See page 324.*)

Suppose you had decided to explain how women's gymnastics is judged to people who enjoy gymnastics but do not know much about it. Your brainstorming notes might appear as follows.

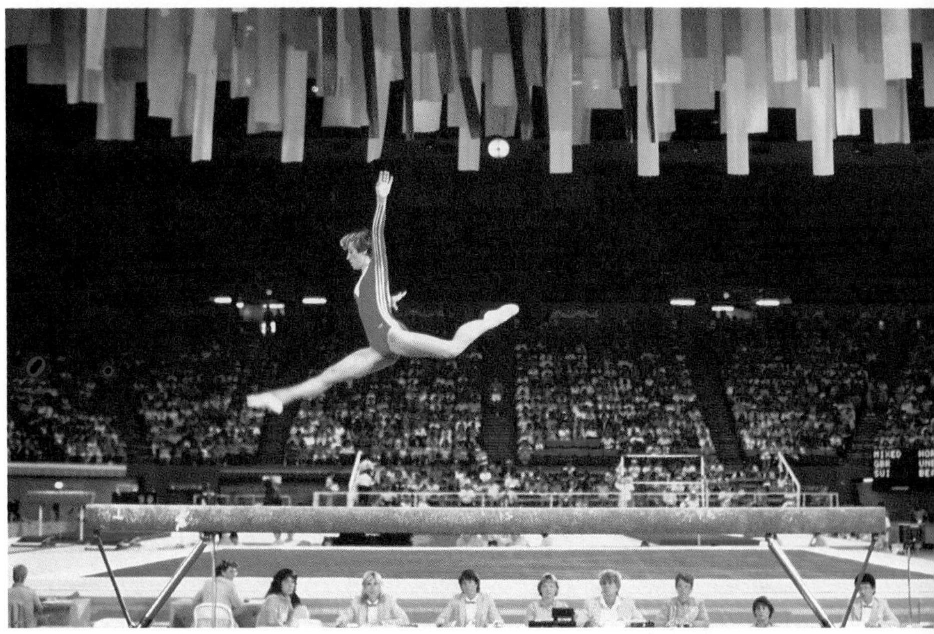

LIMITED SUBJECT how women's gymnastics is judged

BRAINSTORMING NOTES

- originality and composition 2 points
- vaulting scored separately
- perfect score 10 points
- excellent "general impression" earns maximum of 1 point
- difficulty of routine earns 5 points
- execution 2 points
- full 5 points awarded if routine includes variety of easy, medium, and hard movements
- judging standards set by Federation of International Gymnastics

The following chart shows different kinds of details listed according to the essay's purpose.

26e

| **Purpose** | **Kinds of Details** |
|---|---|
| to tell a story | events |
| to describe | sights, sounds, and other details that appeal to the senses |
| to explain | facts, examples, reasons, steps in a process |
| to persuade | reasons, based on fact, that support your opinion |

### EXERCISE 4 Listing Supporting Details

Brainstorm for ideas about each of the following limited subjects. List at least four supporting details for each one. Use the chart above to help you list the kinds of details that suit the purpose.

1. SUBJECT the first party I planned and gave
   PURPOSE to tell a story
   AUDIENCE classmates
2. SUBJECT how to fall asleep at night if you are restless
   PURPOSE to give directions
   AUDIENCE people who have trouble sleeping
3. SUBJECT songs that have a special meaning for me
   PURPOSE to explain
   AUDIENCE music lovers
4. SUBJECT the first warm day of spring
   PURPOSE to describe
   AUDIENCE people in a different region
5. SUBJECT the value of pets
   PURPOSE to persuade
   AUDIENCE people who have no pets

## Arranging Details in Logical Order

When you brainstorm, you write down ideas in the order they occur to you. Chances are they are not in a logical order. In addition, you may have listed ideas that do not strictly relate to your subject. At this last step of the prewriting stage, you can smooth these matters out.

First look over your brainstorming notes and cross out any that do not relate directly to the main idea. Next look for a way to organize your ideas logically. If some items do not fit neatly into the order you have chosen, save them for your introduction or conclusion.

Notice how the brainstorming notes about gymnastics have been grouped and logically arranged.

| | |
|---|---|
| IDEAS SAVED | • judging standards set by Federation of International Gymnastics<br>• vaulting scored separately |
| LARGEST TO SMALLEST POINT VALUE | • perfect score 10 points<br>• difficulty of the routine 5 points<br>• full 5 points awarded if routine includes variety of easy, medium, and hard movements<br>• execution 2 points<br>• originality and composition 2 points<br>• excellent "general impression" earns maximum of 1 point |

26f

**Types of Order**

| | |
|---|---|
| CHRONOLOGICAL | Items are arranged in time order. |
| SPATIAL | Items are arranged in order of location. |
| SIZE OR IMPORTANCE | Items are arranged in order of least to most, or most to least, important or sizable. |
| SEQUENTIAL | Steps in a process are arranged in the order in which they must be performed. |

## EXERCISE 5 Arranging Details in Logical Order

The following brainstorming notes are on the subject of the world's highest waterfalls. Two of the items could be used in the introduction or conclusion. The others can be arranged logically. At the top of your paper, write the two items that do not fit the logical order. Then list the remaining items in logical order. Save your work for Exercise 8.

- largest falls in the world are Angel Falls in Venezuela
- North America has third largest falls, in Yosemite
- waterfalls form when water flowing over land meets an abrupt change in the level of the land
- Angel Falls drops 3,212 feet
- Tugela Falls in South Africa drops 3,110 feet
- Yosemite Falls plunges 2,425 feet
- because of the erosion power built into them, all waterfalls eventually disappear

## EXERCISE 6 On Your Own

Review what you have learned about prewriting on pages 412–417. Then choose and limit a subject for an essay. Brainstorm a list of supporting details, and arrange those details in logical order. Save your work for Exercise 11.

# Writing

When your notes are clearly organized, you can begin the second stage of the writing process—writing the first draft. Use your notes as you write to help you include everything you planned and to help you follow a logical order.

## Writing the Introduction

One of the most important features of a strong introduction is a sentence that states the main idea of the essay. This sentence can come first, last, or in the middle of your introductory paragraph. Following is the introductory paragraph for the essay on gymnastics.

INTRODUCTION

Anyone who has seen a women's gymnastics match knows the excitement of waiting for the judges' scores. When the numbers finally appear, the crowd usually responds with cheers or groans. In most cases the scores from the various judges are very close. To a casual observer, the similarity of the scores may seem surprising. To the judges, however, scoring a gymnastic event is a matter of following the guidelines of the International Gymnastics Federation.

MAIN IDEA

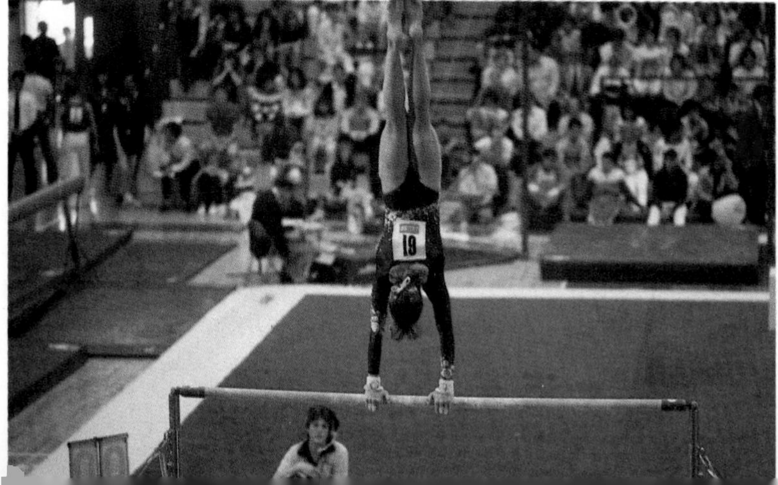

In addition to expressing the main idea, an effective introduction has several other qualities. The following guidelines will help you write strong introductions.

26g

**Writing an Introduction**

A strong introduction
1. catches the reader's attention with an interesting fact, detail, or incident.
2. gives background information if needed.
3. includes a statement of the essay's main idea.
4. does not include such empty expressions as "In this essay I will . . ." or "This essay will be about . . ."

### *EXERCISE 7 Improving a Weak Introduction*

Revise this introduction, using the guidelines above.

How to Give Medicine to a Pet

People have been keeping pets for thousands of years. The first dogs may have been wolves that early hunters tamed. Pets can be interesting and playful. Some pets have even saved lives. Sometimes, however, pets get sick. This essay will be about how to give medicine to a sick pet.

## *Writing the Body*

As you write the body, try to achieve two goals.

26h Use your notes to write complete, varied sentences with vivid words. Use transitions as needed to connect your thoughts smoothly.

Notice how the prewriting notes about gymnastics on page 417 become, with transitions, smooth sentences in the essay body. The transitions are printed in heavy type. (*See pages 348, 364, 379, 382, and 397 for lists of transitions.*)

BODY

All events except vaulting are scored by the same system. A perfect score is 10 points. **By far the most important** category in that score is "difficulty," which is worth 5 points. If the proper number of difficult movements is included in the routine, the gymnast earns the full 5 points. The **next** category, execution, is worth 2 points. If a gymnast fails to perform a movement properly, she may lose tenths of a point in this category. Originality and composition are **also** worth 2 points. For this category the judges look at how the movements are combined in the routine. The category with the **lowest** point value is "general impression," worth 1 point. In this category judges react to the overall performance of the gymnast.

### EXERCISE 8 *Writing a Body Paragraph*

Using your work from Exercise 5, write the body paragraph for an essay about the world's highest waterfalls. Underline each transition that you use.

## Writing the Conclusion

Some paragraphs may not need concluding sentences. All essays, however, need a concluding paragraph. Read the following conclusion to the essay about scoring in gymnastics.

CONCLUSION

A perfect 10 is rare. More often, gymnasts will have tenths of points taken off in one or more categories. Most gymnasts know the scoring system so well that they have a good idea of how well they did even before the judges' cards come up. Still, after the final movement or dismount, all eyes turn anxiously to the scoreboard, wondering if the perfect 10 will somehow appear.

Use the guidelines below to write strong conclusions.

26i

**Writing a Conclusion**

A strong concluding paragraph
1. emphasizes the main idea without restating it exactly.
2. may refer to ideas in the introduction to round out the essay.
3. does not introduce a completely new idea.
4. does not contain empty expressions such as "I have just told you about . . ." or "now you know how . . ."

***Writing a Title.*** When you have completed your first draft, add a title to your essay. The title should be short and catchy. It should suggest the main idea of your essay and invite your readers to read on.

### EXERCISE 9 *Improving a Weak Conclusion*

Read the following weak conclusion to an essay about how watching television affects family life. Then revise it, using the guidelines above.

> As I have shown you, watching television together has given my family members many things to talk about. In our case at least, TV viewing has not cut into family conversations. My family also goes camping together, which we enjoy very much. Spider Lake is our favorite spot.

### EXERCISE 10 *Writing Titles*

Write three possible titles for the essay about women's gymnastics.

### EXERCISE 11 *On Your Own*

Review what you have learned about writing a first draft. Then, using your work from Exercise 6, write the first draft of an essay. Save your work for Exercise 12.

# Revising

The first draft of any writing is a trial copy. Writing that is as good as you can make it usually requires several tries. Use the following checklist to improve the first draft of your essay.

26j

**Checklist for Revising Essays**

Checking Your Essay

1. Do you have an interesting introduction that includes a sentence stating the main idea of the essay?
2. Do all of your sentences relate directly to that main idea? In other words, is your essay unified?
3. Are your ideas organized logically with smooth transitions? In other words, is your essay coherent?
4. Do you have a strong conclusion?

Checking Your Paragraphs

5. If the body of your essay contains more than one paragraph, does each paragraph have a topic sentence?
6. Is each paragraph unified? (*See page 350.*)
7. Is each paragraph coherent? (*See page 351.*)

Checking Your Sentences and Words

8. Did you eliminate short, choppy sentences by combining related sentences? (*See pages 283–287.*)
9. Did you vary the beginnings of your sentences? (*See page 291.*)
10. Did you eliminate rambling sentences? (*See page 294.*)
11. Are your sentences free of repetition and empty expressions? (*See pages 295–296.*)
12. Are your words fresh and vivid? (*See pages 267–277.*)

### EXERCISE 12 *On Your Own*

Use the checklist above to improve the first draft of your essay from Exercise 11. Save your work for Exercise 13.

## Writing Extra

Imagine that you are the editor in charge of the youth newsletter from an animal shelter. A friend of yours has submitted the following short essay about how to discipline a puppy. Revise the essay so that it communicates clearly to young readers. Use the Revision Checklist on page 423 to help you.

Puppy Discipline

A new puppy in your home needs and deserves discipline. My family got a new puppy last year. We also have a cat. In this essay I will tell you some do's and don'ts you should keep in mind while raising a puppy.

Good discipline will make life more pleasant for you and your pup. One of the most important do's is teaching your pup the meaning of no. Using a loud voice will startle your puppy and make him aware that he is doing something wrong. Follow the correction with words of praise. Don't give your puppy an old shoe or item of clothing to play with and chew on. He will not be able to tell the difference between old castoffs and items you do not want destroyed. Another important do is teaching the command "Drop it." Also, do give your puppy many opportunities to go outside. Avoiding housebreaking problems is easier than correcting them. By the way, another don't is this: Don't call your puppy to you to correct him; always go to him. Oh yes, another do is this: Do correct your puppy only when you actually catch him in the act of misbehaving. If corrected too late, puppies do not remember what they did wrong.

Now you know about disciplining a puppy. He wants to learn the rules, so help him with kindness. Cats are harder to train but are usually less mischievous.

After you have completed the revision of the essay about disciplining a puppy, think of a catchy new title for it. (*See page 422.*)

# Editing

By the editing stage, you are satisified with the content and style of your essay. Your main goal now is to polish it. Use the proofreading symbols on page 354 when you edit.

26k

**Editing Checklist**

1. Are your sentences free of errors in grammar and usage?
2. Did you spell each word correctly?
3. Did you use capital letters where needed?
4. Did you punctuate sentences correctly?
5. Did you indent each paragraph?

The appearance of your composition can be almost as important as its content. A paper with uneven margins and words crossed out or crowded together is difficult to read. A neat paper, however, makes a positive impression. The following guidelines will help you prepare the final copy.

26l

**Correct Form for a Composition**

1. Use 8½- by 11-inch white paper. Use one side only.
2. Use blue or black ink. If typing, use a black typewriter ribbon and double-space the lines.
3. Put your name, course title, the name of your teacher, and the date in the upper right-hand corner of page 1.
4. Leave a 1½-inch margin at the left and a 1-inch margin at the right. Also leave a 1-inch margin at the bottom.
5. Starting on page 2, number each page in the upper right-hand corner.

## EXERCISE 13 On Your Own

Use the Editing Checklist to edit your essay from Exercise 12. Make a final, neat copy of your revised and edited essay.

# Spotlight on Writing

**A** **Writing an Essay to Inform.** The following notes are on the subject of handwriting and personality. Use them to write an informative essay.

PURPOSE To explain the theory that handwriting styles sometimes indicate certain personalities

AUDIENCE People your own age

The quick brown fox jumped over the lazy dog.
The quick brown fox jumped over the lazy dog.
The quick brown fox jumped over the lazy dog.
The quick brown fox jumped over the lazy dog.
The quick brown fox jumped over the lazy dog.

**Lines of Writing**

- level lines indicate a person who is "on the level"
- wandering lines may show carelessness
- upward-slanting lines may show optimism
- downward-slanting lines may show moodiness

**Size of Writing**

- tiny handwriting: intellectual
- large writing: generous
- huge writing: conceited but honest

**Slant of Letters**

- leans to the left: distrustful person
- leans far to the right: overly sensitive
- leans slightly to the right: easygoing and friendly

**Ideas Saved for Introduction or Conclusion**

- handwriting experts also study the shape of letters and the spacing between words
- tremendous variety of handwriting styles; no two signatures are exactly the same

**B** **Writing an Essay to Describe.** Look at the picture below of people white-water rafting. Then write an essay that describes the scene. Include details that will create a vivid picture of the event in the minds of your readers. Add sights, sounds, and smells that you think would go along with this scene.

| | |
|---|---|
| PURPOSE | To describe the excitement of white-water rafting by appealing to the senses |
| AUDIENCE | People who have never been white-water rafting and are interested in trying it |

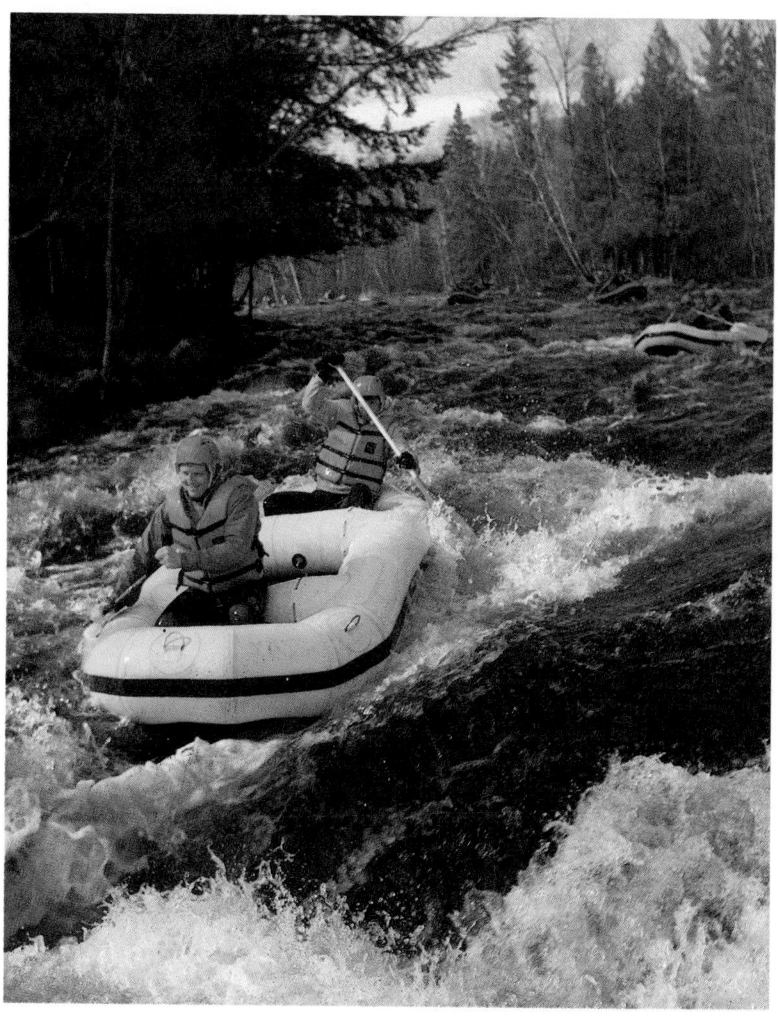

**C Writing an Essay to Relate a Personal Experience** Think of a funny experience you had that you could develop in an essay. Write down all the events that took place. Also include details of time and place. Then write your essay.

PURPOSE To tell an amusing true story
AUDIENCE Readers of a humor magazine

**D Writing an Essay to Persuade.** Think of a change or an improvement that you would like to see at your school. Write down all the reasons why this change would be good for your school. Then write your essay.

PURPOSE To bring about a positive change at school
AUDIENCE Your principal, parents, and teachers

**E Writing from your Writer's Notebook.** Choose a song that you wrote about in your journal. Then write an essay explaining how that song relates to your life.

**F Revising an Essay.** Revise one of the essays you wrote in parts A through E. Use the checklist on page 423.

**G Editing an Essay.** Use the checklist on page 425 to edit the essay you revised in Part F.

**H Writing Ideas.** Write an essay on one of the following subjects or one of your own. Use the Steps for Writing an Essay on page 429 as a guide.

1. working at a friendship
2. my favorite outfit
3. how to enjoy a cold winter
4. my favorite neighborhood spots
5. a time I learned a lesson the hard way
6. New Year's resolutions
7. how to choose a bicycle
8. a dream that came true
9. a famous person I'd like to be and why
10. my favorite time of day

# Steps for Writing an Essay

### Prewriting

1. Make a list of possible subjects by taking inventory or asking yourself questions. (*See page 412.*)
2. Choose one subject from your list. (*See page 413.*)
3. Limit your subject by deciding on your purpose, audience, and focus point. (*See pages 413–414.*)
4. Brainstorm a list of supporting details. (*See pages 414–416.*)
5. Organize your list into a logical order. (*See page 417.*)

### Writing

6. Write an introduction that includes a sentence stating the main idea. (*See pages 419–420.*)
7. Use your notes to write the body of your essay, with smooth transitions between ideas. (*See pages 420–421.*)
8. Add a concluding paragraph. (*See pages 421–422.*)
9. Add a title. (*See page 422.*)

### Revising

10. Use the Revision Checklist on page 423 to improve your first draft.

### Editing

11. Use the Editing Checklist on page 425 to polish your work.

# 27

# Reports

A report and an essay have many features in common. Both have an introduction, a body, and a conclusion. Essays and reports are different, however, in one important way. Essays are developed from the writer's own experience and knowledge. Reports, on the other hand, usually rely on ideas gathered from reading.

27a A **report** is a composition of three or more paragraphs that uses information from books, magazines, and other sources.

## Your Writer's Notebook

One good way to find subjects for a report is to check *The Readers' Guide to Periodical Literature* in the library. (*See pages 557–558.*) It contains thousands of subjects and lists recent magazine articles on them. Write down any interesting subjects you see as you look through the *Readers' Guide.* Also jot down the names of magazine articles about them. Later, in your journal, write down everything you already know about each subject. Write any questions that come to mind.

# Research Reports

One of the most common types of reports is the research report. Students write research reports to learn about new subjects. Workers write research reports to convey important information to company leaders. Since the purpose of a research report is to give information, you will be using the skills of expository writing when you work on your report. (*See Chapter 24.*) You will also be using your library skills as you gather the information you need. (*See Chapter 33.*)

The three main parts of a report are the introduction, the body, and the conclusion. In addition, a report has a title and a page that lists your sources of information. Each part of the report has a special purpose.

**Structure of a Report**

| | |
|---|---|
| **TITLE** | • suggests the subject of the report |
| **INTRODUCTION** | • captures the reader's attention<br>• provides any background information that your reader may need to know<br>• contains a sentence expressing the main idea of the report |
| **BODY** | • supports the main idea stated in the introduction<br>• follows the order of your outline<br>• includes specific information from your sources |
| **CONCLUSION** | • brings the report to a close<br>• summarizes the main idea<br>• includes a comment that shows the importance of your subject |
| **SOURCES** | • list your sources of information<br>• appear at the end of the report |

# Prewriting

In some ways writing a research report is like working on a puzzle. The first step in solving the puzzle is finding pieces of information from books and magazines. The second step is fitting those pieces together into an organized whole. To help you keep track of all the pieces of information, gather the supplies you will need. These include a folder with pockets, index cards, paper clips, and rubber bands.

## Choosing and Limiting a Subject

When you choose a subject for an essay, you try to find one that you know enough about to explain well. When you choose a subject for a report, however, you look for one that requires research in books and magazines.

Compare the following subjects. Only those that require research are suitable for a report.

| PERSONAL EXPERIENCE | RESEARCH |
|---|---|
| how to practice the piano | the history of the piano |
| my best Thanksgiving | the first Thanksgiving |
| why I like sports | televising a sports event |

Once you have several ideas for a subject, use the following guidelines to help you choose one.

27b

**Choosing a Subject**

1. Choose a subject you would like to know more about.
2. Choose a subject your reader might like to know more about.
3. Choose a subject that can be covered adequately in a short report.
4. Choose a subject on which there will be enough information in the library.

Once you have found a general subject that requires research, the next step is to limit it. Your subject should be limited enough to allow you to cover it completely in a short report. To limit your subject, think about the smaller parts that make up your general subject. Also consider limiting it to a specific time or place. The following guidelines will help you limit a subject for a report.

27c

**Ways to Limit a Subject**

1. Divide the general subject into its smaller parts.

   **EXAMPLE** televising a sports event
   **PARTS** setting up the camera crew
   selling commercials
   choosing announcers

2. Limit the subject to a certain time or place.

   **EXAMPLE** the history of the piano
   **TIME** pianos in Mozart's time
   **PLACE** pianos made in Japan

### EXERCISE 1 *Identifying Subjects That Need Research*

Decide whether each subject is a personal experience topic or whether it is a research topic. Indicate your answer by writing *experience* or *research* after the proper number.

1. physical education classes at my school
2. laws requiring physical education in schools
3. why leaves change color in the fall
4. favorite autumn activities at school
5. how an airplane gets off the ground
6. mining the ocean floor
7. your trip to Yellowstone National Park
8. efforts to save the grizzly bears in Yellowstone National Park
9. my favorite records and videos
10. supernovas

### EXERCISE 2 *Limiting a Subject*

For each general subject, write two limited subjects that would be suitable for a short report.

EXAMPLE whales
POSSIBLE ANSWERS how whales breathe
training whales to perform

1. city life
2. American Indians
3. games
4. television shows
5. football
6. zoos
7. computers
8. driving
9. movies
10. hobbies

## Gathering Information

You can begin gathering information once you have a limited subject. The best way to begin the process of gathering information is to make a list of questions. Think about your subject and what you already know about it. Then write a list of questions that you need to answer in order to explain your subject well.

Suppose you had decided to write a report on efforts to protect the bald eagle. Your research questions might appear as follows.

- When did eagles become endangered?
- Why did eagles become endangered?
- How many eagles are left?
- How are people trying to help the eagles?

The following steps will help you find answers to your research questions.

27d

**Steps for Gathering Information**

1. Begin by checking an encyclopedia. This will give you an overview of your subject. It may also contain a list of books with more information.
2. Use the subject cards in the card catalog to find more books on your subject. (*See page 550*.)
3. Check *The Readers' Guide to Periodical Literature* for magazine articles. (*See pages 557–558*.)
4. Make a list of all your sources. For each source record the author, title, publisher's name and location, date of publication, and call number.

Your final list of sources may look like the following.

ENCYCLOPEDIA William H. Drury, "Eagle," *World Book Encyclopedia,* 1982 ed.

BOOKS *Birds of Prey* by Glenys and Derek Lloyd, New York: Grosset and Dunlap, 1970, Y598.2 LL

*The Magnificent Birds of Prey* by Philip S. Callahan, New York: Holiday House, 1974, Y598.9 CA

MAGAZINES *Newsweek,* July 9, 1984, pp. 64–65, "Comeback for a National Symbol" by Sharon Begley with Susan Angrest

*Sierra,* March/April 1983, pp. 68–69, "In Celebration of Eagles" by Tupper Ansel Blake

### *EXERCISE 3 Gathering Information*

Use the library to list three sources for each subject. At least one source should be a magazine. Follow the Steps for Gathering Information above, including step 4.

1. Saturn's rings
2. police dogs
3. the goals of Junior Achievement
4. programming computers in BASIC

## Taking Notes

Before you begin taking notes, skim your sources looking for information that will answer your research questions. When you find the parts of the book that answer your questions, read them carefully, looking for the main ideas. Then use your own words to note those ideas on your card. To help you later when you sort your notes, be sure to prepare your card according to the following guidelines.

27e

**Taking Notes**

1. Write the title of your source in the upper right-hand corner of your index card.
2. Write a heading in the upper left-hand corner of your card to identify the part of the subject being discussed.
3. Begin a new card whenever you start taking notes on a different part of your subject.
4. Summarize main points in your own words.
5. Record the page number from which your information is taken.

Read the following excerpt from the *World Book Encyclopedia* on the subject of eagles. The sample note card on page 437 shows how the information can be summarized on an index card.

> Until the mid-1900s, hunters and trappers killed many bald eagles. The species has been protected by federal law since 1940 in 48 states, and since 1953 in Alaska. However, the continued loss of wilderness regions due to the growth of farms and urban areas has caused a further decline in the bald-eagle population. The number of bald eagles has also dropped because of the pollution of lakes and rivers with pesticides and industrial wastes. These pollutants build up in the bodies of fish, which are then eaten by the eagles. In most cases the pollutants do not kill the birds, but they interfere with the birds' ability to reproduce.

**Sample Note Card**

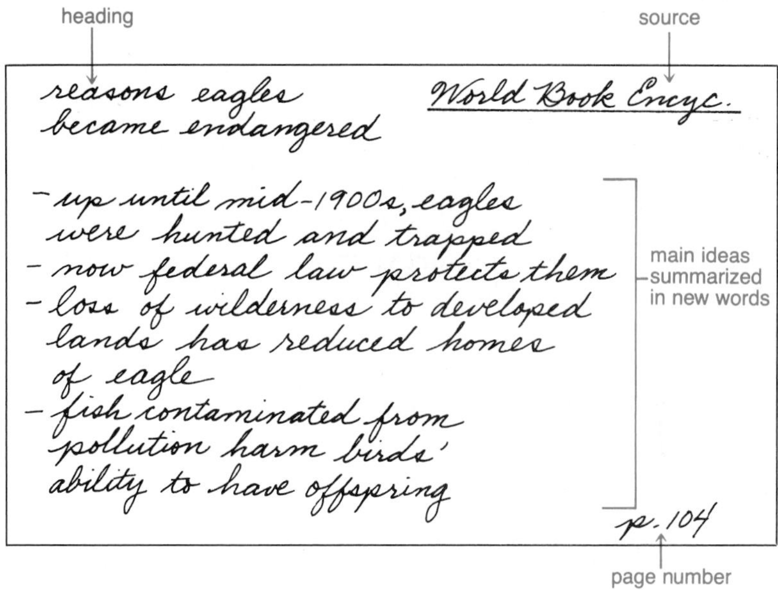

heading
source
reasons eagles became endangered
World Book Encyc.
- up until mid-1900s, eagles were hunted and trapped
- now federal law protects them
- loss of wilderness to developed lands has reduced homes of eagle
- fish contaminated from pollution harm birds' ability to have offspring
main ideas summarized in new words
p. 104
page number


Clip all the note cards from each source separately. Later you will sort them into categories.

### EXERCISE 4 *Taking Notes*

The following information about Eskimo shelters of long ago is from page 278a of the *World Book Encyclopedia*. Make a note card for it. Use the card above as a model.

> **Shelter.** Most Eskimo families had a summer home and a winter home. During the summer almost all Eskimos lived in tents made of sealskin or caribou skin. In winter the Eskimos of most regions lived in sod houses. They also built dome-shaped snowhouses as temporary shelters when they traveled. The Eskimos called snowhouses and sod houses igloos.
>
> The Eskimos built snowhouses with snow that had been packed and hardened by wind and frost. They used a snow knife—a long, straight knife made of bone—to cut blocks of snow about 3 feet (91 centimeters) long, 1½ feet (46 centimeters) wide, and 4 to

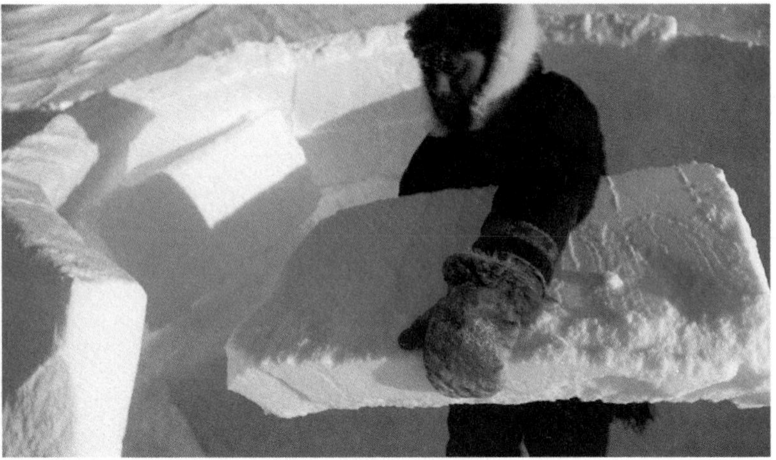

6 inches (10 to 15 centimeters) thick. They stacked the blocks in a continuous, circular row that wound upward, in smaller and smaller circles, to form the dome-shaped house. An Eskimo could build such a house in a couple of hours.

## Outlining

When you have finished your research, you are ready to organize your notes into an outline for the body of your report. Use the following steps as a guide.

27f

### Preparing an Outline

1. Use the headings on your note cards to group the cards into a few categories.
2. Save the cards that do not fit into any category for possible use in the introduction or conclusion.
3. Make a list of your categories. Then, using Roman numerals (I, II, III, etc.), arrange your categories in a logical order. (*See page 417.*)
4. Use the categories as the main topics in your outline.
5. Using your note cards, list subtopics under each main topic. (Use capital letters for subtopics.)

Below are three categories that might be used for the body of a report on efforts to save eagles.

- controlled hatching
- hacking
- preserving wilderness lands

The outline for the body of this report might appear as follows. Notice that the three categories become main topics in the outline.

SUBJECT efforts to save eagles

MAIN TOPIC I. Controlled hatching

SUBTOPICS
- A. Eggs taken from nest
- B. Eggs warmed by a chicken
- C. Hatchlings returned to wild
- D. Hatchlings adopted by foster eagle parents

MAIN TOPIC II. Hacking

SUBTOPICS
- A. Moving eaglets to caged tower in safe location
- B. Caring for eaglets for five or six weeks
- C. Releasing them as free birds

MAIN TOPIC III. Preserving wilderness lands

SUBTOPICS
- A. Importance of Alaska
- B. Protection of southeast Alaska from development

After you have finished your outline, use the following guidelines to check its form.

27g

**Checking an Outline**

1. Did you use Roman numerals for main topics?
2. Did you use capital letters for subtopics?
3. If you include subtopics under main topics, do you have at least two?
4. Did you indent as shown in the above model?
5. Did you capitalize the first word of each entry?

## EXERCISE 5 Outlining

Use the subtopics below to complete the following outline. Place each subtopic under the proper main topic.

SUBJECT how Superman was made to appear to fly

I. The basic equipment
   A.
   B.
II. The backgrounds
   A.
   B.
III. The cape
   A.
   B.

SUBTOPICS

- Miniatures and models of buildings
- Failure of wind machine to make cape flap properly
- Actor Christopher Reeve wearing hip harness with wires
- Wires reaching to track along ceiling of studio
- Radio-controlled device operated rods that moved cape successfully
- Trick photography, in which background shot is combined with shot of Superman flying through studio

## EXERCISE 6 On Your Own

Use the following prewriting steps to plan a report. Save your work for Exercise 11.

STEP 1 Choose and limit a subject for a report. You may want to choose a subject from your writer's notebook.

STEP 2 Gather information from at least three sources and take notes on cards.

STEP 3 Organize your notes into categories.

STEP 4 Use your categories to write an outline for the body of your report.

## Writing Extra

You can use your knowledge of logical order to write a four-line poem. Starter lines are provided for each of the four types of logical order. Think of a general subject to write about. Then finish each line of the poem with an idea about your subject. The example poem may give you ideas for your own poems.

**CHRONOLOGICAL ORDER**
In the earliest times . . .
Later . . .
Soon . . .
Today . . .

**SPATIAL ORDER**
At the bottom . . .
In the middle . . .
Near the top . . .
Way above . . .

**SEQUENTIAL ORDER**
First . . .
Next . . .
Then . . .
Finally . . .

**ORDER OF IMPORTANCE OR SIZE**
The least of all . . .
The next . . .
More than that . . .
The most . . .

My Dad *(Order of Importance)*
The least of all is his funny sneeze,
The next is his great pitching arm,
More than that is his fun way to play,
The most is the love in his eyes.

# Writing

Your goal in writing the first draft of your report is to structure your information into an introduction, a body, and a conclusion. Review the structure of a report on page 431.

## Writing the Introduction

A good introduction is like a promise to your readers. It focuses your readers' attention on the main idea and leads them to expect certain details in the rest of the report. Use the following guidelines to write a strong introduction.

27h

**Writing an Introduction**

A strong introduction
1. captures the reader's attention.
2. provides any background information needed.
3. contains a sentence expressing the main idea of the report.

Read the following two introductions to a report on eagles. Both capture attention and provide background information. The first, however, fails to focus the reader's attention on the main idea.

UNFOCUSED INTRODUCTION

The bald eagle has been the symbol of the United States since 1792. Some early Americans, including Benjamin Franklin, did not like that choice. However, since the eagle is found only in North America, it was voted to receive the high honor of representing the United States. Two hundred years later, President Ronald Reagan declared 1982 "the Year of the Eagle." The eagle is indeed a magnificent bird of prey.

FOCUSED INTRODUCTION

For more than 200 years, the bald eagle has been the symbol of the United States. At the time it was chosen as the national emblem, the eagle numbered about 50,000 in 48 states. By the early 1970s, however, only about 3,000 remained. The last great refuge for bald eagles is Alaska, where an estimated 30,000 still live. Fear for the dwindling population has led to laws protecting eagles in all states, including Alaska. Perhaps even more important, scientists are finding creative ways to increase the eagle population.

MAIN IDEA

Notice that all of the sentences in the second introduction build up to the main idea. No unrelated ideas are included. This introduction provides a clear promise to the readers.

### EXERCISE 7 *Writing Main Idea Statements*

Read each simple report outline. Then write a sentence that clearly expresses the main idea.

1. SUBJECT how cars can be designed to save fuel
   I. Shape of the car
   II. Size of the car
   III. Design of the engine
2. SUBJECT landforms of the United States
   I. Young, rugged mountains in the West
   II. Plateaus in the Southwest
   III. Wide plains in the Midwest
   IV. Old, eroded mountains in the East
3. SUBJECT access for persons who are wheelchair-bound
   I. Ramps and wide doors into buildings
   II. Slanted street curbs for wheelchairs
   III. Buses and trains with lifts for the wheelchairs
4. SUBJECT safety gear worn by football players
   I. Helmets
   II. Padding
   III. Special bandages

## Writing the Body

With your outline as a guide, writing the body of your report is a matter of developing your ideas into smoothly connected sentences and paragraphs. You will use transitions to help guide your readers from idea to idea. (*See pages 348, 364, 379, 382, and 397 for lists of transitions.*)

Notice how the following report body follows the outline on page 439.

FROM ROMAN NUMERAL I IN OUTLINE

One of the most effective ways of increasing the eagle population is by controlling the hatching of eggs. At a research center in Maryland, eggs laid by captive eagles are taken away from the nest. They are then incubated under chickens. Meanwhile, the mother soon lays more eggs. If she had her original brood to watch, she would not lay more eggs. In this way more eaglets can be born from each mother. In some cases the eggs laid by captive eagles are taken into the wild and placed in the nests of other eagles. Most wild eagles seem willing to adopt and care for the new eggs.

FROM ROMAN NUMERAL II

Another technique for increasing the population is called hacking. *Hacking* means "moving young birds to a new, safe habitat." In most cases eaglets are taken from their birthplace and moved to a caged tower in the new location. There they are fed by workers. To prevent these wild birds from becoming dependent on humans, the workers never get close enough to the birds to be seen. When they are old enough to survive on their own, the eagles are released.

FROM ROMAN NUMERAL III

Although these measures have helped the eagle population, they are not enough. The wilderness homes of the eagles must also be protected, especially in Alaska. Many of the birds taken captive for breeding and hacking are taken from Alaska. If water pollution and the use of insecticides become too widespread, Alaska's stock of bald eagles may also become threatened. Some researchers believe that developers should not be allowed to work in the 48,000-acre preserve in southeast Alaska where most bald eagles live.

27i Use your outline to write the paragraphs in the **body** of your report. Write a paragraph for each main topic.

## EXERCISE 8 Recognizing Transitions

Reread the body of the report on pages 444–445. Then write answers to the following questions.

1. What transitional phrase is used to introduce the first main topic?
2. What are the other transitions used in the first paragraph of the body?
3. What transitional word introduces the second main topic?
4. What two transitional words are used in the first two sentences of the third paragraph of the body?

## Writing the Conclusion

A strong conclusion provides a wrap-up of the details in the body of a report. Read the following conclusion to the report on eagles.

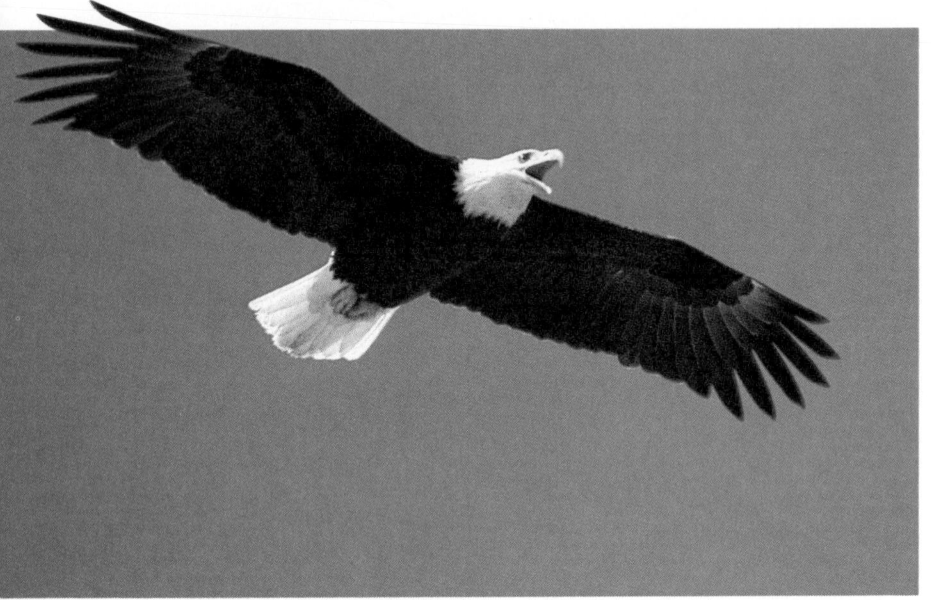

CONCLUSION

In recent years the eagles have found many friends to help them survive. Since 1979, a Bald Eagle Conference has been held every year in the Klamath Basin on the Oregon-California border. The purpose of the conference is to study the eagle and discuss more ways to protect it. In 1982, President Ronald Reagan focused attention on the eagle by declaring the 200th birthday of the national symbol as "the Year of the Eagle." The hatching and hacking programs in many states are also critical to the birds' survival. The more people learn about the needs of the eagle and how to protect it, the greater are the chances that this majestic national symbol will celebrate its 300th birthday next century.

This conclusion adds a strong ending to the report by following several of the guidelines given below. Use these guidelines whenever you write a conclusion to a report.

27j

**Writing a Conclusion**

1. Restate your main idea in new words.
2. Include a comment that shows the importance of your subject.
3. Round out the report by referring to an idea in the introduction without repeating it exactly.
4. Avoid simply repeating the ideas in the body.
5. Avoid adding a completely new idea.
6. Avoid such phrases as "Now you have seen . . ." or "I have just told you . . ."

Once you have finished your first draft, give your report an interesting title. Your title should catch your reader's interest and indicate what your report is about.

### EXERCISE 9 Writing Titles

Write two possible titles for the report on eagles. (*See pages 443, 444–445, and 446.*)

## Listing Sources

As a final step in preparing your report, you need to list your sources of information. This list will be the final page of your completed report. The sources should be listed in alphabetical order according to the author's last name. If no name is given, use the first word in the title for alphabetizing. Write the word *Sources* centered at the top of the page.

The following examples show the correct order of information and punctuation for different types of sources. Notice that page numbers are given only for magazine articles.

27k

**Correct Form for Sources**

| | |
|---|---|
| MAGAZINES | Blake, Tupper Ansel. "In Celebration of Eagles." *Sierra* March–April 1983: 68–69. |
| BOOKS | Callahan, Phillip S. *The Magnificent Birds of Prey*. New York: Holiday House, 1974. |
| ENCYCLOPEDIAS | Drury, William H. "Eagles." *World Book Encyclopedia*. 1982 ed. |
| | "Eagle." *Encyclopaedia Britannica: Micropaedia*. 1983 ed. |

## EXERCISE 10 Preparing a Sources Page

The following sources are on the subject of careers in writing and journalism. Prepare a sources page in correct form. First alphabetize the sources by the author's last name (or the first letter of the title if no author is given). Then use the above models to write each one, using the correct form and punctuation.

1. *Publishing Careers,* a book by Charles Paul May, published in New York by Franklin Watts, Inc., in 1978
2. "Journalism" in *Collier's Encyclopedia,* 1983 edition
3. *Investigative Reporting,* a book by Marilyn Moorcraft published in 1981 by Franklin Watts, Inc., in New York
4. a magazine article by Barry Beyer called "Making the Pen Mightier," published in *Phi Delta Kappan* in the November 1982 issue on pages 193–196

## EXERCISE 11 On Your Own

Use your outline from Exercise 6 to write the first draft of a report, including a sources page and a title. Remember that your outline is for the body of the report. You may find ideas for your introduction and conclusion in the notes you did not use in your outline. Save your work for Exercise 12.

# Revising

In the process of writing your report, you may not have been able to concentrate on all the elements of clear writing. During the revising stage, you can stand back from your report and try to read it with a fresh eye.

27l

**Checklist for Revising Reports**

Checking Your Report

1. Does your introduction contain a sentence expressing the main idea of the report? (*See pages 442–443.*)
2. Does the body of your report support the main idea with specific information and examples?
3. Did you use your own words?
4. Did you use transitions?
5. Does your report have unity? (*See page 350.*)
6. Does your report have coherence? (*See page 351.*)
7. Does your conclusion add a strong ending? (*See pages 446–447.*)
8. Does your report have a title? (*See page 447.*)
9. Does your report have a sources page? (*See pages 447–448.*)

Checking Your Paragraphs

10. Does each paragraph of the body have a topic sentence? (*See page 304.*)
11. Is each paragraph unified and coherent? (*See pages 350 and 444–445.*)

Checking Your Sentences and Words

12. Are your sentences varied? (*See page 291.*)
13. Are your sentences concise? (*See pages 294–296.*)
14. Did you use specific, vivid words? (*See pages 267–268.*)

### EXERCISE 12 On Your Own

Using the Revision Checklist, revise the report you wrote for Exercise 11. Save your work for Exercise 14.

# Editing

The final stage in writing a research report is preparing a finished, polished copy. Use the editing checklist that follows to prepare your final copy. You may want to use the proofreading symbols on page 354 as you edit.

27m

**Editing Checklist**

1. Are your sentences free of errors in grammar and usage?
2. Did you spell each word correctly?
3. Did you capitalize and punctuate correctly?
4. Does your list of sources match the form given on page 448?
5. Did you use correct manuscript form? (*See page 425.*)
6. Did you make a neat final copy of your report?

## EXERCISE 13 *Editing a Concluding Paragraph*

Use the Editing Checklist to polish this final paragraph from a research report about the repairing of the Statue of Liberty. There are 10 errors.

Restoring and repairing the Statue of Liberty cost millions of dollars, and involved many years of hard work. The results, however, was well worth the expense. Miss Liberty is not just an ordanary statue standing in new york harbor. She is a cymbal of the United States of america and a sign of freedom for the rest of the world. Because of the recent alterations, the statue of Liberty is stronger and beautifuller than ever. The contributions made by people across the United States will help keep the famus torch burning brightly. For many years into the future.

## EXERCISE 14 *On Your Own*

Edit your report from Exercise 12 by using the Editing Checklist. Then make a neat final copy of your report.

# Book Reports

Another kind of report is the book report. Most book reports have two main purposes.

27n A **book report** offers a brief summary of the book and an opinion about the quality of the book.

Like other compositions a book report has an introduction, a body, and a conclusion.

27o **Structure of a Book Report**

| | |
|---|---|
| INTRODUCTION | • gives the title and the author's name<br>• tells the subject of the book<br>• may give background information about the author<br>• identifies the time and location of the story in a fictional book<br>• expresses your opinion of the book |
| BODY | • offers specific reasons and examples from the book to support your opinion<br>• includes highlights from the book |
| CONCLUSION | • restates your opinion in new words<br>• adds a strong ending |

When you write a book report, assume that your readers are not familiar with the book. Include a brief summary of what the book is about. Do not try to retell the whole story, however. You will soon run out of room for your opinion of the book if you give too many details.

Also, watch your writing for unnecessary shifts in tense. If you are telling what happened to a character, use the present tense and stick to it. ("The main character, Mark, *tries* to find his father and *searches* throughout the West without giving up.")

Finally, when giving your opinion of the book, avoid stating you like or dislike the book. Instead, try to determine the book's overall effect on you. Were you moved, held in suspense, or bored when you read it? Once you have determined the overall effect, give specific details from the book that show what you mean.

The notes at the left of the following book report show the features to strive for in your book reports.

<u>Across Five Aprils</u>

**INTRODUCTION:** GIVES TITLE, AUTHOR, SUBJECT, AND SETTING

<u>Across Five Aprils</u> is a novel by Irene Hunt about a farm family's living through the Civil War in southern Illinois. Hunt herself spent her early years on a farm in southern Illinois, and the people she describes seem lifelike. The story focuses on Jethro Creighton, a boy of nine years when the story begins, and the tragedies that befall his family during the long war. Jethro's likable character and Hunt's vivid descriptions make the book very involving and realistic.

OVERALL OPINION

BODY: GIVES SPECIFIC HIGHLIGHTS

Jethro learns many hard lessons during the four years of the war. Early in the book, his oldest and best-loved brother, Bill, leaves home to fight for the South. Bill's decision angers Jethro's neighbors, who torment the remaining family. Jethro finds unexpected help, however, from a man who used to be an enemy. From this he learns that people do not divide neatly into good and bad. Jethro's hardest lesson comes when he must decide whether or not to report his cousin Eb to the authorities. Eb had joined the Union army but deserted in despair. Jethro's final decision—writing to President Lincoln for help—shows how mature Jethro has become.

CONCLUSION: SUMS UP AND RESTATES MAIN IDEA

At the end of the book, most of the family is together again. The war, however, has taken its toll on all of them. The author clearly portrays how one small family has been so greatly affected by the larger war. Throughout, the descriptions of the farm in southern Illinois and the stories of the battles ring true. The tenderness in Jethro's family, shown in his mother, father, and sister Jenny especially, helps explain how Jethro grows up to become such an admirable young man.

Use the Steps for Writing a Book Report on page 459 whenever you write a book report.

### EXERCISE 15 *On Your Own*

Choose a book on which to write a book report. Read it carefully. Then jot down answers to the following questions. Save your work for Spotlight on Writing.

1. What was your overall reaction to the book?
2. What scenes stand out in your memory?
3. What are the high points of the story?
4. Would you recommend this book to someone else? Why or why not?

Chris Blanton

# Spotlight on Writing

**A** **Taking Notes.** Imagine that you are planning a report on ESP (extrasensory perception) in animals. Prepare a note card, using the following information from page 9 of a book titled *From Instinct to Intelligence: How Animals Learn* by Gloria Kirshner. Use the card on page 437 as a model.

A headline in a *New York Times* dated June 1968 read, "A Hero Horse's Sense Saves Motorists' Lives." The UPI dispatch from Oviedo, Spain, reported, "A horse received a hero's welcome here for having saved several lives by refusing to enter a tunnel.

"The driver, a local baker, had tried everything to get the animal to move because it was holding up a line of impatient motorists on the road between Ciano and La Nueva.

"Seconds later, the tunnel collapsed."

**B** **Using Your Own Words.** You have decided to include the story of the horse and tunnel in your report. Use your note card to rewrite the story in your own words.

**C** **Outlining.** The notes on pages 455 and 456 are on the subject of ESP in animals. They were taken from *The Strange World of Animals and Pets* by Vincent and Margaret Gaddis. They are not in any order. Follow the steps on page 438 to prepare an outline based on these notes.

homing-dog — *Strange World*

— in the 1920s, collie named Bobbie found his way home to Oregon all the way from Indiana

pp. 130-137

approach of storm-cat — *Strange World*

— cat in Lawrence, Kansas, moved all her kittens days before cyclone came and knocked down old home

p. 185

approach of storm-dog — *Strange World*

— Redsy, a setter, refused to get on boat. Saved his owner, Wm. H. Montgomery, from hurricane in New England in 1938

p. 184

death of owner-bees — *Strange World*

— in April 1961, bees from Sam Rogers' hives in England came to his funeral and sat in funeral wreaths for ½ hour.

p. 208

homing-salmon *Strange World*

– "Indomitable" had to travel up a stream, a canal, a culvert and then straight up a pipe; then had to jump over a 2-ft. net to return home

p.93

approach of storm-birds *Strange World*

–European swifts fly hundreds of miles away several days before storm comes; their young, who can't fly, go into hibernation

p.186

death of owner-geese *Strange World*

–John Gambill once nursed a wounded goose back to health; when Gambill died, flock of geese circled and honked over hospital

p.201

homing-cat *Strange World*

– Tommy traveled 850 miles from Palo Alto, California, to his home in Seattle; took him 14 mos.

p.128

**D** **Revising an Introduction.** The following introduction to a report on ESP in animals needs work. It jumps from point to point. It also fails to focus the reader's attention on the limited subject. Revise it until it meets the guidelines on page 442.

> Animals are very interesting. Pets have long been an important part of many households. Some people believe animals have ESP, or extrasensory perception. Many animals appear to have a sixth sense. Animals are also much more intelligent than many people may give them credit for. Animals can be brave too. ESP in animals is a fascinating subject.

**E** **Writing a Research Report.** Write a research report on one of the following subjects or on one of your choice. (Review your writer's notebook for ideas.) Follow the Steps for Writing a Research Report on page 458.

1. how and when your state was admitted to the Union
2. how the Chicago Fire of 1871 was put out
3. the destruction after Mount St. Helens volcano erupted in 1980
4. how professional football players train
5. Alexander Graham Bell's work with the deaf
6. how cable television works
7. the first space ride of John Glenn
8. friendliness in dolphins
9. Harriet Tubman's role in the Underground Railroad
10. the moons of Jupiter

**F** **Writing a Book Report.** Write a book report on one of the following books or on one of your choice. (You may use your ideas from Exercise 15.) Follow the Steps for Writing Book Reports on page 459.

*Lilies of the Field* by William Barrett
*People of the Dream* by James Forman
*The Chosen* by Chaim Potok
*Julie of the Wolves* by Jean C. George

# Steps for Writing a Research Report

## Prewriting

1. Choose a subject requiring research and limit it. (*See pages 432–433.*)
2. Gather information from encyclopedias, books, and magazines. (*See pages 434–435.*)
3. Take notes on note cards. (*See pages 436–437.*)
4. Organize your notes into categories and use them to outline the body. (*See pages 438–439.*)

## Writing

5. Write an introduction that includes a sentence expressing your main idea. (*See pages 442–443.*)
6. Use your outline to write the body in your own words. (*See pages 444–445.*)
7. Add a concluding paragraph. (*See pages 446–447.*)
8. Add a title. (*See page 447.*)
9. Prepare a list of sources as your final page. (*See pages 447–448.*)

## Revising

10. Use the Checklist for Revising Reports on page 449 to improve your first draft.

## Editing

11. Use the Editing Checklist on page 450 to polish your work.

# Steps for Writing a Book Report

## Prewriting

1. If you are writing about a nonfiction book, briefly summarize the author's main point in your own words. If you are writing about a fiction book, briefly summarize the story in your own words.
2. Describe in a sentence or two the book's overall effect on you. How did you feel when reading it?
3. Skim the book, jotting down specific details that lead to your overall feeling about the book.

## Writing

4. Write an introduction that tells the title, the author, and the subject. Include a sentence that expresses your opinion of the book.
5. Write the body. Include specific details from the book that support your opinion of it and that show the reader more about the book.
6. Write a conclusion that restates your opinion of the book in new words.

## Revising

7. Did you summarize the book briefly?
8. Did you use present tense consistently?
9. Did you avoid stating you liked or disliked the book and instead offer a specific opinion?

## Editing

10. Check your work for errors in grammar, spelling, punctuation, and capitalization.
11. Did you use correct manuscript form? (*See page 425.*)
12. Did you make a neat final copy of your report?

# 28

# Letters

Everyone likes to receive a letter in the mail addressed especially to him or her. Aside from the friendship letters can communicate, they are also widely used to conduct business. In this chapter you will learn the correct form for different kinds of letters. You will also practice shaping your written message to suit both the purpose of the letter and the receiver.

## Your Writer's Notebook

Think about events and people that you would like to remember in the future. Then every day for a week, write a letter to yourself that you will open ten years from now. Record experiences, thoughts, feelings, doubts, and wishes—whatever you want to remember. The following may give you ideas to write about.

1. What changes are happening in your life?
2. What events have given you the most pleasure?
3. What changes do you hope to see in yourself in ten years?
4. What changes do you hope to see in the world around you in ten years?

# Friendly Letters

Some friends write letters just to keep in touch, but the friendly letter can also serve other, more specific purposes. It can be used to thank someone for a gift or to invite someone to a party. It can also be used to express congratulations or sorrow. Whenever it is used, the friendly letter should be courteous and neat.

## Friendly Letter Form

The letter on page 462 shows the correct form for a friendly letter. All friendly letters have five main parts.

28a The parts of a friendly letter are the **heading, salutation, body, closing,** and **signature.**

HEADING The heading includes your full address with ZIP code. Write the full name of your state or use the abbreviation. (*See page 469 for a full listing.*) Always include the date after your address. Remember to follow the rules for capitalizing proper nouns and using commas.

SALUTATION The salutation is your friendly greeting. Always capitalize the first word and all nouns. Use a comma after the salutation.

**D**ear **U**ncle **H**ugh,  **D**ear **M**om,

BODY Your conversational message makes up the body. Remember to indent each paragraph.

CLOSING End with a brief closing, followed by a comma. Capitalize the first word only.

**Y**our friend,  **L**ove always,

SIGNATURE Your signature should be handwritten below the closing.

## Correct Form for a Friendly Letter

heading 1612 Maple Avenue
Grace, MS 38745
January 30, 1987

salutation
Dear Matt,

body Well, nearly a month has passed since New Year's Eve. So far I've done pretty well at sticking to my resolutions. I did join the computer-users club, and I think I've made a few new friends. I still miss everyone in Atlanta very much.

How was your trip to Kentucky to visit your relatives? I hope you had a great time. I am looking forward to hearing about it when you write.

Please say hello to everyone at school for me.

closing Your friend,
signature Janet

NOTE: The envelope for a friendly letter may be handwritten. It should contain the same information as that on the envelope for a business letter. (*See pages 469–470.*) Be sure both addresses are clear and complete.

## Thank-you Notes

When you write a thank-you note, mention the gift and tell how much you appreciate it. The thank-you note below contains the five parts of a friendly letter.

**Thank-you Note**

54 Greeley Avenue
Charlestown, SC 29411
September 13, 1987

Dear Uncle Jason,

Thank you very much for the unusual and thoughtful birthday present. I guess my parents told you how much I wanted to build a telescope. Buying me the supplies was a great idea!

My class at the planetarium begins next Tuesday. In just eight weeks my telescope should be finished. Maybe you could come over some night, and we could do some stargazing together.

Love,

Tim

***Bread-and-butter Notes.*** If you stay overnight or longer with a friend or relative, you should write a special thank-you note called a bread-and-butter note. Using friendly-letter form, tell your host and hostess how much you appreciated their having you. Write a bread-and-butter note as soon as you return home.

### *EXERCISE 1 Writing a Friendly Letter*

Write a letter to a friend or relative you have not seen in a while. Briefly tell him or her the news in your life. Make sure that your completed letter uses the correct form.

### *EXERCISE 2 Writing a Thank-you Note*

Imagine that you have just received a gift from a friend who lives on the planet Zoxtron. The gift is an eebsirf, which is something you enjoyed during your visit there. Write a thank-you note to your friend. Be sure to use the correct form.

### *EXERCISE 3 Writing a Bread-and-butter Note*

Imagine that you have just spent a weekend at the White House. Write a bread-and-butter note telling the President how much you enjoyed the visit.

### EXERCISE 4 On Your Own

Create your own address book. Include the addresses of the friends and relatives you might write to. Use the library or post office to help you find each person's ZIP code if you do not already know it. Then create a design for the cover.

## Writing Extra

Imagine that you are 20 years older than you are now. You have just finished dinner and are getting ready to relax for the evening. Suddenly something makes you think of your seventh-grade English class. You quickly grab a pen and a piece of paper and begin writing a friendly letter to your seventh-grade English teacher. Let him or her know what has happened to you over the past 20 years. You may want to include the following information in your letter.

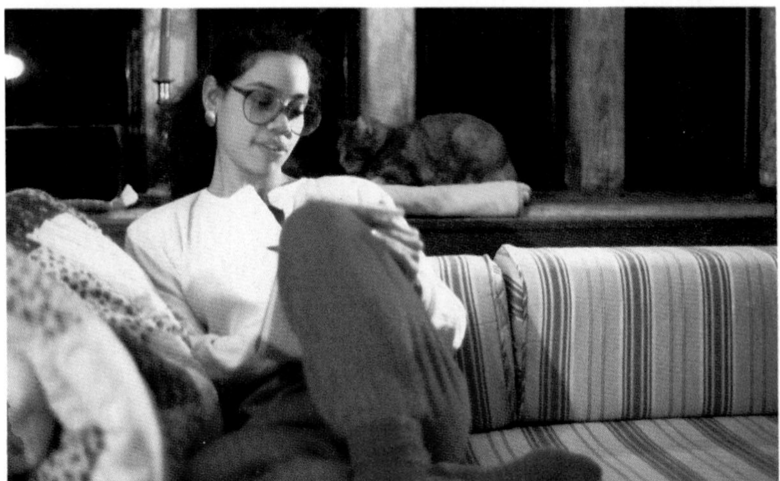

- your career
- your family
- where you live
- any interesting experiences you have had

# Business Letters

Most business letters do more than convey news. They usually call for the receiver of the letter to take some action. To make sure your point is understood, keep your business letters clear and simple.

## Business Letter Form

Most business letters you write will be sent to companies. When a business letter arrives at a company, it is usually taken from its envelope before it reaches the specific person it is addressed to. For this reason a business letter has one more part than a friendly letter has. This part is called the inside address.

28b The parts of a business letter are the **heading, inside address, salutation, body, closing,** and **signature.**

The model on page 468 shows the correct form for a business letter.

HEADING The heading of a business letter is the same as the heading of a friendly letter. Include your full address followed by the date. Remember to follow the rules for capitalizing proper nouns and using commas. You may use the full name of your state or the abbreviation. (*See page 469 for a list of state abbreviations.*) If you choose to use the abbreviation, be sure to abbreviate the state in the inside address too.

INSIDE ADDRESS Start the inside address two to four lines below the heading. Write the name of the person who will receive the letter if you know it. Use *Mr., Ms., Mrs., Dr.,* etc., before the name. If the person has a title, such as *Personnel Director* or *Manager,* write it on the next line. Then write the receiver's address, following the rules for capitalizing proper nouns and using commas.

SALUTATION Start the salutation, or greeting, two lines below the inside address. In a business letter, use a colon after the salutation.

**D**ear **M**s. **M**orley: **D**ear **S**ir or **M**adam:

BODY Two lines below the salutation, begin the body or message of the letter. Skip a line between paragraphs and indent each new paragraph.

CLOSING In a business letter, use a formal closing. Start the closing two or three lines below the body. Line up the closing with the left-hand edge of the heading. Capitalize the first letter only and use a comma.

**S**incerely, **Y**ours truly,
**S**incerely yours, **V**ery truly yours,

SIGNATURE In the signature of a business letter, your name appears twice. First type (or print if your letter is handwritten) your name four or five lines below the closing. Then sign your name in the space between the closing and your typed name. Do not refer to yourself as *Mr.* or *Ms.*

There are many styles for writing business letters. One of the most popular is called the *modified block style.* In this style the heading, closing, and signature are on the right. The inside address, salutation, and body all start at the left margin. Paragraphs are indented. All business letters in this chapter use the modified block style.

When writing a business letter, use white stationery, preferably 8½- by 11-inch paper. Whether you type or write the letter by hand, leave margins at least one inch wide on all sides. Always keep a copy of each business letter you write. You can make a copy with carbon paper or use the copying machines available in most libraries.

**Correct Form for a Business Letter**

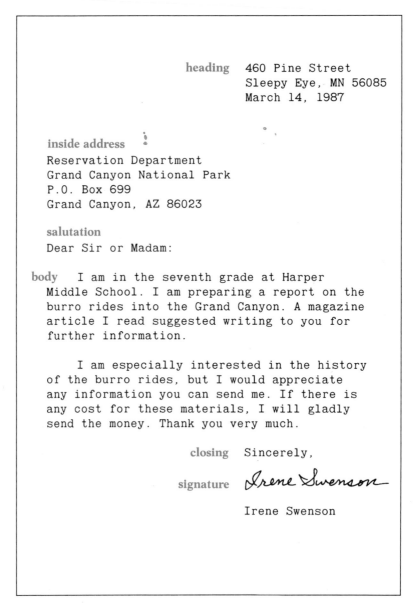

heading
460 Pine Street
Sleepy Eye, MN 56085
March 14, 1987

inside address
Reservation Department
Grand Canyon National Park
P.O. Box 699
Grand Canyon, AZ 86023

salutation
Dear Sir or Madam:

body
I am in the seventh grade at Harper Middle School. I am preparing a report on the burro rides into the Grand Canyon. A magazine article I read suggested writing to you for further information.

I am especially interested in the history of the burro rides, but I would appreciate any information you can send me. If there is any cost for these materials, I will gladly send the money. Thank you very much.

closing
Sincerely,

signature
*Irene Swenson*

Irene Swenson

## Correct Form for Business Envelopes

28c

```
Irene Swenson           your name
460 Pine Street         your address
Sleepy Eye, MN 56085

                 Reservation Department
receiver's       Grand Canyon National Park
address          P.O. Box 699
                 Grand Canyon, AZ 86023
```

### State Abbreviations

|  |  |
|---|---|
| Alabama | AL |
| Alaska | AK |
| Arizona | AZ |
| Arkansas | AR |
| California | CA |
| Colorado | CO |
| Connecticut | CT |
| Delaware | DE |
| District of Columbia | DC |
| Florida | FL |
| Georgia | GA |
| Hawaii | HI |
| Idaho | ID |
| Illinois | IL |
| Indiana | IN |
| Iowa | IA |
| Kansas | KS |
| Kentucky | KY |
| Louisiana | LA |
| Maine | ME |
| Maryland | MD |
| Massachusetts | MA |
| Michigan | MI |
| Minnesota | MN |
| Mississippi | MS |
| Missouri | MO |
| Montana | MT |
| Nebraska | NE |
| Nevada | NV |
| New Hampshire | NH |
| New Jersey | NJ |
| New Mexico | NM |
| New York | NY |
| North Carolina | NC |
| North Dakota | ND |
| Ohio | OH |
| Oklahoma | OK |
| Oregon | OR |
| Pennsylvania | PA |
| Puerto Rico | PR |
| Rhode Island | RI |
| South Carolina | SC |
| South Dakota | SD |
| Tennessee | TN |
| Texas | TX |
| Utah | UT |
| Vermont | VT |
| Virginia | VA |
| Washington | WA |
| West Virginia | WV |
| Wisconsin | WI |
| Wyoming | WY |

## The Envelope

The model on page 469 shows the correct form for an envelope. The envelope should be clearly addressed. If you type the letter, also type the envelope. Place your own name and address in the upper left-hand corner. The receiver's address, which is the same as the inside address in a business letter, is centered on the envelope. Use the postal abbreviation for the state and always include the ZIP code.

How you fold your letter to place it in the envelope depends on the size of your stationery. If you use business-sized envelopes that are the same width as your stationery, fold the letter in thirds, as shown in the following diagrams.

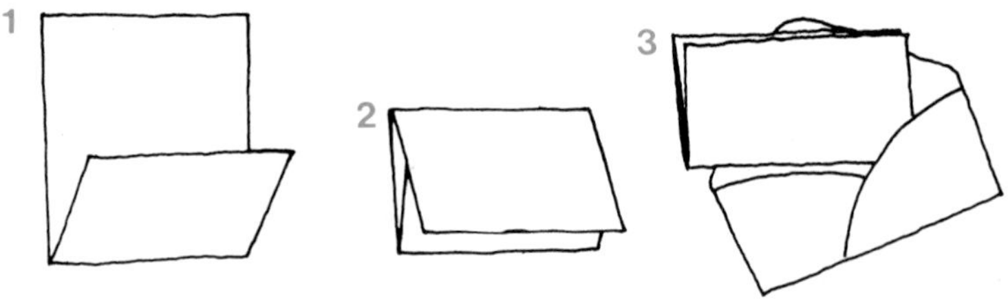


If your envelopes are narrower than your stationery, fold the letter in sixths, as shown below.

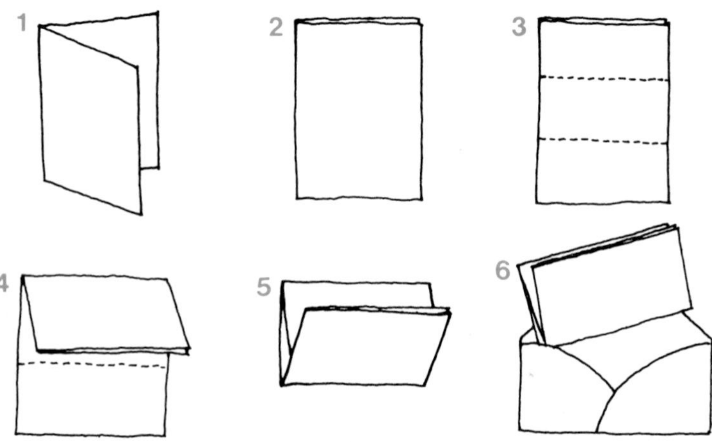

### *EXERCISE 5 Using the Correct Form of a Business Letter*

Using the following information, write a business letter in the proper form. Use the information on pages 466–467 and the model on page 468 to help you.

**Heading:** your address and today's date

**Inside address:** Director of Information, American Youth Hostels, 1332 I Street NW, Washington, DC 20005

**Salutation:** Dear Sir or Madam

**Body:** My club is interested in taking a bicycle tour of (*name of state*). We would like to stay at youth hostels along the way. Would you please send me a listing of the hostels in (*name of state*)? Thank you very much.

**Closing:** Yours truly

**Signature:** your name

## *Letters of Request*

Requesting information is one common purpose of a business letter. The model letter on page 468 is an example of a letter of request. When requesting information, be as specific as you can about what information you need. Also check your letter carefully for errors in grammar, usage, and spelling.

### EXERCISE 6 *Correcting Errors in a Letter of Request*

In the following letter, each line preceded by a number contains an error. Rewrite the letter, correcting each mistake. Then underline the corrections you made.

1 Katherine Smally
2 1132 Winston avenue
Chicago, IL 60688
3

4 Robert Benton
Editorial Director
Bowman Publishing Company
9852 South 83rd Street
5 Milwaukee, Wisconsin 53249

6 Dear Mr. Benson,

I recently read the book Outerspace
Outings by Julia Knowles, published by your
7 company. The book was very enjoyable and I
would like to tell her so. Please send me an
8 adress where I can write to her.

9 I would also like to know what other books
your company has about spaceships. If
possible, please send me a list.

10 Yours Truly,

Katherine Smally

## Order Letters

You can also use a business letter to order merchandise from catalogs and advertisements. Your order letter should give complete information. Be sure to include a description of the item, size, order number, price, and the quantity you want. If you enclose payment for your purchase, your letter should state the amount you have enclosed. Check over your arithmetic to be sure you have enclosed the proper amount. The model on page 474 shows the correct form for an order letter.

### EXERCISE 7 *Writing an Order Letter*

Use the following information to write an order letter.

ADDRESS Order Department, Guitar World, 782 Dayton Drive, Woodbine, Maryland 21797

ORDER 1 complete set of nylon guitar strings, Order #445, $12.95 each; 6 plastic thumb picks, Order #411, $.50 each; $1.75 for shipping and handling

## Order Letter

333 Westmont Drive
Ramer, TN 38367
July 15, 1987

Stowaway Supplies
42 Ridge Avenue
Millington, NJ 07946

Dear Sir or Madam:

Please send me the following items from your 1987 fall catalog.

| | |
|---|---|
| 2 student book bags—1 green, 1 red, Order #356-AZ5, $4.50 each | $ 9.00 |
| 1 navy blue sweat shirt, size medium, Order #455-AM2, $7.50 each | 7.50 |
| TOTAL | $16.50 |

I have enclosed a check for $19.00 to cover the cost of the merchandise plus $2.50 for shipping and handling.

Sincerely,

Martin J. Conway

Martin J. Conway

### EXERCISE 8 On Your Own

Imagine that you are living 100 years ago. Write a letter to a company, ordering merchandise. Use your knowledge of the past to create the company and the merchandise that might have been available.

# Business Forms

You will need to fill out business forms for a variety of reasons. Applying for a library card, sending a money order, or joining a record club are just a few. Following are some guidelines for filling out business forms.

28d

**Completing Business Forms**

1. Read all of the directions carefully before you begin to fill out the form.
2. Check both sides of the form to make sure you do not miss any questions written on the back.
3. Do not leave blanks. If a question does not apply to you, write N/A (not applicable) in the space provided.
4. Always use blue or black pen.
5. Be sure to print neatly and clearly.
6. Remember to sign the form.
7. Read over the form when you are finished to be sure your answers are accurate and complete.

If the form you are filling out is long, you may want to write the answers on a separate sheet of paper first. Then copy the answers onto the form in pen.

The form on pages 476–477 is an application for a Social Security number. You will need a Social Security number to open a bank account or to apply for a job. If you do not already have a Social Security number, now is a good time to apply for one.

### EXERCISE 9 Requesting Business Forms

Write a letter of request to your local Social Security office. (*See page 471.*) Ask for an application form for a Social Security number and any other information you might need. Look in the white pages of your telephone book to find the address of the Social Security office nearest you.

DEPARTMENT OF HEALTH AND HUMAN SERVICES
SOCIAL SECURITY ADMINISTRATION

Form Approved
OMB No. 0960-0066

**FORM SS-5 — APPLICATION FOR A SOCIAL SECURITY NUMBER CARD (Original, Replacement or Correction)**

MICROFILM REF. NO. (SSA USE ONLY)

**Unless the requested information is provided, we may not be able to issue a Social Security Number (20 CFR 422-103(b))**

INSTRUCTIONS TO APPLICANT ▶ Before completing this form, please read the instructions on the opposite page. You can type or print, using pen with dark blue or black ink. Do not use pencil.

| | | First | Middle | Last |
|---|---|---|---|---|
| NAA | NAME TO BE SHOWN ON CARD | John | Joseph | Ficcardi |
| NAB 1 | FULL NAME AT BIRTH (IF OTHER THAN ABOVE) | N/A | N/A | N/A |
| ONA | OTHER NAME(S) USED | N/A | | |

| | | | | | |
|---|---|---|---|---|---|
| STT 2 | MAILING ADDRESS | 1205 Parkedge Road (Street/Apt. No., P.O. Box, Rural Route No.) | | | |
| CTY | CITY: Pittsburgh | STE | STATE: Pennsylvania | ZIP | ZIP CODE: 15220 |

CSP 3 — CITIZENSHIP (Check one only)

- ☑ a. U.S. citizen
- ☐ b. Legal alien allowed to work
- ☐ c. Legal alien not allowed to work
- ☐ d. Other (See instructions on Page 2)

SEX 4 — SEX

- ☑ MALE
- ☐ FEMALE

ETB 5 — RACE/ETHNIC DESCRIPTION (Check one only) (Voluntary)

- ☐ a. Asian, Asian-American or Pacific Islander (Includes persons of Chinese, Filipino, Japanese, Korean, Samoan, etc., ancestry or descent)
- ☐ b. Hispanic (Includes persons of Chicano, Cuban, Mexican or Mexican-American, Puerto Rican, South or Central American, or other Spanish ancestry or descent)
- ☐ c. Negro or Black (not Hispanic)
- ☐ d. Northern American Indian or Alaskan Native
- ☑ e. White (not Hispanic)

| DOB 6 | DATE OF BIRTH | MONTH | DAY | YEAR | AGE 7 | PRESENT AGE | PLB 8 | PLACE OF BIRTH | CITY | STATE OR FOREIGN COUNTRY | FCI |
|---|---|---|---|---|---|---|---|---|---|---|---|
| | | 2 | 14 | 75 | | 12 | | | Pittsburgh | Pennsylvania | ☐ |

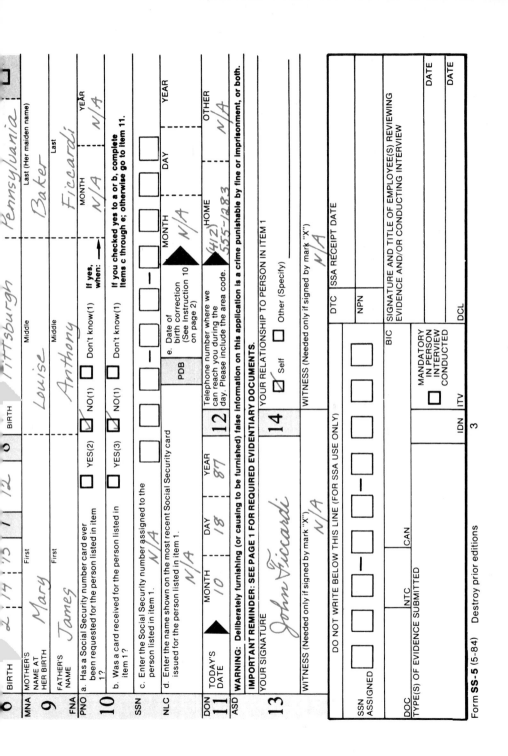

| 6 | BIRTH | 2 / 14 / 75 | 7 | 12 | 8 | BIRTH | Pittsburgh | Pennsylvania |
|---|---|---|---|---|---|---|---|---|

| | | First | Middle | Last (Her maiden name) |
|---|---|---|---|---|
| MNA 9 | MOTHER'S NAME AT HER BIRTH | Mary | Louise | Baker |
| FNA | FATHER'S NAME | First: James | Middle: Anthony | Last: Ficcardi |

**PNO 10**

a. Has a Social Security number card ever been requested for the person listed in item 1? ☐ YES(2) ☑ NO(1) ☐ Don't know(1) **If yes, when:** → MONTH: N/A YEAR: N/A

b. Was a card received for the person listed in item 1? ☐ YES(3) ☑ NO(1) ☐ Don't know(1) **If you checked yes to a or b, complete items c through e; otherwise go to item 11.**

**SSN** c. Enter the Social Security number assigned to the person listed in item 1. N/A ☐☐☐–☐☐–☐☐☐☐

**NLC** d. Enter the name shown on the most recent Social Security card issued for the person listed in item 1. N/A

**PDB** e. Date of birth correction (See Instruction 10 on page 2) ▶ MONTH: N/A DAY: YEAR:

**DON 11** TODAY'S DATE ▶ MONTH: 10 DAY: 18 YEAR: 87

**12** Telephone number where we can reach you during the day. Please include the area code. ▶ HOME: (412) 555-1283 OTHER: N/A

**ASD** **WARNING: Deliberately furnishing (or causing to be furnished) false information on this application is a crime punishable by fine or imprisonment, or both.**

**IMPORTANT REMINDER: SEE PAGE 1 FOR REQUIRED EVIDENTIARY DOCUMENTS.**

**13** YOUR SIGNATURE: John Ficcardi

**14** YOUR RELATIONSHIP TO PERSON IN ITEM 1: ☑ Self ☐ Other (Specify) ____________

WITNESS (Needed only if signed by mark "X") N/A

WITNESS (Needed only if signed by mark "X") N/A

DO NOT WRITE BELOW THIS LINE (FOR SSA USE ONLY)

| SSN ASSIGNED ☐☐☐–☐☐–☐☐☐☐ | | | DTC | SSA RECEIPT DATE |
|---|---|---|---|---|
| | | | NPN | |
| DOC | NTC | CAN | BIC | SIGNATURE AND TITLE OF EMPLOYEE(S) REVIEWING EVIDENCE AND/OR CONDUCTING INTERVIEW |
| TYPE(S) OF EVIDENCE SUBMITTED | IDN | ☐ MANDATORY IN PERSON INTERVIEW CONDUCTED ITV | | DATE |
| | | | | DCL DATE |

Form **SS-5** (5-84) Destroy prior editions 3

# Spotlight on Writing

**A** **Writing a Friendly Letter.** Write a friendly letter to a person from history whom you admire. You may choose a person from the list below or choose someone on your own. Use the Steps for Writing a Letter on page 480 to help you. You may want to include the following information in your letter.

- how the person is remembered today
- what effect the person has had on the world
- how the world is different today
- what things are happening now that would be of particular interest to the receiver of your letter

1. Alexander Graham Bell: inventor of the telephone
2. Jackie Robinson: first black professional baseball player
3. Amelia Earhart: first woman to make a solo flight across the Atlantic Ocean
4. Christopher Columbus: explorer who discovered America
5. Martin Luther King: civil-rights leader
6. Walt Disney: film producer
7. Susan B. Anthony: a leader in the fight for women's right to vote
8. George Washington: first United States president
9. Florence Nightingale: founder of the nursing profession
10. Francis Scott Key: writer of the words to "The Star-Spangled Banner"

**B** **Writing a Friendly Letter.** Choose one of the following purposes for writing a friendly letter. Then write a letter to a friend or relative.

1. congratulating someone on running their first race
2. sending get-well wishes to someone in the hospital
3. inviting someone to a Fourth of July picnic
4. declining an invitation for a weekend camping trip

**C** **Writing a Letter of Request.** Write a letter requesting information about a favorite movie star. Address the letter to Publicity Director, Screen Actors Guild, 7750 Sunset Boulevard, Hollywood, California 90046.

**D** **Writing an Order Letter.** Imagine that you are the set director for a play called *The Haunted Castle.* You have only one hundred dollars to spend for props. Choose from the following items advertised in the Theater Supplies fall catalog. The address of Theater Supplies is 45 Highland Avenue, Lexington, Massachusetts 02173. Add $7.50 for shipping and handling.

| Item | Number | Price |
|---|---|---|
| creaking stairway | #368-B | $65.00 |
| bushel of cobwebs | # 46-9z | $ 9.00 |
| drawbridge | # 55-C | $82.00 |
| dungeon cell | #116-V | $47.50 |
| black curtains | # 99-D | $24.00 |
| ghoulish-laughter tape | # 20-A | $ 3.75 |
| torches | # 67-A | $ 7.50 each |
| portrait with moving eyes | # 21-B | $35.00 |
| motorized rats | # 56-X | $12.00 each |
| puffs of smoke | # 77-221 | $34.00 each |

**E** **Writing from Your Writer's Notebook.** Write a thank-you note to someone that you wrote about in your journal. Imagine you are ten years older than you are now. Thank the person for something that he or she did for you in the past.

# Steps for Writing a Letter

## Friendly Letters

1. Use the proper form for a friendly letter. (*See pages 461–462.*)
2. Edit your letter for errors in usage, capitalization, punctuation, and spelling.
3. Recopy your letter, if necessary, for neatness.
4. Include a return address on the envelope. (*See pages 469–470.*)

## Business Letters

1. Gather the information you need to explain your request or order accurately and completely.
2. Use the proper form for a business letter. (*See pages 466–468.*)
3. Use a formal salutation and the proper closing for a business letter. (*See page 467.*)
4. Express your message briefly and politely in the body of the letter.
5. Use the correct form for the signature. (*See page 467.*)
6. Edit your letter for errors in usage, capitalization, punctuation, and spelling.
7. If possible, type the letter on white 8½- by 11-inch stationery, leaving margins at least 1 inch wide.
8. Keep a copy of your letter.
9. Fold your letter properly. (*See page 470.*)
10. Address the envelope correctly. (*See pages 469–470.*)

# Standardized Test

## COMPOSITION

**Directions:** Decide which sentence best supports the topic sentence. Fill in the appropriate circle on your answer sheet.

SAMPLE By four o'clock the turkey was cooked.
**A** The cranberry sauce was chilled.
**B** Little Laura was demanding peanut butter instead.
**C** It had been in the oven for 3½ hours.

ANSWER Ⓐ Ⓑ Ⓒ

1. A silk garment can usually be washed.
   **A** Just use cold water, a mild soap, and a gentle touch.
   **B** Silk is an expensive but beautiful fabric.
   **C** The cocoon of the silkworm provided the thread.

2. Flight 302 from Chicago to Denver has been canceled.
   **A** Flight 422 out of Denver has just left.
   **B** A serious blizzard has closed the Chicago airport.
   **C** Phil was stuck in the Chicago airport last week.

3. The crowing of a rooster broke the silence of the night.
   **A** That is how every morning began on the Bidwell farm.
   **B** Chickens often cluck, but only roosters crow.
   **C** You never hear roosters crow in the city.

4. Constellations are groups of stars.
   **A** On a clear summer night, it is lovely to look at the stars.
   **B** Virgil did not know that *constellation* has two *l*'s.
   **C** The Big Dipper is one of 88 recognized constellations.

5. The math homework was easier than usual.
   **A** Ms. Costanza is an outstanding teacher.
   **B** It took me only a half hour to do all ten problems.
   **C** There is no science homework tonight.

6. You should maintain good posture in all activities.
   **A** Jeremy is a model for good posture.
   **B** If a person is tired, his or her posture may be poor.
   **C** When you walk, your chin should be up and your shoulders square.

**Directions:** On your answer sheet, fill in the circle of the line in each group that contains an error. If there is no error in the group, fill in the circle containing *4*.

SAMPLE 1) 82 Finney Street
2) East Point, GA, 30344
3) September 9, 1986
4) (No error)

ANSWER ① ② ③ ④

7. 1) 1695 Grand Way
2) Salem, Utah 84653
3) November 28
4) (No error)

8. 1) Dear Aunt Paula:
2) I've been home two days now, but I
3) still miss you. I had a great time.
4) (No error)

9. 1) I cannot imagine a more gracious
2) hostess than you or a more exciting city
3) than San Francisco. I enjoyed every minute.
4) (No error)

10. 1) Thank you for a wonderful week.
2) Love
3) Eva
4) (No error)

**Directions:** You have 20 minutes to write a descriptive paragraph on the topic below. Do not write on any other topic.

My Dream Room

UNIT 7

# Related Language Skills

# Speaking and Listening

A survey once stated that each day the average person speaks about 18,000 words. This number of words would fill about 100 pages of a book! This amazing fact shows how important communication is in everyone's life.

Communication, however, has two parts: speaking and listening. Without one, the other is useless. You could speak for days, but your words would mean nothing if no one were listening. To communicate with others, you must be both a clear speaker and a careful listener.

In this chapter you will learn that speaking and listening are skills. Because they are skills, they can be improved so that *your* 18,000 words a day will communicate more clearly and effectively.

# Informal Speaking

Most of the speaking you do is informal. Telling a friend about a movie you have seen, contributing to a class discussion, or giving directions to the beach are *informal speeches*. Situations such as these are called informal speeches because they are short and require no formal planning or preparation. When speaking informally, however, take the time to organize your thoughts so your message will be clear and to the point.

## Giving Directions

If you have ever been lost, you know how important a clear set of directions can be. Read the two sets of directions below.

UNCLEAR The concert hall? That's not too far from here. Just go down the main street for a while. Turn at the traffic light, go down that street a short way, and it is on your right.

CLEAR To get to the concert hall, continue on Central Street for two blocks. At the second traffic light, take a right onto Grove Avenue. Follow Grove Avenue for one-half mile. You will cross a small bridge, and the concert hall will be on your right.

Notice that the second set of directions gives specific details, such as exact distances, names of streets, and landmarks. The first set of directions does not provide enough information. When you give directions, remember that you may know exactly where a place is located but the other person does not.

Following are some important steps to keep in mind when you give directions.

### Giving Directions

1. Use *right, left,* and *straight* rather than *north, south, east,* or *west.*
2. Use names of streets if you know them.
3. Mention landmarks whenever possible.
4. Include the approximate number of miles.
5. If possible, draw a map.
6. Do not give directions for a difficult shortcut.
7. If you are unsure of the correct directions, direct the person to someone who might know.
8. Repeat the directions or have the other person repeat the directions to you.

When you give directions, keep in mind that most people cannot easily remember more than three to five steps of directions. If the directions are long and complicated, sometimes the best thing to do is to give directions to a halfway point. Then tell the person to ask for additional directions from there. Whatever directions you give, make sure they are clear and accurate.

## EXERCISE 1 *Improving Directions*

List five errors in the directions below. Then rewrite the directions using specific details of your own choice.

> Oh, the Crown Building! Go south on the main street through town for a while. Turn at the streetlight and go for another mile or so. After you cross a bridge, go north. The Crown Building should be on your left.

## EXERCISE 2 *Giving Directions*

Write directions from your classroom to the following places in your school. Include as many specific details as possible. Then read your directions to a classmate. Discuss ways the directions could be improved.

1. cafeteria
2. gymnasium
3. auditorium

# Formal Speaking

Have you ever given an oral book report or made a nomination speech during a school assembly? Situations such as these are called *formal speeches*. A formal speech is usually longer than an informal speech, and it requires preparation in advance.

The steps that you follow when you prepare a formal speech are much the same as those that you follow when you prepare a written report. (*See Chapter 27.*) The main difference is that you will practice your speech and deliver it orally rather than write it.

## Knowing Your Audience

Before you choose a subject for a speech, think about who your audience will be. Throughout your school years, most of your speeches will be delivered to your classmates. Once in a while, however, you may be asked to give a short speech before teachers or give a talk to a group of younger students who will soon be entering your school.

Following are some questions to ask yourself about your audience. Answering these questions will help you decide what subject will be suitable for your audience. Doing this will also help you decide what information you should include in your speech.

**Knowing Your Audience**

1. What are the interests of my audience? Are they similar to mine?
2. What will my audience already know about the subject I would like to talk about?
3. Is my audience coming to learn, to be persuaded, or to be entertained?

## Choosing and Limiting a Subject

To choose a subject, first make a list of subjects that you know something about. Then choose one that both you and your audience will be interested in. For example, if you were speaking to younger students about your school, you might tell them about the courses your school offers. If you were speaking to your classmates, however, this subject would not interest them. A better subject for your classmates might be new courses the school should offer.

Once you have decided on a subject, think about how much time you have to deliver your speech. If you have only ten minutes, you cannot give a speech on all the courses you would like to see your school offer. Instead, you might talk about the importance of offering computer courses.

### EXERCISE 3 *Finding a Subject*

Number your paper from 1 to 6. Then write the subject of a speech that could be included under each area.

EXAMPLE personal experiences
POSSIBLE ANSWER the day I appeared on television

1. personal experiences
2. current events or issues
3. how to do something
4. experiences of others
5. past events or people
6. how to make something

### EXERCISE 4 *Limiting a Subject*

Number your paper 1 to 10. Then limit each subject so that it is suitable for a ten-minute speech.

EXAMPLE foods rich in vitamins
POSSIBLE ANSWER citrus fruits rich in Vitamin C

1. books by Mark Twain
2. unusual birds
3. science fiction movies
4. American Indians
5. the solar system
6. noise pollution
7. poisonous snakes
8. famous rock groups
9. gymnastic events
10. American heroines

## Understanding Your Purpose

Before you gather information for your speech, you should think about your purpose. Most speeches have one of the following three purposes.

**Purposes of a Speech**

| PURPOSE | EXAMPLES |
|---|---|
| TO INFORM | • to explain how the Special Olympics began<br>• to explain how the Egyptian pyramids were built |
| TO PERSUADE | • to encourage people to vote for a certain person for president<br>• to encourage others to try out for the school musical |
| TO ENTERTAIN | • to tell about the time you played the lead in a play and forgot your lines<br>• to tell about the time you went sailing without a sail |

### EXERCISE 5 Determining a Purpose for a Speech

Number your paper 1 to 10. Then label the purpose of each speech: *to inform, to persuade,* or *to entertain.*

1. to explain how exercise and diet affect people's health
2. to give information about the life of a professional athlete
3. to encourage more students to attend school basketball games
4. to tell about the time you went fishing and ended up going swimming instead
5. to encourage your listeners to buy Wam-o running shoes
6. to explain how to make a flying machine from a milk carton

7. to explain the plot in Steven Spielberg's science fiction movie *ET*
8. to tell about the time you spent the day with your favorite movie star
9. to encourage teachers to make a computer available in every classroom
10. to tell about your first dance class

## Gathering and Organizing Your Information

The next steps in preparing your speech are to gather information and then organize it. These steps are similar to those you follow when writing a report. (*See pages 434–439.*) Following are some helpful reminders as you gather and organize your information.

**Gathering Information**

1. List what you already know about your subject.
2. Gather more information in the library or through an interview.
3. Find interesting examples and quotations to include.
4. Write your information on note cards. (*See pages 436–437.*)

**Organizing Information**

1. Make an outline of your speech. (*See pages 438–439.*)
2. The **introduction** of your speech should capture the attention of your audience. It should also include the main idea of your speech. (*See pages 442–443.*)
3. The **body** of your speech should include your supporting points. Arrange your points in a logical order. Use transitions to connect your ideas. (*See pages 444–445.*)
4. The **conclusion** of your speech should summarize your main idea. (*See pages 446–447.*)

### EXERCISE 6 Gathering and Organizing Information

Choose and limit a subject for a ten-minute speech. Write what you know about it on note cards. Next go to the library and find information for at least four more note cards. Then organize your cards and write an outline of your speech. Save your outline for Exercise 7.

## Practicing Your Speech

Practicing your speech aloud is a very important step in delivering a successful speech. Following are some helpful suggestions to think about as you practice.

**Practicing Your Speech**

1. Read your complete outline several times until you are familiar with all the information.
2. Make a few notes to use as you practice.
3. Practice in front of a long mirror so that you will be aware of your facial expressions and gestures, such as clenching your hands or biting your lips.
4. Practice looking around the room as you talk. Good eye contact is important.
5. Time the length of your speech. If it is too long, find information that you can omit. If it is too short, you should find more information.
6. Practice over a period of several days.

After practicing your speech several times, try it before members of your family or some friends and ask for suggestions. If possible, tape-record your speech. Listen especially for how often you say "um" or "ah" or how often you connect sentences with *and* or *well.*

The more you practice your speech aloud, the more self-confident you will become. When you are more self-confident, you will be less nervous when it comes time to give your speech.

### EXERCISE 7 *Practicing Your Speech*

Your teacher will assign you to work with another student in the class. Practice the speech you prepared for Exercise 6 and discuss your speech with your classmate. Then listen to your classmate's speech and discuss that speech as well. Point out how the presentation might be improved.

## Delivering Your Speech

Most speakers feel a little nervous before they begin to make a speech. However, if a speaker is well prepared, he or she is less likely to feel so nervous. Following are some helpful suggestions to keep in mind when you deliver your speech.

**Delivering Your Speech**

1. Be well prepared and have all the necessary materials.
2. Wait until your audience is quiet and settled.
3. Take a deep breath and begin.
4. Stand with your weight evenly divided between both feet. Avoid swaying back and forth.
5. Speak slowly, clearly, and loudly enough to be heard.
6. Use rehearsed gestures and facial expressions to emphasize your main points.
7. Look directly at the people in your audience, not over their heads. Try to make eye contact.
8. Use pictures and other audiovisual aids to increase the attention of your audience.

### EXERCISE 8 *Delivering Your Speech*

Present the speech you practiced for Exercise 7 before a group of four to six students in your class. Afterward, write a brief evaluation of your speech. List things that you think you did well and things you would like to improve in your next speech.

# Listening

Most people spend over 50 percent of each day just listening. Surprisingly, however, most people remember only about one fourth of what they hear. This section will help you improve your listening skills.

### EXERCISE 9 *Listening Carefully*

Stop all classroom activity for several minutes and listen for sounds. Identify each sound you hear and list it on your paper. Next, write words that describe the sounds you heard, such as "shrill whistle," "rumbling subway," "gentle wind." Compare your descriptions with those of your classmates.

### EXERCISE 10 *Developing Good Listening Habits*

Think about people you like to talk to because they are good listeners. Then make a list of the habits good listeners show during a conversation. Discuss your ideas in class. Think about ways you can improve your listening skills.

## Taking Notes While Listening

Taking notes on speeches helps you to listen more carefully. Following are some guidelines for taking notes.

**Taking Notes on Speeches**

1. Write the main idea presented in the introduction.
2. Write the main topics, using Roman numerals.
3. Under each main topic, write the subtopics or supporting points. Listen for clues, such as "There are three main reasons why . . ." or "I will explain the four main causes of . . . ."
4. In the conclusion of the speech, write the restatement of the main idea.

Following is an outline of a ten-minute speech about how video games are designed.

**Main idea:** Designing video games is a complex, carefully planned procedure.

MAIN TOPIC I. Games developed around one theme

SUBTOPIC A. Ideas from books, magazines, movies, dreams, life experience

B. Ideas suggested by other popular games

II. Idea or theme developed on paper

A. Sequence of sketches or drawings called storyboards

B. Flow charts or block diagrams showing a game in words and boxes

III. Next, game programmed into computer

A. Game coded in *assembly* or *machine* computer language, not BASIC

B. *Assembly* languages give game its speed and exactness

IV. Game tested and marketed

A. Children play new games, and their reactions are studied

B. Games put in arcades and records kept on use

C. If popular, game produced in large quantities

**Summary statement:** Designing video games includes several steps. They are (1) developing a theme, (2) putting it down on paper, (3) programming the game into the computer, and (4) testing and marketing the game.

When you take notes, never try to write everything down. If you do, you might miss important points. Write only the information that is necessary to remember accurately. Your notes will then help you remember the other details.

### *EXERCISE 11* *Listening and Taking Notes*

Prepare a brief explanation of how to do something, such as how to do a certain dance step or how to make an omelet. Then take notes as each student presents an explanation to the class. Later compare notes to see if you have included the same topics.

### *EXERCISE 12* *Listening and Taking Notes*

Work with a classmate who attends the same science or social studies class you do. Working separately, listen carefully during the next discussion period and take notes. Then compare your notes with your classmate's. Did you miss any important ideas?

## *Listening Critically*

When listening to a speech, always evaluate what is being said. The following sections will help you sort out misleading information from facts.

***Hasty Generalizations.*** A hasty *generalization* is a misleading statement. It is a broad judgment based on only a few examples. A hasty generalization does not consider individual differences.

| | |
|---|---|
| HASTY GENERALIZATIONS | All football games are boring. |
| | The buses never leave on time. |
| | Taxes are unfair for everyone. |

Such words as *all, always, never, none, everyone,* and *only* often signal a hasty generalization. Although *some* football games may be boring, *all* are not. Although buses may *sometimes* be late, it is unlikely that they *never* leave on schedule. In the same way, the tax system may treat *some* people unfairly, but not *everyone.* Since a hasty generalization may contain some truth, it can sound entirely true—if you are not listening carefully.

### EXERCISE 13 Rewriting Hasty Generalizations

Number your paper 1 to 5. Then rewrite the following hasty generalizations so that they are not misleading.

EXAMPLE The city is always noisy.
POSSIBLE ANSWER Sometimes the city is noisy.

1. That rock group never sings songs I like.
2. The service at Bob's Grill is always slow.
3. Only people who read the newspaper are informed.
4. All teenagers are irresponsible.
5. Everyone in our neighborhood likes dogs.

***Fact and Opinion.*** A *fact* is a statement that can be proved, but an *opinion* is a personal feeling or judgment.

FACT Albany is the capital of New York.
OPINION Albany is a wonderful city.

FACT The rock group the Mobots will tour the United States this summer.
OPINION The Mobots is the best rock group in the world.

Very often *opinions* are stated as facts. Sometimes it is only a careful listener who can tell them apart.

### EXERCISE 14 Understanding Fact and Opinion

Number your paper 1 to 10. Label each statement *fact* or *opinion*.

1. Our school has a girls' basketball team.
2. Christopher Hamilton is a poor actor.
3. Our school is the oldest school in the city.
4. Maria won the state spelling contest.
5. Everyone should go to college.
6. Our cafeteria serves terrible food.
7. California is the best state to live in.
8. Water expands when it is frozen.
9. My mother and father were born in Oklahoma.
10. Everyone today wants something for nothing.

# Chapter Review

**A** **Giving Directions.** Choose a place of interest in your city or town. Write directions to that place from your school. Be sure to include specific details. Your teacher may ask you to read your directions to the class and ask your classmates to try to repeat them. If time permits, discuss why some directions were easier to follow than others.

**B** **Giving a Speech.** Prepare a ten-minute speech about one of the following topics or one of your choice. Your teacher may ask you to deliver your speech to the class.

1. the story of Amelia Earhart, the first woman to cross the Atlantic Ocean by air
2. how astronauts are trained
3. learning to canoe
4. Houdini's famous tricks
5. how people dream
6. the life of the Pueblo Indians
7. how Chinese food and Japanese food are different
8. how tornadoes are formed
9. how to purchase a computer
10. how bats fly using sonar

**C** **Listening for Fact and Opinion.** As students deliver their speeches for Exercise B, take notes. Then discuss whether the speech included any generalizations or opinions that were stated as facts.

**D** **Listening and Taking Notes.** As your teacher reads an article from an encyclopedia, listen carefully and take notes in outline form. Then use your notes to write a short quiz. Give your quiz to several of your classmates.

# 30

# Vocabulary

You may have heard the expression "the power of words." In what ways are words powerful? For one, you can use them to persuade people. During the time of the American Revolution, Thomas Paine wrote a small book called *Common Sense.* His words stirred thousands of people to join the fight for independence. Words are also powerful in another way. They give you control over your surroundings. When you were a baby, for example, you learned the word *water.* Suddenly you had the power to request exactly what you wanted when you were thirsty. The more words you know, the more "word power" you have.

### EXERCISE 1 Previewing the Vocabulary List

Turn to the vocabulary list on page 511. Choose five words and write a sentence using each. If you do not know the meanings of the words you chose, look them up in a dictionary before writing your sentences.

# Word Meaning

What do you do when you come across words that are new to you? Suppose you came across this sentence.

The short story took place in a bucolic setting.

Perhaps you know that *bucolic* means "rural" or "countrylike," but more likely it is a new word to you. One way to learn its meaning is to look it up in a dictionary. In this chapter you will learn several other ways to unlock the meaning of new words.

## Context Clues

Often you can pick up clues about a word's meaning from its context. The *context* of a word is the sentence, the surrounding words, or the situation in which a word is used. Use the surrounding words to determine the meaning of *automaton* in the following sentence.

CONTEXT CLUES Dr. Sawyer's mechanical servant, Robbie, is the ideal **automaton.**

The clue *mechanical servant* tells you that an automaton is a robot.

There are several kinds of context clues. You have probably often seen the following types in your science and social studies textbooks.

DEFINITION Animals that feed on plants are **herbivores.**

EXAMPLE The **conifers,** like the cone-bearing pine and spruce trees, are found in cooler climates.

SYNONYM The **Isle** of Wight lies off the coast of England. The island is famous for its scenery and mild climate.

In the first item, the word *herbivores* is defined in the sentence. In the second item, examples of *conifers* appear in the sentence. In the third item, a synonym for the word *isle* is used in the following sentence. All of these examples show how the surrounding words can be used to determine the meaning of new words.

### EXERCISE 2 *Using Context Clues*

Number your paper 1 to 10. Then write the letter of the answer that is closest in meaning to the underlined word.

1. Kathleen is reading the biography of Thomas Edison because she is interested in his life as well as in his inventions.
   (A) book (B) life story (C) encyclopedia
   (D) paperback (E) journal
2. Be sure to save your receipt; it will show when you bought your sweater and how much you paid for it.
   (A) credit card (B) money (C) package
   (D) sales slip (E) price tag
3. James was nicknamed "Stretch" because he was so lean and lanky.
   (A) ugly (B) fat (C) irritable (D) handy
   (E) tall
4. "I can't predict the outcome of the game," the coach said, "but I can tell you that our players are ready to put up a good fight."
   (A) foretell (B) explain (C) justify
   (D) forgive (E) undo
5. Superman didn't even flinch when the boulder came tumbling down on him; he just stood there, hands on hips, unmoved.
   (A) cry out (B) fly (C) duck (D) moan
   (E) stare
6. While all the other members of the jury thought the man was guilty, a single juror held on to her "not guilty" vote.
   (A) witness (B) judge (C) jury member
   (D) defense lawyer (E) officer

7. After several accidents, a new school law was passed that prohibits skateboards on school grounds.
   (A) encourages (B) forbids (C) requires
   (D) produces (E) permits
8. In areas of high elevation, such as the Rocky Mountains, the air is thin and breathing is difficult.
   (A) scenery (B) height above sea level
   (C) trees (D) temperature changes
   (E) rainfall
9. When you fill out the order form, specify the size and color of the T-shirt you want so your order can be filled accurately.
   (A) name exactly (B) leave out (C) cross out
   (D) reduce (E) pick out
10. The train sat stationary out in the middle of nowhere, while the anxious passengers wondered if it would ever move again.
    (A) heavy (B) unmoving (C) loaded
    (D) sliding (E) rotating

### EXERCISE 3 *Using Context Clues*

Number your paper 1 to 10. Write each underlined word and its meaning. Use the context of the paragraph to help you. Then check your answers in a dictionary.

The aging monarch sat on his throne with his head bowed. Outside, the thunder of distant armies carried an ominous warning. The king knew that soon he would have to yield his throne to his enemies, who were now strong enough to overpower him. His only hope was the band of loyal, brave soldiers who had been summoned from fighting in a distant land. Would they materialize in time? Suddenly the quiet of the throne room was shattered by a great commotion outside the palace. Were the cheers and hoofbeats those of his valiant troops, or were they the victory sounds of his treacherous enemies? Rousing himself from despair, the king raced toward the palace gate to discern his fate.

## Prefixes and Suffixes

Another way to discover the meanings of unfamiliar words is to break the words down into their parts. Suppose, for example, that you come across the word *disobey.* Chances are you recognize one part of this word, *obey.* This part is called the root. A *root* is the part of the word that carries the basic meaning. The roots in the following words are in heavy type.

ROOTS mis**trust** un**drink**able dis**agree**ment **joy**ful

### EXERCISE 4 Finding Roots

Number your paper 1 to 15. Then write each word and underline the root.

1. distasteful
2. unreachable
3. unwise
4. prerecorded
5. truthful
6. unhappy
7. visualize
8. debtor
9. unbearable
10. dishonest
11. misfire
12. subtopic
13. displease
14. prepayment
15. dependence

**Prefixes.** The part of the word that comes before the root is called a *prefix.* In the word *disobey,* the prefix is *dis-*. If you know that *dis-* means "not," then you can figure out that *disobey* means "not obey." Following are some common prefixes and their meanings.

| Prefix | Meaning | Example |
|---|---|---|
| anti- | against | anti + freeze = antifreeze |
| dis- | not | dis + agree = disagree |
| in- | not | in + human = inhuman |
| mis- | incorrect | mis + spell = misspell |
| pre- | before | pre + school = preschool |
| re- | again | re + appear = reappear |
| sub- | under | sub + way = subway |
| un- | not | un + healthy = unhealthy |

## EXERCISE 5 Using Prefixes

Number your paper 1 to 10. Write the prefix that has the same meaning as the underlined word. Then write the complete word defined after the equal sign.

EXAMPLE again + copy = copy again
ANSWER re-, recopy

1. before + view = to see something ahead of time
2. against + war = opposed to war
3. incorrect + pronounce = to use the wrong pronunciation
4. again + freeze = to freeze a second or third time
5. not + approve = to judge unfavorably
6. incorrect + print = an error in a published work
7. not + popular = not pleasing to most people
8. under + average = lower than average
9. not + direct = roundabout
10. again + capture = to seize again

## EXERCISE 6 Using Prefixes

Write as many words as you can by combining each prefix with as many roots as possible. Use a dictionary to be sure you have made real words.

EXAMPLE dis-
POSSIBLE ANSWERS disconnect, dislocate, disorganize

| PREFIXES | | ROOTS | | | |
|---|---|---|---|---|---|
| anti- | re- | view | treat | place | connect |
| mis- | sub- | take | human | divide | organize |
| pre- | un- | do | judge | group | locate |
| | | heat | gravity | develop | freeze |

***Suffixes.*** The part of the word that comes after the root is called a *suffix*. Like prefixes, suffixes can have one or more syllables. Unlike prefixes, many suffixes can change a word from one part of speech to another. In the following list, notice how suffixes can create different parts of speech.

| Noun Suffixes | Meaning | Examples |
|---|---|---|
| -ance, -ence | state of | depend + ence |
| -er, -or | one who or that | debt + or |
| -ment | state of | resent + ment |
| -ness | state of | kind + ness |
| **Verb Suffixes** | **Meaning** | **Examples** |
| -ize | make or cause | final + ize |
| -en | make or become | sharp + en |
| **Adjective Suffixes** | **Meaning** | **Examples** |
| -able | capable of | break + able |
| -ful | full of | care + ful |
| **Adverb Suffix** | **Meaning** | **Example** |
| -ly | in a certain way | slow + ly |

### EXERCISE 7 *Using Suffixes*

Number your paper 1 to 10. Write the suffix that has the same meaning as the underlined words. Then write the complete word defined after the equal sign.

EXAMPLE bold + state of = daring
ANSWER -ness, boldness

1. train + capable of = able to be taught
2. catch + one who = ball player behind batter
3. strength + make or become = to make stronger
4. rapid + in a certain way = quickly
5. hospital + make or cause = to place in a hospital
6. develop + state of = growth
7. soul + full of = filled with feeling
8. confine + state of = the state of being restricted
9. resist + state of = efforts to fight back
10. sick + state of = disease

## EXERCISE 8 *Using Suffixes*

Number your paper 1 to 20. Then add two different suffixes to each word to create different parts of speech. After each word write its part of speech. Use the list of suffixes on page 504 to help you.

EXAMPLE bright
POSSIBLE ANSWERS brighten—verb, brightly—adverb

| | | | |
|---|---|---|---|
| 1. fair | 6. collect | 11. like | 16. sad |
| 2. employ | 7. rude | 12. treat | 17. natural |
| 3. light | 8. read | 13. flat | 18. teach |
| 4. visual | 9. moral | 14. legal | 19. quiet |
| 5. deep | 10. personal | 15. firm | 20. kind |

## EXERCISE 9 *Using Prefixes and Suffixes*

Number your paper 1 to 10. Then write the letter of the answer that is closest in meaning to the word in capital letters. The prefixes and suffixes you have learned in this chapter will help you figure out the meanings of the capitalized words.

1. INFREQUENT (A) again and again (B) often (C) not often
2. REFRESH (A) not fresh (B) to become fresh again (C) to become fresh before
3. SUBMARINE (A) under water (B) across water (C) above water
4. PREPAID (A) paid late (B) paid in advance (C) not paid
5. DISPLEASE (A) not please (B) please again (C) please after
6. AVIATOR (A) state of flying (B) one who pilots (C) to cause to fly
7. HASTEN (A) to make haste (B) one who hurries (C) state of hurrying
8. CHANGEABLE (A) state of changing (B) to make a change (C) capable of change

9. CHEERINESS (A) capable of being cheery (B) state of cheer (C) one who is cheery
10. SORROWFUL (A) against sorrow (B) to cause sorrow (C) full of sorrow

## Synonyms

Because English has so many words, you can choose words that express your meaning exactly. Sometimes two or more words will have similar meanings. A word that has nearly the same meaning as another word is called a *synonym.*

In the following sentences, the words *tall* and *towering* are synonyms. Although they have similar meanings, *towering* paints a more precise picture.

The shade from the **tall** tree kept us cool.
The shade from the **towering** tree kept us cool.

Dictionaries often include synonyms for words. Some also explain the slight differences in the meanings of synonyms. When you write, search for the word that conveys your meaning exactly and use your dictionary for help.

### EXERCISE 10 Recognizing Synonyms

Number your paper 1 to 10. Write the letter of the answer that is closest in meaning to the word in capital letters. Then check your answers in a dictionary.

1. CONVICTION (A) infection (B) prison (C) belief (D) offering (E) revenue
2. NEUTRAL (A) electric (B) indifferent (C) sharp (D) lifeless (E) hardy
3. FATAL (A) deadly (B) earnest (C) pale (D) wishful (E) empty
4. SANITIZE (A) wrap (B) mock (C) worship (D) sterilize (E) wax

5. MOBILE (A) energetic (B) movable (C) graceful (D) sturdy (E) relaxed
6. FEAT (A) deed (B) game (C) hunt (D) cheer (E) gossip
7. ABSOLUTELY (A) carelessly (B) quickly (C) totally (D) possibly (E) doubtfully
8. ALTOGETHER (A) wholly (B) solely (C) tightly (D) separately (E) partly
9. CONCLUSION (A) continuation (B) ending (C) secret (D) promise (E) injury
10. DECOY (A) sticker (B) warning (C) flash (D) sacrifice (E) lure

## EXERCISE 11 *Choosing the Better Word*

Number your paper 1 to 10. Then write the synonym in parentheses that fits the meaning of each sentence. Use a dictionary for help.

EXAMPLE My aunt collects (aged, antique) dolls.
ANSWER antique

1. Our friends were so deep in (conversation, discourse) that they barely noticed us.
2. Lara has a (shiny, brilliant) mind.
3. Samuel (spotted, detected) a hint of disapproval in his father's voice.
4. The glass figurines were very (flimsy, fragile).
5. For his report Ian prepared a (graph, picture) showing the average monthly temperatures in Mexico City.
6. Marissa hoped a (lullaby, song) would calm her baby sister.
7. The speaker bored everyone with his (repetitious, monotonous) voice.
8. The decorator chose (neutral, indifferent) colors for the living room.
9. Kim's library books are (expected, overdue).
10. The baby (scribbled, wrote) all over the mural.

### EXERCISE 12 Using Synonyms

Write as many synonyms as you can for the underlined word in each phrase.

1. a nice person
2. a big boat
3. a great day
4. a good movie
5. a little fish
6. a tall building
7. a bad time
8. a hot sun
9. a sad story
10. a super game

## Antonyms

An *antonym* is a word that means the opposite of another word. Dictionaries list antonyms for many words. All of the following are antonyms.

amateur: professional
discard: save
stationary: movable
resident: visitor
resistance: willingness
continuous: interrupted
vanity: modesty
routine: unusual
resemble: differ
reduce: increase

Antonyms show a contrast between extremes. Often, however, there are words in between that show a smaller degree of contrast. Between *wet* and *dry*, for example, we can find such words as *damp, moist,* and *humid.* Knowing the whole range of words between antonyms will help you choose exactly the right word when you write.

### EXERCISE 13 Recognizing Antonyms

Number your paper 1 to 10. Write the letter of the answer that is most nearly opposite in meaning to the word in capital letters. Then check your answers in a dictionary.

1. SUSPICION (A) crime (B) trust (C) worry (D) suspense (E) kindness
2. TRIUMPHANT (A) victorious (B) disappointed (C) musical (D) defeated (E) loud

3. VILLAIN (A) character (B) joker (C) hero (D) criminal (E) resident
4. THOROUGH (A) total (B) narrow (C) straight (D) lasting (E) incomplete
5. STRICT (A) tight (B) old (C) permissive (D) striped (E) rigid
6. MATURE (A) wise (B) eager (C) childish (D) ripe (E) respected
7. GALLANT (A) courteous (B) friendly (C) daring (D) cowardly (E) similar
8. CHANGEABLE (A) steady (B) unreliable (C) nervous (D) cranky (E) upset
9. BLUNT (A) dull (B) rude (C) wide (D) heavy (E) sharp
10. EXHALE (A) relax (B) snore (C) inhale (D) greet (E) decline

## Analogies

At various times during your years in school, you will be tested on your vocabulary. Some vocabulary tests will ask you to identify relationships between pairs of words. These relationships are called *analogies.* Following is an item from a test of analogies.

KIND : CRUEL :: (A) tired : sleepy (B) late : tardy (C) top : bottom

The first step in answering this question is to identify the relationship between the two capitalized words. In this case the words are antonyms, since the meaning of *cruel* is nearly opposite the meaning of *kind.*

The next step is to find another pair of words with the same relationship. The words *tired* and *sleepy* mean about the same thing, so they are synonyms. The words *late* and *tardy* are also synonyms. Letter *C, top* and *bottom,* is the correct answer. *Top* and *bottom* are antonyms, just as *kind* and *cruel* are.

The capitalized words may also be synonyms.

RAPID : SWIFT :: (A) shallow : deep
(B) simple : difficult (C) polite : courteous

The first two pairs of words are antonyms, so they cannot be correct. The correct answer is *C,* since *polite* and *courteous,* like *rapid* and *swift,* are synonyms.

## EXERCISE 14 Recognizing Analogies

Number your paper 1 to 10. Write *synonyms* or *antonyms* to tell how the words in capital letters are related. Then write *A, B,* or *C* to tell which pair of words is related in the same way.

EXAMPLE NIGHT : DAY :: (A) violin : fiddle
(B) health : illness (C) dish : plate

ANSWER antonyms—B

1. TREACHEROUS : DANGEROUS :: (A) brave : afraid
(B) shaky : unsteady (C) hungry : full
2. DAZE : STUN :: (A) walk : stroll (B) work : play
(C) come : go
3. PROHIBIT : ALLOW :: (A) guard : protect
(B) save : keep (C) wash : soil
4. STATIONARY : IMMOVABLE :: (A) hard : difficult
(B) chilly : warm (C) dark : light
5. YIELD : RESIST :: (A) sew : stitch (B) listen : hear
(C) sink : float
6. HASTEN : HURRY :: (A) sing : dance
(B) sit : stand (C) cry : sob
7. RESEMBLE : DIFFER :: (A) arrive : leave
(B) eat : dine (C) grow : mature
8. GALLANT : BRAVE :: (A) soft : hard
(B) easy : simple (C) many : few
9. REDUCE : INCREASE :: (A) spend : save
(B) win : triumph (C) recollect : remember
10. STRICT : PERMISSIVE :: (A) sad : sorrowful
(B) quick : slow (C) distant : far

# Increasing Your Vocabulary

You can work on building your vocabulary every day. When you come across an unfamiliar word, look it up in the dictionary. Try to use that word in speaking and writing so that it becomes very familiar to you.

Another way to enlarge your vocabulary is to keep a notebook of new words. Add new words and their definitions as you come across them. Look over your list from time to time to refresh your memory.

## Vocabulary List

The following list contains words that you are likely to find in your reading. All the words have appeared earlier in the chapter. If you are unsure of any of these words, add them to your vocabulary notebook.

**Vocabulary List**

| | | | |
|---|---|---|---|
| absolutely | detect | lullaby | resistance |
| altogether | disagree | mature | rouse |
| amateur | dishonest | mobile | routine |
| aviator | displease | monarch | sanitize |
| biography | elevation | monotonous | specify |
| blunt | exhale | neutral | stationary |
| brilliant | fatal | ominous | strict |
| commotion | feat | overdue | submarine |
| conclusion | flinch | predict | suspicion |
| continuous | fragile | preview | thorough |
| conviction | gallant | prohibit | treacherous |
| daze | graph | receipt | triumphant |
| debtor | hasten | reduce | vanity |
| decoy | juror | refresh | villain |
| dependence | lanky | resemble | yield |

# Chapter Review

**A** **Context Clues.** Number your paper 1 to 4. Then write the letter of the answer that is closest in meaning to the underlined word.

1. Thomas didn't know the exact number, but he thought there were approximately 28 grams in an ounce.
   (A) certainly (B) usually (C) about
   (D) mainly (E) undoubtedly
2. The solitary wolf crossed miles of trackless snow with no companions, no playmates, and no offspring.
   (A) tame (B) happy (C) baby (D) lone
   (E) sacred
3. Soon the doors to his memory opened, and the old man had a clear recollection of his fourth birthday.
   (A) reflection (B) memory (C) present
   (D) fear (E) development
4. The corridor, or passageway, echoed with footsteps.
   (A) room (B) camp (C) playground
   (D) ship (E) hallway

**B** **Prefixes and Suffixes.** Number your paper 1 to 10. Write the prefix or suffix that has the same meaning as the underlined word or words. Then write the complete word defined after the equal sign.

1. before + historic = before written records were kept
2. not + approve = not think well of
3. not + certain = not sure
4. again + write = to write a second time
5. incorrect + place = to put in the wrong spot
6. conduct + one who = a person who runs a train
7. govern + state of = organized rule of law
8. grace + full of = not clumsy
9. length + make or become = to make longer
10. fulfill + state of = completion

**C** **Synonyms.** Number your paper 1 to 10. Write the letter of the answer that is closest in meaning to the word in capital letters.

1. BRILLIANT (A) stubborn (B) nervous (C) bright (D) wholesome (E) tired
2. OMINOUS (A) friendly (B) polite (C) cloudy (D) threatening (E) outgoing
3. MATURE (A) grown (B) empty (C) smart (D) weary (E) youthful
4. THOROUGH (A) partial (B) near (C) old (D) complete (E) respected
5. FLINCH (A) drive (B) soar (C) wait (D) hitch (E) duck
6. OVERDUE (A) above (B) late (C) simple (D) heavy (E) distant
7. ROUSE (A) interfere (B) waken (C) drift (D) fix (E) reduce
8. VANITY (A) anger (B) peace (C) pride (D) weakness (E) courage
9. COMMOTION (A) disturbance (B) direction (C) building (D) cause (E) travel
10. BLUNT (A) sharp (B) dull (C) short (D) careful (E) bulky

**D** **Antonyms.** Number your paper 1 to 15. Then write an antonym for each of the following words.

1. reduce
2. blunt
3. exhale
4. mature
5. strict
6. mobile
7. fragile
8. gallant
9. prohibit
10. thorough
11. dishonest
12. suspicion
13. dependence
14. stationary
15. resistance

# 31

# Studying and Test-Taking Skills

When you learn to play a musical instrument, you learn a set of skills. You can then use those skills to play almost any piece of music. Studying and taking tests also requires a set of skills. Once you learn these skills, you can use them to improve your performance in all your subjects.

### *EXERCISE 1 Studying and Test-Taking Skills*

Number your paper 1 to 10. Read the list of studying and test-taking skills below. On your paper write *Yes* if the skill would be helpful to practice. Write *No* if it would not be helpful to practice.

1. Review often the notes you take in class.
2. Study in a place with loud music and a telephone.
3. Read test directions carefully before beginning.
4. Take notes on your textbook assignments.
5. Study hard only on the night before a test.
6. Make up questions you think might be on the test.
7. Study hard without taking a break.
8. Review unit and chapter summaries.
9. Keep all study materials together.
10. Get a good night's sleep before a test.

# Studying Skills

Much of the information you need to learn comes from books, especially textbooks. Textbooks contain special sections that help you use the book efficiently. Always become familiar with the table of contents, the index, the glossary, and any other special sections in your textbooks.

## Reading a Textbook

When you read an adventure story, you usually read it only once. When you read a textbook, you need to learn and remember what you have read. One way to help you to do this is the SQ3R method. SQ3R stands for *Survey, Question, Read, Recite,* and *Review.*

**Steps for Reading a Textbook**

| | |
|---|---|
| **Survey** | First get a general idea of what the selection is about. Begin by reading titles, subtitles, and words set off in a different type or color. Look at maps, tables, charts, or other illustrations. Then read the introduction and summary. |
| **Question** | Decide what questions you should be able to answer after reading the selection. Look at any study questions in the book. Also think of your own questions, based on your survey. |
| **Read** | Now read the selection. As you read, try to answer your questions. Also look for important information that is not included in your questions. Take notes as you read. (*See page 516.*) |
| **Recite** | Answer each question in your own words by reciting or writing the answers. |
| **Review** | Answer the questions again without looking at your notes or the selection. Then check your answers. Continue reviewing until you can answer each question correctly. |

### EXERCISE 2 Reading a Textbook

Use the SQ3R method to study the passage about families.

1. **Survey** the passage. What tells you the general idea?
2. Write **questions** that you can answer later.
3. **Read** the passage and take notes.
4. **Recite** the answers to your questions.
5. **Review** your answers by writing them without looking at your notes. Then check them against the passage.

---

**Family Ties**

For many people in the United States, the word *family* means parents and their children. Such a family is a small, central group. It is sometimes called a **nuclear family,** which is another way of saying a central family.

In many African societies, the word *family* means parents, grandparents, aunts, uncles, brothers, sisters, and cousins. These family members often live close to one another, sometimes even in the same household. This kind of family is an **extended family.** Almost half the people in Africa live in extended families.

---

## Taking Notes

Another way to understand and remember what you read is to take notes. Taking notes helps you focus on the most important ideas. Use the strategies below as a guide.

**Strategies for Taking Notes**

1. Read the selection first. Then review it, taking notes in your own words.
2. Include only the main ideas and important details.
3. Write key words and phrases, not complete sentences.
4. Look for key words set off in different type.
5. Look for words that mark main points, such as *first, next, then, one, another important, finally.*

## EXERCISE 3 *Taking Notes*

The passage below is about glaciers. Review the strategies for taking notes. Then take notes on the passage by following the directions below.

1. Read the passage once.
2. Write the title of the passage.
3. Write the words that appear in dark type.
4. Write one phrase that marks an important point in the passage.
5. Write three abbreviations that you might use in your notes.
6. Using the strategies on page 516, take notes on the passage.

---

**Moving Ice**

The movement of ice is another important force that reshapes the earth. This action is carried on by **glaciers** (glā′ shərz). A glacier is formed when snow on a mountain presses down older layers of snow beneath. The pressure turns the snow into ice. As the weight of the ice increases, the ice starts to slide down the mountain.

Glaciers differ in their rate of movement. Many glaciers in the Alps move only 30 centimeters (1 foot) a day. Some in Alaska travel as much as 15 meters (about 50 feet) a day in the summer.

Moving down the mountain, a glacier carves its own valley. As it moves, it picks up huge rocks and blocks of earth. The rocks carried by the glacier gouge and groove the earth as they travel. Like a giant sheet of sandpaper, the moving ice grinds down the land. The valleys of Yosemite (yō sem′ ət ē) National Park in California were formed in this way.

As a glacier moves farther and farther down a mountain, it meets warm air and begins to melt. When a glacier melts, it is said to **retreat.** As a glacier retreats, it deposits a ridge made of the dirt and rock it has been carrying. Such a ridge is called a **moraine** (mə rān′). Long Island, New York, was formed in this way.

---

# Test-Taking Skills

"I studied hard, but then I got confused and nervous during the test." Has that ever happened to you? Knowing how to take a test can be as important as knowing the material. Test-taking, like studying, involves certain skills. Once you acquire them, you will feel more relaxed and confident during any test.

## Classroom Tests

Tests may include objective questions and essay questions. An objective question has only one correct answer, and the answer is always short. Common objective questions are true-false and multiple-choice.

***True-False Questions.*** A true-false question is in the form of a statement. You are asked to decide whether the statement is true or false. Every word of the statement is important.

__**F**__ All families in the United States are nuclear families. [Many families are, but not *all.*]

__**T**__ Many Africans live in extended families.

**Strategies for True-False Questions**

1. Read each word carefully. Just one word can make the statement true or false.
2. Look for words such as *always, never, all, none, no.* They mean the statement can have no exceptions.
3. Look for words such as *many, some, sometimes, usually, may.* They mean the statement can have exceptions and still be true.
4. Think carefully about each part of the statement. If any part is false, then the entire statement is false.

## EXERCISE 4 Answering True-False Questions

Number your paper 1 to 10. Then write *T* if the statement is true and *F* if it is false. You may look in other parts of this book for the answers.

1. The subject of a sentence sometimes follows the verb.
2. Some nouns should be capitalized.
3. Indefinite pronouns always have an antecedent.
4. Action verbs always express physical action.
5. The verbs *grow* and *turn* may be used as linking verbs.
6. A verb never has more than one helping verb.
7. *Is* and *was* may be either linking or helping verbs.
8. A verb phrase is never interrupted by other words.
9. Adjectives can modify only nouns.
10. Adverbs modify verbs, adjectives, and other adverbs.

**Multiple-Choice Questions.** A multiple-choice question gives you several possible answers. You are asked to choose the best one. Try to choose the best answer to the following multiple-choice question.

Which word is a compound noun?
a. left-handed c. independence
b. replacement d. lighthouse

If you remember what a compound noun is, you may be able to choose the right answer immediately. If you are not sure, however, you may be able to eliminate some of the choices. For example, *left-handed* is an adjective, not a noun. *Replacement* is a noun with a prefix and a suffix. Could it be a compound noun? *Independence,* however, is also a noun with a prefix and a suffix. There cannot be two correct answers. *Lighthouse,* choice *d,* must be the answer. *Lighthouse* is the only compound noun.

The following example shows another type of multiple-choice question. This type asks you to complete a sentence.

A country in Central America is ______.
a. Japan b. Costa Rica c. Canada d. Havana

Begin by reading all of the choices and eliminating those you know are wrong. You may know that Japan is in Asia, not in Central America. Canada, although in America, is north of the United States and so would not be considered central. Havana is not a country but a city. Costa Rica, *b*, is the only possible choice.

**Strategies for Multiple-Choice Questions**

1. Read every word of the question carefully.
2. Read all of the choices before answering.
3. Eliminate choices that you know are wrong.
4. Choose the best answer from the remaining choices.
5. Find a reason for your choice. Do not guess wildly.

### EXERCISE 5 *Answering Multiple-Choice Questions*

Number your paper 1 to 10. Then write the letter of the correct answer to each question.

1. Madrid is the capital of what country?
   a. Tokyo
   b. Asia
   c. the Mediterranean
   d. Spain
2. Find the pair of antonyms.
   a. sudden, gradual
   b. awkward, clumsy
   c. your, you're
   d. courageous, brave
3. How many sides does a pentagon have?
   a. 1
   b. 3
   c. 4
   d. 5
4. Which word would be listed last in a dictionary?
   a. supersonic
   b. supernova
   c. supercharge
   d. superpower
5. Which planet is closest to the sun?
   a. Earth
   b. Mercury
   c. Milky Way
   d. Sirius
6. Who was the only president to be elected four times?
   a. Franklin Roosevelt
   b. Martin Luther King
   c. John F. Kennedy
   d. George Washington

7. Find the word spelled incorrectly.
   a. already
   b. eighth
   c. mispell
   d. weird
8. What is another way of writing 49?
   a. 4 + 9
   b. 40 + 9
   c. 4 + 90
   d. 40 + 90
9. What keeps penguins warm?
   a. body fat and feathers
   b. thick fur
   c. flying
   d. warm ocean water
10. Which is an example of a moraine left by a glacier?
   a. Long Island, New York
   b. Alaska
   c. Yosemite National Park
   d. California

***Essay Questions.*** An essay question asks you to write out a full answer. The answer may be a paragraph or more. Essay questions test not only your knowledge of facts but also your ability to organize them. The steps on page 522 explain how to take an essay test.

### ***EXERCISE 6 Understanding Essay Questions***

Number your paper 1 to 5. Read the Steps for Writing an Essay Answer on page 522. Then read each essay question below. Write the key word and one sentence that explains what each question asks you to do.

EXAMPLE Explain the formation of glaciers.
ANSWER Explain—Tell what glaciers are and how and why they are formed.

1. Describe one way in which glaciers change the land.
2. Summarize the plot of Robert Louis Stevenson's novel *Treasure Island.*
3. Compare Canada and the United States.
4. What are the important contrasts between the nuclear family and the extended family?
5. Write a paragraph that defines the term *algae.*

## EXERCISE 7 Answering an Essay Question

Choose one of the questions in Exercise 6 and write an answer for it. Follow the steps below.

## EXERCISE 8 Answering Your Own Essay Question

Write an essay question based on a subject you have studied in one of your courses this year. Then answer the question, following the steps below.

### Steps for Writing an Essay Answer

1. Plan your time and strategy. Spend more time on questions that are worth more points. Begin with the questions you find easiest to answer. If you have a choice of questions, read each one carefully before you choose.
2. Read the directions carefully. Be sure you understand what the question is asking before you write your answer. Look for key words such as the following.

| | |
|---|---|
| **Compare** | Point out similarities and differences. |
| **Contrast** | Point out differences. |
| **Describe** | Give details. |
| **Define** | Make the meaning clear. |
| **Discuss** | Examine in detail. |
| **Explain** | Tell how, what, or why. |
| **Summarize** | Briefly review the main points. |

3. Organize your answer. Write a simple outline by jotting down your main points and supporting details.
4. Write the essay. Use the strategies below.
   - State the main idea of the essay in your introduction.
   - Follow the order of your outline.
   - Be specific. State each main point in a complete sentence. Then back up each main point with facts, examples, and other supporting details. Be sure all your details relate to the main point.
   - Write a conclusion that summarizes the main idea of your essay.
   - Edit your answer, correcting any errors.

# Standardized Tests

Classroom tests are used as a measure of what you have just learned in a course. Standardized tests are printed tests that measure your overall knowledge and abilities in various subjects. These tests are given to large numbers of students in different schools across the country.

The best way to prepare for standardized tests is to keep up with your schoolwork. It is also important to become familiar with the form and the types of questions asked. This part of the chapter will show you how to take standardized tests.

**Hints for Taking Standardized Tests**

1. Listen closely to the examiner's instructions.
2. Fill in your name on the answer sheet.
3. Read the directions and sample questions carefully. Be sure you understand them before you begin.
4. Begin working when the examiner tells you.
5. Read each question carefully. Be aware of details.
6. Don't spend too much time on any one question.
7. You may write on the test form, but always mark your answers on the separate answer sheet. Most tests ask you to shade the circle that contains the letter of your answer.

   ANSWER SHEET 1. Ⓐ Ⓑ Ⓒ Ⓓ
8. Most standardized tests are scored by machine. Mark only one answer for each question. Make sure your mark is dark. To change an answer, erase it fully.
9. Be sure the number on the answer sheet matches the number of the question.
10. Stop when you reach a stop signal on the test or time is called.
11. If you have time, check your work.

***Vocabulary Tests.*** One kind of vocabulary test asks you to recognize a **synonym**—a word that has nearly the same meaning as another word. Following is one example. Try to find the synonym of the underlined word.

frequently late
**A** sometimes **B** often **C** hardly **D** always

All of the words make sense when used with *late*. Only one word, however, is close in meaning to *frequently*. The answer is *B, often*. To answer this question, you would fill in the circle with the letter *B* on your answer sheet.

ANSWER SHEET Ⓐ Ⓑ Ⓒ Ⓓ

## EXERCISE 9 *Answering Vocabulary Questions*

Number your paper 1 to 5. Then write the letter of the synonym of the underlined word.

1. glittering stars
   **A** sparkling **B** waving **C** famous **D** visible
2. conceal the letter
   **A** hide **B** write **C** mail **D** open
3. department supervisor
   **A** store **B** schedule **C** secretary **D** manager
4. a colorful ornament
   **A** poster **B** occasion **C** decoration **D** tale
5. disappear suddenly
   **A** scream **B** vanish **C** leap **D** change

***Tests on Mechanics and Usage.*** Following are some examples of standardized test questions on mechanics and usage. The correct answers are shaded.

CHOOSE THE CORRECT ANSWER.

I ______ a gray cat.
**A** sees **B** seen **C** seed Ⓓ saw

CHOOSE THE BEST WAY TO WRITE THE UNDERLINED PART.

Marilyn carried the biggest of the two suitcases.
(A) bigger  B biggest  C most big  D more bigger

FIND THE ERROR IF THERE IS ONE.

My mother and I met steven yesterday. No error
A B (C) D

## EXERCISE 10 Answering Questions on Mechanics and Usage

Number your paper 1 to 10. Then write the letter of the best choice for the underlined part.

1. Charlie break one of the pink glasses.
   A break  B breaked  C broke  D broken
2. Do you know the name of that beautiful orange flower.
   A flower.  B flower?  C flower  D flower!
3. Please don't eat anything just before dinner.
   A anything  B nothing  C none  D no food
4. Harold is meeting aunt fay at twelve o'clock.
   A aunt fay  B Aunt Fay  C aunt Fay  D Aunt fay
5. Which of the two cars is most oldest?
   A most oldest  B oldest  C more older  D older
6. Unfortunately, Carol is feeling worser today.
   A worser  B more worse  C worse  D badder
7. The driver said, "there are no seats left."
   A "there  B There  C there  D "There
8. I haven't spoke to Carlos in a week.
   A spoke  B spoken  C spoked  D speaked
9. One of the girls had lost their flashlight.
   A their  B there  C her  D hers
10. Which of the reports is yours?
    A yours  B you'res  C your's  D yours'

## EXERCISE 11 Answering Questions on Mechanics and Usage

Number your paper 1 to 5. Then write the letter of the underlined part that has an error. If there is no error, write *D*.

1. Cora, (A) Kevin, (B) and ben (C) are all late. No error (D)

2. Her (A) has forgotten (B) her umbrella again. (C) No error (D)

3. Each of your (A) costumes (B) are (C) handmade. No error (D)

4. No one has (A) written (B) to Adam (C) yet. No error (D)

5. He (A) isnt (B) coming to school (C) today. No error (D)

***Tests of Writing Ability.*** Standardized tests also measure the skills you use when you put sentences together into paragraphs. Some questions ask you to find the sentence that does not belong in the paragraph. Others ask you to choose the best supporting detail for a topic sentence. Another type of question asks you to choose the best order for the sentences in a paragraph. Notice in the following example that the sentences are numbered. The numbers below the sentences show various ways the sentences can be ordered.

(1) Crack two eggs into a cup and add a little milk.
(2) Scrambled eggs are very easy to make.
(3) Cook in a hot, buttered skillet for a few minutes.
(4) Beat the eggs and milk thoroughly.

**A** 1 - 2 - 3 - 4 **C** 3 - 1 - 4 - 2
**B** 4 - 1 - 2 - 3 **D** 2 - 1 - 4 - 3

The answer is *D*. Choice *D* shows the steps for making scrambled eggs in the correct order.

## EXERCISE 12 Answering Questions on Writing

Number your paper 1 to 5. Then write the letter that shows the best order for the sentences.

1. (1) Be sure to start the computer properly.
   (2) Next, insert the disk.
   (3) Then you are ready to begin.
   (4) First, turn on the switch.

   **A** 1 - 4 - 2 - 3 **C** 2 - 4 - 3 - 1
   **B** 4 - 1 - 3 - 2 **D** 3 - 4 - 1 - 2

2. (1) The school band led the marchers.
   (2) From my window I watched the parade go by.
   (3) Behind the band strutted the smiling children.
   (4) A line of fabulous floats ended the celebration.

   **A** 4 - 1 - 2 - 3 **C** 2 - 1 - 3 - 4
   **B** 3 - 1 - 4 - 2 **D** 1 - 2 - 3 - 4

3. (1) Gradually the water level falls back to low tide.
   (2) This rise and fall of water is called a tide.
   (3) About twice a day, the level of the ocean rises.
   (4) The raised water level is known as high tide.

   **A** 1 - 3 - 2 - 4 **C** 3 - 4 - 1 - 2
   **B** 3 - 2 - 4 - 1 **D** 4 - 1 - 2 - 3

4. (1) Muscles are made up of long cells called fibers.
   (2) When a fiber receives a message from a nerve, it shortens, or contracts.
   (3) This shortening and lengthening of muscle fiber is what causes your body to move.
   (4) When the message stops, the fiber lengthens.

   **A** 3 - 1 - 4 - 2 **C** 1 - 2 - 4 - 3
   **B** 2 - 4 - 3 - 1 **D** 4 - 2 - 1 - 3

5. (1) Each bird found its own egg.
   (2) To find out, researchers exchanged their eggs.
   (3) It moved the egg back to the original spot.
   (4) Can some birds identify their own eggs?

   **A** 4 - 2 - 1 - 3 **C** 3 - 2 - 1 - 4
   **B** 4 - 3 - 2 - 1 **D** 1 - 2 - 3 - 4

# Chapter Review

**A Answering True-False Questions.** Number your paper 1 to 10. Then write *T* if the statement is true and *F* if it is false.

1. Dictionaries list words in alphabetical order.
2. *Angel* and *axle* come before *arch* in the dictionary.
3. To find *stork,* look for the guide words *stem/stick.*
4. Dictionaries never list proper nouns.
5. Most dictionaries list the preferred spelling first.
6. The letter *a* is always pronounced the same way.
7. All words contain only one accented syllable.
8. A word may have more than one definition.
9. Some words may be used as different parts of speech.
10. Many words in English come from other languages.

**B Answering Vocabulary Questions.** Number your paper 1 to 10. Then write the letter of the synonym of the underlined word.

1. unpleasant <u>odor</u>
   **A** smell **B** event **C** experience **D** sight
2. to her <u>amazement</u>
   **A** surprise **B** rehearsal **C** house **D** eyes
3. <u>annual</u> event
   **A** pleasant **B** formal **C** yearly **D** familiar
4. official <u>declaration</u>
   **A** welcome **B** parade **C** uniform **D** statement
5. <u>absolutely</u> empty
   **A** almost **B** completely **C** still **D** frequently
6. The <u>origin</u> of the word
   **A** pronunciation **B** end **C** meaning **D** source
7. looked <u>drenched</u>
   **A** unhappy **B** soaked **C** forward **D** around

8. train departed
   A derailed B roared C halted D left

9. vacant chair
   A empty B broken C wooden D comfortable

10. despise it
   A harm B lift C hate D hide

**C Answering Questions on Mechanics and Usage.** Number your paper 1 to 10. Then write the letter of the underlined part that has an error. If there is no error, write *D*.

1. The class elected (A) I (B) as its (C) president. No error (D)
2. Twelve beautiful roses were (A) delivered on Aunt (B) Betty's (C) birthday. No error (D)
3. Is (A) this your (B) seat, or is it her's (C)? No error (D)
4. Senator Harris, (A) thank (B) you for you're (C) efforts on our behalf. No error (D)
5. Each one were (A) wearing the school jacket, tie, (B) and hat at the graduation ceremony. (C) No error (D)
6. In Washington (A) Becky and I (B) saw many interesting and beautiful sights? (C) No error (D)
7. Most of the students will (A) take standardized tests in English (B) and mathematics (C) next week. No error (D)
8. My (A) essay has the title "under (B) the Night (C) Sky." No error (D)
9. Neither camel has (A) had (B) any (C) water for days. No error (D)
10. Hasn't nobody (A) eaten (B) yet? (C) No error (D)

# The Dictionary

The reference book that you use most often is probably the dictionary. A dictionary can tell you how to spell a word, what it means, how to pronounce it, and much more.

SPELLING — **as tro naut** (as'trə nôt), *n.* pilot or member of the crew of a spacecraft. [< Greek *astron* star + *nautēs* sailor] — WORD ORIGIN

**at las** (at'ləs), *n.* **1** book of maps. **2** book of plates or tables illustrating any subject. **3 Atlas,** (in Greek myths) a Titan whose punishment for revolt against Zeus was to support the heavens on his shoulders. **4** the first cervical vertebra, which supports the skull. [< Latin < Greek] — CAPITALIZATION

ABBREVIATIONS —

**atty.,** attorney.

**Au,** gold. [for Latin *aurum*]

**Aug.,** August.

PRONUNCIATION / PART OF SPEECH — **awk ward** (ôk'wərd), *adj.* **1** not graceful or skillful in movement; clumsy; ungainly: *The seal is very awkward on land, but graceful in the water.* See synonym study below. **2** not well suited to use; unhandy: *The handle of this pitcher has an awkward shape.* **3** not easily managed: *an awkward bend in the road.* **4** inconvenient: *an awkward moment.* **5** unpleasant to deal with. **6** ill at ease. — DEFINITIONS

**—awk'ward ly,** *adv.* **—awk'ward ness,** *n.* — RELATED FORMS

**Syn. 1 Awkward, clumsy** mean not graceful. **Awkward** means lacking grace, ease, quickness, and skill: *An awkward person may find it difficult to become a good dancer.* **Clumsy** suggests moving heavily and stiffly: *The clumsy child bumped into all the furniture.* — SYNONYM

# Word Location

A dictionary is organized in alphabetical order to help you find the information you need quickly. Guide words tell you at a glance which words can be found on each page.

## Guide Words

The two words printed in heavy type at the top of each dictionary page are called *guide words.* Each pair of guide words shows the first and last words defined on the page. The guide words **duet** and **dungaree,** for example, show you that *dugout* and *dune buggy* are listed on that page. The words *dungeon* and *dunk shot,* however, would appear on the next page.

### EXERCISE 1 Using Guide Words

Make two columns on your paper. Write the guide words **babble—badminton** at the top of the first column and **baffle—balloon** at the top of the second column. Then write each word in the proper column.

| | | | |
|---|---|---|---|
| baboon | Bahamas | balcony | ballerina |
| babysit | bachelor | badly | backpack |
| baggage | backyard | ballet | Badlands |
| backgammon | balance | bald eagle | ballad |
| bagpipe | bacteria | bakery | badger |

## Alphabetical Order

Once you have located the right page, you can find the word you need by following a strict, letter-by-letter alphabetical order. Compound words are alphabetized as if there were no space or hyphen.

| | |
|---|---|
| SINGLE WORD | space |
| ONE-WORD COMPOUND | spacecraft |
| TWO-WORD COMPOUND | space station |
| HYPHENATED COMPOUND | space-time |

The dictionary also lists proper nouns, prefixes, suffixes, phrases, and abbreviations. Abbreviations are alphabetized letter by letter and not by the word they stand for. The abbreviation *rd.* for *road* would fall between the words *razor* and *read.* It would not be placed next to *road.*

## EXERCISE 2 Alphabetizing Words

Number your paper 1 to 10. Then arrange the underlined words in each phrase in alphabetical order.

EXAMPLE as wild as a winter wind
ANSWER wild, wind, winter

Tongue Twisters

1. the mystery of the missing meatball
2. millions of mighty mice
3. the wicked witch of the West
4. the case of the cagey canary
5. a band of baboons playing banjos
6. eleven elephants in an elevator
7. selling seashells by the seashore
8. a gaggle of gawky geese
9. buggy bumpers for bouncing baby buggies
10. Peter Piper picked a peck of pickled peppers.

## EXERCISE 3 Alphabetizing Words

Make three columns on your paper. Then write the words in each column in alphabetical order.

| 1. | 2. | 3. |
|---|---|---|
| seafloor | moonstruck | snowball |
| sea legs | moonrise | snow job |
| seamanship | moonlit | snow-white |
| seabed | moonbeam | snow leopard |
| seagoing | moonstone | snow tire |
| seafowl | moonlight | SNOBOL |
| seascape | moonward | snowshoe |
| seasick | moon shot | snow-blind |
| sea dog | moonflower | Sno-Cat |
| seawall | moonquake | snowcap |

# Information in an Entry

All of the information given for a word is called an *entry*. The entry is made up of four main parts: (1) the entry word, (2) the pronunciation, (3) the definitions, and (4) the word origin. The following entry for *porpoise* shows these four main parts.

ENTRY WORD
PRONUNCIATION

**por poise** (pôr′pəs), *n., pl.* **-pois es** or **-poise. 1** a sea mammal with a blunt, rounded snout, of the same order as the whale but smaller and living in groups in the northern Atlantic and Pacific. **2** any of several other small sea mammals, especially the dolphin. [< Old French *porpeis,* ultimately < Latin *porcus* pig + *piscis* fish]

DEFINITIONS
WORD ORIGIN



## The Entry Word

The entry word provides three kinds of information. It shows (1) how to spell a word, (2) whether a word should be capitalized, and (3) where a word breaks into syllables.

**Spelling.** The entry word shows how to spell a word correctly. Some words have more than one correct spelling. The most common spelling, called the *preferred spelling,* is given first. The second spelling is called the *variant spelling.* Always use the preferred spelling of a word in your writing.

A dictionary entry also shows how to spell the plurals of nouns, the principal parts of verbs, and the comparative and superlative degrees of adjectives and adverbs. These are given only if the form or spelling is irregular.

**gup py,** (gup′ ē), *n., pl.,* **—pies.** — NOUN PLURAL
**gur gle,** (gėr gəl), *v.,* **—gled, —gling.** — PRINCIPAL PARTS
**gus ty,** (gus′ tē), *adj.,* **gust i er, gust i est.** — ADJECTIVE FORMS

Words formed by adding a prefix or suffix to the entry word are often shown at the end of the entry. These related forms are called *derived words.*

**nois y** (noi′zē), *adj.,* **nois i er, nois i est. 1** making much noise: *a noisy crowd.* **2** full of noise: *a noisy street.* **3** having much noise with it: *a noisy quarrel.* **—nois′i ly,** *adv.* **—nois′i ness,** *n.* — DERIVED WORDS



## EXERCISE 4 *Checking Spelling*

Number your paper 1 to 20. Write each word with the ending given in parentheses. Use a dictionary to check your spelling.

EXAMPLE drive (ing)
ANSWER driving

1. spy (s)
2. wolf (s)
3. tomato (s)
4. quiz (s)
5. cloudy (ness)
6. bus (s)
7. charity (s)
8. busy (er)
9. compass (s)
10. lonely (ness)
11. satisfy (ed)
12. refer (ed)
13. continue (ing)
14. bury (ing)
15. omit (ing)
16. lovely (est)
17. lazy (ness)
18. monkey (s)
19. crispy (est)
20. precede (ed)

***Capitalization.*** If a word should be capitalized, the entry word will be printed with a capital letter. If a word should only be capitalized sometimes, the word will be shown with a capital letter near the appropriate definition.

CAPITAL LETTERS

**north** (nôrth), *n.* **1** direction to which a compass needle points; direction to the right as one faces the setting sun. **2** Also, **North.** the part of any country toward the north. **3 the North,** the northern part of the United States; the states north of Maryland, the Ohio River, and Missouri, making up most of the states that formed the Union side in the Civil War. [Old English]

**North Star,** the bright star almost directly above the North Pole, formerly much used as a guide by sailors; Polaris; polestar; lodestar.



***Syllables.*** When you write your final copy of a report or composition, you will sometimes need to divide a word at the end of a line. The dictionary shows you how a word breaks into syllables.

**as•tro•naut** **I•tal•ian** **pri•va•cy**

Always divide a word between syllables. *(See the rules for dividing words on page 259.)*

### EXERCISE 5 Dividing Words into Syllables

Number your paper 1 to 10. Using a dictionary, write each word with a small dot between syllables.

EXAMPLE resourceful
ANSWER re•source•ful

1. majestic
2. discolor
3. justify
4. coincide
5. immunity
6. assistant
7. usually
8. lawmaker
9. article
10. exhibit

# Pronunciation

If you are not sure how to pronounce a word, you can look it up in the dictionary. A phonetic spelling is shown in parentheses after each entry word. The phonetic spelling shows how to pronounce the word correctly.

**knee** (nē) **ra•di•o** (rā′ dē ō)

At the front of the dictionary is a complete pronunciation key to help you understand the letters and symbols used in the phonetic spellings. Most dictionaries also provide a shortened form of the key on every other page for easy reference.

**PARTIAL PRONUNCIATION KEY**

| | | | | | | | | | |
|---|---|---|---|---|---|---|---|---|---|
| **a** | hat | **i** | it | **oi** | oil | **ch** | child | | a in about |
| **ā** | age | **ī** | ice | **ou** | out | **ng** | long | | e in taken |
| **ä** | far | **o** | hot | **u** | cup | **sh** | she | ə = | i in pencil |
| **e** | let | **ō** | open | **ů** | put | **th** | thin | | o in lemon |
| **ē** | equal | **ô** | order | **ü** | rule | **ŦH** | then | | u in circus |
| **ėr** | term | | | | | **zh** | measure | < = | derived from |



***Diacritical Marks.*** In the pronunciation key above, there are marks over some of the vowels. These are called *diacritical marks* and show the different sounds a vowel can make. For example, the different sounds of the vowel *a* are shown in the following ways.

DIACRITICAL MARKS

**a** as in hat **ā** as in age **ä** as in far

***The Schwa.*** Sometimes vowels are pronounced like the sound *uh*. Dictionaries use the symbol ə to represent this sound. This symbol is called a *schwa*.

**a•bove** (ə buv′) **lem•on** (lem′ ən) **to•ken** (tō′ kən)

### EXERCISE 6 Marking Pronunciation

Number your paper 1 to 10. Using a dictionary, write the pronunciation of each word. Be sure that you include all diacritical marks.

EXAMPLE adrift
ANSWER (ə drift′)

1. rate
2. film
3. dust
4. mild
5. final
6. strike
7. provide
8. benefit
9. canteen
10. feline

***Accent Marks.*** An accent mark shows which syllable should be stressed in the pronunciation. Accent marks appear in the phonetic spelling of a word.

**fa • mous** (fā′məs) **in • jus • tice** (in jus′tis)

Some words will have two accent marks. The darker one, called the *primary accent,* tells you which syllable receives more stress. The lighter one, called the *secondary accent,* receives slightly less stress.

**in • ex • pen • sive** (in′ ik spen′ siv)

PRIMARY ACCENT
SECONDARY ACCENT

### EXERCISE 7 Placing Accent Marks

Number your paper 1 to 10. Using a dictionary, write the pronunciation of each word. Leave space between syllables and mark both primary and secondary stresses.

EXAMPLE hydrochloride
ANSWER hī′ drə klôr′ īd

1. composition
2. vegetarian
3. navigation
4. scientific
5. desperation
6. territory
7. dictionary
8. interstate
9. afternoon
10. helicopter

## Definitions

Most words have more than one meaning. The following entry for *trunk* gives five definitions.

**trunk** (trungk) *n.* **1.** the main stem of a tree: *The huge trunk supported many branches.* **2.** a large box used for storing or moving household items: *We packed the clothes in a trunk.* **3.** the long flexible snout of an elephant. **4.** the storage compartment of a car: *The spare tire is in the trunk.* **5.** the body of a human or animal not including the head, arms, and legs: *A giraffe's trunk is shorter than its neck.*

To find the definition that fits the sentence you have in mind, read all of the definitions and examples carefully. Then decide which meaning makes sense in your sentence.

### EXERCISE 8 Choosing an Appropriate Meaning

Using the entry for *trunk* above, write the definition that tells what *trunk* means in each sentence.

EXAMPLE Its trunk explored the ground for peanuts.
ANSWER the long flexible snout of an elephant

1. Please help me carry this trunk to the attic.
2. We always put the groceries in the trunk.
3. The mother elephant was showing by example how her baby should use its trunk.
4. Richard had the trunk of an athlete, with broad shoulders and slim hips.
5. A gash in the trunk showed the forest ranger where lightning had struck.
6. Drew locked the extra set of keys in the trunk.
7. In a fight the elephant's trunk grasps the enemy.
8. Moss grew on the trunk of the old oak tree.
9. I helped pack my sister's winter clothes in a trunk before she left for college in New England.
10. The trunk of some camels has two humps.

***Part of Speech Labels.*** Dictionaries use the following abbreviations to tell what part of speech a word is.

| | | | |
|---|---|---|---|
| *n.* | noun | *pron.* | pronoun |
| *v.* | verb | *prep.* | preposition |
| *adj.* | adjective | *conj.* | conjunction |
| *adv.* | adverb | *interj.* | interjection |

Since many words can be more than one part of speech, two or more abbreviations may appear in a single entry.

> **back** (bak), *n.* **1.** The part of the human body from the back of the shoulders to the end of the spine. **2.** the upper part of an animal's body from the neck to the end of the backbone. **3.** the rear part: *the back of the house.* **4.** the part which supports the back: *the back of the chair.* **5.** the opposite side: *the back of an envelope.* —*v.* **1.** to cause to move backward: *She backed the car out of the garage.* **2.** to support or help: *to back a candidate.* —*adj.* at the rear: *back door.* —*adv.* toward the rear: *step back.*

The entry above shows that the word *back* can be used as four parts of speech. Be sure to find the right part of speech when searching for the definition of a word.

## ***EXERCISE 9 Finding Different Meanings of Words***

Using the definition of *back* above, write the part of speech of each underlined word. If the word is a noun or a verb, also write the number of the definition that tells what *back* means in the sentence.

EXAMPLE The cat arched its back.
ANSWER noun, 2

1. The line curled all the way around the back of the movie theater.
2. The fire fighters told the crowd to stand back.
3. On the back of the letter, the spy wrote a message in code.
4. The lawyer tried to back the case with solid evidence.
5. The ball soared over the back fence.

***Synonyms.*** Words with almost the same meaning are called *synonyms*. Dictionaries often list synonyms at the end of an entry and explain the special meaning of each. This information is usually signaled by the abbreviation *syn.*

**tired** (tīrd), *adj.* weary; fatigued; exhausted. **—tired′ly,** *adv.* **—tired′ness,** *n.*

SYNONYMS — **Syn. Tired, weary, exhausted** mean drained of strength, energy, or power of endurance. **Tired** is the general word: *I am tired, but I must get back to work.* **Weary** implies feeling worn out and unable to go on: *Weary shoppers wait for buses and streetcars.* **Exhausted** implies without enough energy left to be able to go on: *Exhausted by near starvation and bitter winds, the lost hikers lay in a stupor.*



## Word Origins

The English language is constantly changing and growing. The dictionary provides information about the history of words that have long been part of our language. It also gives the sources of new words. The following entry shows that the word *centipede* comes from two Latin words meaning "one hundred feet."

**cen ti pede** (sen′tə pēd′), *n.* any of a class of flat, wormlike arthropods with many pairs of legs, the front pair of which are clawlike and contain poison glands; chilopod. Centipedes vary in length from an inch (2.54 cm.) to nearly a foot (30 cm.).

WORD ORIGIN — [< Latin *centipeda* < *centum* hundred + *pedem* foot]

**centipede**
about 1 in. (2.5 cm.) long



Many of the words we use come from Latin and Greek. The English language, however, also contains words from many other languages.

**Words from Other Languages**

| | | | |
|---|---|---|---|
| **AMERICAN INDIAN** | chipmunk<br>opossum | hickory<br>raccoon | moccasin<br>skunk |
| **DUTCH** | cookie<br>slim | cruise<br>waffle | iceberg<br>wagon |
| **FRENCH** | garage<br>parachute | menu<br>picnic | liter<br>souvenir |
| **GERMAN** | hamster<br>noodle | nickel<br>pretzel | zinc<br>waltz |
| **ITALIAN** | confetti<br>pizza | lagoon<br>stanza | opera<br>volcano |
| **MEXICAN SPANISH** | burrito<br>guacamole | cafeteria<br>stampede | canyon<br>taco |
| **SPANISH** | alligator<br>tornado | fiesta<br>rodeo | mosquito<br>tuna |

***Words with Unusual Origins.*** Borrowing words from other languages is only one way our language grows. New words come into our language in a variety of other ways. Some words, called compound words, are formed by combining two words.

weekend    birthday    sunglasses    moonlight

Some words are a blend of two words.

breakfast + lunch = brunch    twist + whirl = twirl
guess + estimate = guesstimate    smoke + fog = smog

Some words are shortened forms of longer words.

| Shortened Form | Longer Form |
|---|---|
| plane | airplane |
| super | superior |
| fan | fanatic |
| sub | submarine |

Some words imitate sounds.

Ping-Pong    hiss    sizzle    swish    pitter-patter

Some names of people have also become words.

Levi Strauss—maker of **Levi's** blue jeans
George Ferris—inventor of the **Ferris** wheel
Louis Pasteur—first to **pasteurize** milk

Some words are acronyms. Acronyms are words that are formed from the first letter or syllables of other words.

**NASA** **N**ational **A**eronautics and **S**pace **A**dministration
**VISTA** **V**olunteers **i**n **S**ervice **t**o **A**merica
**radar** **ra**dio **d**etecting **a**nd **r**anging

The word origin is usually listed at the end of an entry. Keep in mind, however, that all dictionaries do not arrange information in exactly the same way. All dictionaries provide an explanation of their arrangement at the front of the book.

### EXERCISE 10 *Finding Word Origins*

Number your paper 1 to 10. Then use the dictionary to write the origin of each of the following words.

1. walrus
2. vanilla
3. chocolate
4. technique
5. kindergarten
6. piano
7. helicopter
8. trampoline
9. patio
10. toboggan

### EXERCISE 11 *Finding Unusual Origins*

Number your paper 1 to 20. Then tell how each of the following words came into the English language by writing *compound, blend, shortened form, sounds, person's name,* or *acronym.* Use the dictionary and the examples on pages 541–542 to help you.

1. splash
2. moped
3. raincoat
4. scuba
5. tangelo
6. newspaper
7. lab
8. squiggle
9. saxophone
10. diesel
11. deli
12. motel
13. SAT
14. whoosh
15. chortle
16. chuckle
17. shoelace
18. sandwich
19. limo
20. ZIP code

# Chapter Review

**Using the Dictionary.** Number your paper 1 to 15. Then answer each question using the entries shown below.

**Bad lands** (bad′landz′), *n. pl.* **1** rugged, barren region in SW South Dakota and NW Nebraska in which erosion has produced unusual land formations. **2** **badlands,** any similar region.
**Band-Aid** (band′ād′), *n.* trademark for a small adhesive bandage.
**ban dan na** or **ban dan a** (ban dan′ə), *n.* a large, gaily colored kerchief often worn on the head or neck.
**bar be cue** (bär′bə kyü), *n., v.,* **-cued, -cu ing.** —*n.* **1** an outdoor meal in which meat is roasted over a fire. **2** grill or fireplace for cooking meat. —*v.* **1** roast over an open fire.
**bar ra cu da** (bar′ə kü′də), *n.,* a salt-water fish with a long, narrow body, sharp teeth, and a jutting lower jaw. [< Spanish]
**BA SIC** (bāsik), *n.* language using English words and algebraic notation for programming and communicating with computers. [< *b(eginner's) a(ll-purpose) s(ymbolic) i(nstruction) c(ode)*]
**bd.,** **1** board. **2** bond. **3** bound.
**beau ti ful** (byü′tə fəl), *adj.* delighting the mind or senses. **—beau′ti ful ly,** *adv.* **—beau′ti-ful ness,** *n.*
**Syn. Beautiful, lovely, handsome** mean pleasing the senses or mind. **Beautiful** suggests delighting the senses by excellence and harmony: *Looking at a beautiful painting always gives one satisfaction.* **Lovely** suggests appealing to the emotions: *Her lovely smile shows a sweet disposition.* **Handsome** means pleasing to look at: *That is a handsome phonograph.*



1. When should *badlands* be capitalized?
2. Which entry word has two accepted spellings?
3. Which entry word has four syllables?
4. How many syllables in *barracuda* are stressed?
5. What do the letters in the word *BASIC* stand for?
6. What are two synonyms for *beautiful*?
7. What are the three meanings of the abbreviation *bd.*?
8. What two parts of speech can *barbecue* be?
9. Which entry word comes from Spanish?
10. Which entry word is always plural?
11. What two derived words are listed under *beautiful*?
12. If this were a complete dictionary page, what would the two guide words be?
13. How many syllables in *beautiful* contain a schwa?
14. What are two principal parts of the verb *barbecue*?
15. Which definition of *barbecue* is used below?
    My brother and I cleaned the barbecue after the cookout.

# 33

# The Library

When you need to choose a novel for a book report or a topic for a science project, the library is the best place to start. The library contains a wide variety of resources, and it is arranged so you can find them quickly. For example, if you were writing a science report about sea otters, the information you would need could be found in the following materials.

- The *Dictionary of Animals* explains that the sea otter is the largest of all otters.
- The *Atlas of Wildlife* contains maps that show that sea otters live along the Pacific Coast from California to Alaska.
- The *Encyclopedia of North American Wildlife* explains how sea otters wrap seaweed around their bodies when they sleep so they will not drift far out to sea.
- *The Guinness Book of World Records* identifies the sea otter as the slowest-swimming marine mammal.

In addition to the books listed above, the library contains many other materials for you to use. This chapter will tell you what these materials are and will show you how to find them easily.

# Library Arrangement

A library arranges books on the shelves so you can find them easily. Books of fiction are organized in alphabetical order. Nonfiction books are arranged by numbers and filed in a separate section.

## Fiction

Books of fiction include novels and stories that are partly or totally imaginary. These books are put on the shelves in alphabetical order by the author's last name. The following rules will help you find books of fiction.

- Two-part names are alphabetized by the first part of the name.

  **Da**Rosa  **Mac**Mahon  **O**'Leary  **Van** Dam

- Names beginning with *Mc* or *St.* are alphabetized as if they began with *Mac* and *Saint.*
- Books by the same author are alphabetized by title, skipping *a, an,* and *the* at the beginning.

### Exercise 1 *Arranging Fiction*

Number your paper 1 to 10. Then write the novels in the order they should be placed on the shelves.

*M. C. Higgins, the Great,* Virginia Hamilton
*Across Five Aprils,* Irene Hunt
*Little Women,* Louisa May Alcott
*Dr. Doom: Superstar,* T. Ernesto Bethancourt
*Tina Gogo,* Judie Angell
*Arilla Sun Down,* Virginia Hamilton
*The Wolves of Willoughby Chase,* Joan Aiken
*The Empire Strikes Back,* Donald F. Glut
*The Wonderful Wizard of Oz,* L. Frank Baum
*The Blind Colt,* Glen Rounds

### Exercise 2 *Solving Shelving Problems*

Number your paper 1 to 10. Then write the following fiction authors in the order that their books would appear on the shelves.

Mary O'Hara
Ursula Le Guin
Scott O'Dell
Patricia A. McKillip
Jean Van Leeuwen
Madeleine L'Engle
Robert O'Brien
Helen MacInnis
Scott O'Neill
Betty MacDonald

## Nonfiction

Nonfiction books contain facts about real people and events. Most libraries use the Dewey decimal system to arrange nonfiction books on the shelves. In this system each book is assigned a number according to its subject. There are ten general categories in the Dewey decimal system.

This system makes finding a book about a certain subject easy. A subject that falls under science—such as astronomy—is assigned a number between 500 and 599. A book

**Dewey Decimal System**

| | |
|---|---|
| 000–099 | General Works (reference books) |
| 100–199 | Philosophy |
| 200–299 | Religion |
| 300–399 | Social Science (law, education, economics) |
| 400–499 | Language |
| 500–599 | Science (mathematics, biology, chemistry) |
| 600–699 | Technology (medicine, inventions) |
| 700–799 | Fine Arts (painting, music, theater) |
| 800–899 | Literature |
| 900–999 | History (biography, geography, travel) |

about robots would be listed under technology. It would be assigned a number between 600 and 699. This number is written on the spine—the part of the book that faces you when it is on the shelf. The books are then arranged on the shelves in numerical order.

**Science: 500–599**

Biographies and autobiographies are usually kept in a separate section. Most libraries label each book with a *B* for biography or with the Dewey decimal number 920. They are arranged in alphabetical order by the last name of the subject, not the author.

## EXERCISE 3 Understanding the Dewey Decimal System

Number your paper 1 to 10. Then for each of the following nonfiction books, write the range of numbers and the category it falls under in the Dewey decimal system. Use the chart on page 547.

EXAMPLE *The History of Rock 'n' Roll*
ANSWER 700–799 Fine Arts

1. *Laws, Courts, and Lawyers*
2. *The Life of John F. Kennedy*
3. *The Philosophy of Plato*
4. *The Invention of Ordinary Things*
5. *Religions of the World*
6. *Math and Logic Games*
7. *Heart Transplants*
8. *Hit Broadway Plays*
9. *You Can Speak French*
10. *Famous American Poets*

## EXERCISE 4 Solving Shelving Problems

Number your paper 1 to 10. Then write the following Dewey decimal numbers and book titles in the order that the books would appear on the shelves. Remember that nonfiction books are arranged in numerical order, not in alphabetical order.

590.7 *A Zoo for All Seasons*
581.4 *The Life of a Forest*
598.2 *Birds of the Ocean*
594.5 *Kingdom of the Octopus*
582.3 *What's in the Names of Flowers*
591.9 *Animals of the Antarctic*
595.7 *Familiar Insects of America*
586 *Plants without Leaves*
597.3 *The Natural History of Sharks*
593.9 *The Living Wilderness*

# The Card Catalog

The card catalog is a cabinet of small drawers that contain a file card for every book in the library. The drawers also contain cards for other types of material, such as filmstrips, tapes, and records. Each drawer is labeled to show what part of the alphabet it covers.

There are three cards for each book in the catalog. You can look up an *author card,* a *title card,* or a *subject card* to find the book you need.

**Card Catalog File Drawer**

## Author Cards

Sometimes you know the author of a book but not the title. You can look in the card catalog under the author's last name. To find a book by Kenneth Gatland, for example, you look in the drawer that covers the letter *G*.

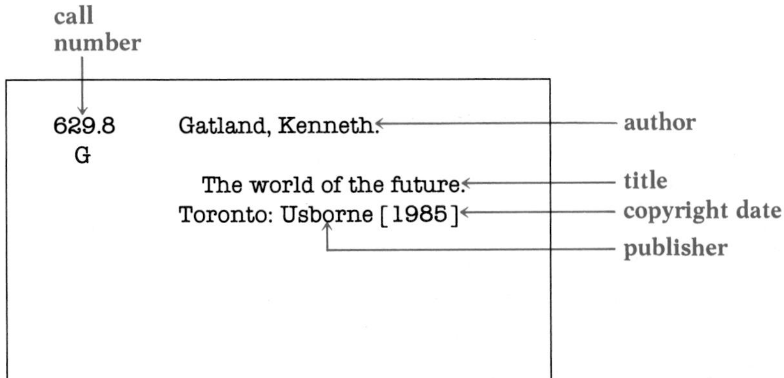

## Title Cards

Sometimes you know the title of a book but not the author. You can find the book by looking up the first word in the title (except *a, an,* and *the*). To find *The World of the Future,* look in the drawer containing the letter *W.*

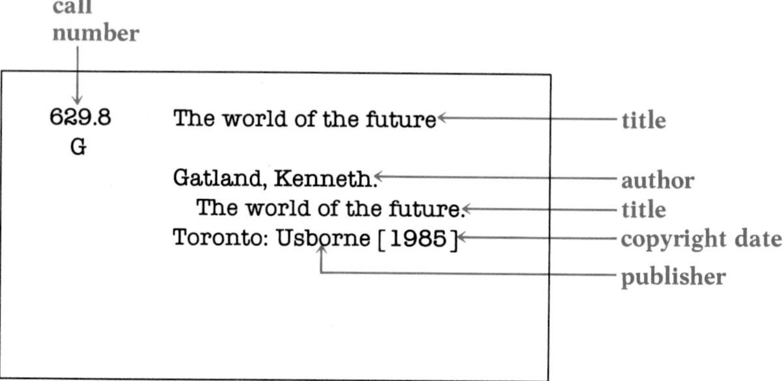


## Subject Cards

When you are looking for books for a report, you will use subject cards more than title or author cards. If your subject were robots, you would look in the drawer that covers the letter *R.* There you would find cards for all of the books about robots available in that library.

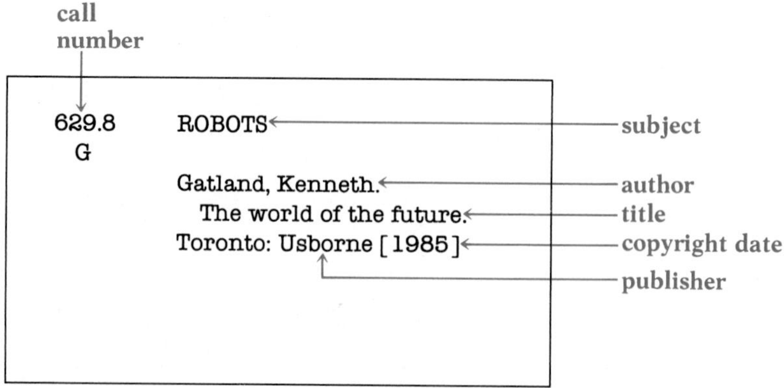


Notice that all three cards for *The World of the Future* provide the same information.

**Steps for Finding Books**

1. Find out if the library has the book you want by finding the author card, the title card, or the subject card in the card catalog.
2. Read the card to see if the book is likely to contain the information you need. Check the copyright date to see how current the information is.
3. On a slip of paper, copy the call number, the title, and the name of the author for each book you want to find.
4. Use the call number to find each book. The first line of the call number tells which section of the library to look in.

| | |
|---|---|
| F or FIC | fiction section |
| B or 920 | biography section |
| Dewey number | nonfiction section |

Then find each book on the shelves by looking for its call number, located on the spine.

## *EXERCISE 5 Using the Card Catalog*

Number your paper 1 to 10. Then write the letter or letters of the drawer in which you would find each of the following in the card catalog.

EXAMPLE *The Hobbit*
ANSWER He–I

1. *The Mysterious Planet*
2. Kristin Hunter
3. photography
4. computers
5. robots
6. Isaac Asimov
7. *Search for Bigfoot*
8. Rudyard Kipling
9. magic
10. Italy

**EXERCISE 6** ***Writing Catalog Cards***

Write an author card, a title card, and a subject card using the following information.

> *Baseball's Hottest Hitters,* published in Minneapolis by Lerner Publications, Dewey decimal number 796.35, copyright date 1983, written by Nathan Aaseng.

## Cross-Reference Cards

In addition to author, title, and subject cards, a card catalog contains "see" and "see also" cards. A "see" card will tell you that the subject you need is listed under another heading. A "see also" card will list other subjects that also have information about your subject.

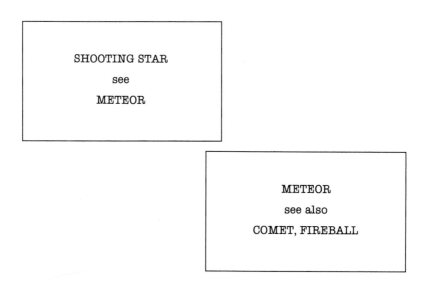

SHOOTING STAR
see
METEOR

METEOR
see also
COMET, FIREBALL

## Guide Cards

Guide cards, like the ones shown in the file drawer on page 549, are blank cards with a word or a letter printed at the top. These cards are arranged in alphabetical order in each file drawer of the card catalog. Using guide cards will help you find title, author, and subject cards quickly.

# Reference Materials

Reference books, such as encyclopedias, dictionaries, atlases, and almanacs, are kept in a separate section of the library. Since these books cannot be checked out, there are usually study tables set up in the reference section.

## Encyclopedias

When you are gathering information for a report, encyclopedias are a good place to start. These are works that contain general information on a wide variety of subjects. Following are some popular general encyclopedias.

ENCYCLOPEDIAS *Collier's Encyclopedia*
*Compton's Pictured Encyclopedia*
*Encyclopedia Americana*
*Encyclopaedia Britannica*
*World Book Encyclopedia*

The information in most encyclopedias is arranged alphabetically by subject. Guide letters on the spine show which letter or letters are covered in each volume. Guide words at the top of each page help you find your subject.

When looking for information in an encyclopedia, be sure to check the *index*. It will tell you if your subject is discussed in more than one volume or if it is listed under another name. Most encyclopedias put the index in a separate volume or at the end of the last volume.

## Specialized Encyclopedias

Specialized encyclopedias have the same organization as general encyclopedias. Specialized encyclopedias, however, concentrate on one specific subject. They provide more complete information than general encyclopedias do. Following are some specialized encyclopedias.

| | |
|---|---|
| SPECIALIZED ENCYCLOPEDIAS | *The Baseball Encyclopedia*<br>*Encyclopedia of Animal Care*<br>*International Wildlife Encyclopedia*<br>*Encyclopedia of Modern Art*<br>*Encyclopedia of Beekeeping*<br>*Encyclopedia of Comic Book Heroes*<br>*The Encyclopedia of Dance and Ballet*<br>*The Illustrated Encyclopedia of World Coins*<br>*The McGraw-Hill Encyclopedia of Science and Technology* |

## Biographical References

Biographical reference works give you information about the lives of famous people. Check your library to see which of the following biographical reference books it has.

| | |
|---|---|
| BIOGRAPHICAL REFERENCES | *Current Biography*<br>*Who's Who*<br>*Who's Who in America*<br>*Webster's Biographical Dictionary*<br>*Dictionary of American Biography*<br>*Contemporary Authors*<br>*Twentieth Century Authors*<br>*Men and Women of Science* |

### EXERCISE 7 Using Biographical References

Each of the following Americans was the first at what he or she did. Using a biographical reference, briefly explain what this famous first was.

1. Jackie Robinson
2. Sally Ride
3. Guion Bluford
4. Geraldine Ferraro
5. Robert E. Peary
6. George Washington
7. Sandra Day O'Connor
8. Neil Armstrong
9. Amelia Earhart
10. Charles Lindbergh

## Atlases

Atlases are books of maps. They also contain facts about oceans, deserts, mountains, climate, population, and natural resources. All atlases do not contain the same maps and information. The pages at the front of each atlas will tell you what the atlas contains and how the information is presented. Following is a list of commonly used atlases.

ATLASES *Collier's World Atlas and Gazetteer*
*Hammond's Medallion World Atlas*
*Rand McNally: The International Atlas*
*Goode's World Atlas*
*Atlas of World History*

## Almanacs and Yearbooks

Almanacs and yearbooks include facts about many subjects. They contain world records, noteworthy achievements, facts about famous people, and much more. Since almanacs and yearbooks are published every year, they usually contain up-to-date information. Following are the names of some well-known almanacs and yearbooks.

ALMANACS AND YEARBOOKS *Information Please Almanac*
*World Almanac and Book of Facts*
*Hammond's Almanac*
*Guinness Book of World Records*
*Collier's Yearbook*

## Specialized Dictionaries

These specialized dictionaries contain entries related to one specific subject. Some, for example, list only synonyms. Some list only those terms that are used in mathematics, or computers, or even sports. Following are a few of the many specialized dictionaries available.

| | |
|---|---|
| SPECIALIZED DICTIONARIES | *The New Roget's Thesaurus in Dictionary Form*<br>*Webster's New Dictionary of Synonyms*<br>*Abbreviations Dictionary*<br>*Compton's Illustrated Science Dictionary*<br>*Dictionary of American History* |

### EXERCISE 8 Using Reference Materials

Following is a list of library resources. Number your paper 1 to 10. Then write the best source for answering each question.

| | |
|---|---|
| specialized encyclopedia | atlas |
| specialized dictionary | almanac or yearbook |
| biographical reference | |

1. For which president's inauguration did Robert Frost write a poem?
2. Who is the subject of Andrew Wyeth's famous painting *Christina's World*?
3. How many people can the Rose Bowl in Pasadena, California, seat when it is filled to capacity?
4. Lorraine Vivian Hansberry was the first black woman to have a play produced on Broadway. What was the name of the play?
5. In tennis, what is a foot fault?
6. During what years was the American buffalo nickel made?
7. Name the countries partly covered by the Alps.
8. What cities were sites of the Olympic Games from 1968 to 1984?
9. In what state is Kalamazoo, and what large city is directly north of it?
10. In music, what does the term *rockabilly* mean?

### EXERCISE 9 Finding Facts in Reference Books

Use the library's reference materials to find the answers to the ten questions in Exercise 8.

## Readers' Guide to Periodical Literature

Magazines can give you information on most subjects. They are especially useful for providing the most recent information available. The *Readers' Guide to Periodical Literature* is an index that can tell you which magazines have articles on your subject. It indexes approximately 175 magazines. Bound volumes of the *Readers' Guide* are published every year, and paperback volumes are issued during the year. A list of all the magazines covered is in the front of each volume.

Entries in the *Readers' Guide* are listed by subject and author. Following are several entries from one issue.

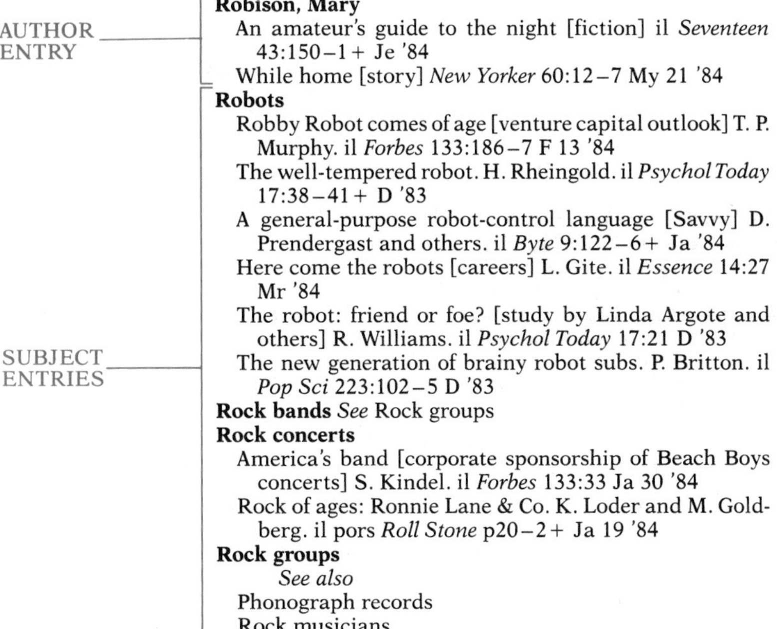

AUTHOR ENTRY
**Robison, Mary**
An amateur's guide to the night [fiction] il *Seventeen* 43:150–1+ Je '84
While home [story] *New Yorker* 60:12–7 My 21 '84
SUBJECT ENTRIES
**Robots**
Robby Robot comes of age [venture capital outlook] T. P. Murphy. il *Forbes* 133:186–7 F 13 '84
The well-tempered robot. H. Rheingold. il *Psychol Today* 17:38–41+ D '83
A general-purpose robot-control language [Savvy] D. Prendergast and others. il *Byte* 9:122–6+ Ja '84
Here come the robots [careers] L. Gite. il *Essence* 14:27 Mr '84
The robot: friend or foe? [study by Linda Argote and others] R. Williams. il *Psychol Today* 17:21 D '83
The new generation of brainy robot subs. P. Britton. il *Pop Sci* 223:102–5 D '83
**Rock bands** *See* Rock groups
**Rock concerts**
America's band [corporate sponsorship of Beach Boys concerts] S. Kindel. il *Forbes* 133:33 Ja 30 '84
Rock of ages: Ronnie Lane & Co. K. Loder and M. Goldberg. il pors *Roll Stone* p20–2+ Ja 19 '84
**Rock groups**
*See also*
Phonograph records
Rock musicians




Each entry in the *Readers' Guide* provides all the information you need to locate articles on a particular subject. Notice how the information is listed in the following entry on *robots*.

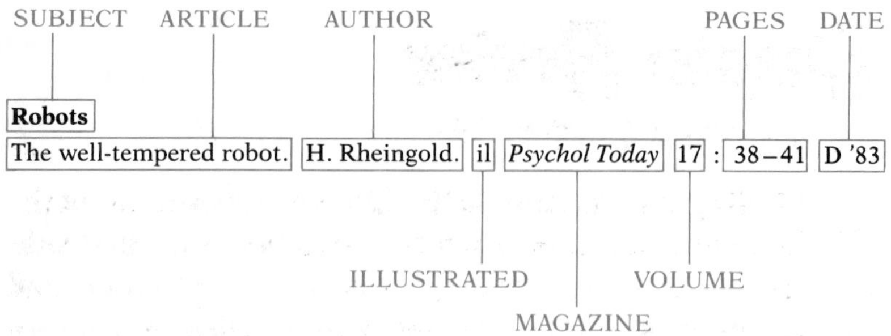


### EXERCISE 10 *Using the* Readers' Guide

Use the entries from the *Readers' Guide* on page 557 to answer the following questions.

1. What are the titles of two stories by Mary Robison?
2. What are the names of the two magazines that published these stories?
3. What are the titles of the two articles published in the December, 1983 issue of *Psychology Today?*
4. In what volume of *Popular Science* does the article about robot submarines appear?
5. On what pages in *Forbes* magazine does the article "Robby Robot Comes of Age" appear?
6. What subject heading would you look under if you wanted information on rock bands?
7. Who is the author of the article about the Beach Boys' concerts?
8. On what page in *Forbes* magazine can this article be found?
9. What are two cross-references listed under rock groups?
10. How many of the articles listed are illustrated?

## The Vertical File

Libraries also keep pamphlets, catalogs, newspaper clippings, and other kinds of leaflets. These are usually kept in a filing cabinet called the vertical file. Items are placed in file folders and arranged alphabetically by subject.

# Chapter Review

**A** **Finding Information in the Library.** Choose one of the following subjects. Then find two books on that subject and write their authors, titles, copyright dates, and call numbers. Next find two magazine articles on that subject. Write the name of the magazine, the date of the magazine, the title and author of the article, and the page numbers on which the article can be found.

1. television comedies
2. dogs
3. tennis
4. Chicago
5. the solar system
6. national parks
7. cross-country skiing
8. dinosaurs
9. motion pictures
10. the police

**B** **Choosing Reference Materials.** Write the best resource for answering each of the following questions.

specialized encyclopedia
biographical reference
atlas
almanac or yearbook
specialized dictionary
*Readers' Guide*
vertical file

1. What are two synonyms for *friendly*?
2. What is the most mountainous state in the United States?
3. Why is Mary Lou Retton famous?
4. What computer courses are offered this summer in the University of Pittsburgh catalog?
5. What are the world's three tallest buildings?
6. What is the name of a pamphlet on bicycle safety?
7. What is the birthplace of rock star Bruce Springsteen?
8. What does a baseball player have to do in order to receive the Cy Young Award?
9. What magazine articles were published on mountain climbing within the last three months?
10. What is the climate like in the Gobi Desert?

# 34

# Spelling

When you write, you want readers to concentrate on what you are saying. You do not want them to be distracted or confused by spelling errors. This chapter will help you improve your spelling of commonly used words.

### EXERCISE 1 *Spelling Warm-Up*

Number your paper 1 to 10. Then write the correct spelling of each underlined word.

Hiking

Hikers enjoy many (1) benifits from their activity. Hiking is good (2) exsercise, as the body moves up and down and around obstacles. Hikers are almost (3) allways out in the open, in the fresh air of parks and woods. This wholesome activity helps keep the senses alert, for there are (4) intresting sights, sounds, and smells all around. From hills and mountains, hikers can enjoy the breathtaking (5) scenry. As they walk along forest trails, they are (6) broght close to nature. They can (7) excape the hustle and bustle of city life. Deep in the forest, they can find peace and (8) quite. I (9) beleive hiking is so good that I would (10) reccomend it to anyone.

# Spelling Improvement

The English language has at least 500,000 words. If you tried to learn to spell them all, you would make little progress. Even if you tried to learn the spellings of ten words a day, it would take you more than 130 years!

A much better way to improve your spelling is to concentrate on the words you use often. The following suggestions will help you become an accurate speller.

**Methods for Improving Your Spelling**

1. Start a spelling notebook. List the words you find difficult to spell. By reviewing your list often, you will master each word.
2. When writing, use a dictionary to check the spelling of words you are unsure of. Avoid guessing.
3. Proofread your writing carefully. In the rush of putting your thoughts on paper, you may put an extra letter in a word or leave a letter out.
4. Sound out each syllable to avoid dropping letters.

   in **ter** est ing    lab **o** ra to ry    an ni ver **sa** ry

5. Use memory tricks for words you often misspell. The most useful memory tricks are ones you think of yourself. Following are some examples.

   biscuits  **U** and **I** like bisc**ui**ts.
   ache  **I ache** from **a che**st cold.

## EXERCISE 2 Using a Dictionary

Number your paper 1 to 10. Write the word that is spelled correctly in each pair. Then check your answer in a dictionary. Enter in your notebook any words you misspelled.

Tears

1. Most people know that tears (releive, relieve) tension.
2. Few people (realize, relize) how important tears are in keeping eyes in good working order.

3. Because eyes can be (easyly, easily) injured, they need good protection.
4. Tears can keep the eye clean and carry away harmful (particles, particals).
5. Other parts of the eye (assist, assisst) tears in the job of keeping the eye safe.
6. The eyelashes are the first line of (defense, defens) for the eye.
7. Eyelashes act like (minature, miniature) filters in keeping out dust.
8. The eyebrows help keep (perspiration, prespiration) and rain from entering the eye.
9. Eyelids help keep the eyes (iriggated, irrigated) with tears and cover them when necessary.
10. Tears are an important part of the (desine, design) of the eye.

### *EXERCISE 3 Recognizing Misspelled Words*

Number your paper 1 to 10. Write the letter that comes before the misspelled word in each group. Then write the word correctly. Check your answers in a dictionary and enter in your notebook any words you misspelled.

EXAMPLE (A) eighth (B) pamplet (C) unique
ANSWER (B) pamphlet

1. (A) occurrence (B) neice (C) stretch
2. (A) fiery (B) drought (C) arial
3. (A) condemn (B) weight (C) interupt
4. (A) courtesy (B) milage (C) regrettable
5. (A) assistence (B) biscuit (C) carriage
6. (A) immigrant (B) fasinate (C) pitiful
7. (A) business (B) bargain (C) campain
8. (A) ilustrate (B) seize (C) reference
9. (A) chord (B) luxury (C) napsack
10. (A) analyze (B) ordinery (C) cooperate

# Spelling Rules

If you learn a few spelling rules, you can spell hundreds of words correctly. To help you remember the rules, write them in your spelling notebook with examples. Also write down any exceptions. Reviewing these rules often will help you conquer many spelling demons.

## Spelling Patterns

You have probably heard the rhyme that helps you spell words with *ie* or *ei*.

Put *i* before *e*
Except after *c*
Or when sounded like *a*
As in *neighbor* and *weigh.*

The following examples show this rule in action.

| ***i* before *e*** | **except after *c*** | **sounded like *a*** |
|---|---|---|
| believe | ceiling | eight |
| niece | deceive | freight |
| piece | perceive | sleigh |
| thief | receive | weight |

Following are some exceptions to this rule.

| | | | |
|---|---|---|---|
| either | protein | height | ancient |
| neither | foreign | their | conscience |
| leisure | seize | weird | species |

Other words that sometimes cause spelling problems are those that end with a "seed" sound. This sound can be spelled *-sede, -ceed,* or *-cede.* By far the greatest number of words ending with the "seed" sound are spelled with *-cede.* The following chart shows the *only* words that have the other endings.

| -sede | -ceed | -cede |
|---|---|---|
| supersede | exceed<br>proceed<br>succeed | all others |

### EXERCISE 4 Using Spelling Patterns

Number your paper 1 to 20. Then write each word, adding either *ie* or *ei*.

| | | | |
|---|---|---|---|
| 1. r__ndeer | 6. v__n | 11. l__sure | 16. p__ce |
| 2. ach__ve | 7. w__rd | 12. n__ther | 17. s__ze |
| 3. rec__ve | 8. th__r | 13. h__ght | 18. th__f |
| 4. anc__nt | 9. f__ld | 14. dec__t | 19. bel__f |
| 5. n__ghbor | 10. w__gh | 15. __ther | 20. __ght |

### EXERCISE 5 Using Spelling Patterns

Number your paper 1 to 10. Then write each word, adding *-sede, -ceed,* or *-cede.*

| | | | | |
|---|---|---|---|---|
| 1. re__ | 3. ac__ | 5. suc__ | 7. pre__ | 9. super__ |
| 2. ex__ | 4. se__ | 6. con__ | 8. pro__ | 10. inter__ |

## Plurals

The following rules will help you form the plurals of nouns correctly. When in doubt about an exception, check a dictionary.

***Regular Nouns.*** To form the plural of most nouns, simply add *s.* If a noun ends in *s, ch, sh, x,* or *z,* add *es* to form the plural.

| | | | | |
|---|---|---|---|---|
| SINGULAR | room | computer | sofa | pencil |
| PLURAL | room**s** | computer**s** | sofa**s** | pencil**s** |
| SINGULAR | bo**ss** | mat**ch** | wi**sh** | bo**x** |
| PLURAL | boss**es** | match**es** | wish**es** | box**es** |

***Nouns Ending in y.*** Add *s* to form the plural of a noun ending in a vowel and *y*.

| | | | | |
|---|---|---|---|---|
| SINGULAR | bo**y** | tra**y** | dec**oy** | pla**y** |
| PLURAL | boy**s** | tray**s** | decoy**s** | play**s** |

Change the *y* to *i* and add *es* to a noun ending in a consonant and *y*.

| | | | | |
|---|---|---|---|---|
| SINGULAR | batte**ry** | cad**dy** | assemb**ly** | courte**sy** |
| PLURAL | batter**ies** | cadd**ies** | assembl**ies** | courtes**ies** |

### EXERCISE 6 *Forming Plurals*

Number your paper 1 to 20. Then write the plural of each noun.

1. lady
2. dish
3. fox
4. day
5. kiss
6. maze
7. waltz
8. ash
9. cross
10. canary
11. reflex
12. anxiety
13. stick
14. stitch
15. trolley
16. discovery
17. whisper
18. century
19. speech
20. journey

***Nouns Ending in o.*** Add *s* to form the plural of a noun ending in a vowel and *o*.

| | | | | |
|---|---|---|---|---|
| SINGULAR | rad**io** | ster**eo** | kangar**oo** | rat**io** |
| PLURAL | radio**s** | stereo**s** | kangaroo**s** | ratio**s** |

The plurals of nouns ending in a consonant and *o* do not follow a regular pattern.

| | | | | |
|---|---|---|---|---|
| SINGULAR | pota**to** | he**ro** | torna**do** | ta**co** |
| PLURAL | potato**es** | hero**es** | tornado**s** | taco**s** |

Add *s* to form the plural of a musical term ending in *o*.

| | | | | |
|---|---|---|---|---|
| SINGULAR | sol**o** | alt**o** | pian**o** | cell**o** |
| PLURAL | solo**s** | alto**s** | piano**s** | cello**s** |

If you are unsure about how to form the plural of a noun

ending in *o*, check the dictionary. If the plural is not formed by simply adding *s*, the dictionary will show the correct spelling. (*See pages 533–534.*)

***Nouns Ending in* f *or* fe.** To form the plural of some nouns ending in *f* or *fe*, simply add *s*.

| | | | | |
|---|---|---|---|---|
| SINGULAR | gul**f** | belie**f** | gira**ffe** | fi**fe** |
| PLURAL | gulf**s** | belief**s** | giraffe**s** | fife**s** |

To form the plural of other nouns ending in *f* or *fe*, change the *f* to *v* and add *es*.

| | | | | |
|---|---|---|---|---|
| SINGULAR | cal**f** | el**f** | thie**f** | wi**fe** |
| PLURAL | cal**ves** | el**ves** | thie**ves** | wi**ves** |

There is no sure way to tell how to form the plural of nouns ending in *f* or *fe*. Use a dictionary to check the plural forms of these words when you write them.

***Other Plural Forms.*** The following box lists examples of nouns that do not form the plural by adding *s* or *es*. Study these words so that you will remember them when you write them.

**Irregular Plurals**

| | | |
|---|---|---|
| tooth, teeth | child, children | ox, oxen |
| foot, feet | woman, women | mouse, mice |
| goose, geese | man, men | die, dice |

**Same Form for Singular and Plural**

| | | |
|---|---|---|
| Chinese | deer | scissors |
| Japanese | sheep | headquarters |
| Portuguese | moose | corps |
| Swiss | salmon | series |
| Sioux | surf | politics |

### EXERCISE 7 Forming Plurals

Number your paper 1 to 20. Write the plural of each noun. Then check your answers in a dictionary.

1. cuckoo
2. studio
3. trio
4. ditto
5. rodeo
6. hero
7. soprano
8. half
9. sheriff
10. roof
11. knife
12. leaf
13. shelf
14. man
15. mouse
16. Sioux
17. goose
18. woman
19. scissors
20. child

## Prefixes and Suffixes

A *prefix* is one or more syllables placed in front of a root to form a new word. When you add a prefix, do not change the spelling of the root.

im + mature = immature
dis + appoint = disappoint
mis + spell = misspell
re + enter = reenter

A *suffix* is one or more syllables placed after a root to change its part of speech. In many cases, you simply add the suffix. In others, however, you must change the spelling of the root before adding the suffix. The following rules will help you spell words with suffixes correctly.

**Words Ending in e.** Drop the final *e* before a suffix that begins with a vowel.

save + ing = saving
create + ed = created
nerve + ous = nervous
close + est = closest

Keep the final *e* before a suffix that begins with a consonant.

state + ment = statement
lone + some = lonesome
grace + ful = graceful
price + less = priceless

Note the following exceptions to these rules.

courage—courageous
pronounce—pronounceable
argue—argument
true—truly

***Words ending in y.*** To add a suffix to most words ending in a vowel and *y*, keep the *y*.

joy + ful = joyful play + ing = playing

To add a suffix to most words ending in a consonant and *y*, change the *y* to *i* before adding the suffix.

hurry + ed = hurried rely + able = reliable

### EXERCISE 8 Adding Prefixes and Suffixes

Number your paper 1 to 15. Then write each word, adding the prefix or suffix shown. Remember to make any necessary spelling changes.

1. dis + appear
2. ir + regular
3. re + arrange
4. argue + ment
5. smile + ing
6. drive + ing
7. true + ly
8. joy + ous
9. ship + ment
10. create + ion
11. deny + al
12. stay + ing
13. care + ful
14. merry + ly
15. place + ment

***Doubling the Final Consonant.*** The final letter in a word is sometimes doubled before a suffix is added. Before doubling a consonant, check to make sure the word meets both of the following tests.

- The word has only one syllable or is stressed on the final syllable.
- The word ends in one consonant preceded by one vowel.

hit + ing = hi**tt**ing begin + ing = begi**nn**ing

### EXERCISE 9 Adding Suffixes

Number your paper 1 to 9. Then write each word, adding the suffix shown. Remember to make any necessary spelling changes.

1. slim + est
2. wait + er
3. slip + ing
4. forget + able
5. dip + er
6. clean + est
7. stop + able
8. regret + ing
9. boat + er

# Commonly Misspelled Words

The following sections contain lists of words that are commonly misspelled. Learning them now will help you avoid spelling errors in your writing.

## Homonyms

The words below are *homonyms,* words that sound the same. Notice, however, that they have different spellings and different meanings. Learn the meaning and spelling of each word so that you can use it correctly in your writing.

**Commonly Confused Homonyms**

| | |
|---|---|
| its | belonging to it [possessive pronoun] |
| it's | it is or it has [contraction] |
| their | belonging to them [possessive pronoun] |
| there | at a certain place [adverb] |
| they're | they are [contraction] |
| theirs | belonging to them [possessive pronoun] |
| there's | there is [contraction] |
| to | in a direction toward [preposition] |
| too | excessively; also [adverb] |
| two | a number [adjective] |
| whose | belonging to whom [possessive pronoun] |
| who's | who is [contraction] |
| your | belonging to you [possessive pronoun] |
| you're | you are [contraction] |

### EXERCISE 10 Using the Right Word

Number your paper 1 to 10. Then write the word that fits the meaning in each sentence.

1. Is this (their, there, they're) house?
2. Jamie is (to, too, two) silly sometimes.

3. (Its, It's) time to go to the movies.
4. (Whose, Who's) book are you going to borrow?
5. You can always count on (your, you're) best friend.
6. Will Marcos go (to, too, two) the movies with you?
7. (Their, There, They're) arriving tonight at ten o'clock.
8. (Whose, Who's) at the door?
9. When (your, you're) on vacation, please write to me.
10. (Theirs, There's) some juice in the refrigerator.

## Spelling Demons

The words in the following list are often spelled incorrectly. Study the words carefully, following the suggestions on page 561.

**Spelling Demons**

| | | | |
|---|---|---|---|
| accompany | courtesy | kerchief | quiet |
| acquaint | deceive | knapsack | receipt |
| aerial | definition | lieutenant | reference |
| allegiance | dependent | luxury | regrettable |
| altogether | drought | mileage | reign |
| analyze | eighth | mischievous | remembrance |
| anniversary | emphasize | monitor | responsibility |
| assistance | environment | niece | satchel |
| bargain | fascinate | occasion | satisfactory |
| beautiful | feud | occurrence | scenery |
| biscuit | fiery | opponent | seize |
| boulevard | gauge | ordinary | separate |
| business | genuine | pamphlet | similar |
| campaign | guilty | paralyze | squawk |
| carriage | handicap | particle | stretch |
| chauffeur | heiress | perspiration | sufficient |
| chord | illustrate | phantom | thief |
| complexion | immigrant | pitiful | unique |
| condemn | interrupt | priest | vehicle |
| convenient | irregular | professional | weight |
| cooperate | jealous | pursuit | weird |

# Chapter Review

**A** **Using a Dictionary.** Number your paper 1 to 10. Write the word that is spelled correctly in each pair. Then check your answer in a dictionary.

Keeping Time

1. Some of the (earlyest, earliest) clocks were sundials.
2. Sundials were (populer, popular) 7,000 years ago.
3. Sundials are so (accurate, acurrate) that until 1900 French railroad workers set their watches by them.
4. Other (timepeices, timepieces) used water, sand, or wax.
5. In water clocks, a pointer on a (flote, float) marked off the hours.
6. Our modern egg timers are (similar, simular) to the old sand clocks.
7. Burning candles was another (anceint, ancient) way to measure the passing of time.
8. In the 1200s, mechanical clocks made timekeeping more (conveniant, convenient).
9. Many of the old mechanical clocks are still keeping time in some European (cities, citys).
10. In recent years, an atomic clock was (devised, deviced) that measures time precisely.

**B** **Using Spelling Patterns.** Number your paper 1 to 20. Write the word that is spelled correctly in each pair.

1. achieve, acheive
2. sliegh, sleigh
3. believe, beleive
4. leisure, liesure
5. yield, yeild
6. deceive, decieve
7. wieght, weight
8. neither, niether
9. thier, their
10. hieght, height
11. field, feild
12. breif, brief
13. receipt, reciept
14. consceince, conscience
15. nieghbor, neighbor
16. excede, exceed
17. proceed, procede
18. supercede, supersede
19. precede, presede
20. succede, succeed

**C** **Forming Plurals.** Number your paper 1 to 20. Then write the correct plural form of each word.

1. sash
2. radio
3. day
4. fly
5. mouse
6. tariff
7. rodeo
8. reflex
9. tooth
10. cameo
11. roof
12. self
13. leaf
14. taco
15. jury
16. potato
17. soprano
18. volcano
19. journey
20. Chinese

**D** **Adding Prefixes and Suffixes.** Number your paper 1 to 10. Then write each word, adding the prefix or suffix shown. Remember to make any necessary spelling changes.

1. mis + pronounce
2. dis + satisfied
3. play + ful
4. silly + ness
5. true + ly
6. taste + ful
7. tasty + er
8. courage + ous
9. trim + est
10. upset + ing

**E** **Using the Right Word.** Number your paper 1 to 5. Then write the word that fits the meaning in each sentence.

1. (Their, There, They're) here!
2. You can come along, (to, too, two).
3. We gave our dog (its, it's) dinner.
4. (Whose, Who's) in (your, you're) homeroom this year?
5. (Theirs, There's) often a silver lining in a dark cloud.

**F** **Spelling Demons.** Number your paper 1 to 20. Then write the correct spelling of each word.

1. eigth
2. wierd
3. arial
4. firey
5. queit
6. fewd
7. neice
8. seeze
9. sqawk
10. theif
11. pityful
12. ocasion
13. vehical
14. oponant
15. seprate
16. fasinate
17. beautyful
18. copperate
19. dependant
20. sufficent

# Standardized Test

## VOCABULARY AND SPELLING

**Directions:** Choose the word that is most nearly *opposite* in meaning to the word in capital letters. In the appropriate row on your answer sheet, fill in the circle containing the same letter as your answer.

SAMPLE MATURE (a) adult (b) childish (c) ready (d) unwilling

ANSWER ⓐ ● ⓒ ⓓ

1. VANITY (a) modesty (b) disappointment (c) pride (d) intelligence
2. FRAGILE (a) important (b) unimportant (c) delicate (d) sturdy
3. YIELD (a) improve (b) lose (c) resist (d) collapse
4. VILLAIN (a) hero (b) enemy (c) friend (d) soldier
5. DISPLEASE (a) cooperate (b) satisfy (c) disappoint (d) separate
6. MOBILE (a) moving (b) stationary (c) enormous (d) strong
7. LANKY (a) long (b) stout (c) foolish (d) sane
8. DEPENDENCE (a) happiness (b) sadness (c) independence (d) sleep
9. TREACHEROUS (a) cowardly (b) safe (c) interesting (d) dangerous
10. TRIUMPHANT (a) defeated (b) victorious (c) unimportant (d) undecided
11. CONTINUOUS (a) annoying (b) humorous (c) natural (d) interrupted
12. CONCLUSION (a) beginning (b) indecision (c) satisfaction (d) ending
13. COMMOTION (a) uproar (b) unhappiness (c) information (d) peacefulness
14. STRICT (a) sorrowful (b) independent (c) intelligent (d) permissive
15. SUSPICION (a) improvement (b) intelligence (c) trust (d) politeness

**Directions:** Decide which word in each numbered group is misspelled. In the appropriate row on your answer sheet, fill in the circle containing the same number as the misspelled word. If no word is misspelled, fill in *5*.

SAMPLE 1) reference
2) luxery
3) occasion
4) pamphlet
5) (No errors)

ANSWER ① ❷ ③ ④ ⑤

16. 1) eighth
2) guage
3) squawk
4) phantom
5) (No errors)

17. 1) occurence
2) illustrate
3) carriage
4) professional
5) (No errors)

18. 1) emphasize
2) irregular
3) assistance
4) perspiration
5) (No errors)

19. 1) boulevard
2) drout
3) responsibility
4) beautiful
5) (No errors)

20. 1) campaign
2) altogether
3) satisfactery
4) paralyze
5) (No errors)

21. 1) opponent
2) particle
3) handicap
4) hieress
5) (No errors)

22. 1) similar
2) satchel
3) chord
4) persuit
5) (No errors)

23. 1) gilty
2) jealous
3) biscuit
4) genuine
5) (No errors)

24. 1) business
2) analyze
3) reign
4) bargain
5) (No errors)

25. 1) cooperate
2) aerial
3) ordnary
4) unique
5) (No errors)

# Index

## A



## B



## C

## D

## T

# Tab Index

## Grammar



## Usage

## Chapter 11 Using Pronouns



## Chapter 12 Subject and Verb Agreement



## Chapter 13 Using Adjectives and Adverbs



# Mechanics

## Chapter 14 Capital Letters



## Chapter 15 End Marks and Commas



## Chapter 16 Underlining and Quotation Marks



## Chapter 17 Other Punctuation

# Composition

## Chapter 18 Words



## Chapter 19 Sentences



## Chapter 20 Paragraph Structure



## Chapter 21 The Writing Process



## Chapter 22 Narrative Paragraphs



## Chapter 23 Descriptive Paragraphs



## Chapter 24 Expository Paragraphs

## Chapter 25 Persuasive Paragraphs



## Chapter 26 Essays



## Chapter 27 Reports



## Chapter 28 Letters

## Acknowledgments

The authors and editors have made every effort to trace the ownership of all copyrighted selections found in this book and to make full acknowledgment of their use. Grateful acknowledgment is made to the following authors, publishers, agents, and individuals for their permission to reprint copyrighted materials.

**Page 25.** From *The 2nd Mammoth Book of Trivia,* by Bruce D. Witherspoon, copyright © 1982 by Hart Associates. Reprinted by permission of A & W Publishers, Inc.
**Page 205.** "The Bat," copyright 1938 by Theodore Roethke, from *The Collected Poems of Theodore Roethke.* Reprinted by permission of Doubleday and Company, Inc.
**Page 363.** "The Saint Elena Canyon," from *America's Majestic Canyons,* by Tor Eigeland, copyright © 1979 by the National Geographic Society. Reprinted by permission of the publisher.
**Pages 436–438.** Excerpts from *The World Book Encyclopedia,* copyright © 1983, U.S.A., by World Book, Inc. Reprinted by permission of the publisher.

### Photo Credits

*Photo Research:* Laurel Anderson

***Unit 1:* 1, *Unit 2:* 133, *Unit 3:* 203:** William Smith

***Unit 4:* 265:** William Smith. **Chapter 18: 270:** Laurel Anderson (Odyssey Productions). **272:** Nicholas Devore (Photographers Aspen). **273:** Jack Fields (Photo Researchers, Inc.). **275:** David Hiser (Photographers Aspen). **276:** Nicholas Devore (Photographers Aspen). **279:** Richard Hutchings (Photo Researchers, Inc.). **Chapter 19: 288:** Mi Seitelman (Woodfin Camp Associates). **289:** J. C. LeJeune (Stock, Boston Inc.). **293:** Charles Seaborn (Odyssey Productions). **297:** Julie Habel (Woodfin Camp Associates). **300:** Fred McConnaughey (Photo Researchers, Inc.). **Chapter 20: 304:** Tony Suarez (Woodfin Camp Associates). **305:** Brown Bros. **306:** Courtesy of NASA. **308:** Tom McHugh (Photo Researchers, Inc.). **312:** Robert Frerck (Odyssey Productions). **315:** George Fischer of Visum (Woodfin Camp Associates). **317:** Grant Wood, *America Gothic,* 1930. Oil on beaver board, 29⅞" × 25", 1930.34. Friends of American Art Collection © The Art Institute of Chicago. All rights reserved.

***Unit 5:* 321:** William Smith **Chapter 21: 324:** Tim Eagan (Woodfin Camp Associates). **331:** Richard Howard. **Chapter 22: 334:** Mark Newman (Earth Images). **336:** Donald Smetzer (Click/Atoz). **343:** Alan Carey (Image Works). **357:** Paul Chesley (Photographers, Aspen). **Chapter 23: 361:** Clyde H. Smith (f-Stop Productions, Inc.). **365:** Bettman Archive Inc. **367:** William Smith. **370:** *l* Robert Frerck (Odyssey Productions); *r* Sepp Seitz (Woodfin Camp Associates). **371:** Laurel Anderson (Odyssey Productions). **Chapter 24: 377:** Eric Roth (The Picture Cube. **384:** North Wind Picture Archives. **390:** John Bova (Photo Researchers, Inc.). **Chapter 25: 400:** Steven Spellman. **401:** Eastcott/Momatiuk (The Image Works). **403:** Lou Jones.

***Unit 6:* 409:** William Smith **Chapter 26: 412:** Stephanie Maze (Woodfin Camp Associates). **415:** Bill Ross (Woodfin Camp Associates). **418:** C. T. Seymour (The Picture Cube). **419:** Cathlyn Melloan (Click/Atoz). **427:** Steve Leonard (Click/Chicago). **Chapter 27: 434:** Alan Carey (The Image Works). **438:** William Strode (Woodfin Camp Associates). **440:** TMS © DC Comics Inc. (Camera 5). **441:** Jeff Dunn (The Picture Cube). **444:** Robert Hernandez (Photo Researchers, Inc.). **446:** Pat and Tom Leason (Photo Researchers, Inc.) **452:** North Wind Picture Archive. **454:** Owen Franken (Stock, Boston Inc.). **Chapter 28: 465:** Ted Cordingley. **471:** George Robinson (f-Stop Pictures, Inc.). **473:** Lenor Weber (Omni-Photo Communications). ***Unit 7:* 483:** William Smith. **Chapter 29: 484:** Donald Smetzer/Click/Atoz.

### Illustration Credits

**278, 283, 284, 295, 303:** Caroline White. **312, 325:** George Ulrich. **345, 346, 347, 352, 366, 380:** Caroline White. **383, 389:** George Ulrich. **395, 426, 464:** Caroline White. **470:** George Ulrich. **479:** Caroline White. **540, 545, 547, 549, 551:** George Ulrich.